A

TREATISE

ON THE

RIGHT USE OF THE FATHERS

IN THE

Decision of Controversies

EXISTING AT THIS DAY IN RELIGION.

BY JOHN DAILLÉ,

MINISTER OF THE GOSPEL IN THE REFORMED CHURCH OF PARIS.

WITH A

PREFACE

BY THE REV. G. JEKYLL, LL.B.

SECOND AMERICAN EDITION,

REVISED AND CORRECTED BY THE EDITOR OF THE BOARD.

PHILADELPHIA:

PRESBYTERIAN BOARD OF PUBLICATION,

No. 265 CHESTNUT STREET.

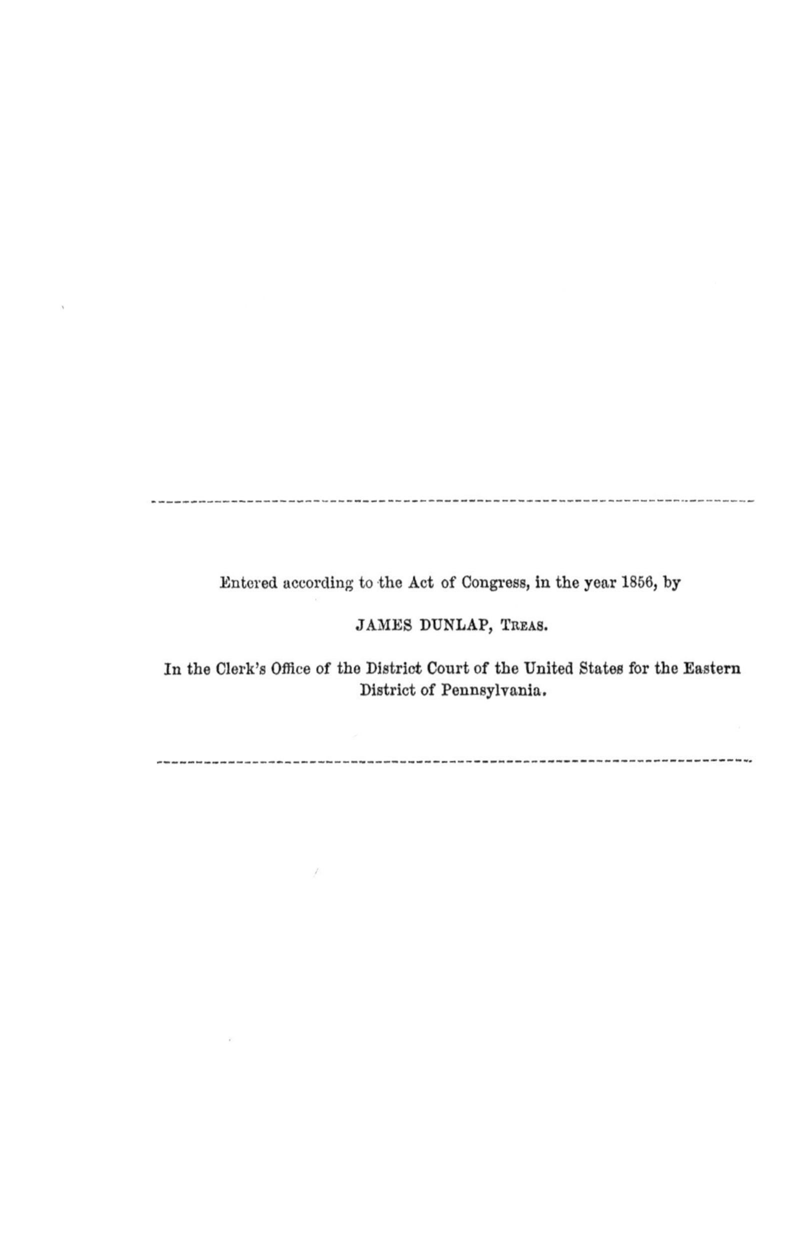

CONTENTS.

CHAPTER X.

CHAPTER XI.

BOOK II.

THE FATHERS ARE NOT OF SUFFICIENT AUTHORITY FOR DECIDING CONTROVERSIES IN RELIGION.

CHAPTER I.

CHAPTER II.

CHAPTER III.

CHAPTER IV.

CHAPTER V.

CHAPTER VI.

PREFACE

BY THE REV. G. JEKYLL, LL.B.

"The authority of the Fathers (says Bishop Warburton, in his Introduction to Julian,) had for many ages been esteemed *sacred.* These men, by taking the Greek Philosophers to their assistance, in explaining the nature and genius of the gospel, had unhappily turned religion into an *art;* and their successors the schoolmen, by framing a body of theology out of them, instead of searching for it in the Scriptures, soon after turned it into a *trade.* But (as in all affairs where reason does not hold the balance) that which had been extravagantly advanced, was, on the turn of the times, as extravagantly undervalued. It may not therefore be amiss to acquaint the English reader, in few words, how this came to pass.

"When the avarice and ambition of the Romish clergy had, by working with the superstition and ignorance of the people, erected what they call their hierarchy, and digested an ecclesiastical policy on the ruins of gospel liberty, for the administration of it they found nothing of such use for the support of this lordly system, as the making the autho-

2

rity of the Fathers sacred and decisive. For having introduced numerous errors and superstitions, both in rites and doctrine, which the *silence* and the *declarations* of Scripture equally condemned, they were obliged to seal up those living oracles, and open this new warehouse of the dead. And it was no wonder if in that shoal of writers (as a poet of our own calls it) which the great drag-net of time hath inclosed, and brought down to us, under the name of *Fathers*, there should be some amongst them of a character suited to countenance any kind of folly or extravagance. The decisions of the *Fathers*, therefore, they thought fit to treat as laws, and to collect them into a kind of code, under the title of the *Sentences.*

"From this time everything was tried at the bar of the Fathers; and so unquestioned was their jurisdiction, that when the great defection was made from the Church of Rome back again to the Church of Christ, the Reformed, though they shook off the tyranny of the Pope, could not disengage themselves from the unbounded authority of the Fathers; but carried that prejudice with them, as they did some others of a worse complexion, into the Protestant religion. For in sacred matters, as novelty is suspicious, and antiquity venerable, they thought it for their credit to have the Fathers on their side. They seemed neither to consider antiquity in general as a thing relative, nor Christian antiquity as a thing positive: either of which would have shown them that the Fathers themselves were modern, compared to that authority on which the Reformation was founded; and that the gospel was that true antiquity on which all its followers should repose themselves. The consequence of which unhappy error was, that, in the long appeal to reason, between Protestants and Papists, both of them going on a common principle, of the decisive authority of the Fathers, the latter were enabled to support their credit against all the evidence of common sense and sacred Scripture.

"At length an excellent writer of the *Reformed*, observing that the controversy was likely to be endless; for though the gross corruptions of Popery were certainly later than the third, fourth, and fifth centuries, to which the appeal was usually made, yet the seeds of them being then sown, and beginning to pullulate, it was but too plain there was hold enough for a skilful debater to draw the *Fathers* to his own side, and make them water the sprouts they had been planting: observing this, I say, he wisely projected to shift the ground, and force the disputants to vary their method, both of attack and defence. In order to this he composed a discourse of the *True Use of the Fathers;* in which, with uncommon learning and strength of argument, he showed that the Fathers were incompetent deciders of the controversies now on foot; since the points in question were not formed into articles till long after the ages in which they lived. This was bringing the *Fathers* from the bench to the table; degrading them from the rank of judges into the class of simple evidence; in which, too, they were not to speak, like *Irish* evidence, in every cause where they were wanted, but only to such matters as were agreed to be within their knowledge. Had this learned critic stopped here, his book had been free from blame; but at the same time his purpose had in all likelihood proved very ineffectual; for the obliquity of old prejudices is not to be set straight by reducing it to that line of right which barely restores it to integrity. He went much further; and by showing, occasionally, that they were absurd interpreters of holy writ; that they were bad reasoners in morals, and very loose evidence in facts; he seemed willing to have his reader infer, that even though they had been masters of the subject, yet these other defects would have rendered them very unqualified deciders.

"However, the work of this famous foreigner had great consequences; and especially with us here at home. The more learned amongst the nobility (which, at that time, was of the republic of letters,) were the first who emancipated themselves from the general prejudice. It brought the excellent Lord *Falkland* to think moderately of the Fathers, and to turn his theological inquiries into a more useful channel; and his great rival in arts, the famous Lord *Digby*, found it of such use to him, in his defence of the Reformation against his cousin Sir *Kenelm*, that he has even epitomized it in his fine letter on that subject. But what it has chiefly to boast of is, that it gave birth to the two best defences ever written on the two subjects, *religion* and *liberty:* I mean Mr. *Chillingworth's Religion of Protestants*, and *Dr. Jer. Taylor's Liberty of Prophesying.* In a word, it may be truly said to be the storehouse from whence all who have since written popularly on the character of the *Fathers*, have derived their materials."

Deeply impressed with the sound views taken by the acute and learned bishop, and believing that this work may be very useful in this age of the Church, when the simple doctrines of our most holy religion bid fair to be made of none effect by tradition, the editor ventures to introduce it, in a corrected and amended state, to the notice of the public.

Jean Daillé, one of the most learned divines of the seventeenth century, was born at Chatelleraut, in Poitou, January 6th, 1594. Having been designed by his father, who was receiver of consignments at Poitiers, to succeed him in his business, his early education was neglected; but his natural thirst for learning could not be restrained, and at the age of eleven, he was sent to school to learn the first rudiments. Close application, assisted by a good understanding, soon enabled him to retrieve the lost time; and when only eighteen years of age he was received into the family of the illustrious M. Du Plessis Mornay, as tutor to his two grandsons, whom he accompanied some years after in a tour to Italy. One of the brothers dying at Padua, he travelled with his remaining pupil through Switzerland, Germany, Flanders, and Holland; and thence to England—returning to France about the end of the year 1621. He always in after life regretted the two years spent in travelling, which he reckoned almost as lost, because he might have spent them more usefully in his closet; the only advantage he received being the acquaintance of Father Paul at Venice, to whom he had been recommended by M. Du Plessis. He was called to the ministry in 1623, and officiated first in the house of his patron, at whose death, in the November of the same year, he was removed to the church of Saumur, and in 1626 to that of Paris. The remainder of his life was spent in the service of this last church. He died 1670, aged 77 years.

Daillé's early love of learning continued through life. We read of him, "that his books and studies were his chief recreation and delight. He rose very early, and by that means had five or six hours free from the common hurry of life which he could spend in his closet."* The daily husbanding of so many hours through a long life—and those hours devoted to reading and meditation—enabled him to acquire so extraordinary a stock of learning, that he was considered one of the best read men of his age.

* Abrégé de la Vie de Daillé.

What is recorded of Pliny might be truly said of Daillé—"he read nothing without making extracts, for he was wont to say, that no book was so bad, that he could not gain some profit from it."

In 1631 he published his first work, "Du Vrai Emploi des Pères." This performance excited considerable attention and controversy, and has generally been considered his master-piece. It contains a very strong chain of arguments, which form a moral demonstration against those who would have differences of religion to be decided by the authority of the Fathers.*

An English translation of this work appeared in 1651, which has usually been attributed to the learned Thomas Smith, M. A., Fellow of Christ's College, Cambridge; although from a remark which appears in the preface to that edition under the signature of T. S. "that he commended it to the world, as faithfully translated by a judicious hand," we might infer that the translation was merely submitted to his editorial revision; or probably he undertook the translation jointly with others. M. Mettayer however, who only four years after published a Latin translation of the work, says, in the dedication to Daillé, that Smith himself was the translator of the English edition;† thus contradicting the

* Encyclopædia Britannica.

† [Mettayer does *not* assert "that Smith himself was the translator." His words are "*Accepi* hoc ipsum opus ab ornatissimo viro Thos. Smith in Anglicum idioma translatum;" which amounts to nothing more than a mere hearsay.

In a copy of the English edition of 1651, now in the Loganian Library in Philadelphia, a note on the title-page, in the hand-writing of the learned James Logan, says, "Translated (as some say) by Thos. Smith of Oxford; but undoubtedly it was not he, though he seems to have signed the Preface "T. S."]—*Editor of the Board of Publication.*

assertion of Scrivener, "that Mr. Smith had told him that the translation was not made by himself, but by an Oxford man, and that he himself would have confuted the work if he had thought it worth the while."* Now, Smith, in his address to the reader, after introducing the recommendatory testimonies of Lord Falkland, Lord Digby, Bishop Jeremy Taylor, and others, says, "*Et siquis cuculo locus inter oscines*, I must ingenuously profess, that it was the reading of this rational book which first convinced me that my study in the French language was not ill employed." The truth is, that Scrivener wished to excite a prejudice against Daillé's work, in answer to which he was writing his "Apology for the Fathers;" and in his Preface he made the above mentioned assertion of the English translation by Smith. Lord Clarendon however, in his answer to Cressy, shows what degree of credit is to be attached to the statements of Scrivener; and the learned Du Moulin, in his "Patronus bonæ fidei in causâ Puritanorum contra Hierarchos Anglos," inflicts a severe chastisement on Daillé's semi-papistical opponent.

It may here be observed, that although a simple reprint of this standard work would have been desirable, it has been thought advisable to alter and amend the translation, the language of which was frequently obscure, and had become too antiquated and obsolete for modern times. The notes have been re-arranged, and the typography modernized; so as to render the reading of the volume more pleasant and agreeable.

The Editor thinks he shall be promoting the best interests of the Church, by the republication of a work which did her good service when attacked by her enemies from

* Scriveneri Apol. pro Sanctæ Eccles. Patribus. London, 1672.

without, and which he believes to be eminently calculated to serve her now, when her foundations are being sapped by some of her sons from within. To conclude, in the words of Bishop Hurd, "May the eyes of the more candid and intelligent inquirers be opened, and the old principle be for ever established, that the Bible, and that only (interpreted by our best reason) is the Religion of Protestants."*

* Bishop Hurd on Proph. vol. ii. p. 217.

☞ This edition has been carefully compared with the French original, and occasionally with the Latin translation, and several hundred errors, both typographical and editorial, have been corrected.—*Editor of the Board of Publication.*

AUTHOR'S PREFACE.

All the difference of religion, which is at this day between the Church of Rome and the Protestants, lies in some certain points which the Church of Rome maintains as important and necessary articles of the Christian faith: whereas the Protestants, on the contrary, neither believe nor will receive them as such. For as for those matters which the Protestants believe, which they conceive to be the fundamentals of religion, they are evidently and undeniably such, that even their enemies admit and receive them as well as they: inasmuch as they are both clearly delivered in the Scriptures, and expressly admitted by the ancient councils and Fathers; and are indeed unanimously received by the greatest part of Christians in all ages, and in different parts of the world. Such, for example, are the maxims, "That there is a God who is supreme over all, and who created the heavens and the earth:—that he created man after his own image; and that this man, revolting from his obedience, is fallen, together with his whole posterity, into most extreme and eternal misery, and become infected with sin, as with a mortal leprosy, and is therefore obnoxious to the wrath of God, and liable to his curse:—that the merciful Creator, pitying man's estate, graciously sent his Son Jesus Christ into the world:—that his Son is God eternal with him; and that having taken flesh upon himself in the womb of the

Virgin Mary, and become man, he has done and suffered in this flesh all things necessary for our salvation, having by this means sufficiently expiated for our sins by his blood; and that having finished all this, he ascended again into heaven, and sitteth at the right hand of the Father; from whence he shall one day come to judge all mankind, rendering to every one according to their works;—that to enable us to communicate of this salvation by his merits, he sends us down his Holy Spirit, proceeding both from the Father and the Son, and who is also one and the same God with them; so that these three persons are notwithstanding but one God, who is blessed for ever;—that this Spirit enlightens our understanding, and generates faith in us, whereby we are justified:—that after all this, the Lord sent his Apostles to preach this doctrine of salvation throughout the whole world:—that these have planted churches, and placed in each of them pastors and teachers, whom we are to hear with all reverence, and to receive from them Baptism, the sacrament of our regeneration, and the holy Eucharist, or Lord's Supper, which is the sacrament of our communion with Jesus Christ:—that we are likewise all of us bound fervently to love God and our neighbour; observing diligently that holy doctrine which is laid down for us in the books of the New Testament, which have been inspired by his Spirit of truth; as also those other of the Old; there being nothing, either in the one or in the other, but what is most true.

These articles, and there may be some few others of a similar nature, are the substance of the Protestant's whole belief: and if all other Christians would but content themselves with these, there would never be any schism in the Church. But now their adversaries add to these many other points, which they press and command men to believe as necessary; and such as, without believing in, there is no possible hope of salvation. As for example : that the Pope of Rome is the head and supreme monarch of the whole Christian Church throughout the world:—that he, or at least the Church which he acknowledges a true one, cannot possibly err in matters of faith :—that the sacrament of the Eucharist is to be adored, as being really Jesus Christ, and not a piece of bread :—that the mass is a sacrifice, that really expiates the sins of the faithful:—that Christians may and ought to have in their churches the images of God and of saints, to which, bowing down before them, they are to use religious worship:—that it is lawful, and also very useful, to pray to saints departed and to angels:—that our souls after death, before they enter into heaven, are to pass through a certain fire, and there to endure grievous torments; thus making atonement for their sins :—that we neither may nor ought to receive the holy Eucharist, without having first confessed in private to a priest: that none but the priest himself that consecrated the Eucharist is bound by right to receive it in both kinds:—with a great number of other opinions, which their adversaries plainly protest that they cannot with a safe conscience believe.

These points are the ground of the whole difference between them; the one party pretending that they have been believed and received by the Church of Christ in all ages as revealed by him; and the other maintaining the contrary.

Now, seeing that none of these tenets have any ground from any passage in the New Testament, (which is the most ancient and authentic rule of Christianity) the maintainers are glad to fly to the writings of the doctors of the Church, who lived within the first four or five centuries after the Apostles, who are commonly called the Fathers: my purpose in this treatise is to examine whether or not this be good and sufficient means for the decision of these differences. For this purpose I must first presuppose two things, which any reasonable person will easily grant me. The first is, that the question being here about laying a foundation for certain articles of faith, upon the testimonies or opinions of the Fathers, it is very necessary that the passages which are produced out of them be clear, and not to be doubted; that is to say, such as we cannot reasonably scruple at, either as regards the author, out of whom they are alleged; or the sense of the place, whether it signify what is pretended. For a deposition of a witness, and the sentence of a judge, being of no value at all, save only for the reputation of the witness or judge, it is most evident, that if either proceed from persons unknown, or suspected, they are invalid, and prove nothing. In like manner, if the deposition of a witness or sentence of a judge be obscure, and in doubtful terms, it is clear, that in this case the business must rest undecided; there being another doubt first to be cleared, namely, what the meaning of either of them was.

The second point that I shall here lay down for a foundation to the ensuing discourse, is no less evident than the former: namely, that to allow a sufficiency to the writings of the Fathers for the deciding of those controversies, we must necessarily attribute to their persons very great authority; and such as may oblige us to follow their judgment in matters of religion. For if this authority be wanting, however clear and express their opinions be, in the articles now controverted, it will do nothing towards their decision. We have therefore here two things to examine in this business. The first is, whether or not we may be able to know, with certainty and clearness, what the opinion of the Fathers has been on the differences now in hand. The second, whether their authority be such, that every faithful person who shall clearly and certainly know what their opinion has been in any one article of Christian religion, is thereby bound to receive that article for true. For if the Church of Rome be but able to prove both these points, it is then without all dispute that their proceeding is good, and agreeable to the end proposed; there being so many writings of the ancient Fathers at this day adduced by them. But if, on the contrary, either of these two things, or both of them, be indeed found to be doubtful, I should think that any man, of a very mean judgment, should be able to conclude of himself, that this way of proof, which they have hitherto made use of, is very insufficient; and that therefore they of necessity ought to have recourse to some other more proper and solid way of proving the truth of the said opinions, which the Protestants will not by any means receive.

TO THE

NOBLE LADY ANNE MORNAY,

LADY OF TABARIERE, BARONESS OF ST. HERMINE, &C.

MADAM:—It is now nearly four years since your son, the late Baron of St. Hermine, acquainted me with what kind of discourse he was usually entertained at court by those who laboured to advance the Romish religion, or rather to excite his disgust against the Reformed; and told me that the chief argument which they urged against him was *Antiquity*, and the *general consent* of all the Fathers of the first ages of Christianity. Although he himself understood well enough the vanity of this argument of theirs, yet, notwithstanding, for his own fuller satisfaction, he requested that I would discover to him the very depth of this matter. This therefore I did, as minutely as I possibly could, and gave him my judgment at large in this particular. This treatise of mine he was pleased so much to approve, that he conceived some hopes from thence, that it might also haply be of some use to others.

Shortly afterwards I put pen to paper, and digested it into the treatise you now see. It having therefore been composed at first for his service, I had resolved also with myself to have dedicated it to his name; purporting, by this small piece of service, to testify to the world the continuation of the affection I bare to his progress in piety. But that deadly blow which snatched him from us, in the flower of his age, about two years since, at the famous seige of Boisleduc, having left us nothing of him now, save only the spoils of his mortality, and the memory of his virtue, together with our great sorrow for having enjoyed him here so short a time, I am constrained, Madam, to change my former resolution. I shall therefore content myself with cherishing and preserving, whilst I live, the precious memory of his worth, the excellency of his wit, the soundness of his judgment, the sweetness of his nature, the fairness of his carriage, and those other choice parts, wherewith he was accomplished; but, above all, his singular piety, which clearly shone forth in his words and actions, till the hour of his death.

As for this small treatise, Madam, which was at first conceived and composed for him, I thought I could not, without being guilty of a piece of injustice, present it to any other but yourself: seeing it has pleased God, notwithstanding the common order of nature, to make you heir to him to whom it belonged. This consideration only has emboldened me to present it to your hands; knowing that the nature of this discourse is not so suitable to that sorrow which has of late cast a cloud over your house; it having pleased God, after the death of the son, to deprive you of the father; and to the loss of your children, to add that also of your noble husband. But my desire to avoid being unjust has forced me to be thus uncivilly troublesome: seeing I accounted it a kind of theft, should I have any longer withheld from you that which was your right, by this sad title of inheritance. Be pleased, therefore, Madam, to receive this book as a part of the goods of your deceased son; which I now honestly restore, in the view of the whole world, after concealment of it for some time in my study. This name, I know, will oblige you to afford it some place in your closet, which is all that I can at present desire. For as for the reading of it, besides that your exquisite piety (which is built upon infinitely much firmer grounds than these disputes,) has no need at all of it; I know also that your present condition is such, that it would be very troublesome to you. And if you shall chance to desire to spend some hours in the perusal of it, it must be hereafter, when the Lord, by the efficacy of his Spirit, shall have comforted yours, and shall have allayed the violence of your grief; to whom I pour out my most earnest prayers, that he would vouchsafe powerfully to effect the same, and to shed forth his most holy grace upon you and yours; and that he would by his great mercy preserve, long and happily, that which remains of that goodly and blessed family, which he has bestowed upon you.

This, Madam, is one of the most hearty prayers of

Your most humble

And obedient servant,

DAILLÉ.

PARIS, *August* 15, 1631.

ON THE

RIGHT USE OF THE FATHERS.

BOOK I.

CHAPTER I.

Reason I.—On the difficulty of ascertaining the opinions of the Fathers in reference to the present controversies in religion, deduced from the fact that there is very little of their writings extant of the first three centuries.

If we should here follow the same course of argument which some writers of the Church of Rome pursue against the Holy Scriptures, it would be very easy to bring in question, and render very doubtful and suspected, all the writings of the Fathers; for when the Old or New Testament is quoted, these gentlemen instantly demand, how or by what means we know that any such books were really written by those Prophets and Apostles whose names they bear? If therefore, in like manner, when these men adduce Justin, Irenæus, Ambrose, Augustine, and others, we should at once demand of them, how and by what means we are assured that these Fathers were the authors of those writings which at this day bear their names, there is little doubt but that they would find a harder task of it than their adversaries would, in justifying the writings of the sacred volume; the truth whereof is much more easy to be demonstrated than of any human writings whatsoever. But I shall pass by this too artificial way of proceeding, and only say, that it is not very easy to find out, by the writings of the Fathers, what has really been their opinion, in any of those controversies which are now in dispute between the Protestants and the Church of Rome. The considerations, which render the knowledge of this so difficult, are many; I shall therefore, in this first Part, discuss some of them only, referring the rest to the second Part, examining them one after another.

The first reason, therefore, which I shall lay down for the proving of this difficulty, is the little we have extant of the writings of the ancient Fathers, especially of the first, second, and third centuries; which are those we are most especially to regard. For, seeing that one of the principal reasons that moves the Church of Rome to adduce the writings of the Fathers, is to show the truth of their tenets by their antiquity, which they consider as indicative of it; it is evident that the most ancient ought to be the most noticed. And indeed there is no question but that the Christian religion was more pure and without mixture in its beginning and infancy, than it was afterwards in its growth and progress: it being the ordinary course of things to contract corruptions, more or less, according as they are more or less removed from their first institution: as we see by experience in states, laws, arts, and languages, the natural propriety of all which is continually declining, after they have once passed the point of their vigour, and as it were the flower and prime of their strength and perfection. Now, I cannot believe that any faithful Christian will deny but that Christianity was in its zenith and perfection at the time of the blessed Apostles; and indeed it would be the greatest injury that could be offered them, to say that any of their successors have either had a greater desire or more abilities to advance

Christianity than they had. It will hence follow then, that those times which were nearest to the Apostles were necessarily the purest, and less subject to suspicion of corruption, either in doctrine, or in manners and Christian discipline: it being but reasonable to believe, that if any corruptions have crept into the Church, they came in by little and little, and by degrees, as it happens in all other things. Some may here object, that even the very next age, immediately after the times of the Apostles, was not without its errors, if we may believe Hegesippus; who, as he is cited by Eusebius, witnesses, that the Church continued a virgin till the emperor Trajan's time; but that after the death of the Apostles the conspiracy of error began to discover itself with open face. *Ὡς ἀρα μεχρι των τοτε χρονων παρθενος καθαρα και ἀδιαφθορος ἐμεινεν ἡ ἐκκλησια,* &c. *ὡς δ' ὁ ἱερος των ἀποστολων χορος διαφορον εἰληφει του βιου τελος, παρεληλυθει τε ἡ γενεα ἐκεινη των αὐταις ἀκοαις της ἐνθεου σοφιας ἐπακουσαι κατηξιωμενων, τηνικαυτα της ἀθεου πλανης την ἀρχην ἐλαμβανεν ἡ συστασις δια της των ἑτεροδιδασκαλων ἀπατης, οἱ και ἁτε μηδενος ἐτι των ἀποστολων λειπομενου, γυμνῃ λοιπον ἠδη τῃ κεφαλῃ τῳ της ἀληθειας κηρυγματι την ψευδωνυμον γνωσιν ἀντικηρυττειν επεχειρουν.**

I shall not oppose anything against this testimony, but shall only say, that if the enemy, immediately upon the setting of these stars of the Church, their presence and light being scarcely shut in, had yet the boldness presently to fall to sowing his evil seed; how much more had he the opportunity of doing this in

* "The Church continued until then as a pure and uncorrupt virgin; * * * but when the sacred choir of apostles became extinct, and the generation of those that had been privileged to hear their inspired wisdom, had passed away, then also the combinations of impious error arose by the fraud and delusions of false teachers. These also, as there was none of the apostles left, henceforth attempted, without shame, to preach their false doctrine against the gospel of truth."—Euseb. Hist. Eccles. lib. 3. cap. 32.

those ages which were further removed from their times; when (the sanctity and simplicity of these great teachers of the world, having now by little and little vanished out of the memories of men) human inventions and new fancies began to take place? So that we may conclude that even supposing the first ages of Christianity have not been altogether exempt from alteration in doctrine, yet are they much more free from it than the succeeding ages can pretend to be, and are therefore consequently to be preferred to them in all respects; it being here something like what the poets have fancied of the four ages of the world, where the succeeding age always came short of the former. As for the opinion of those men* who think the best way to find out the true sense of the ancient Church, will be to search the writings of those of the Fathers chiefly who lived between the time of Constantine the Great and Pope Leo, or Pope Gregory's time, (that is to say, from the end of the third century to the beginning of the seventh,) I consider this as an admission only of the small number of books that are left us of those ages before Constantine, and not that these men allow that the authority of these three later ages ought to be preferred to that of the three former.

If we had but as much light and as clear evidences of the belief of the one as we have of the other, I make no question but they would prefer the former. But if they mean otherwise, and are indeed of a persuasion that the Church was really more pure after Constantine's time than before, they must excuse me, if I think that they by this means confess the distrust they have of their own cause, seeing that they endeavour to fly as far as they can from the light of the primitive times; retreating to those ages, wherein it is most evident there were both less perfection and light than before; running altogether contrary to that

* Cassand. Consult. Ferdinan. p. 894. Perron. Epist. to Casaub.

excellent rule which Cyprian has given us:* That we should have recourse to the fountain, whenever the channel and stream of doctrine and ecclesiastical tradition are found to be the least corrupted. But, however, let their meaning be what it will, their words, in my judgment, do not a little advance the Protestants' cause; it being a very clear confession that those opinions, about which they contest with them, do not at all appear clearly in any of the books that were written during the first three centuries. For if they were found clearly in the same, what policy were it then in them to appeal to the writers of the three following centuries, to which they very well know that their adversaries attribute less than to the former? But beside this tacit confession of theirs the thing is evident; namely, that there is left us at this day very little of the writing of the Fathers of the first three centuries of Christianity, for the deciding of our differences.

The blessed Christians of those times contented themselves, for the greatest part, with writing the Christian faith in the hearts of men, by the beams of their sanctity and holy life, and by the blood shed in martyrdom, without much troubling themselves with the writing of books; whether it were because, as the learned Origen† elegantly gives the reason, they were of opinion that the Christian religion was to be defended by innocency of life and honesty of conversation, rather than by sophistry and the artifice of words: or whether, because their continual sufferings gave them not leisure to take pen in hand and to write books; or else, whether it were for some other reason perhaps, which we know not. But of this we are very well assured, that, except the writings of the Apostles, there was very little written by others in these primitive times; and this was the cause of so much trouble

* Cypr. ep. 74. p. 195.
† Orig. Præf. Operis contra. Cels. p. 1, 2.

to Eusebius in the beginning of his history, who had little or no light to guide him in his undertaking; treading, as he saith, *Οἷα τινα ἐρημην και ἀτριβη ἰεναι ὁδον ἐγχειρουμεν*; "in a new path, unbeaten by any that had gone before him."*

Besides, the greatest part of those few books which were written by the Christians of those times, have not come down to our hands, but were lost, either through the injury of time, that consumes all things; or else have been destroyed by the malice of men, who have made bold to suppress whatsoever they met with that was not altogether to their taste. Of this sort were those five books of Papias bishop of Hierapolis, the apology of Quadratus Atheniensis, and that other of Aristides, the writings of Castor Agrippa against the twenty-four books of the heretic Basilides, the five books of Hegesippus, the works of Melito bishop of Sardis, Dionysius bishop of Corinth, Apollinaris bishop of Hierapolis, the epistle of Pinytus Cretensis, the writings of Philippus, Musanus, Modestus, Bardesanes, Pantænus, Rhodon, Miltiades, Apollonius, Serapion, Bacchylus, Polycrates bishop of Ephesus, Heraclius, Maximus, Hammonius, Tryphon, Hippolytus, Julius Africanus, Dionysius Alexandrinus, and others; of whom we have nothing left but their names and the titles of their books, which are preserved in the works of Eusebius, Jerome, and others.† All that we have left us of these times, which is certainly known to be theirs, and of which no man doubts, are some certain discourses of Justin, the philosopher and martyr, who wrote his second apology a hundred and fifty years after the nativity of our Saviour Christ; the five books of Irenæus, who wrote not long after him; three excellent and learned pieces of Clemens Alexandrinus, who lived towards the end of the

* Euseb. Hist. Eccles. l. 1. c. 1.

† Hieron, 1. de Scriptor, &c. Euseb. in Hist. passim. Tertul. aliquorum meminit.

second century; divers books of Tertullian, who was famous about the same time; the epistles and other treatises of Cyprian bishop of Carthage, who suffered martyrdom about the year of our Saviour 261; the writings of Arnobius, and of Lactantius his scholar, and some few others. As for Origen, Cyprian's contemporary—who alone, had we but all his writings entire, would be able perhaps to give us more light and satisfaction in the business we are now engaged in than all the rest—we have but very little of him left, and the greatest part of that too most miserably abused and corrupted; the most learned and almost innumerable writings of this great and incomparable person not being able to withstand the ravages of time, nor the envy and malice of men, who have dealt much worse with him, than so many ages and centuries of years that have passed from his time down to us.

Thus have I given you an account of well nigh all that we have left us, which is certainly known to have been written by the Fathers of the first three centuries. For as for those other pieces, which are pretended to have been written in the same times, but are indeed either confessed to be supposititious by the Romanists themselves, or are rejected by their adversaries, and that upon very good and probable grounds; these cannot have any place or account here, in elucidating the controversy we have now in hand.

The writings of the fourth and fifth centuries have, I confess, surpassed the former in number and good fortune too; the greatest part of them having been transmitted safely to our hands; but they come much short of the other in weight and authority, especially in the judgment of the Protestants, who maintain, and that upon very probable grounds, that the Christian religion has from the beginning had its declinings by little and little, losing in every age some certain degree of its primitive and native purity. And besides, we have good reason perhaps to fear lest the number of writers of these two ages trouble us as much as the paucity of them in the three preceding: and that, as before we suffered under scarcity, we now may be overwhelmed by their multitude. For the number of words and of books serves as much sometimes to the suppressing of the sense and opinion of any public body, as silence itself; our minds being then extremely confounded and perplexed, while it labours to comprehend what is the true and common opinion of the whole, amidst so many differently biassed details, whereof each endeavours to express the same; it being most certain, that amongst so great and almost infinite variety of spirits and tongues, you shall hardly ever meet with two persons that shall deliver to you one and the same opinion, (especially in matters of so high a nature as the controversies in religion,) after the same form and way of representation, how unanimous soever their consent may otherwise be in the same opinion. And this variety, although it be but in the circumstances of the thing, makes, notwithstanding, the foundation itself also appear different.

CHAPTER II.

REASON II.—Those writings which we have of the Fathers of the first centuries, treat of matters far different from the present controversies in religion.

BUT suppose that neither the want of books in the first three centuries, nor yet the abundance of them in the three following, should produce these inconveniences; it will nevertheless be very hard to discover from them what the opinion of their authors has been concerning those points of the Christian religion now controverted. For the matters whereof they treat are of a very different nature; these authors, according as the necessity of the times required, employing themselves either in justifying the Christian religion, and vindicating it from the aspersion of such crimes, wherewith it was most falsely and injuriously charged; or else in laying open to the world the absurdity and impiety of Paganism; or in convincing the hard-hearted Jews, or in confuting the prodigious fooleries of the heretics of those times; or in exhortations to the faithful to patience and martyrdom; or in expounding some certain passages and portions of the Holy Scripture: all which things have very little concern with the controversies of these times; of which they never speak a syllable, unless they accidentally or by chance let a word drop from them toward this side or that side, yet without the least thought of us or of our controversies; although both the one and the other party sometimes light upon passages, wherein they conceive they have discovered their own opinions clearly delivered, though in vain for the most part, and without ground: precisely as he did, who on hearing the ringing of bells, thought they perfectly sounded out what he in his own thoughts had fancied. Justin Martyr and Tertullian, Theophilus and Lactantius, Clemens and Arnobius, show the heathen the vainness of their religion, and of their gods; and that Jupiter and Juno were but mortals, and that there is but one only God, the Creator of heaven and earth. Irenæus bends his whole forces against the monstrous opinions of Basilides, the Valentinians, and other Gnostics, who were the inventors of the most chimerical divinity that ever came into the fancy of man. Tertullian also lashes them, as they well deserve; but he especially takes Marcion, Hermogenes, Apelles, Praxeas, and others to task, who maintained that there were two Gods, or two principles, and confounded the persons of the Father and the Son. Cyprian is wholly upon the discipline and the virtues of the

Christian Church. Arius, Macedonius, Eunomius, Photinus, Pelagius, and afterwards Nestorius and Eutyches, made work for the Fathers of the fourth and fifth centuries.

The blasphemies of these men against the person or the natures of our Saviour Christ, or against the Holy Ghost and his grace, which have now of a long time lain buried and forgotten, were the matters controverted in those times, and the subject of the greatest part of the books then written, that have come to our hands. What relation has anything of all this to the doctrines of transubstantiation, and the adoration of the eucharist, or the monarchy of the Pope, or the necessity of auricular confession, or the worshipping of images, and similar points, which are those of the present controversies, and which none of the ancients have treated expressly and by design, or perhaps ever so much as thought of? It is very true indeed, that the silence of these Fathers on these points, which some set so much value by, is not wholly mute, and perhaps also it may pass for a very clear testimony, but certainly not on their side who maintain them affirmatively. But, however, this is a most certain truth, that throughout the whole body of the genuine writings of these Fathers, you shall not meet with anything expressly urged either for or against the greatest part of these opinions. I shall most willingly confess, that the belief of every wise man makes up but one entire body, the parts whereof have a certain correspondence and relation to each other, to such a degree that a man may be able by those things which he delivers expressly, to give a guess what his opinion is concerning other things of which he says nothing; it being utterly improbable that he should maintain any position which shall manifestly clash with his other tenets, or that he should reject anything that necessarily follows upon them. But, besides, this manner of disputation presupposes that the belief of the ancient Fathers is uniform, no one position contradicting another, but having all its parts united, and depending one upon another, which indeed is very questionable, as we shall show elsewhere. Besides all this, I say it requires a quick discernment, which readily and clearly apprehends the connections of each distinct point, an excellent memory to retain faithfully whatever positions the ancients have maintained, and a solid judgment free from all pre-occupation, to compare them with the tenets maintained at this day. And the man who is endued with all these qualities I shall account the fittest to make profitable use of the writings of the Fathers, and the likeliest of any to search deeply into them. But the mischief is, that men so qualified are very rare and difficult to be found.

I shall add here, that if you will believe certain writers of the Church of Rome,* this method is vain and useless, as is also that which makes use of argumentation and reason; means which are insufficient, and unable (in the judgment of these doctors) to arrive at any certainty, especially in matters of religion. Their opinion is, that we are to rely upon clear and express texts only. Thus, according to this account, we shall not, if we be wise, believe that the Fathers held any of the aforenamed points, unless we can find them in express terms in their writings; that is to say, in the very same terms that we read them in the decrees and canons of the Council of Trent. Seeing then that, according to the opinion of these men, those testimonies only are to be received which are express, and likewise that of these points now controverted there is scarcely any thing found expressly delivered by the Fathers, we may, in my opinion, very logically and reasonably conclude, that it is at least a very difficult if not impossible thing (according

* Gontery, Veron, and others.

to these men) to come to the certain knowledge of the opinion of the ancients concerning the greatest part of the tenets of the Church of Rome, which are at this day rejected by the Protestants.

CHAPTER III.

REASON III.—Those writings which bear the names of the ancient Fathers, are not all really such; but a great portion of them supposititious, and forged, either long since or at later periods.

I NOW enter upon more important considerations; the two former, though they are not in themselves to be despised or neglected, being yet but trivial ones compared with those which follow. For there is so great a confusion in the most part of these books of which we speak, that it is a very difficult thing truly to discover who were their authors, and what is their meaning and sense. The first difficulty proceeds from the infinite number of forged books, which are falsely attributed to the ancient Fathers; the same having also happened in all kinds of learning and sciences; insomuch that the learned at this day are sufficiently puzzled to discover, both in philosophy and humanity, which are forged and supposititious pieces, and which are true and legitimate. But this abuse has not existed anywhere more grossly, and taken to itself more liberty, than in the ecclesiastical writers. All men complain of this, both on the one side and on the other, and labour to their utmost to deliver us from this confusion, oftentimes with little success, by reason of the warmth of their feelings by which they are carried away; ordinarily judging of books according to their own interest rather than the truth, and rejecting all those that any way contradict them, but defending those which speak on their side; how good or bad soever they otherwise chance to be. So that, to say the truth, they judge not of their own opinions by the writings of the Fathers, but of the writings of the Fathers by their own opinions. If they speak with us, it is then Cyprian and Chrysostom; if not, it is some ignorant modern fellow, or else some malicious person, who would fain cover his own impurity under the rich garment of these excellent persons.

Now, were it mere partiality that rendered the business obscure, we should be able to quit our hands of it, by stripping it and laying it open to the world; and all moderate men would find enough to rest satisfied with. But the worst of it is, that this obscurity oftentimes happens to be in the things themselves; so that it is a very difficult and sometimes impossible thing to elucidate them, whether it be by reason of the antiquity of the error, or by reason of the near resemblance of the false to the true. For these forgeries are not new, and of yesterday; but the abuse has existed above fourteen hundred years. It is the complaint of the greatest part of the Fathers, that the heretics, to give their own dreams the greater authority, promulgated them under the names of some of the most eminent writers in the Church, and even of the Apostles themselves.* Amphilochius, bishop of Iconium, who was so much esteemed by the great Basil, archbishop of Cæsarea, wrote a particular tract on this subject,† alleged by the Fathers of the seventh council against a certain passage produced by the Iconoclasts out of I know not what idle treatise, entitled, "The Travels of the Apostles." And I would that that tract of this learned prelate were now extant! If it were, it would perhaps do us good service in discovering the vanity of many ridiculous pieces, which now pass current in the world under the names

* Hegesippus apud Euseb. l. 4. c. 22.
† Concil. 7. Act. 5. tom. 3. p. 552.

of the primitive and most ancient Christians. Jerome rejects divers apocryphal books,* which are published under the names of the Apostles, and of their first disciples; as those of St. Peter, of Barnabas, and the others. The gospel of St. Thomas, and the epistle to the Laodiceans, are classed in the same category by the seventh council.†

Now, if these knaves have thus taken such liberty with the Apostles as to make use of their names, how much more likely is it, that they would not hesitate to make as free with the Fathers? And indeed this kind of imposture has always been common. Thus we read that the Nestorians sometime published an epistle under the name of Cyril of Alexandria,‡ in the defence of Theodorus, bishop of Mopsuestia, who was the author and first broacher of their heresy: and likewise that the Eutychists also circulated certain books of Apollinaris, under the title of "The Orthodox Doctors," namely, to impose on the simplicity of the people.§ Leontius has written an express tract on this subject;|| wherein he shows that these men abused particularly the names of Gregory of Neocæsarea, of Julius bishop of Rome, and of Athanasius bishop of Alexandria; and he also says particularly, that the book entitled, *Ἡ κατα μερος Πιστις* (A particular Exposition of the Faith,) which is delivered to us by Turrianus the Jesuit, Gerardus Vossius, and the last edition of Gregorius Neocæsariensis, for a true and legitimate piece of the said Gregory¶ is not truly his, but the bastard issue of the heretic Apollinaris. The like judgment do the publishers of the *Bibliotheca Patrum* give of the twelve Anathemas, which are

* Hier. l. de Script. Eccles. tom. 1. p. 346, et 350.

† Concil. 7. Act. 6. ‡ Concil. 5. Collat. 5.

§ Marian. ep. ad Mon. Alex. ad calcem Concil. Chalc. t. 2. p. 450. E.

|| Leont. lib. extat Bibl. SS. PP. t. 4. par. 2.

¶ Greg. Thaumat. op. Par. an. 1622, p. 97. ubi vide Voss.

commonly attributed to the same Gregory.* The Monothelites also, taking the same course, forged an oration under the name of Menas, patriarch of Constantinople, and directed to Vigilius, bishop of Rome:† and two other books under the name of the same Vigilius, directed to Justinian and Theodora; wherein their heresy is in express terms delivered; and these three pieces were afterwards inserted in the body of the fifth council, and kept in the library of the Patriarch's palace in Constantinople.‡ But this imposture was discovered and proved in the sixth council: for otherwise, who would not have been deceived by it, seeing these false pieces in so authentic a copy?

I bring but these few examples, to give the reader a sample only of what the heretics not only dared but were able also to do in this particular: and all these things were done before the end of the seventh century, that is to say, above nine hundred years ago. Since which time, in all the disputes about the images in churches,§ and in the differences betwixt the Greek and Latin churches, and indeed in the most part of all other ecclesiastical disputations, you shall find nothing more frequent than the mutual reproaches that the several parties cast at each other,|| accusing one another of forging the pieces of authors which they produced each of them in defence of their own cause. Judge you, therefore, whether or not the heretics, using the same artifice and the same diligence, now for the space of so many centuries since, though in different causes, may not in all probability have furnished us with a sufficient number of spurious pieces published under the names of the ancient Fathers by their professed enemies. And only con-

* Bibl. SS. PP. t. 1. Gr. Lat.

† Concil. 6. Act 3. et Act 14. t. 3. Concil.

‡ Ibid.

§ Concil. 7. Act 6. Refut. Iconoclast. tom. 5.

|| Concil. Florent. Sess. 20. t. 4.

sider whether or no we may not chance to commune with a heretic sometimes, when we think we have a Father before us; and a professed enemy disguised under the mask of a friend. Thus it will hence follow that it may justly be feared, that we sometimes receive and deliver for maxims and opinions of the ancient Church, no better than the mere dreams of the ancient heretics. For we must suppose that they were not so foolish as to discover their venom at the first, in their heretical writings; but rather that they only cunningly infused here and there some sprinklings of it, laying the foundation of their heresy as it were a far off only; which makes the knavery the more difficult to be discovered, and consequently the more dangerous. But supposing that this juggling deception of the heretics may have very much corrupted the old books; yet notwithstanding, had we no other spurious pieces than what had been forged by them, it would be no very hard matter to distinguish the true from the false. But that which renders the evil almost irremediable is, that even in the Church itself this kind of forgery has both been very common and very ancient.

I impute a great part of the cause of this mischief to those men who, before the invention of printing, were the transcribers and copiers of manuscripts: of whose negligence and boldness, in the corrupting of books, Jerome very much complained even in his time: "Scribunt non quod inveniunt, sed quod intelligunt; et dum alienos errores emendare nituntur, ostendunt suos;"* that is, "they write not what they find but what they understand: and whilst they endeavour to correct other men's errors they show their own."

We may very well presume, that the liberty these men took in corrupting, they also took the same in forging, books: especially since this last course was beneficial to them, while the other was not. For, by

* Hier. Ep. 28. ad Lucin. tom. 1.

altering or corrupting the books they wrote, they could not make any advantage to themselves: whereas, in forging new books, and disposing of them under great and eminent names, they sold them more readily and dearer. So likewise, if there came to their hands any book that either had no author's name; or having any, it was but an obscure or a tainted one; to the end that these evil marks might not prejudice the selling of it, they would erase it without any more ado, and inscribe it with some one of the most eminent and venerable names in the Church; that thus the reputation and favour, which that name had found in the world, might be a means for better passing off their false wares. As for example, the name of Novatianus, who was the head of a schism against the Roman Church, became justly odious to Christian ears: as that of Tertullian was the more esteemed, both for the age, wit, and learning of the person. Now the transcriber, considering this, without any other design or end than that of his own private gain, has, in my judgment, made an exchange, attributing to Tertullian that book of the Trinity which is in reality the production of Novatianus; as we are also given to understand by Jerome.* And I am of opinion, that both the birth and fortune of that other piece, "De Pœnitentia," have been, if not the very same, yet at least not much unlike that of the other. So likewise the book, entitled "De Operibus Cardinalibus Christi,"† (which was composed and sent by its author to one of the Popes, without giving his name, as he there testifies,) has been circulated abroad under the name of Cyprian, merely because by this means it was the more profitable to the manuscript-monger; and has always passed, and does pass, for his: notwithstanding that, in my judgment, it is clear enough that it

* Hier. Apol. 2. cont. Ruff.

† Auctor operis, De Operibus Card. Christi, inter Cyprian. oper. p. 444.

cannot be his, as is ingenuously confessed by many of the learned of both parties.* Ruffinus had some name in the Church, though nothing near so great as Cyprian had: and this is the reason why the afore-named merchants have inscribed with Cyprian's name that treatise upon the Apostles' Creed, which was written by Ruffinus.

Besides the avarice of these Librarii, their own ignorance, or at least of those whom they consulted, has in like manner produced no small number of these spurious pieces. For when either the likeness of the name, or of the style, or of the subject treated of, or any other seeming reason, gave them occasion to believe that such an anonymous book was the work of such or such an ancient author, they presently copied it out, under the said author's name; and thus it came from thenceforth to be received by the world for such, and by them to be transmitted for such to posterity.

All the blame, however, is not to be laid upon the transcribers only in this particular: the authors themselves have contributed very much to the promoting of this kind of imposture; for there have been found in all ages some so sottishly ambitious, and so desirous, at any rate, to have their conceptions published to the world, that, finding they should never be able to please, and get applause abroad of themselves, they have issued them under the name of some of the Fathers; choosing rather to see them received and honoured under this false guise, than disguised and slighted under their own real name. These men, according as their several abilities have been, have imitated the style and sentiments of the Fathers either more or less happily; and have boldly presented these productions of their own brain to the world under

* Erasmus in edit. Cyp. suâ. Sixtus Senens. Biblioth. l. 4. Bellar. de Euchar. l. 2. c. 9. De amiss. grat. l. 6. c. 2. Possevin. in Apparat. Scult. Medulla Patr. Andr. Rivet. l. 2. c. 15. Crit. Sacr. Aubert de Euchar. 1. 2. ch. 8.

their names. The world, of which the greatest part has always been the least reflecting, has very readily collected, preserved, and cherished these fictitious productions, and has by degrees filled all their libraries with them. Others have been induced to adopt the same artifice, not out of ambition, but some other irregular fancy; as those men have done, who, having had a particular affection, either to such a person, or to such an opinion, have undertaken to write of the same, under the name of some author of good esteem and reputation with the world, to make it pass the more currently abroad: precisely as that priest did, who published a book, entitled "The Acts of St. Paul, and of Tecla;"* and being convicted of being the author of it, in presence of the Apostle John, he plainly confessed, that the love that he bare to Paul was the only cause that incited him to do it. Such was the boldness also of Ruffinus, a priest of Aquileia, (whom Jerome justly reprehends so sharply, and in so many places,†) who, to vindicate Origen's honour, wrote an apology for him, under the name of Pamphilus, a holy and renowned martyr; although the truth of it is, he had taken it partly out of the first and sixth books that Eusebius had written upon the same subject, and partly made use of his own invention in it. Some similar fancy it was that moved him also to put forth the life of one Sextus, a Pythagorean philosopher, under the name of St. Sixtus the martyr,‡ to the end that the work might be received the more favourably. What can you say to this? namely, that in the very same age there was a personage of greater note than the former; who, disliking that Jerome had translated the Old Testament out of the

* Hier. de Script. Eccl. tom. 1. p. 350. ex Tertul. lib. de Baptisma. cap. 17.

† Hier. l. 2. Apol. contr. Ruffin. tom. 2. p. 334. et Ep. 69. t. 2. et Apol. contr. Ruff. ad. Pammach. et Marc. tom. 2.

‡ Hier. in Ierem. com. 4. tom. 4.

Hebrew, framed an epistle under his name, wherein he represents him as repenting of having done it; which epistle, even in Jerome's lifetime, though without his knowledge, was published by the said author, both at Rome and in Africa? Who could believe the truth of this bold attempt, had not Jerome himself related the story, and made complaint of the injury done him therein?* I must impute also to a fancy of the same kind, though certainly more innocent than the other, the spreading abroad of so many predictions of our Saviour Jesus Christ, and his kingdom, under the names of the Sibyls; which was done by some of the first Christians, only to prepare the Pagans to relish this doctrine the better; as it is objected against them by Celsus in Origen.† But that which is yet of greater consequence is, that even the Fathers themselves have sometimes made use of this artifice, to promote either their own opinions or their wishes. Of this we have a notable example, which was objected against the Latins by the Greeks, above two hundred years since, of two Bishops of Rome, Zosimus and Boniface;‡ who, to authorize the title which they pretended to have, of being universal bishops, and heads of the whole Christian Church, and particularly of the African, forged, about the beginning of the fifth century, certain canons in the council of Nice, and frequently quoted them as such in the councils in Africa;§ which, notwithstanding, after a long and diligent search, could never yet be found in any of the authentic copies of the said council of Nice, although the African bishops had taken the pains to send as far as Constantinople, Alexandria, and Antioch, to obtain the best and most genuine copies they could. Neither indeed do the canons

* Hier. l. 2. Apol. contra Ruff. tom. 2.
† Orig. contra Cels. lib. 7.
‡ Concil. Flor. Sess. 20, p. 457. § Concil. Afric. 6. cap. 3.

and acts of the council of Nice at this day, though they have since that time passed through so many various hands, contain any such thing; no, not even the editions of those very men who are the most interested in the honour of the Popes, as that of Dionysius Exiguus, who published his Latin collection of them about the year of our Saviour 525: nor any other, either ancient or modern.

As to that authentic copy of the council of Nice, which one Friar John, at the council of Florence, pretended to have been the only copy that had escaped the corruptions of the Arians,* and which had for this cause been always kept under lock and key at Rome, with all the safety and care that might be, (out of which copy they had transcribed the said canons,) I confess it must needs have been kept up very close, under locks and seals, seeing that three of their Popes namely, Zosimus, Boniface, and Celestine, could never be able to produce it for the justification of their pretended title against the African Fathers, though in a case of so great importance. And it is a strange thing to me that this man, who came a thousand years after, should now at last make use of it in this cause; whereas those very persons who had it in their custody never so much as mentioned one syllable of it: which is an evident argument that the seals of this rare book were never opened, save only in the brains of this Doctor, where alone it was both framed and sealed up; brought forth, and vanished all at the same instant; the greatest part of those men that have come after him being ashamed to make use of it any longer, having laid aside this chimerical invention. To say the truth, that which these men answer, by way of excusing the said Popes, is not any whit more probable, namely, that they took the council of Nice and that of Sardica, in which those canons they allege are

* Concil. Flor. Sess. 20.

really found, for one and the same council. For whom will these men ever be able to persuade, that two Ecclesiastical Assemblies, (between which there passed nearly twenty-two whole years, called by two several emperors, and for matters of a far different nature—the one of them for the explanation of the Christian faith, and the other for the re-establishing of two Bishops on their thrones; and in places very far distant from each other—the one at Nicæa in Bithynia, the other at Sardica a city of Illyricum—the canons of which two councils are very different, both in substance, number, and authority—the one of them having always been received generally by the whole Church, but the other having never been acknowledged by the Eastern Church,) should yet, notwithstanding, be but one and the same council? How can they themselves endure this, who are so fierce against the Greeks, for having offered to attribute (which they do, notwithstanding, with more appearance of truth) to the sixth council, those one hundred and two canons, which were agreed upon ten years after at Constantinople, in an assembly wherein one party of the Fathers of the sixth council met? How came it to pass, that they gave any credit to the ancient Church, seeing that in the Greek collection of her ancient canons, those of the council of Sardica are entirely omitted; and in the Latin collection of Dionysius Exiguus, compiled at Rome eleven hundred years since, they are placed, not with those of the council of Nice, or immediately after, as making one entire collection with them; but after the canons of all the general councils that had been held till that very time he lived in?* And how comes it to pass that these ancient Popes, who quoted these canons, if they believed these councils to be both one, did not say so?

The African bishops had frequently declared that

* Codex Can. Ec. Dionys. Exig. p. 99.

these canons, which were by them referred to, were not at all to be found in their copies. Certainly therefore, if those who had cited them had thought the council of Nice and that of Sardica to have been both but one council, they would no doubt have made answer, that these canons were to be found in this pretended second part of the council of Nice, among those which had been agreed upon at Sardica; especially when they saw that these careful Fathers, for the clearing of the controversy between them, had resolved to send for this purpose, as far as Constantinople and Alexandria. And yet, notwithstanding all this, they do not utter a word on the subject.

Certainly if the canons of the council of Sardica had been in those days reputed as a part of the council of Nice, it is a very strange thing, that so many learned and religious prelates as there were at that time in Africa, (as Aurelius, Alypius, and even Augustine, that glorious light, not of the African only but of the whole ancient Church,) should have been so ignorant in this particular. But it is strange beyond all belief, that three Popes and their Legates should leave their party in ignorance so gross, and so prejudicial to their own interest; it being in their power to have relieved them in two words. We may safely then conclude that these Popes, Zosimus, and Boniface, had no other copies of the council of Nice than what we have; and also, that they did not believe that the canons of the council of Sardica were a part of the council of Nice; but that they rather purposely quoted some of the canons of Sardica, under the name of the canons of the council of Nice. And this they did, according to that maxim which was in force with those of former times, and is not entirely laid aside even in our own, that for the advancing of a good and godly cause, it is lawful sometimes to use a little deceit, and to have recourse to what are called *pious frauds*. As they therefore firmly believed that the supremacy of their see over all other Churches, was a business of great importance, and would be very profitable to all Christendom, we are not to wonder if, for the establishing this right to themselves, they made use of a little legerdemain, in adducing Sardica for Nice: reflecting that if they brought their design about, this little failing of theirs would, in process of time, be abundantly repaired by the benefit and excellency of the thing itself.

Notwithstanding the opposition made by the African Fathers against the Church of Rome, Pope Leo, not many years after, writing to the emperor Theodosius,* omitted not to make use of the old forgery, citing one of the canons of the council of Sardica, for a legitimate canon of the council of Nice; which was the cause, that the emperor Valentinian also, and his empress Galla Placidia, writing in behalf of the said Pope Leo to the emperor Theodosius,† affirmed to him for a certain truth, that both all antiquity, and the canons of the council of Nice also had assigned to the Pope of Rome the power of judging of points of faith, and of the prelates of the Church; Leo having before allowed that this canon of the council of Sardica was one of the canons of Nice. And thus, by a strong perseverance in this pious fraud, they have at length so fully persuaded a great part of Christendom, that the council of Nice had established this supremacy of the Pope of Rome, that it is now generally urged by all of them whenever this point is controverted.

I must request the reader's pardon for having so long insisted on this particular; and perhaps somewhat longer than my design required: yet, in my judgment, it may be of no small importance to the

* Leo in ep. ad Theodos. Imp. tom. 2 Concil.

† Valentin. in ep. ad Theodos. tom. 2. Concil. Galla Placid. in ep. ad Theodos. tom. 2.

business in hand; for, (will the Protestants here say) seeing that two Popes, Bishops, and Princes, which all Christians have approved, have notwithstanding, thus foisted in false wares, what ought we to expect from the rest of the Bishops and Doctors? Since these men have done this, in the beginning of the fifth century, an age of so high repute for its faith and doctrine, what have they not dared to do in the succeeding ages? If they have not forborne so foully to abuse the sacred name of the council of Nice, (the most illustrious and venerable monument of Christianity next to the Holy Scriptures,) what other authors can we imagine they would spare? And if, in the face of so renowned an assembly, (and in the presence of whatever Africa could show of eminency, both for sanctity and learning, and even under the eye of the great Augustine too,) they had no compunctions of conscience in making use of so gross a piece of forgery; what have they not since, in these later times, while the whole world for so many ages lay covered with thick darkness, dared to do? But as for my part, I shall neither accuse nor excuse at present these men's proceedings, but shall only conclude, that, seeing the writings of the Fathers, before they came to us, have passed through the hands of those who have sometimes been found to use these juggling tricks, it is not so easy a matter, as people may imagine, to discover, out of those writings which now pass under the names of the Fathers, what their opinions were.

Similar motives produced the very same effects in the fifth council;* where a letter, forged under the name of Theodoret, respecting the death of Cyril, was read, and by a general silence approved by the whole assembly; which, notwithstanding, was so evidently spurious, that those very men, who caused the body of the general councils to be printed at Rome,

* Concil. 5. Act. 5. tom. 2. Concil.

have convicted it of falsehood, and branded it as spurious.

Such another precious piece is that foolish story of a miracle, wrought by an image of our Saviour Christ in the city Berytus, which is related in very ample manner in the seventh council,* and bears, forsooth, the name of Athanasius; but is indeed so tasteless a piece, and so unworthy the gallantry and clearness of that great wit, that he must not be thought to have common sense who can find in his heart to attribute it to him. Therefore we see that, notwithstanding the authority of this council, both Nannius, Bellarmine, and Possevine have plainly confessed that it was not written by Athanasius.†

I shall place in this rank the so much vaunted deed of the donation of Constantine, which has for so long a time been accounted as a most valid and authentic evidence, and has also been inserted in the decrees, and so pertinaciously maintained by the Bishop of Agobio, against the objections of Laurentius Valla.‡ Certainly those very men, who at this day maintain the donation, do notwithstanding disclaim this evidence as a piece of forgery.

Of the same nature are the epistles attributed to the first Popes,§ as Clemens, Anacletus, Euaristus, Alexander, Sixtus, Telesphorus, Hyginus, Pius, Anicetus, and others, down to the times of Siricius; that is to say, to the year of our Saviour, 385, which the world read, under these venerable titles, at the least for eight hundred years together; and by which have been decided, to the advantage of the Church of Rome, very many controversies, and especially the

* Concil. 7. Act. 4. tom. 3. Concil.

† Nanni. in edit. op. Athan. Bellar. de imag. l. 2. c. 10. et lib. de Script. Eccles. in Athan. Possevin. in appar. in Athan.

‡ D. 96. C. Constantino nostro. 14. Augusti. Steuchius de Dona. Constant.

§ Baron. in annal. Melchior Canus locor. Theolog. l. 11. p. 511.

most important of all the rest, that of the Pope's monarchy. This shows plain enough the motive, (shall I call it such !) or rather the purposed design of the trafficker that first circulated them. The greatest part of these are accounted forged by men of learning, as Henricus Kaltheisen, Nicolas Cusanus, Jo. de Turrecremata (both cardinals,) Erasmus, Jo. Driedo, Claudius Espensæus, Cassander, Simon Vigor, Baronius, and others:* for indeed their forgery appears clear enough from their barbarous style, the errors met with at every step in the computation of times and history, the pieces they are patched up of, stolen here and there out of different authors, whose books we have at this day to show; and also by the general silence of all the writers of the first eight centuries, among whom there is not one word mentioned of them.

Now I shall not here meddle at all with the last six or seven centuries; where, in regard to various articles of faith, most eagerly professed and established by them, there has been more need than ever of the assistance of the ancients; and whereas, owing to the dark ignorance of those times, and the scarcity of opposers, they had much better opportunity than before, to forge what books they pleased. This abuse the world was never free from, till the time when the light broke forth in the last century; when Erasmus gives us an account,† how he himself had discovered one of these wretched knaves, whose ordinary practice it was to lay his own eggs in another man's nest, putting his own fooleries on Jerome particularly, and

* Hen. Kaltheis. ap. Magdeb. cent. 2. Nic. Cusan. Conc. Cath. l. 2. c. 34. Io. de. Turrecr. de Eccl. lib. 2. c. 101. Io. Driedo de dogm. et Scrip. Eccl. l. 1. c. 2. Cl. Espens. de Contin. l. 1. c. 2. G. Cassand. defens. lib. de officio pii viri, p. 843. Sim. Vig. ex resp. Syn. Basil. &c. en la lettre contr. Durand. Baron. Annal. t. 2. an. 102, et an. 805.

† Erasm. præfat. in Hieron.

on Augustine and Ambrose. And who knows what those many books are, that are daily issued out of the self same shops, that of old were wont to furnish the world with these kind of deceptions? Is it not very probable that both the will and the dexterity in forging and issuing these false wares, will rather in these days increase than abate in the professors of this trade? So that (if besides what the malice of the heretics, the avarice and ignorance of transcribers of manuscripts, and the ambition and affection of men have brought forth of this kind, there have yet so many others turned their endeavours this way, and that in a manner all along for the space of the last fourteen hundred years, although they had their several ends,) we are not to wonder at all if now, in this last age, we see such a strange number of writings falsely fathered upon the ancients; which, if they were all put together, would make little less than a fourth or a fifth part of the works of the Fathers.

I am not ignorant that the learned have noticed a great number of them, and do ordinarily cast them into the later tomes of editions; and that some have written whole books upon this subject; as Ant. Possevine's Apparatus, Bellarmine's Catalogue, Scultetus' Medulla Patrum, Rivet's Critic, and the like, both of the one and the other religion. But who can assure us that they have not forgotten anything they should have noted? Besides that it is a new labour, and almost equal to the former to read so many books of the moderns as now exist. And when all is done, we are not immediately to rest satisfied with their judgment without a due examination. For each of them having been prepossessed with the prejudices of the party in which they were brought up, before they took this work in hand, who shall assure us that they have not delivered anything, in this case, in favour of their own particular interest, as we have before noticed? The justness of this suspicion is so clear, that I presume that no man, any way versed in these matters, will desire me to prove my assertion. Neither shall I need to give any other reason for it, than the conflicts and disagreement in judgments which we may observe in these men: the one of them oftentimes letting pass for pure metal what the other perhaps will throw by for dross; which differences are found not only between those that are of quite opposite religions, but, which is more, even between those that are of the self-same persuasion.

Those whom we named not long before, who were all of the Roman Church, depreciate, as we have said, the greatest part of the decretals of the first Popes. Franciscus Turrianus, a Jesuit, receives them, and defends them all, in a tract written by him to that purpose. Baronius calls the Recognitions, which are attributed to Clemens Romanus, "A gulf of filth and uncleanness; full of prodigious lies and frantic fooleries."* Bellarmine says that this book was written either by Clemens or some other author as learned and as ancient as himself.† Some of them consider those fragments, published by Nicol. Faber, under the name of St. Hilary, as good and genuine productions; and some others again reject them. Erasmus, Sixtus Senensis, Melchior Canus, and Baronius, are of opinion that the book "Of the Nativity of the Virgin Mary," is falsely attributed to Jerome. Christophorus à Castro, a Spanish Jesuit, maintains the contrary. Cardinal Cajetan, Laurentius Valla, Erasmus, and some others, hold the books of Dionysius the Areopagite, as suspected and spurious. Baronius, and almost all the rest of their writers, maintain that they are true and legitimate. Turrianus, Bovin, and some others, recommend to us the "Constitutions of

* Baron. Annal. tom. 1. an. 51.

† Nos fatemur librum esse corruptum, &c. Sed tamen vel esse Clementis Romani, vel alterius æquè docti ac antiqui.—*Bellar. de lib. arbit. t. 5. c. 25.*

the Apostles," as a genuine production; but Baronius, Possevine, Petavius, and a great many others, speak doubtfully of them.

We find in the writings of those of the Church of Rome an infinite variety of judgments in such cases as these. He that desires to furnish himself with examples of this kind, may have recourse to their books, and particularly to the writings of the late Cardinal Perron, who differs as much from the rest, in this point of criticism, as he does for the most part in the method he observes in his disputations. Now, I would willingly be informed what a man should do, amidst these diversities of judgment; and what path he should take, where he meets with such disagreeing guides.

Yet suppose that these authors have done their utmost endeavour in this design, without any particular affection or partiality; how, notwithstanding, shall we be satisfied concerning their capability for the performance of their undertaking? Is it a light business, think you, to bring the whole stock of antiquity to the crucible, and there to purify and refine it, and to separate all the dross from it, which has so deeply, and for the space of so many ages, been not only, as it were, tied and fastened on to it, but even thoroughly mixed, united, and incorporated with it? This work requires the most clear and refined judgment that can be imagined; an exquisite wit, a quick piercing eye, a perfect ear, a most exact knowledge in all history, both ancient and modern, ecclesiastical and secular; a perfect knowledge of the ancient tongues; and a long and continued acquaintance with all kinds of writers, ancient, mediæval, and modern, to be able to judge of their opinions, and which way their pulse beats: to understand rightly the manner of their expression, invention, and method in writing: each age, each nation, and each author, having in all these things their own peculiar ways. Now such a man as this is hardly produced in a whole age.

As for those men who in our times have taken upon them this department of criticism, who knows, who sees not, that only reads them, how many of the qualifications just enumerated are wanting in them? But, suppose, that such a man were to be found, and that he should take in hand this discovery, I do verily believe that he would be able very easily to find out the imposture of a bungling fool, that had ill counterfeited the stamp, colour, and weight, in the work which he would father upon some other man; or that should, for example, endeavour to represent Jerome or Chrysostom with a stammering tongue, and should make them speak barbarous language, bad Latin, and bad Greek; or else perhaps should make use of such terms, things, or authors, as were not known to the world, till a long time after these men; or should make them treat of matters far removed from the age they lived in, and maintain opinions which they never thought of; or reject those which they are notoriously known to have held: and of this sort, for the most part, are those pieces which our critics have decried, and noted as spurious. But if a man should chance to bring him a piece of some able master, that should have fully and exactly learned both the languages, history, manners, alliances, and quarrels of the family into which he has boldly obtruded himself, and should be able to make happy use of all these, be assured that our Aristarchus would be here as much puzzled to discover this juggler, as they were once in France, to prove the impostures of Martin Guerre.

Now, how can we imagine, but that among so many several persons, that have for their several purposes employed their utmost endeavours in these kinds of forgeries, there must needs have been, in so many centuries, very many able men, who have had the skill so artificially to copy the manner and style of the persons whom they imitate, as to render it impossible to discover them? Especially, if they made choice of such a name, as was the only thing remaining in the world of that author; so that there is no mark left us, either of his style, discourse, or opinions, to guide us in our examination. And, therefore, in my judgment, he was a very cunning fellow, and made a right choice, that undertook to write, under the name of Dionysius the Areopagite; for, not having any true legitimate piece of this author left us, by which we may examine the cheat, the discovery must needs be difficult; and it would have proved so much the more hard, if he had but used a more modest and less swelling manner of expression; whereas for those others, who, in the ages following, made bold with the names of Jerome, Cyprian, Augustine, and the like, (of whose legitimate writings we have very many pieces left us,) a man may know them at the first sight, merely by their style; those Gothic and rude spirits being no more able to counterfeit the graces and elegances of these great authors, than an ass is to imitate the warblings of the nightingale.

I confess there is another help, which, in my judgment, may better answer our purpose in this particular than all the rest; namely, the light and direction of the ancients themselves, who oftentimes make mention of other writers of the Church, that lived either before or in their own times; Jerome, among the Latins, having taken the pains to make a catalogue of all those with whose names and writings he was acquainted, from the apostles to his own time, which was afterwards continued by Gennadius. To this we may also add that incomparable work of the patriarch Photius, which he calls his *Bibliotheca*, and which is now published in this our age; where this great person has given us his judgment of most of the authors of the Greek Church. Now, this aid we may make use of in two different ways; the one in justifying a book, if it be found mentioned by these authors; the other in rejecting it, if they say nothing of it. As for the first of these, it concludes only according to the quality of the authors who make mention of a suspected book. For some of the Fathers themselves have made use of these kinds of forgeries, as we have formerly said; others have favoured them because they served their turn; some have not been able to discover them; and some others have not been willing to do so, whatsoever their reason has been.

I shall not here repeat the names of any of those who have done these things themselves. As for those that have favoured them, there are numerous examples; as Justin Martyr, Theophilus, and others, who adduce the Sybils' verses as oracles; the greatest part of which, notwithstanding, are forged. As to Clemens Alexandrinus, the most learned and most polished of all the Fathers, in Jerome's judgment,* how often does he make use of those apocryphal pieces, which go under the names of the apostles and disciples, to whom they were most falsely attributed; citing, under the name of Barnabas,† and of Hermes,‡ such writings as have been forged under their names. And did not the seventh council in like manner make use of a supposititious piece attributed to Athanasius, as we have shown before; and likewise of divers others, which are of the same stamp?

That even the Fathers themselves therefore have not been able always to make a true discovery of these false wares, no man can doubt; considering that of those many necessary qualifications, which we enumerated before, as requisite in this particular,

* Hier. ep. 84. ad Magn. tom. 2. † Clem. Alex. Strom. l. 2.
‡ Clem. Alex. Strom. l. 1. & l. 2. et alibi passim.

they may oftentimes have failed in some. Jerome himself, the most knowing man among all the Latin Fathers, especially in matters of this nature, sometimes lets them pass without examination: as where he speaks of a certain tract against mathematicians, attributed to Minutius Fœlix, "If at least (saith he) the inscription represent unto us the right author of the book."* In another place, whatsoever his reason was, he delivers to us, for legitimate pieces, the epistles that go under the name of St. Paul to Seneca, and of Seneca to St. Paul;† which, notwithstanding, Cardinal Baronius holds for suspected and spurious, as doubtless they are.‡ But even those men who have been able to discover these false pieces have not sometimes been willing to do it; either being unwilling to offend the authors of them, or else not daring to cast any disrepute upon those books which, having many good things in them, had not in their judgment maintained any false or dangerous positions. This is the reason why they chose to let such things pass, rather than, out of a little tenderness of conscience, to oppose them: there being, in their apprehension, no danger at all in the one, but much trouble and invidiousness in the other. Therefore I am of opinion, that Jerome, for example, would never have taken the pains, nor have undergone the invidiousness, of laying open the forgeries of Ruffinus, if the misunderstanding that happened to be between them had not urged him to it. Neither do I believe that the African Fathers would ever have troubled themselves to prove the false allegation of Zosimus, but for their own interest, which was thereby called into question. For wise and sober men are never wont to fall into variance with any without necessity: neither do they quickly take notice of any injury or abuse offered

* Hier. ep. 84. ad Magn. tom. 2.

† Id. in Catal. tom. 1. ‡ Baron. Annal. tom. 1. an. 66.

them, unless it be a very great one, and such as has evident danger in it: which was not at all perceived or taken notice of at first, in these forgeries, that have nevertheless at length, by little and little, in a manner borne down all the good and legitimate books.

These considerations, in my opinion, make it clearly appear, that the title of a book is not sufficiently justified by a passage or two being cited out of it by some of the ancients, and under the same name. As for the other way, which renders the authority of a book doubtful, from the ancients not having made any mention of it, I confess it is no more demonstrative than the other: as it is not impossible, that any one, or divers of the Fathers, may not have met with such a certain writer that was then extant: or else perhaps that they might omit some one of those very authors which they knew. Yet this is, notwithstanding, the much surer way of the two: there being less danger in this case, in rejecting a true piece, than in receiving a forged one; the want of the truth of the one being doubtless much less prejudicial than the receiving the opposite falsehood of the other. For as it is a less sin to omit the good, than to commit the evil that is opposed to it; in like manner is it a less error not to believe a truth than to believe the falsehood which is contrary to it. And thus we see what confusion there is in the books of the ancients, and what defect in the means which is requisite in distinguishing the false from the true: insomuch that, as it often happens, it is much easier to judge what we ought to reject, than to resolve upon what we may safely receive. Let the reader therefore now judge, whether or not, these writings having come down through so many ages, and passed through so many hands, which are either known to have been notoriously guilty, or at least strongly suspected of forgery—the truth in the mean time having made on its part but very weak resistance against these impostures—it be not a very difficult matter to discover, amidst the infinite number of books that are now extant, and go under the names of the Fathers, which are those that truly belong to them, and which, again, are those that are falsely imposed upon them. And if it be so hard a matter to discover in gross only which are the writings of the Fathers, how much more difficult a business will it be to find out what their opinions are, on the several controversies now in agitation. We are not to imagine, that it is no great matter from which of the Fathers such an opinion has sprung, so that it came from any one of them: for there is altogether as much difference amongst these ancient doctors, both in respect of authority, learning, and goodness, as among the modern. Besides that, an age being higher or lower either raises or lessens the repute of these writings, in the esteem both of the one party and of the other, as it were so many grains as years: and certainly not altogether without good reason; it being most evident to any one that has been but the least versed in the reading of these books, that time has by degrees introduced very great alterations, as well in the doctrine and discipline of the ancients, as in all other things.

Our conclusion therefore must be, that if any one shall desire to know what the sense and judgment of the primitive Church has been, as regards our present controversies, it will be first in a manner as necessary for him as it is difficult, exactly to find out both the name and the age of each of these several authors.

CHAPTER IV.

REASON IV.—The writings of the Fathers, which are considered legitimate, have been in many places corrupted by time, ignorance, and fraud, pious and malicious, both in the early and later ages.

BUT now suppose that you have, by long and judicious investigation, separated the true and genuine writings of the Fathers, from the spurious and forged; there would yet rest upon you a second task, the result of which is likely to prove much more doubtful, and more replete with difficulty, than the former. For it would behove you, in the next place, in reading over those authors which you acknowledge as legitimate, to distinguish what is the author's own, and what has been foisted in by another hand; and also to restore to your author whatsoever either by time or fraud has been taken away, and to take out of him whatsoever has been added by either of these two. Otherwise you will never be able to assure yourself that you have discovered, out of these books, what the true and proper meaning and sense of your author has been; considering the great alterations that in various ways they may have suffered at different times.

I shall not here speak of those errors which have been produced by the ignorance of the transcribers, "who write," as Jerome has complained of them, "not what they find, but what themselves understand;"* nor yet of those faults which necessarily have grown up out of the very transcribing; it being impossible that books which have been copied out an infinite number of times, during the space of ten or twelve centuries, by men of different capacities and handwriting, should all this while retain exactly and

* Jer. ep. 28. ad Lucin. tom. i.

in every particular the self-same style, the same form and body, that they had when they first came forth from the author's own hand.

I shall say nothing of the damage sustained by these books from moths and a thousand other injuries of time, by which they have been corrupted; while all kinds of learning, for so many ages together, lay buried as it were in the grave; the worms on one side feeding on the books of the learned, and on the other, the dust defacing them; so that it is impossible now to restore them to their first condition. This is the fate that all kinds of books have been exposed to; whence have originated so many various readings found almost in all authors. I shall not here take any advantage of this; though there are some doctors in the world that have showed us the way to do it; with the intention of lessening the authority that the Holy Scriptures of themselves ought to have in the esteem of all men; under that plea, that even in these sacred writings there are sometimes found various readings, which yet are of very little or no importance as to the ground-work. If we would tread in these men's steps, and apply to the writings of the Fathers what they say and conclude of the Scriptures, we could do it upon much better terms than they; there being no reason on earth to imagine but that the books of the ancient writers have suffered very much more than the Scriptures have, which have always been preserved in the Church with much greater care than any other books, and which have been learned by all nations, and translated into all languages; which all sects have retained, both Orthodox and Heretics, Catholics and Schismatics, Greeks and Latins, Moscovites and Ethiopians; each observing diligently the revisions and transcriptions of the other; so that there could not possibly happen any remarkable alteration in them, without the whole world as it were instantly exclaiming against it, and making their complaints to resound through the universe. Whereas, on the contrary, the writings of the Fathers have been kept, transcribed, and read in as careless a manner as could be; and that too by but very few, and in few places: being but rarely understood by any, save those of the same language; this being the cause that so many faults have the more easily crept into them, and likewise that they are the more difficult to be discovered. Besides that the particular style and obscurity of some of them render the errors the more important. As for example, take a Tertullian, and you will find that one little word added or taken away, or altered ever so little, or a full point or comma put out of its place, will so confound the sense, that you will not be able to discover his meaning: whereas in books of an easy, smooth, clear style, as the Scriptures for the most part are, these faults are much less prejudicial; for they cannot in anywise so darken the sense but that it will be still easy enough to comprehend it.

But I shall pass by all these minute particulars, as more suitable to the inquiries of the Pyrrhonians and Academics, whose business it is to question all things, than of Christians who only seek, in simplicity and sincerity of heart, whereon to build their faith. I shall only here take notice of such alterations as have been knowingly and voluntarily made in the writings of the Fathers, purposely to conceal or disguise their sense, or else to make them speak more than they meant. This forgery is of two sorts; the one has been made use of with a good intention, the other out of malice. Again, the one has been committed in times long since past, the other in this last age, in our own days and the days of our fathers. Lastly, the one is in the additions made to authors, to make them speak more than they meant; the other, in subtracting from the author, to eclipse and darken what he would be understood to say. Neither ought we to wonder, that even those of the honest, innocent, primitive times also made use of these deceits; seeing that, for a good end, they made no great scruple to forge whole books, taking a much stranger and bolder course, in my opinion, than the other. For without doubt it is a greater crime to coin false money, than to clip or alter the true. This opinion has always been in the world, that to fix a certain estimation upon that which is good and true, (that is to say, upon what we account to be such,) it is necessary that we remove out of the way whatsoever may be a hinderance to it, and that there can be no great danger either in putting in, or at least in leaving any thing in, that may yield assistance to it; whatsoever the issue of either of these may in the end prove to be. Hence it has come to pass, that we have so many ancient forgeries, and so many strange stories of miracles and of visions; many taking a delight in feigning (as Jerome says) "great combats which they have had with devils in deserts,"* all of which are merely fabulous in themselves, and acknowledged to be so by the most intelligent of them. Yet, notwithstanding, they are tolerated, and sometimes also recommended, as they account them useful, for the settling or increasing the faith or devotion of the people.

What will you say, if at this day there are some even of those men who make profession of being the greatest haters in the world of these subtilties, who cannot nevertheless put forth any book, without lopping off or falsifying whatsoever does not wholly agree with the doctrine they hold for true; fearing, as they say, lest such things, coming to the eye of the simple common people, might infect them, and possess their heads with new fancies. So firmly has this opinion been of old rooted in the nature of man.

* Dæmonum contra se pugnantium portenta confingunt.—*Hier. ep.* 4. *ad Rustic.* tom. 1.

Now, I will not here dispute whether this proceeding of theirs be lawful or not. I shall only say by the way that in my judgment it is shameful for the truth to be established or defended by such falsifications and evasions, as if it had not sufficient weapons, both defensive and offensive of its own, but that it must borrow of its adversary. It is a very dangerous course moreover, because the discovery of one cheat oftentimes renders the cause of those who practised it wholly suspected. So that, by making use of such sleights as these in the Christian religion, either for the gaining or confirming the faith of some of the simpler people, it is to be feared, that you may give distaste to the more intelligent; and by this means at length may chance to lose also the affections of the more ignorant. But whatsoever this course of deception be, either in itself, or in its consequences, it is sufficient for my purpose, that it has long been the practice in the Church, in matters of religion; and for proof of which I shall here produce some instances.

The heretics have always been accused of using this artifice: but I shall not here notice what alterations have been made by the most ancient of them, even in the Scriptures themselves. If you would have a sample of this practice of theirs, only go to Tertullian and Epiphanius, and you will there see how Marcion had mutilated and altered the Gospel of Luke, and those Epistles of Paul, which he allowed to be such. Nor have the ages following been a whit more conscientious in this particular; as appears by those complaints made by Ruffinus,* in his expositions upon the Apostles' Creed; and in another treatise written by him purposely on this subject; which is indeed contradicted by Jerome,†

* Ruffi. in Expos. Symbol. et lib. de adult. script. Origen.
† Hier. ep. 65, tom. 2, et Apol. 2. contr. Ruffi.

but only in his hypothesis, as to what concerned Origen, but not absolutely in his thesis; and by similar complaints of Cyril,* and various others of the ancients; and among the moderns by those very persons also who have put forth the general councils at Rome; who inform us, in the preface to the first volume,† that time and the fraud of the heretics have been the cause that the acts of the said councils, as far as they exist, have not come to our hands either entire or pure and perfect: and they grievously bewail that we should be thus deprived of so great and so precious a treasure. Now this testimony, coming from such, is to me worth a thousand others; they, in my opinion, being evidently interested to speak otherwise. For if the Church of Rome, who is the pretended mistress and trustee of the faith, has suffered any part of the councils to perish and be lost, which is esteemed by them as the code of the Church, what then may the rest have also suffered? what may not the heretics and schismatics have been able to do? And if all these evidences have been altered by their fraud, how shall we be able by them to come to the knowledge of the opinions and judgment of the ancients? I confess I am much surprised to see these men make so much account of the acts of the councils; and to make such grievous complaints against the heretics for having suppressed some of them. For if these things are of such use, why then do they themselves keep from us the acts of the council of Trent; which is the most important council, both for them and their party, that has been held in the Christian Church these eight hundred years? If it be a crime in the heretics to have kept from us these precious jewels, why are not they afraid, lest the blame which they lay on others may

* Cyril. ep. ad Ioh. Antioch. in Act. Conc. Eph.

† In Præfat. in tom. 1. Concil. Gen.

chance to revert upon themselves? But, doubtless, there is something in the business that renders these cases different; and I confess I wonder they publish it not: the simpler sort, for want of being otherwise informed, thinking perhaps, though it may be without cause, that the reason why the acts of this last council are kept close from them, is because they know that the publishing of them would be either prejudicial, or at least unprofitable, to the greatness of the Church of Rome. They also again, on the other side, conceive that in those other acts, which they say have been suppressed by the heretics, there were wonderful matters to be found, for the advancing and supporting of the Church of Rome. Whatsoever the reason be, I cannot but commend the ingenuity of these men, who, notwithstanding their interest which seemed to engage them to the contrary, have nevertheless confessed, that the councils which we have at this day are neither entire nor uncorrupted.

Let us now examine whether even the orthodox party themselves have not also contributed something to this alteration of the writings of the primitive Church. Epiphanius reports, that in the true and most correct copies of Luke, it was written, that "Jesus Christ wept;" and that this passage had been quoted by Irenæus; but that the Catholics had blotted out this expression, fearing that the heretics might abuse it. *'Ορθοδοξοι δε ἀφειλοντο το ρητον, φοβηθεντες, και μη νοησαντες αὐτου το τελος, και το ἰσχυροτατον.**

Whether this relation be true or false, must rest upon the credit of the author. But this I shall say, that it seems to me a clear argument, that these ancient Catholics would have made no great scruple of blotting out of the writings of the Fathers any word that they found to contradict their own opinions and judgment; and that with the same liberty that

* Epiphanius in Anchor.

they inform us the heretics used to do. For seeing that, as this Father informs us, they made no conscience of making such an attempt upon the gospel of the Son of God himself, with how much greater confidence would they adventure to mangle the books of men? Certainly Ruffinus, a man so much applauded by Jerome,* before their falling out, and so highly esteemed by Augustine,† who very much bewails the breach between those two, (and whom Gennadius‡ has placed, with a very high eulogy of his worth, in his Catalogue of Ecclesiastical writers) has so filthily mangled, and so licentiously confounded the writings of Origen, Eusebius, and others, which he has translated into Latin, that you will hardly find a page in his translations, where he he has not either cut off, or added, or at least altered something. Jerome also, although his opponent, yet agrees with him in this point;§ confessing in several places that he had indeed translated Origen, but in such a manner that he had taken liberty to cut away that which was dangerous, and had left only that which was useful, and had interpreted only what was good, and had left out the bad; that is to say, that if he found anything there that was not consonant to the common judgment and opinions of his time, and so might possibly give offence to the common people, he suppressed it in his translation. He also affirmed that Hilary, and Eusebius, bishop of Vercelli, had done the like.|| And again, in his preface to Eusebius, "De locis Hebraicis," he confesses that he left out that which he conceived was not worth remembering; and that he had altered the greatest part of it. To make it evident that this has been his constant practice, we need but

* Hier. ep. 5. ad Flor. et. ep. 41. ad Ruffin.

† Aug. ep. ad Hier. quæ est inter ep. Hier. 93, et iterum ep. 97.

‡ Gennad. in Catal. inter op. Hier.

§ Hier. ep. 62. ad Theoph. Alex. et lib. 2. Apol. contra Ruffin.

|| Hier. ep. 75. Id. præfat. in lib. Euseb. de loc. Hebr.

compare his Latin chronology with the Greek fragments which remain of Eusebius; where you may plainly see what license these ancients allowed themselves in the writings of others.

What doubt can there be but that those men who came after them, following the authority of so great an example, carefully took out of their copies, or else left out of their translations, the greatest part of whatever they found to be dissonant to the opinions and customs which were received in the Church in the times they lived in? and likewise, that for imparting the greater authority to them, some have had the boldness to add, in some places, what they conceived to be wanting? Whence else could it proceed, that we should have so many unreasonable breakings off in many places, and so many impertinent additions in others, as are frequently to be met with in the ancient authors? Whence otherwise should we have those many coarse patches in the midst of their soft satin and velvet; and that inequality which we observe in one and the same author in a quarter of an hour's reading?

It would be a tedious matter to bring in here all the examples of this kind that might be mentioned; there being scarcely any of the moderns that have taken any pains in writing upon the Fathers, but have noticed and complained of this abuse. Hence it is, that we oftentimes meet with such notices as this, in the margins of the Fathers: "*Hic videtur aliquis assuisse nugas suas*," and the like;* and that also which is observed by Vives upon the twenty-first Book of Augustine de Civitate Dei; namely, that ten or twelve lines, which we find at this day in the twenty-fourth chapter of that Book, containing a possitive assertion of purgatory, were not to be found in

* Tom. 4. op. Ambr. p. 211. lib. 2, de Abra. in marg. annot.

the ancient manuscripts of Bruges, and of Cologne;* no, nor yet in that of Paris, as is noted by those that printed Augustine, anno 1531. One Holsteinius also, a Dutchman, testifies that he had met with divers pieces among the manuscripts of the king's library, of Chrysostom, Proclus, and others, that had in like manner been scratched in divers places by the like hands, by some interpolators of the later and worse ages.†

But I may not here forget to observe, that this alteration has also taken place, even in the most sacred and public pieces, as in the liturgies of the Church, and the like: and I shall give you this observation, in order that it may carry with it the greater gracefulness and weight, in the expressions of Andreas Masius, a man of singular and profound learning, yet of such candour and integrity as renders him more admired than his knowledge; and which, together with his other excellencies, endears him to all moderate men of both professions. This learned person, observing that the Liturgy of St. Basil was not so long in the Syriac as in the Greek, assigns this reason—"For," saith he, "men have always been of such a humour and disposition in matters of religion, that you shall scarcely find any that have been able to content themselves with the ceremonies prescribed unto them by their Fathers, however holy they have been in themselves: so that we may observe that in course of time, according as the prelates have thought fittest to unite the affections of the people to piety and devotion, many other things have been either added or altered, and (which is much worse,) many supersti-

* In antiquis libris Brug. et Colon. non leguntur isti decem aut duodecim qui sequuntur versus.—*Lud. Vives in lib.* 21. *de Civ. Dei*, c. 24.

† Neque solius Athanasii ea fortuna, ut ineptissimorum interpolatorum manus subiret, cùm Chrysostomi, Procli, aliorumque homilias similibus sequiorum sæculorum ineptiis fœdatas, in iisdem regiis codicibus invenerim.—*Holstein. op. lim. præf. tom. op. Athan.*

tious things have been also introduced; in which particular I conceive the Christians of Syria have been more moderate and less extravagant than the Greeks and Latins, from not having the opportunity of enjoying that quiet and abundance of life which the others had."* Thus the learned Masius. Cassander also,† who searched the writings of the ancients with good intentions, acknowledges, and proves out of other authors, that the ancient liturgies have by little and little been enlarged by the several additions of the moderns.

Thus proportionably as the world itself has changed, so would it have whatever there remained of antiquity to undergo its alterations also; imagining that it was but reasonable that these books should in some measure accommodate their language to the times; as the authors of them in all probability would have done themselves, (believing and speaking with the times,) had they been now living. Now to render them the more acceptable, they have used those arts upon them, that some old men are wont to practice; they have new-coloured their beard and mustachios, cutting off the rude and scattered hairs; have smoothed their skin, and given it a fresh complexion, and taught them to speak with a new voice, having changed also the colour of their habit: insomuch that it is much to be feared, that we oftentimes do but lose our labour, when we search, in these disguised faces and mouths, for the complexion and language of true antiquity. Thus have they taught Eusebius to tell us in his Chronicon, that the fast of Lent was instituted by Telesphorus, and the observation of the Lord's day by Pius, both bishops of Rome: which is a thing Eusebius never so much as dreamt of, as may appear out of some manuscripts of his, where you find him wholly

* Andr. Masius, Præf. in Litur. Syr.
† Cassand. in Liturg. cap. 2.

silent as to these points, with which the moderns are much pleased.*

But to return, and take up the thread of time, we may observe that this license grew stronger daily as the times grew worse; because that the greater the distance of time was from the author's own age, the more difficult the discovery of those forgeries must necessarily be: the example also of some of the most eminent persons among the ancients, who had sometimes made use of these sleights, adding on the other side boldness to every one, and courage to venture upon what they had done before them. For indeed, is it not a strange thing, that the legates of Pope Leo, in the year 451, in the midst of the council of Chalcedon, where were assembled six hundred bishops, the very flower and choice of the whole clergy, should have the confidence to quote the sixth canon of the council of Nice in these very words—"That the Church of Rome has always had the primacy:"† words which are no more found in any Greek copies of the councils, than are those other pretended canons of Pope Zosimus: neither do they appear in any Greek or Latin copies, nor so much as in the edition of Dionysius Exiguus, who lived about fifty years after this council. When I consider that the legates of so holy a Pope would at that time have fastened such a wen upon the body of so venerable a canon, I am almost ready to think that we scarcely have any thing of antiquity left us that is entire and uncorrupt, except it be in matters of indifference, or which could not have been corrupted without much noise; and to take this proceeding of theirs, which is come to our knowledge, as an advertisement purposely given us by Divine Providence, to let us see with how much

* Euseb. in Chro. edit. num. 2148. & 2158. Vide Scalig. in loc. p. 198. a. & 201. a. See also Card. Perron's Reply to K. James, Observ. 2. c. 8.

† Concil. Chalced. Act. 16. tom. 2. Concil.

consideration and advisedness we ought to receive for the Council of Nice, and of Constantinople, and for Cyprian's and Jerome's writings, that which goes at this day for such.

About seventy-four years after the council of Chalcedon, Dionysius Exiguus, whom we before mentioned, made his collection at Rome, which is since printed at Paris, *cum privilegio regis*, out of very ancient manuscripts. Whosoever will but look diligently into this collection, will find various alterations in it, one of which I shall instance merely to show how old this artifice has been among Christians.

The last canon of the council of Laodicea, which is the hundred and sixty-third of the Greek code of the Church universal, forbidding to read in churches any other books than those which are canonical, gives us a long .catalogue of them. Dionysius Exiguus, although he has indeed inserted in his collection (Num. 162) the beginning of the said canon, which forbids to read any other books in the churches besides the sacred volumes of the Old and New Testament, yet has wholly omitted the catalogue, or list of the said books: fearing, as I conceive, lest the tail of this cataloguê might scandalize the Church of Rome, where many years before Pope Innocent had, by an express degree to that purpose, put into the canon of the Old Testament* the Maccabees, the Wisdom of Solomon, Ecclesiasticus, Tobit, Judith, &c.; of which books the Fathers of the council of Laodicea make no mention at all, naming but twenty-two books of the Old Testament; and in the catalogue of the New, utterly omitting the Apocalypse.

If any man can show me a better reason for this suppression, let him speak. For my part I conceive this the most probable that can be given. However, we are not bound to divine what the motive should be,

* Innocent I. ep. 3. ad exup. Tholos. c. 7.

that made Dionysius cut off that part of the canon. For, whatsoever the reason was, it serves the purpose well enough to make it appear that at that time they felt no compunction of conscience in curtailing, if need were, the very text of the canons themselves. So that if we had not had the good fortune to have this canon entire and perfect, in divers other monuments of antiquity, (as in the collections of the Greeks, and also in the councils of the French Church,) we should at this day have been wholly ignorant what the judgment of the Fathers of Laodicea was respecting the canon of the Holy Scriptures, which is one of the principal controversies of these times.

It is true, I confess, that the Latins have their revenge upon the Greeks, reproaching them in like manner, that in their translation of the code of the canons of the African Church, they have left the books of the Maccabees quite out of the roll of the books of Scriptures, which is set down in the twenty-fourth canon of their collection, expressly against the faith of all the Latin copies in this collection, both printed and manuscript, as Cardinal Perron affirms.* Yet there are some others† who assure us that no book of Maccabees appears at all in this canon, in the collection of Cresconius, a bishop of Africa, not yet printed.

The Greek code represents to us seven canons of the first council of Constantinople; which are in like manner found both in Balsamon and in Zonaras, and also in the Greek and Latin edition of the general councils, printed at Rome. The last three of these do not appear at all in the Latin code of Dionysius; though they are very important ones as to the business they relate to, which is, the order of proceeding,

* Perron Repl. l. 1. c. 50.

† Christ. Justel. in Not. ad Can. 24. Cod. Gr. Eccles. Afric.

in passing judgment upon bishops accused, and in receiving such persons, who, forsaking their communion with heretics, desire to be admitted into the Church. It is very difficult to say, what should move the collector to alter this council thus. But this I am very well assured of, that in the sixth canon, which is one of those he has omitted, and which treats of judging of bishops accused, there is not the least mention made of *appealing to Rome*, nor of any *reserved cases*, wherein it is not permitted to any, save only to the Pope himself, to judge a bishop; the power of hearing and determining all such matters being here wholly and absolutely referred to provincial diocesan synods. Now whether the Greeks made this addition to the council of Constantinople, (which yet is not very probable,) or whether Dionysius or the Church of Rome curtailed this council, it will still appear evident that this boldness in exscinding or making additions to ecclesiastical writings, is not at all a modern invention. After the canons of Constantinople, there follow, in the Greek code, eight canons of the general council of Ephesus, set down also both by Balsamon and Zonaras, and printed with the acts of the said council of Ephesus, in the first volume of the Roman edition. But Dionysius Exiguus has discarded them all, not giving us any one of them: and you will hardly be able to give a probable guess what his reason should be, unless perhaps it were because the business of the eighth canon displeased him; which is, that the bishops of Cyprus had their ordinations within themselves, without admitting the patriarch of Antioch to have anything to do with it; and that the same course ought to be observed in all other provinces and dioceses; so that no bishop should have power to intrude into a province which had not from the beginning been under his and his predecessor's jurisdiction: "For fear, that under the pretence of the administration of sacred offices, the pride of a secular power should thrust itself into the Church; and by this means we should lose," say these good Fathers, "by little and little, before we were aware, the liberty that our Lord Jesus Christ hath purchased for us with his own blood." Ἱνα μη των πατερων οἱ κανονες παραβαινωνται, μηδε ἐν ἱερουργιας προσχηματι, ἐξουσιας κοσμικης τυφος παρησδυηται μηδε λαθωμεν την ἐλευθεριαν κατα μικρον απολεσαντες ἡν ἡμιν ἐδωρησατο τῳ ἰδιῳ αἱματι ὁ Κυριος ἡμων Ἰησους Χριστος.*

I know not, whether this constitution, and these words have put the Latins into any fright or not; or whether any other reason has induced them not to receive the canons of the council of Ephesus into their code. But this is certain that they do not appear any where among them; and it is now at the least seven hundred and fifty years and upward, that Anastasius Bibliothecarius,† the Pope's library-keeper, testified, that these canons were not anywhere to be found in the most ancient Latin copies; accusing moreover the Greeks of having forged them. Let them settle this dispute among themselves. Whether these canons were forged by the Greeks; or whether they have been blotted out of this council, by the Latins; it is still a clear case, that the cheat is very near eight hundred years standing. But in the next example that follows, the business is evidently clear. For whereas the Greek code, Num. 206, sets before us, in the 28th canon of the general council of Chalcedon, a decree of those Fathers, by which, conformably to the first council of Constantinople, they ordained, that "seeing the city of Constantinople was the seat of the senate, and of the empire, and enjoyed the same privileges with the city of Rome; therefore it should in like manner be advanced to the same height and greatness in ecclesiastical affairs, being the second church

* Concil. Eph. Can. 8. qui in 7. Gr. est 178. Cod. Can. Eccl.
† Anastas. Biblioth. Præf. in Synod. 8. tom. 3. Concil. Gen.

in order, after Rome: and that the bishop of it should have the ordaining of Metropolitans in the three dioceses of Pontus, Asia, and Thrace." *Την βασιλεια και συγκλητῳ τιμηθεισαν πολιν, και των ἰσων ἀπολαυουσαν πρεσβειων τῃ πρεσβυτερᾳ βασιλιδι Ρωμῃ, και ἐν τοις ἐκκλησιαστικοις ὡς ἐκεινην μεγαλυνεσθαι πραγμασι, δευτεραν μετ' ἐκεινην ὑπαρχουσαν.**

This canon is found both in Balsamon and Zonaras; and has also the testimony of the greatest part of the ecclesiastical historians, both Greek and Latin, that it is a legitimate canon of the council of Chalcedon; in the acts of which council, at this day also extant, it is set down at large: yet, notwithstanding, in the collection of Dionysius Exiguus this canon appears not at all, no more than if there had never been any such thing thought of at Chalcedon. We know very well, that Pope Leo and some others of his successors rejected it; but he that promised us that he would make an orderly digest of the canons of the councils, and translate them out of the Greek, why or how did he, or ought he, to omit this so remarkable a canon? If all other evidences had been lost, how should we have been able so much as to have guessed that any such thing was ever treated of at Chalcedon? Where, or by what means, could we have learned what the opinion was of the six hundred and thirty Fathers, who met there together respecting this point, which is the most important one of all those that are at this day controverted among us? It is now eleven hundred years and upward, since this omission was first made. And who will pass his word to us, that among so many other writings, whether of councils or particular men's works, whether Greek or Latin, similar liberty has not been at any time used? Rather by these forgeries which have come to our knowledge, who can doubt but that

* Conc. Chalc. Can. 28. Cod. Græc. Eccl. Univ. 206.

there have been many others of the same kind, which we are ignorant of? You have gone along innocently perhaps, reading these books of the ancients, and believing you there find the pure sense of antiquity; and yet you see here, that from the beginning of the sixth century they have made no scruple of cutting off, from the most sacred books they had, whatsoever was not agreeable to the taste of the times. And therefore, though we had no more against them than this, it were, in my judgment, a sufficient reason to induce us to go on here very warily, and, as they say, with a tight rein, through this whole business.

In the next place there is a very observable corruption in the epistle of Adrian I. to the Emperor Constantine, in the time of the second council of Nice.* For in the Latin collection of Anastasius, made about seven hundred and fifty years since, Adrian is there made to speak very highly and magnificently of the supremacy of his see; and he rebukes the Greeks very shrewdly, for having conferred upon Tarasius, the patriarch of Constantinople, the title of Universal Bishop; and all this while there is not so much as one word of this to be found either in the Greek edition of the said seventh council, nor yet in the common Latin ones. The Romanists accuse the Greeks of having suppressed these two clauses; and the Greeks again accuse the Romanists of having foisted them in: neither is it easy to determine on which side the guilt lies. However, it is sufficient for me, that wheresoever the fault lies, it evidently appears hence, that this curtailing and adding to authors, according to the interest of the present times, has now a very long time been in practice amongst Christians. It appears also very evidently, in the next piece following in the same council, namely, the Epistle of Adrian to Tarasius, that it is quite another thing in

* Concil. 7, Act. 2, tom. 3, Concil.

the Greek from what it is in Anastasius's Latin translation; and that in points too of as high importance as those others before mentioned. So in the fifth act likewise, where both in the Greek text, and also in the old Latin translation, Tarasius is called Universal Bishop,* this title appears not at all in Anastasius's translation.

In the same act, the Fathers accuse the Iconoclasts† of having cut many leaves out of a certain book in the library at Constantinople; and that at a certain city called Photia, they had burned to the number of thirty volumes; that besides this, they had erased the annotations out of a certain book; and all this out of the malice they bore against images, of which these books spoke well and favourably.

Yet I do not see how we can excuse the Romanists from being guilty of corrupting Anastasius in those passages above noted; nor yet of the injury they do Eusebius, in the exposition which they give of certain words of his, only to render him odious; objecting against him, because he says, that "the carnal form of Jesus Christ was changed into the nature of the Deity:"—*Ὅτι μετεβληθη ἡ ἐνσαρκος αὐτου μορφη εἰς την της θειοτητος φυσιν.* Whereas all that he says is, "that it was changed by the Deity dwelling in it:" *ἡ ἐνσαρκος αὐτου μορφη προς της ἐνοικουσης αὐτη θειοτητος μεταβληθεισα.*‡

Hence it appears how much credit we are to give to these men, when they instance here and there divers strange and unheard of pieces; and on the contrary scornfully reject whatever their adversaries bring; as, for example, that remarkable passage quoted by them out of Epiphanius; which passage they refused as supposititious: "Because, (said they,) if Epiphanius had been of the same judgment with the Iconoclasts,

* Concil. 7, Act. 5, tom. 3, Concil. † Ib. p. 557.
‡ Concil. 7, Act. 6, advers. Synod. Iconocl. Sect. 5.

he would then in his *Panarium* have reckoned the reverencing of images among the other heresies:" *Εἰ την των εἰδωλων ποιησιν ἀλλοτριαν του Χριστου ἐγινωσκεν, εἰς τον ἀριθμον των αἱρεσεων ταυτην κατεταξεν ἀν.**

May not a man, by the same reason, as well conclude that Epiphanius was a favourer of the Iconoclasts? for otherwise he would have included their doctrine among the rest of the heresies enumerated by him. I shall not here say anything of their refusing so boldly and confidently those passages quoted from Theodotus Ancyranus, and others. Since that time you will find nothing more common in the books both of the Greeks and the Latins, than the like reproaches, that they mutually cast upon each other, of having corrupted the writings and evidences wherein their cause was the most concerned. As, for example, at the council of Florence;† Mark, bishop of Ephesus, disputing concerning the procession of the Holy Ghost, had nothing to answer to two passages that were alleged against him, (the one out of that piece of Epiphanius which is intitled *Anchoratus*, the other out of Basil's writings against Eunomius,) but that "that piece of Epiphanius had been long since corrupted," (*τουτο το βιβλιον ἐστι διεφθαρμενον προ πολλων χρονων*:) and so likewise of that other passage out of Basil, that "some one or other who favoured the opinion of the Latins, had accommodated it to their views;" moreover protesting,‡ that in all Constantinople there were but four copies of the said book that had that passage quoted by the Latins; but that there were in the said city above a thousand other copies wherein those words were not to be found at all.

The Latins had nothing to retort upon them more

* Concil. 7, Act. 6, advers. Synod. Iconocl. p. 616.
† Concil. Florent. Act. 18, tom. 4, Conc. ‡ Ib. Act. 20.

readily than that it had been the ordinary practice, not of the West but of the East, to corrupt books; and for proof thereof, they cite a passage out of Cyril, which we have heretofore noticed: where, notwithstanding, he says not anything but of the heretics, (that is, the Nestorians,) who were said to have falsified the epistle of Athanasius to Epictetus; but not a word there of all the Eastern men, much less of the whole Greek Church. The Greeks then retorted upon the Latins the story of Pope Zosimus, mentioned in the preceding chapter. Thus did they unceremoniously assail each other, having, as may be easily perceived, much more appearance of reason and of truth in their accusation of their adversaries, than in excusing or defending themselves.

I shall here also give you another similar answer, made by one Gregorius, a Greek monk, a strong maintainer of the union made at Florence, to a passage cited by Mark, bishop of Ephesus, out of a certain book of John Damascene; affirming that "the Father only is the cause," to wit, in the Trinity.* "These words (saith this monk) are not found in any of the ancient copies," which is an evident argument, that it had been afterwards foisted in by the Greeks, to bring over this doctor to their opinion. Petavius has in like manner lately rid himself of an objection, taken out of the sixty-eighth canon of the Apostles, against the fasting on Saturdays, which is observed in the Romish Church, pretending that the Greeks have falsified this canon.†

But whosoever desires to see how full of uncertainty the writings of this later antiquity are, let him but read the eighth council, which is pretended by the Western Church to be a general council, and but com-

* Apol. Gregor. Mon. Protosyn. contra Ep. Marc. Eph. in tom. 4, Concil.

† Petavius Not. in Epiphan.

pare the Latin and the Greek copies together;—taking especial notice also of the preface of Anastasius Bibliothecarius; who (after he has very sharply reproved the ambition of the Greeks, and accused the canons which they produce of the third general council as forged and supposititious,) to make short work with them says, in plain terms, that the Greeks have corrupted all the councils except the first.

What then have we now left us to build upon, seeing that this corruption has prevailed even as far as on the councils, which are the very heart of the ancient monuments of the Church? Nor yet has the Nicene creed, which has been approved and made sacred in so many general councils, been able to escape these alterations. Not to say anything of these expressions, which are of little importance, *de cœlis*, from heaven; *secundum Scripturas*, according to the Scriptures; *Deum de Deo*, God of God; which cardinal Julian affirmed at the council of Florence* were to be found in some creeds, and in some others were not: it is now the space of some ages past, since the Eastern Church accused the Western of having added *Filioque* (and the Son) in the article on the procession of the Holy Ghost: the Western men as senselessly charging upon them again, that they have cut it off;† which is an alteration, though but trivial in appearance, of vast importance to both sides, for the decision of that great controversy which has hitherto caused a separation betwixt them; namely, "Whether or not the Holy Ghost proceeds from the Son as well as from the Father:" which is an evident argument, that either the one or the other of them has, out of a desire to do service to their own side, laid false hands upon this sacred piece.

* Concil. Flor. Sess. 12.

† Concil. Flor. Ses. 4 et 5, et Concil. 7, Act. 7, quo loco vidend. annot. marg.

Now whatever has been attempted in this kind by the ancients, may well pass for innocence, if compared with what these later times have dared to do: their passion being of late years so much heated, that, laying all reason and honesty aside, they have most miserably and shamelessly corrupted all kinds of books and of authors. Of those men that go so desperately to work, we cannot certainly speak of their baseness as it deserves: and in my judgment, Laurentius Bochellus, in his preface to the *Decreta Ecclesiæ Gallicanæ*, had all the reason in the world to detest these men, as "people of a most wretched and malicious spirit, who have most miserably mutilated an infinite number of authors, both sacred and profane, ancient and modern; their ordinary custom being to spare no person, no not kings; nor even St. Louis himself; out of whose *Pragmatica Sanctio* (as they call it) they have blotted out certain articles (principally those which concerned the state of France,) from that library of the Fathers, the *Constitutiones Regiæ*, and others also from the Synodical Decrees of certain Bishops, lately printed at Paris. Wo, wo, (to speak with the prophet) to these mischievous knaves who do not only lay such treacherous snares for the venerable chastity and integrity of the Muses, but do also most impudently and wickedly deflower, under a false and counterfeit pretence of religion, even the Muses themselves, accounting this juggling to be but a kind of pious fraud."*

* Taceo innumeros auctores sacros, profanos, veteres, recentiores ab istis tam improbi quàm infœlicis ingenii hominibus miserabiliter decurtatos, vel ipsis regibus parcere non assuetis, nedum S. Ludovico, cujus *Pragmaticæ* (ut vocant) *Sanctionis* articulos nonnullos, maximè ad rei Gallicæ statum pertinentes, abs bibliotheca illa SS. PP. *Constitutionibus Regiis;* et statutis Episcoporum quorundam Synodalibus reginæ urbium Lutetiæ nuper impressis, expunxerunt. Væ, iterum væ, ut cum Vidente exclamem, nebulonibus, qui tales Musarum castitati et integritati venerandæ non solum insidias struunt, sed et Musas ipsas impudenter, et nequiter subdolo religionis

We do not here write against these men; it is sufficient for us to give a hint only of that which is as clear as the sun; namely, that they have altered and corrupted, by their additions in some places, and curtailing in others, very many of the evidences of the ancient belief. These are they, who in this part of the twelfth epistle of Cyprian, written to the people of Carthage—"I desire that they would but patiently hear our council, &c. that our fellow bishops being assembled together with us, we may together examine the letters and desires of the blessed martyrs, according to the doctrine of our Lord, and in the presence of the confessors, *et secundum vestram quoque sententiam*, (and according as you also shall think convenient)"*—have maliciously left out these words, *et secundum vestram quoque sententiam:* by which we may plainly understand, that these men would not by any means have us know, that the faithful people had ever anything to do with, or had any vote in, the affairs of the Church. These are the same, who, in his fortieth epistle, have changed *Petram* into *Petrum;*† (a *Rock* into *Peter;*) and who, following the steps of the ancient corrupters, have foisted into his tract *De Unitate Ecclesiæ*, wherever they thought fit, whole periods and sentences, against the faith of the best and most uncorrupted manuscripts: as, for example in this place;

zelo, nullius frontis homines devirginant, fucumque istum pietatis nomen ementitum, inter pias fraudes numerant.—*Laur. Bochel. Præfat. in decret. Eccles. Gal.*

* Audiant quæso patienter consilium nostrum; expectent regressionem nostram, ut cum ad vos per Dei misericordiam venerimus, convocati coëpiscopi plures secundum Domini doctrinam, et confessorum præsentiam, beatorum Martyrum literas et desideria examinare possimus. (*Cypr. Ep.* 14. *Extr.*)—Cypr. Pamel. et Gryph. Lugd. an. 1537, l. 3, ep. 16, p. 148; aliæ editiones, ut Manutii, item Morelli, Par. an. 1564, p. 158, legunt "secundum vestram quoque sententiam."

† Cathedra una super *Petrum* Domini voce fundata. (*Cypr. Pamel. Epist.* 40, *p.* 76.)—Gryph. an. 1537, p. 52, Morel. an. 1564, p. 124, habebant *super Petram.*

"He built his Church on Him alone, (Peter,) and commanded him to feed his sheep;* and in this; "He established one sole chair:"† and this other; "The primacy was given to Peter, to show that there was but one church, and one chair of Christ:‡ and this; "Who left the chair to Peter, on which he had built his church."§ These being additions which every one may see the object of.

These are the men who cannot conceal the regret they have for not having suppressed an epistle of Firmilianus, archbishop of Cæsarea in Cappadocia, who was one of the most eminent persons of his time; which epistle Manutius had indeed omitted in his Roman edition of Cyprian;|| but was afterwards inserted by Morellius in his, amongst the epistles of Cyprian, to whom it was written; and all because it informs us how the other bishops in ancient times had dealt with the Pope. Thus we may hence observe of what temper these men have always been, and may guess how many similar pieces have been killed in the nest. Out of the like storehouse it is, that poor Ambrose is sent abroad, but so ill accoutred, and in so pitiful a plight, that Nicolas Faber has very much bewailed the corruption of him.¶ For those gentle-

* Super illum unum ædificat Ecclesiam suam, et illi pascendas mandat oves suas. (*Cypr. Pamel. p.* 254)—Quæ verba desiderantur in edit. Gryph. anno 1537, et Morel. anno. 1564.

† Unam cathedram constituit. (*Cypr. Pamel. ibid.*)—Quæ verba desiderabantur in editione Gryphii, anno 1537, et Morel. anno 1564.

‡ Primatus Petro datur, ut una Ecclesia Christi, et cathedra una monstretur; et pastores sunt omnes; sed unus grex ostenditur, qui ab Apostolis omnibus unanimi consensione pascatur. (*Cypr. Pamel. ibid.*)—Quæ verba omnia, exceptis illis (ut una Ecclesia monstretur) non habebantur in edit. Gryph. neque Morel. uti sup.

§ Qui cathedram Petri super quam fundata est Ecclesia. (*Cypr. Pamel. p.* 254.)—Absunt à Gryph. et Morel. edit.

|| Atque adeo fortassis consultius foret, nunquam editam fuisse hanc epistolam; ita ut putem, consulto illam omisisse Manutium.—*Pamel. in arg. ep.* 75. *Cypr.*

¶ Nic. Faber, in ep. ad Front. Ducæum in Opusc. p. 216.

men who have published him being over ingenious (as he saith) in another man's works, have changed, mangled, and transposed divers things: and especially have they separated the books of the "Interpellation of Job, and of David," which were put together in all other editions; and to do this they have, by no very commendable example, foisted in and altered divers things: and they have likewise done as much in the "First Apology of David;" and more yet in the second; where they have erased out of the eighth chapter five or six lines which are found in all the ancient editions of this Father.* They have also attributed to this author certain tracts which are not his; as that "Of the Forbidden Tree;" and that other upon the last chapter of the Proverbs. We may, by the way, also take notice, that this is the edition which they followed, who printed Ambrose's works at Paris, anno 1603. They were such hands as these that so villainously curtailed the book "Of the Lives of the Popes," written by Anastasius, or rather by Damasus; leaving out, in the very entry of it, the author's epistle dedicatory, written to Jerome, because it did not so well suit with the present temper of Rome; omitting, in like manner, in the life of Peter, the passage which I shall here quote as it is found in all manuscripts; "He consecrated St. Clement Bishop, and committed to his charge the ordering of his seat, or of the whole Church, saying, As the power of binding, and loosing, was delivered to me by my Lord Jesus Christ; in like manner do I commit to thy charge the appointing of such persons as may determine such ecclesiastical causes as may arise; that thou thyself mayest not be taken up with worldly cares, but mayest apply thy whole studies only to prayer, and preaching to the people. After he had thus disposed

* Nic. Faber, ibid. p. 215.

of his seat, he was crowned with martyrdom."* This is the testament that Peter made; but it has been suppressed and kept from us, because in it he has charged his successors with such duties as are quite contrary both to their humour and practice. In another place, in the same book, instead of *Papa Urbis*, (that is to say, "the Pope or Bishop of the city," namely, of Rome, as all manuscripts have it) these worthy gentlemen will needs have us read *Papa Orbis*, that is, "the Bishop of the whole world:"† inasmuch as this is now the style of the court, and this has long since become the title of the bishop of Rome.

These are the men, who in Fulbertus, bishop of Chartres,‡ (where he cites that remarkable passage of Augustine, "This then is a figure commanding us to communicate of the passion of the Lord,") have inserted these words, "Figura ergo est, dicet hæreticus:" (It is a figure then, will a heretic say:) cunningly making us believe this to be the saying of a heretic, which was indeed the true sense and meaning of Augustine himself, and so cited by Fulbertus. These are the very men also, who in St. Gregory have changed *exercitus sacerdotum* into *exitus sacerdotum;* reading, in the 38th epistle of his fourth book, thus: "All things, &c. which have been foretold, are accomplished. The king of pride (he speaks of Antichrist) is at hand; and, which is horrible to be spoken, the

* Hic B. Clementem Episcopum consecravit, eique cathedram, vel ecclesiam omnem disponendam commisit, dicens: Sicut mihi gubernandi tradita est à Domino meo Jesu Christo potestas ligandi solvendique; ita et ego tibi committo, ut ordines dispositores diversarum causarum, per quos actus ecclesiasticus profligetur; et tu minimè in curis seculi deditus reperiaris, sed solummodo ad orationem, et prædicationem populi vacare stude. Post hanc dispositionem Martyrio coronatur.—Habentur hæc ex Euchar. Salm. ad Sirmond. cap. 5. Editio Par. anno 1621, p. 664.

† Dei ordinante providentia Papa Orbis consecratus est. (*Anastas. in Stephano* v. p. 215.)—MSS. habent, *Papa Urbis,* ex Salm. in Euchar. ad Sirmond. pag. 464.

‡ Vid. Fulbert. Carnot. Edit. à Villerio, anno 1608, Par. p. 168.

failing (or end) of priests is prepared: whereas the manuscripts (and it is so cited by Bellarmine too) read, "An army of priests is prepared for him."*

These are they who have made Aimoinus to say, that the Fathers of the pretended eighth general council "had ordained the adoration of images, according as had been before determined by the orthodox doctors:" whereas he wrote quite contrary, "that they had ordained otherwise than had been formerly determined by the orthodox doctors;" as appears plainly, not only by the manuscripts, but also by the most ancient editions of this author; and even by Card. Baronius, quoting this passage also, in the tenth tome of the Annals, anno Domini 869.†

These are they who have entirely erased this following passage out of Œcumenius: "For they who defended and favoured the law, introduced also the worshipping of angels; and that because the law had been given by them. And this custom continued long in Phrygia, insomuch that the council of Laodicea made a decree, forbidding to make any addresses to angels, or to pray to them: whence also it is that we find many temples among them erected to Michael the Archangel." *Οἱ γαρ τῳ νομῳ συνηγορουντες, και τους ἀγγελους σεβειν εἰσηγουντο, ὁτι δἰ ἀυτων και ὁ νομος ἐδοθη. Ἐμεινε δε τουτο κατα Φρυγιαν το ἐθος, ὡς και την ἐν Λαοδικεια συνοδον νομῳ κωλυσαι το προσιεναι ἀγγελοις, και προσευχεσθαι, ἀφ᾽ οὑ και ναοι παρ᾽ ἀυτοις του ἀρχιστρατηγου Μιχαηλ πολλοι.*

* Omnia, &c. quæ prædicta sunt, fiunt. Rex Superbiæ prope est; et quod dici nefas est, Sacerdotum ei præparatur exitus. (*Gregor M. ep. l.* 4. *ep*. 38.)—MSS. habent, 'Sacerdotum ei præparatur exercitus;' ex Tho. James. in Vindic. Gregor. loc. 666; quomodo citatur etiam à Bellarmino hic locus, lib. 3. de Rom. Pont. c. 13. Sect. Addit. et extr. c. Sect. pari ratione.

† In quâ Synodo, (quam Octavam Universalem illuc convenientes appellarunt) de imaginibus adorandis, secundum quod orthodoxi doctores antea definierant, statuerunt. (*Aimon. de Gest. Franc. lib.* 5, *c*. 8.)—Legendum; "Aliter quàm orthodoxi definierant; sic enim legit ipse Baron. Annal. tom. 10. an. 869.

This passage David Hœschelius, in his notes upon the books of Origen against Celsus, p. 483, witnesses that he himself had seen and read in the manuscripts of Œcumenius; and yet there is no such thing to be found in any of the printed copies. Who would believe but that the Breviaries and Missals should have escaped their pruning-knife? Yet, as it has been observed by persons of eminent learning and honesty, where it was read, in the collect on St. Peter's day heretofore thus: "Deus, qui B. Petro Apostolo tuo, collatis clavibus regni cœlestis, animas ligandi, et solvendi Pontificium tradidisti:" (that is, O God, who hast committed to thy Apostle St. Peter, by giving him the keys of the heavenly kingdom, the episcopal power of binding and loosing souls:*) in the later editions of these Breviaries and Missals, they have wholly left out the word *animas* (souls;) to the end that people should not think that the Pope's authority extended only to spiritual affairs, and not to temporal also. So likewise in the Gospel upon the Tuesday following the Third Sunday in Lent, they have printed, "Dixit Jesus discipulis suis;"† (that is, "Jesus said to his disciples;") whereas it was in the old books "Respiciens Jesus in discipulos dixit Simoni Petro, Si peccaverit in te frater tuus:"‡ (Jesus looking back upon his disciples, said unto Simon Peter, If thy brother have offended against thee, &c.,) cunningly omitting those words relating to Simon Peter, for fear it might be thought that our Saviour Christ had made St. Peter, that is to say, the Pope, subject to the tribunal of the Church to which he there sends him.

If the council of Trent would but have hearkened to Thomas Passio, a canon of Valencia, they should

* Simon Vigor. l. 1. de la Monarch. Ecclesiastique, ch. 1. F. Paolo di Vinet, Apol. contr. Bellarm. Sic legitur in Brev. Clement. VIII. jussu recognitis, p. 937.

† Sic legitur in Breviar. Clem. VIII. jussu recogn. p. 369.

‡ Sic legebatur in Brev. impres. Paris. 1492, per Jo. de Prato.

have blotted out of the Pontifical all such passages as make any mention of the people's giving their suffrage and consent in the ordination of the ministers of the Church: and, among the rest, that where the bishop, at the ordination of a priest, saith, "That it was not without good reason, that the Fathers had ordained that the advice of the people should be taken in the election of those persons who were to serve at the altar; to the end that having given their assent to their ordination, they might the more readily yield obedience to those who were so ordained."* The meaning of this honest canon was, that to take away all such authorities from the heretics, the best way would be to blot them all out of the Pontifical; to the end that there might be no trace or footstep of them left remaining for the future.

They have not, however, contented themselves with merely corrupting in this manner certain books, out of which perhaps we might have been able to discover what the opinion and sense of the ancients has been:† but they have also wholly abolished a very great number of others. And for the better understanding of this, we should notice that the emperors of the first ages took all possible care to suppress and abolish all such writings as were declared prejudicial to the true faith; as the books of the Arians and Nestorians and others, which were forbidden to be read under a great penalty, but were to be wholly suppressed and abolished by the appointment of these ancient princes.

The Church itself also sometimes called in the books of such persons as had been dead long before, by the

* Neque enim fuit frustra à patribus institutum, ut de electione illorum, qui ad regimen altaris adhibendi sunt, consulatur etiam populus; quia de vita et conversatione præsentandi, quod nonnunquam ignoratur à pluribus, scitur à paucis; et necesse est, et facilius ei quis obedientam exhibeat ordinato, cui assensum præbuerit, ordinando.—*Pontif. Rom. de Ordinat. Presbyt.* fol. 38.

† Pet. Soave, Hist. Concil. Trident. l. 7.

common consent of the Catholic party, as soon as they perceived anything in them that was not consonant to the present opinion of the Church: as it did at the fifth general council,* in the business of Theodorus, Theodoretus, and Ibas, all three bishops, the one of Mopsuestia, the other of Cyrus, and the third of Edessa; anathematizing each of their several writings, notwithstanding these persons had been all dead long before: dealing also, even in the quiet times of the Church, with Origen in the same manner, after he had been dead about three hundred years.†

The Pope hath not failed to imitate, for the space of many ages, both the one and the other of these rigorous courses; increasing moreover the harshness of them from time to time: insomuch that, in case any of the opinions of the ancients has been by chance found at any time to contradict his, there is no doubt but that he has very carefully and diligently suppressed such writings, without sparing any, more than the others, though they were written perhaps two, three, four, or five hundred years before. As for example, it is at this time disputed, whether or not the primitive Church had in their temples, and worshipped, the images of Christ and of saints. This controversy has been sometimes very warmly, and with much heat, and for a long time together, disputed in the Greek Church. That party which maintained the affirmative, bringing the business before the seventh council held at Nicæa,‡ it was there ordained, that it should be unlawful for any man to have the books of the other party, and charging every man to bring what books they had of that party to the Patriarch of Constantinople, to do with them, as we may imagine, according as had been required by the legates of Pope Adrian; that is, "That they should burn all

* Conc. 5. Col. 8. † Id. Col. 5. et Col. 8. Anath. 11.
‡ Concil. 7, Act. 8, Can. 9.

those books which had been written against the venerable images:" Ἵνα παντα τα συγγραμματα τα κατα των σεπτων εἰκονων γενομενα μετα ἀναθεματισμου λειανθωσιν, ἢ τῳ πυρι παραδοθωσι:* including no doubt, within the same condemnation, all such writings of the ancients as seemed not to favour images; as the epistle of Eusebius to Constantia; and that of Epiphanius to John of Jerusalem, and others which are not now extant, but were in all probability at that time abolished. As for the epistle of Epiphanius, that which we now have is only Jerome's translation of it, which happened to be preserved in the western parts, where the feeling in behalf of images was much less violent than it was in the eastern: but the original Greek of it is no where to be found. Adrian II. in his council ordained, in like manner, that the council held by Photius against the Church of Rome should be burnt, together with his other books, and all the books of those of his party which had been written against the see of Rome: and he commanded the very same thing also in the eighth council, which is accounted by the Latins for a general council.†

It is impossible but that in these fires very many works must needs have perished that might have been of great use to us for discovering what the opinion of the ancients was, whether respecting images, which was the business of the seventh council; or that other controversy respecting the power of the Pope, which was the principal point debated in the synod held by Photius; some of whose writings, for the self-same reason, they at this day keep at Rome under lock and key; which doubtless they would long ere this have published, had they but told as much for the Pope as in all probability they tell against him. This rigorous proceeding against books at length arrived to such a

* Concil. 7, Act. 5.

† Cap. 1, habetur in Concil. 8, Act. 7. Ibid. Act. 1, in Ep. Adriani.

height, that Leo X., at the council of Lateran, which broke up in the year 1518, decreed, "that no book should be printed but what had first been diligently examined at Rome by the Master of the Palace, in other places by the bishop, or some other person deputed by him for the same purpose, and by the Inquisitor, under this penalty, That all booksellers offending herein should forfeit their books, which should be burnt in public, and should pay a hundred ducats, when it should be demanded, towards the fabric of St. Peter, (a kind of punishment this, which we find no example of in all the canons of the ancient Church ;) and should also be suspended from exercising his function, for the space of a whole year."*

This is a general sentence, and which comprehends as well the works of the Fathers as of any others; as appears plainly by this, that the bishop of Malfi, having given in his opinion, saying, that he concurred with them in relation to new authors but not to the old, all the rest of the Fathers voted simply for all;† neither was there any limitation at all added to this decree of the council. This very decree has been since strongly confirmed by the council of Trent,‡ which appointed also certain persons to take a review of the books and censures, and to make a report of them to the company, "to the end that there might be a separation made between the good grain of Christian verity and the tares of strange doctrines:"§ that is, in plain terms, that they might suppress in all kinds of books whatever relished not well with the taste of the Church of Rome. But these fathers,

* Conc. Later. sub Leone X. Sess. 10.

† Responderunt omnes placere, excepto R. P. D. Alexio, episcopo Melfitano, qui dixit, Placere de novis operibus, non autem de antiquis.—*Ibid.*

‡ Concil. Trid. Sess. 5. Decreto de Edit. et usu Sacror. libr.

§ Quo facilius ipsa possit varias et peregrinas doctrinas, tanquam zizania, à Christianæ veritatis tritico separare.—*Idem. Sess.* 18.

having not the leisure themselves to look to this pious work, appointed certain commissaries who should give an account of this matter to the Pope:* whence, afterwards it came to pass, that first Pope Pius IV. and afterwards Sixtus V. and Clement VIII. published certain rules and indexes of such authors and books as they thought fit should be either quite abolished or purged only, and have given such strict order for the printing of books, as that in those countries where this order is observed, there is little danger that ever anything should be published, that is either contrary to the doctrine of the Church of Rome, or which advances anything in favour of their adversaries.

All these instructions, which are too long to be inserted here, may be seen at the end of the council of Trent where they are usually given in full. To enforce these rules they have put forth their *Indices Expurgatorii* (as they call them;) namely, that of the Low Countries, and of Spain and other places; where these men sit in judgment upon all kinds of books, erasing and altering, as they please, periods, chapters, and often whole treatises, and that too in the works of those men who for the most part were born, and educated, and died also, in the communion of their own Church.

If the Church, eight or nine hundred years since, had razors sharp as these men now have, it is then a vain thing for us to search any higher what the judgment of the primitive Christians was on any particular point: for whatsoever it was, it could not have escaped the hands of such masters. And if the ancient Church had not heretofore any such institution as this, why then do we, who pretend to be such observers of antiquity, practise these novelties? I know very well that those men make profession of reforming

* Concil. Trident. Sess. 25, decreto de Indice libr.

only the writings of the moderns: but who sees not that this is but a cloak which they throw over themselves, lest they should be accused as guilty of the same cruelty that Jupiter is among the poets, for having behaved himself so insolently to his own father? Those pieces which they erase so scrupulously from the books of the moderns, are the cause of the greater mischief to themselves, when they are found in the writings of the ancients, as sometimes they are. For what a senseless thing is it to leave them in where they hurt most, and to erase them where they do little harm?

The inquisition at Madrid* omits these words in the index of Athanasius, "Adorari solius Dei est;" (that is, God alone is to be worshipped:) *Οὐκουν θεου ἐστι μονου το προσκυνεισθαι*:† and yet, notwithstanding, these words are still expressly found in the text of Athanasius. The same Father saith, "that there were some other books, besides those which he had before set down, which, in truth, were not of the canon, and which the Fathers had ordained should be read to those who were newly come into the Christian communion, and desired to be instructed in the word of piety." *Ἐστι και ἑτερα βιβλια τουτων ἐξωθεν, οὐ κανονιζομενα μεν, τετυπωμενα δε παρα των πατερων ἀναγινωσκεσθαι τοις ἀρτι προσερχομενοις και βουλομενοις κατηχεισθαι τον εὐσεβειας λογον.*‡

They reckoned in this number the Wisdom of Solomon, Ecclesiasticus, Judith, Esther, Tobit, and some others. Nevertheless these very censors erased, in the index of Athanasius's works, those words which affirm that the said books are not at all canonical. In the index of Augustine they erased these words: "Christ hath given the sign of his body:" which yet are evidently to be seen in the text of this Father, in his

* Ind. Expurgat. Sandoval. in Athanas. Ind. 1.
† Athanas. Orat. 3, contra Arian. ‡ Id. in Frag. et Fest.

book against Adimantus, chap. 12.* They erased, in like manner, these words: "Augustine accounted the Eucharist necessary to be administered to infants:" which opinion of Augustine is very frequently found expressed either in these very words, or the like, throughout his works, as we shall see hereafter. They likewise erased these words: "We ought not to build temples to angels:" and yet the very text of Augustine says, "If we should erect a temple of wood or of stone to any of the holy angels, should we not be anathematized?"†

This is the practice of the censors, both in the Low Countries and in Spain, in many other particulars, which we shall not here notice. Now if you cut off such sentences as these from the indexes of these holy Fathers, why do you not as well erase them from the text also? Or if you leave them in the one, why do you blot them out in the other? What can the meaning be of so strange a way of proceeding in such wise men? Yet who sees not the reason of it? The sentences which these men thus boldly and rudely correct, are as displeasing to them in the ancients as in the moderns; and where they may safely do it they expunge them, as well from the one as the other. But this they dare not do openly, for fear of incurring scandal, which they are willing to avoid; because if they should deal so unceremoniously, and take such liberty with antiquity, they would destroy that respect which all people bear towards it; which being a matter that very nearly concerns themselves, it is a special point of wisdom in them, carefully to preserve its reputation. But in lashing the poor moderns, who have made indexes to all the works of the Fathers, they

* Id. in August.

† Nonne si templum alicui sancto angelo excellentissimo de lignis et lapidibus faceremus, anathematizemur à veritate Christi, et ab ecclesia Dei, &c.—*Infr. l.* 1. *c.* 8. *Ind. Exp. Sandov. in August. contr. Maxim. lib.*

save their credit, and do their business too; ruining the opinions which they hate by chastising the one, and still preserving the venerable esteem of antiquity, which they cannot exist without, by sparing the other.

I cannot however see why Bertram, a priest, who lived in the time of the emperor Charles the Bald, which is about seven hundred and fifty years since, should be classed among the moderns: and yet his book, "De Corpore et Sanguine Domini," is absolutely, and without any limitation, forbidden to be read, in the index of the council of Trent, in the letter B, among the authors of the second *classis*, as they call them. But the censors of the Low Countries have dealt with him more gently, shall I say, or rather more cruelly; not quite taking his life away, but only maiming him in the several parts of his body, and leaving him in the like sad condition with Deiphobus in the poet:—

> "Lacerum crudeliter ora,
> Ora manusque ambas populataque tempora, raptis
> Auribus, et truncas inhonesto vulnere nares."

For they have cut off, with one single dash of their pen, two long passages, consisting each of them of twenty-eight or thirty lines, and which are large enough to make up a very considerable part of a small treatise, such as his.

That the reader may the better judge of the business, I shall here extract one of these passages entire as it is:

"We ought further to consider (says Bertram, speaking of the holy Eucharist) that in this bread is represented not only the body of Christ, but the body of the people also that believe in Him. And hence it is that it is made up of many several grains of wheat, because the whole body of believing people is united together, and made into one, by the word of Christ. And therefore as it is by a mystery that we receive this bread for the body of Christ, in like manner it is

9*

by a mystery also, that the members of the people believing in Christ are here figured unto us. As this bread is called the *body of believers*, not corporeally but spiritually; so is the *body of Christ* also necessarily to be understood as represented here, not corporeally but spiritually. In like manner is it in the wine, which is called the blood of Christ, and with which it is ordained that water be mixed; it being forbidden to offer the one without the other: because as the head cannot subsist without the body, nor the body without the head, in like manner neither can the people be without Christ, nor Christ without the people. So that in this sacrament the water represents the image of the people. If then the wine, after it is consecrated by the office of ministers, be corporeally changed into the blood of Christ, of necessity then must the water also be changed corporeally into the body of the believing people: because that where there is but one only, and the same sanctification, there can be but one and the same operation; and where the reason is equal, the mystery also that follows it is equal. But as for the water, we see that there is no such corporeal change wrought in it: it therefore follows that neither in the wine is there any corporeal transmutation. Whatsoever then of the body of the people is signified unto us, by the water, is taken spiritually: it follows therefore necessarily that we must, in like manner, take spiritually whatsoever the wine represents unto us of the blood of Christ. Again, those things, which differ among themselves, are not the same. Now the body of Christ which died, and was raised up to life again, dies no more, having become immortal; and death having no more power over it, it is eternal and free from further suffering. But this, which is consecrated in the Church, is temporal, not eternal; corruptible, not free from corruption; in its journey, and not in its native country. These two things therefore are different, one from the other, and consequently cannot be one and the same thing. And if they be not one and the same thing, how can any man say that this is the real body and real blood of Christ? If it be the body of Christ, and if it may be truly said that this body of Christ is really and truly the body of Christ—the real body of Christ being incorruptible and impassible, and therefore eternal; consequently this body of Christ, which is consecrated in the Church, must of necessity also be both incorruptible and eternal. But it cannot be denied but that it doth corrupt, seeing it is cut into small pieces and distributed (to the communicants,) who bruise it very small with their teeth, and so take it down into their body."*

* Considerandum quoque, quòd in pane illo non solùm corpus Christi, verum etiam corpus in eum credentis populi figuretur: unde multis frumenti granis conficitur, quia corpus populi credentis multis per verba Christi fidelibus augmentatur, (al. coagmentatur.) Qua de re sicut mysterio panis ille Christi corpus accipitur: sic etiam in mysterio membra populi credentis in Christum intimantur. Et sicut non corporaliter, sed spiritualiter panis ille credentium corpus dicitur: sic quoque Christi corpus non corporaliter sed spiritualiter necesse est intelligatur. Sic et in vino, qui sanguis Christi dicitur, aqua misceri jubetur, nec unum sine altero permittitur offerri, quia nec populus sine Christo, nec Christus sine populo, sicut nec caput sine corpore, vel corpus sine capite valet existere. Igitur si vinum illud, sanctificatum per ministrorum officium, in Christi sanguinem corporaliter convertitur, aqua quoque, quæ pariter admixta est, in sanguinem populi credentis necesse est corporaliter convertatur. Ubi namque una sanctificatio est, una consequenter operatio; et ubi par ratio, par quoque consequitur mysterium. At videmus in aqua secundum corpus nihil esse conversum, consequenter ergo et in vino nihil corporaliter ostensum. Accipitur spiritualiter quicquid in aqua de populi corpore significatur; accipiatur ergo necesse est spiritualiter quicquid in vino de Christi sanguine intimatur. Item, quæ à se differunt, idem non sunt: corpus Christi, quod mortuum est, et resurrexit, et immortale factum jam non moritur, et mors illi ultrà non dominabitur, æternum est, jam non passibile. Hoc autem, quod in ecclesia celebratur temporale est, non æternum; corruptibile est, non incorruptibile, in via est, non in patria. Differunt igitur à se, quapropter non sunt idem. Quòd si non sunt idem, quomodo verum corpus Christi dicitur, et verus sanguis? Si enim corpus Christi est, et hoc dicitur verè, quia corpus Christi in veritate cor-

Thus Bertram. His other passage, which is longer yet than this, is of the same nature; but I shall not here set it down, to avoid prolixity.*

Now these gentlemen, finding that the language of both these passages did very ill accord with the doctrine of Transubstantiation, thought it the best way to erase them entirely: for fear lest, coming to the people's knowledge, they might imagine that there had been Sacramentarians in the Church ever since the time of Charles the Bald.

Then, whoever you may be that think yourself bound to search the writings of the Fathers for the doctrine of salvation, learn from this artifice of theirs, and those many other cheats which we, to their great mortification, are now investigating, what an extreme desire they have to keep from us the opinion and sense of the ancients in all those particulars where they ever so little contradict their own doctrines; and remembering moreover, how every day they have had, and still have, such opportunities of doing what they please in this way, you cannot doubt, but that they have struck deep enough where there was cause. These blows of theirs, together with the alterations and changes that time, the malice of heretics, the innocent and pious frauds of the primitive Church, and the sentiments of the later Christians, have long since produced, have rendered the writings and venerable

pus Christi est, et si in veritate corpus Christi, incorruptibile est, et impassibile, ac per hoc æternum. Hoc igitur corpus Christi quod agitur in ecclesia necesse est ut incorruptibile sit, et æternum. Sed negari non potest corrumpi, quod per partes commutatum dispartitur ad sumendum, et dentibus commolitum in corpus trajicitur.—*Bertram. Presbyt. lib. de Corp. et Sang. Dom.*

* Non malè aut inconsultè omittantur igitur omnia hæc à fine paginæ: 'Considerandum quoque quod in pane illo,' &c.; usque ad illud multò post, 'Sed aliud est quod exteriùs geritur,' &c. in ead. pag. Et seq. pag. omnia illa sequentia, 'Item quæ idem sunt, unâ definitione comprehenduntur,' &c.; usque ad illud, 'Hoc namque quod agitur in viâ, spiritualiter,' &c. seq. pag.—*Index Expurg. Belg.* an. 1571, *in Bertramo.*

monuments of antiquity, so jumbled and confused, that it will be a very difficult matter for any man to make a clear and perfect discovery of those things which so many different parties have endeavoured to conceal from us.

CHAPTER V.

Reason V.—The writings of the Fathers are difficult to be understood, on account of the languages and idioms in which they wrote, and the manner of the writing, which is encumbered with rhetorical flourishes and logical subtleties, and with terms used in a sense far different from what they now bear.

If any man, either by the mere light of his own mind, or by the assistance and direction of some able and faithful hand, shall at length be able, as by the help of the clew of which the poets speak, to extricate himself happily from these two labyrinths, and to find any pieces of the ancients that are not only legitimate, but also entire and uncorrupt; certainly that man has just reason to rejoice at his own good fortune, and to give God hearty thanks. For I must needs confess that it is no very small satisfaction to a man to have the opportunity of conversing with those illustrious persons of ages passed, and to learn of them what their opinions were, and to compare our own with theirs:

"Verasque audire et reddere voces."

But yet this I dare confidently pronounce, that if he would know from them what their sense and opinions have truly been, as to the differences now in agitation, he will find that he is now but at the very beginning and entrance of his business; and that there remain behind many more difficulties to be overcome in his passage, than he has yet grappled with. One of the two disagreeing parties refusing the Scriptures for the judge of controversies by reason of its obscurity, lays this for a ground, (and indeed rationally enough) that no obscure books are proper for the decision of controversies.

Now I do not know why a man may not, with as much reason, say of most of the writings of the Fathers, as Jerome did of some certain expositors of some parts of the Scriptures, "That it was more trouble to understand them well, than those very things which they took upon them to expound:"* that is to say, that it is much harder rightly to understand them than the Scriptures themselves. For a man fully to comprehend them, it is in the first place necessary that he have perfect and exact skill in those languages wherein they wrote; that is to say in the Greek and Latin, which are the tongues in which most of them wrote. As for those of the Fathers who have written either in Syriac or Arabic, or Ethiopian, or the like vulgar tongues of their own, whose writings perhaps would be as useful to us in the discovery of the opinions of the ancient Church as any others; we have not, that I know, any of those monuments now publicly to be seen abroad, but only some translations of them in Greek or Latin: as, for instance, the works of St. Ephrem, (if at least those books, which go abroad under his name, be truly his:) and the "*Comment. de Paradiso*," of Moses Bar-Cephas, translated into Latin by Masius, and perhaps some few others.

I know very well, that for the most part, men trust to the translations of the Fathers, whether they be in Latin or in vulgar languages; and that the world is now come to that pass, that people will not hesitate to take upon them to judge of the Greek Fathers,

* Plerisque nimium disertis accidere solet, ut major sit intelligentiæ difficultas in eorum explanationibus, quàm in iis quæ explanare conantur.—*Hier. ep.* 139. *ad Cypr.*

without having (at least, that can be perceived out of their writings,) any competent knowledge of the Greek tongue,* which cannot in my judgment be accounted anything less than the highest presumption. The thing is clear enough of itself, that to be able to reach the conceptions and sense of a man, especially in matters of importance, it is most necessary that we understand the language he delivers himself in, his terms, and the manner of their coherence; there being in every particular language a certain peculiar force, and power of significancy, which can scarcely ever be so preserved in translation but that it will lose in the passage something of its natural lustre and vigour, however learned and faithful the interpreter may be. But this, which is very useful indeed in all other cases, is most necessary in the particular business before us, by reason of the little care and fidelity that we find in the translations of the greatest part of the interpreters of the Fathers, whether ancient or modern.

We have before seen how Ruffinus, and even Jerome himself, have laboured in this particular; and long after them, Anastasius also, in his translation of the seventh council, who, notwithstanding in his preface to the eighth gives us this for a most infallible rule; namely, that whatsoever is found in his translation is true and legitimate, and, on the contrary, whatsoever the Greeks have said, either more or less, is supposititious and forged.

If all the other interpreters of the councils and Fathers had been men of the same temper that Anastasius here would have us believe him to be, we might then indeed very well lay by the Greek text, and content ourselves with such dull Latin as he has furnished us with in his translation. But the mischief of it is, that all the world does not believe this testimony which he has given of himself; and that, although he has such

* Bellarmine.

a special gift in valuing his own translation above the original; yet this will hardly ever be allowed to other translators, especially the modern, who, having been men that have been for the most part carried away by their affection to their own party, he must needs be a very weak man that should trust to them in this case, and rely upon what they say.

Whosoever hath yet a mind to be further satisfied how far these men's translations are to be trusted, let him but take the pains to compare the Greek preface to Origen's books against Celsus, with the Latin translation of *Christophorus Persona;* and, if he please, he will do well to run over some part of the bocks themselves; and if he is desirous of exposing himself to the laughter of the Protestants, let him but produce, upon the honest word of this worthy interpreter, this passage out of the fifth book for the Invocation of Angels:—"We ought to send up our vows, and all our prayers and thanksgivings to God, by the angel who has been set over the rest by him who is the Bishop, the living Word, and God:"* in which words he seems to intimate that Jesus Christ hath appointed some one of the angels to hear our prayers, and that by him we ought to present them to God; whereas Origen says the direct contrary; namely, "That we ought to send up to God, who is above all things, all our demands, prayers, and requests, by the great High Priest, the living Word, and God, who is above all the angels." *Πασαν μεν γαρ δεησιν, και πασαν προσευχην, και ἐντευξιν και εὐχαριστιαν ἀναπεμπτεον τῳ επι πασι θεῳ, δια του ἐπι παντων ἀγγελων ἀρχιερεως, ἐμψυχου λογου, και θεου.*†

You have a sufficient discovery also of the affections of translators, who many times make their

* Vota namque et preces omnes, et gratiarum insuper actiones ad Deum, sunt per Angelum transmittendæ, qui per Pontificem, et vivens verbum, et Deum, angelis præfectus est cæteris.—*Origen. Christoph. Persona, lib. 6. contr. Celsum..*

† Orig. contr. Cels. l. 5. p. 239.

authors speak more than they meant, in Jo. Christophorson's translation of the ecclesiastical historians: as likewise in most of the translators of these later times, excepting only some very few of the more moderate sort. But we shall not need to insist any longer on this particular, which has been sufficiently proved already by the several parties of both sides discovering the falseness of their adversaries' translations, as every man must know who is any way conversant with that kind of writings, where you shall meet with nothing more frequent than these mutual reprehensions of each other.

Now, in the midst of such distraction, and contrariety of judgments, how can a man possibly assure himself that he hath the true sense and meaning of the Fathers, unless he hear them speak in their own language, and have it from their own mouth? I shall here lay down then, for a most sure ground and undeniable maxim—

That to be able rightly to apprehend the judgment and sense of the Fathers, it is necessary that we first understand the language they write in; and that too, not slightly and superficially, but exactly and fully; there being in all languages certain peculiar terms and idioms, familiarly used by the learned, which no man shall ever be able to understand thoroughly and clearly, that has but a superficial knowledge of the said languages, and has not dived even to the depth and very bottom of them. If you would see how necessary the knowledge of an author's language is, and how prejudicial the want of it, do but turn to that passage of Theodoret, where, speaking of the Eucharist, he saith thus:—*Οὐδε γαρ μετα τον ἁγιασμον τα μυστικα συμβολα της οἰκειας ἐξισταται φυσεως, μενει γαρ ἐπι της προτερας οὐσιας, και του σχηματος, και του εἰδους.** The Protestants, and all their adversaries

* Theod. Dial. 2.

(before cardinal Perron,) interpret this place thus: "The mystical symbols, after consecration, do not leave their proper nature; for they continue in their first substance, figure, and form." Now what can be said more expressly against transubstantiation? But yet the above named cardinal, having, it seems, consulted those old friends of his among the grammarians, who had heretofore taught him, that *μιαινειν* signified *to smoke*, or *evaporate*,* will needs persuade us, that this passage is to be interpreted otherwise; namely, that "the signs in the Eucharist continue in the figure and form of their first substance:" which would be tacitly and indirectly to allow transubstantiation. Now it is true that this exposition is contrary, not only to the design and purpose of the author, but to the usual way of speaking also among the Greeks. But in case you had not exact skill in the language, how should you be able to judge of this interpretation? especially seeing it put upon you with so much confidence and unparalleled boldness, according to the ordinary custom of this doctor, who never affirms or recommends anything to us more confidently, than when it is most doubtful and uncertain.

It is out of the same rare and unheard-of grammar, that the said cardinal has elsewhere taken upon him to give us that notable correction of his, of the inscription of an epistle written by the emperor Constantine to Miltiades, bishop of Rome, set down in the tenth book of Eusebius's Ecclesiastical History, (c. 5,) reading it thus: "Constantinus Augustus, to Miltiades, bishop of the Romans, wisheth long time or long opportunity:" whereas all copies, both manuscript and printed, have it, "Constantinus Augustus, to Miltiades, bishop of the Romans, and to Mark," (*Κωνσταντινος Σεβαστος, Μιλτιαδῃ ἐπισκοπῳ Ρωμαιων,*

* Perron Repl. p. 709. Answ. to the 2 Instit. where he takes this word to signify *to smoke;* whereas the true signification is, *to pollute*, or *defile*.

και Μαρκω:)* fearing, I suppose, lest some might accuse the emperor of not understanding himself aright, in here making this Mark companion to the Pope, who in all things ought to march without a compeer.

I should never have done, if I should undertake to notice all those other passages, in which the cardinal has used the same arts, in wresting the words of the ancients to a wrong sense, which otherwise would seem to favour the Protestants: whence it may plainly appear, how necessary a knowledge of the languages is, for the right understanding of the sense of the Fathers. So that, in my judgment, the result of all this will clearly be, that, as we have before said, it is a difficult thing to come to the right understanding of them. For who knows not what pains it will cost a man to attain to a perfect knowledge of these two tongues; what abilities are necessarily required in this case? A happy memory, a lively conception, a good education, continual application, and much and diligent reading; all which very rarely meet in any one person. The truth of this is clearly proved, by the continual debates and disputes among those who, though they have referred the judgment of their differences to the decision of the Fathers, do yet notwithstanding still implead each other at their bar, and cannot possibly be brought to any agreement whatever.

Many of the writers of the Church of Rome, object against the Protestants, as an argument of the obscurity of the Scriptures, the controversies that are betwixt themselves and the Lutherans, against the Calvinists, as regards the Eucharist; and of the Calvinists

* Perron, in his Reply, says we ought to read it thus: *Κωνσταντινος Σεβαστος, Μιλτιαδη επισκοπω Ρωμαιων και προν μακρον.* But it seems more probable that we should read, *και Μεροκλει*, and to Merocles, who was at that time bishop of Milan, as is observed by Optatus, lib. 1, p. 334.

against the Lutherans and the Arminians, in the point of predestination. If this argument of theirs be of any force at all, who sees not that it clearly proves that which we maintain in this particular? For the Greeks and the Latins, who both of them make profession of submitting themselves to the authority of the Fathers, and to plead all their causes before them, have not as yet been able to come to any agreement. Do but observe the passages between these two, at the council of Florence,* where the strongest and ablest champions on both sides were brought into the lists; how they wrangled out whole sessions, about the exposition of a certain short passage in the council at Ephesus, and some similar one out of Epiphanius,† Basil,‡ and others: and after all their disputes, how clearly and powerfully soever each party vaunted that the business was carried on, they have yet left us the sense of the Fathers much more dark and obscure than it was before; their contests having rendered the business much more perplexed. Each side has indeed very much the appearance of reason in what they urged against their adversaries, but very little solidity in what they have said severally for themselves. Certainly the Latins, who are thought to have had the better cause of the two, (and who, upon a certain passage of Basil adduced by themselves, *Οὐ λαμβανομεν τινα παρα του πνευματος, ὥσπερ παρα του υἱου το πνευμα,*§ triumphed as if they had gained the day—baffling and affronting the Greeks in a very disdainful manner, and giving them very harsh language,) used, notwithstanding, such an odd kind of logic, to persuade the receiving of the exposition which they gave, as that even at this day, in the last edition of Basil's works, printed at Paris, and revised

* Concil. Flor. Sess. 5, de Decreto quodam Concil. Eph. Act. 6, Sess. 11 et 12.

† Concil. Flor. Sess. 18, 20.

‡ Ibid. Sess. 21.

§ Ibid. locus Basil.

by Fronto Ducæus,* the Latin translation follows, in this particular, not their exposition, but that of the Greek schismatics.

Some of the Protestants having also had the same success in some particular points controverted betwixt themselves, it lies open to every man's observation, how much obscurity there is found in the passages cited by both sides. If Tertullian was of the opinion of the Church of Rome, in the point concerning the Eucharist, what could he have uttered more dark and obscure than this passage of his, in his fourth book against Marcion; "Christ having taken bread, and distributed it to his disciples, made it his body, in saying, This is my body; that is to say, The figure of my body."† If Augustine held transubstantiation, what can the meaning be of these words of his, "The Lord hesitated not to say, This is my body, when he delivered the sign of his body?"‡

If these passages, and an infinite number of the like, do really and truly mean that which Cardinal Perron pretends they do, then was there never any thing of obscurity either in the riddles of the Theban Sphinx, or in the oracles of the Sybils.

If you look on the other side, you will meet with some other passages in the Fathers, which seem to speak point blank against the Protestants; as, for example, where they say expressly, "That the bread changes its nature; and that by the almighty power of God, it becomes the flesh of the Word:" and the like. And so in all the controversies between them, they produce such passages as these, both on the one

* Basil. in Orat. in Sacr. Baptis. p. 511, tom. 1. Edit. Paris. apud Michael. Sonnium anno 1618.

† Acceptum panem, et distributum discipulis, corpus suum illum fecit, Hoc est corpus meum, dicendo, id est, Figura corporis mei. —*Tertul. contr. Marc. l.* 4, *c.* 40.

‡ Non enim Dominus dubitavit dicere, Hoc est corpus meum, cùm signum daret corporis sui.—*Aug. cont. Adimant. c.* 12.

side and on the other: some whereof seem to be irreconcilable to the sense of the Church of Rome, and some others to the sense of their adversaries.

If cardinal Perron, and those other sublime wits of both parties, can have the confidence to affirm that they find no difficulty at all in these particulars, we must needs think that either they speak this merely out of bravado, setting a good face upon a bad matter; or else, that both the wits and eyesight of all the rest of the world are marvellously dull and feeble, in finding nothing but darkness, where these men see nothing but light. Yet for all this, if there be not obscurity in these writings of the Fathers, and that very great too, how comes it to pass, that even these very men find themselves ever and anon so puzzled to discover the meaning of them? How comes it to pass, that they are fain to use so many words, and make trial of so many tricks and devices, for the clearing of them? Whence proceeds it, that so often, for fear of not being able to satisfy their readers, they are forced to cry down either the authors or the pieces out of which their adversaries produce their testimonies?

What strange sentences and passages of authors are those that require more time and trouble in elucidating them, than in deciding the controversy itself, and which multiply differences rather than determine them; oftentimes serving as a covert and retreating place to both parties? Thus the sense and meaning of these words is debated: "This is my body." For the explaining of them, there is brought this passage out of Tertullian; and that other out of Augustine. Now I would have any man speak in his conscience what he thinks, whether or not these words are not as clear, or clearer, than those passages which they quote from these Fathers, as they are explained by the different parties. I desire, reader, no other judge than yourself, whosoever you are; only provided that you will but vouchsafe to read and examine that which is now said upon these places, and consider the strange turnings and contortions that they make us take, to bring us to the right sense and meaning of them. In a word, if the most able men that exist did not find themselves extremely puzzled and perplexed in distinguishing the genuine writings of the Fathers from the spurious, it is not likely that the censors of the Low Countries, who are all choice and select men, should be obliged to show us so ill an example of finding a way to help ourselves, when the authority of the ancients is strongly pressed against us by our adversaries, as they do, in excusing the expressions of the Fathers sometimes, by some handsomely contrived invention, and in putting some convenient probable sense upon them.*

What has been said, I am confident, is sufficient to convince any reasonable man of the truth of the assertion, that it is a very difficult matter to understand the sense and opinions of the Fathers by their books. But that we may leave no doubt behind us, let us briefly consider some few of the principal causes of this difficulty.

Certainly the Fathers, having been wise men, all of them both spoke and wrote to be understood; insomuch that, having both the will and the ability to do it, it seems very strange that they should not be able to attain the end they aimed at. But we must here call to mind what we have said before, that these controversies of ours having not in their time sprung up, they had no occasion, nor was it their design, either to speak or write anything respecting them. For these sages raised as few doubts in matters of religion as they could. Besides their times furnished them

* Plurimos in Catholicis veteribus errores excogitato commento persæpe negamus, et commodum iis sensum affingimus, dum opponuntur in disputationibus, aut in conflictibus cum adversariis.—*Ind. Exp. Belg. in Bertr.*

with sufficient matter of dispute, in points which were then in agitation, without so much as thinking of those of ours now on foot. And they have very clearly delivered their sense in all those controversies on which they have entered. Even Tertullian himself, who is the most obscure amongst them all, has notwithstanding delivered himself so clearly in the disputes between him and Marcion and others, that there is no place left to doubt what his opinions were on the points discussed. I am therefore fully persuaded that if they had lived in our times, or if the present controversies had been agitated in their times, they would have delivered their judgment upon them very plainly and expressly. But seeing that they have not touched upon them, or only slightly, and as they came accidentally in their way, rather than from any design, we are not to think it strange, if we find them not to have spoken decidedly, and given their sense clearly as to these disputes of ours. As any man may easily observe in the ordinary course, those things that happen without design are never clear and full, but ambiguous and doubtful; and oftentimes contrary, perhaps, either to the sense or the sentiment of the person from whom they proceeded. Thus before the springing up of that pernicious doctrine of Arius, who so much troubled the ancient Church, there was very little said of the eternity of the divine nature of Jesus Christ: or if the Fathers said anything at all of it, it was only by the way, and not by design: and hence it is also that what they have delivered in this particular, is as obscure and difficult to be rightly understood, as those other passages of theirs that relate to our present controversies.

Do but explain the meaning, if you can, of this passage of Justin Martyr, in his treatise against Trypho; where he saith that "The God which appeared to Moses and to the Patriarchs, was the Son and not the Father;"* inasmuch as the Father is not capable of locomotion, neither can he properly be said to ascend or descend: and that "No man ever saw the Father, but only heard his Son, and his angel, who is also God, by the will of the Father." *Οὐτε οὐν Ἀβρααμ, οὐτε Ισαακ, οὐτε Ἰακωβ, οὐτε ἀλλος ἀνθρωπων εἰδε τον πατερα και ἀρρητον κυριον των παντων ἁπλως, και αὐτου του Χριστου, ἀλλ' ἐκεινον, τον κατα βουλην την ἐκεινου και θεον ὀντα, υἱον αὐτου, και ἀγγελον, ἐκ του ὑπηρετειν τῃ γνωμῃ αὐτου*, &c.†

These words of his cannot be very well explained, without allowing a difference of nature in the Father and the Son; which were to establish Arianism.

Observe what Tertullian also says, in this particular, namely, "That the Father, bringing him forth out of himself, made his Son;"‡ and, "That the Father is the whole substance, and the Son a portion, and a derivation of that whole;"§ and many other similar passages, which you meet with here and there, in that excellent piece of his, written against Praxeas, which will scarcely be reconciled to good sense. In like manner does Dionysius Alexandrinus call the Son, "The work, or workmanship, of the Father:" *Ποιημα και γενητον εἰναι τον υἱον του θεου*:|| which are the very terms that were so much quarrelled about in Arius. The eighty Fathers, who condemned Paulus Samosatenus, bishop of Antioch, said expressly, "That the Son is not of the same essence with the Father:"¶ that is to say, they in express terms denied the

* Just. contr. Tryph. p. 283, et 356, edit. Paris. 1615.

† Ibid. p. 357.

‡ Quem ex semetipso proferendo, Filium fecit.—*Tertul. lib.* 2, *contr. Marc. c.* 27.

§ Pater tota substantia est, filius verò derivatio totius et portio. —*Id. l. cont. Prax. cap.* 9, *et passim in eo opere.*

|| Dion. Alex. apud Athanas. ep. de fide Dion. Alex. Vide et Basil. ep. 41, t. 2. p. 802.

¶ Octoginta Episcopi olim respuerunt το ὁμοουσιον.—*Athan. ep. de Syn. Arim. et Selcu. Vide et Hilar. de Syn. fol.* 97.

ὁμοουσιον, or *consubstantiality* of the Son, which was afterwards established in the council of Nice.

It would be no difficult matter to make good the assertion in reference to all the other disputes that have arisen in the Church against Macedonius, Pelagius, Nestorius, Eutyches, and the Monothelites; that the Fathers have spoken very obscurely of these matters, before the controversies were started; as persons that spoke only incidentally thereof, and not with previous design. It is now long since that Jerome said, "That before Arius, that impudent devil, appeared in the world, the Fathers had said many things innocently, and without taking much heed of their words, as they might have done; and indeed some things that can hardly escape the cavils of wrangling spirits."* This has also been observed by some of the most learned among the moderns; as cardinal Perron,† and also the Jesuit Petavius (a man highly esteemed by those of his own party) who, writing upon Epiphanius, and endeavouring to clear Lucian the Martyr from the suspicion of being an Arian and a Samosatenian, says, "That in this question respecting the Trinity, as also in various others, it has so happened that most of the ancient Fathers, who wrote before the rise of those particular heresies in the Church, have in their writings let fall here and there such things as are not very consonant to the rule of the orthodox faith."‡

* Vel certè antequam in Alexandria quasi dæmonium meridianum Arius nasceretur, innocenter quædam, et minus cautè locuti sunt, et quæ non possint perversorum hominum calumniam declinare.—*Hier. Apol.* 2, *contr. Ruff.*

† Perron. Repl. Obs. 4. c. 5.

‡ Quod idem plerisque veterum Patrum, cùm in hoc negotio (Trinitatis,) tum in aliis fidei Christianæ capitibus, usù venit, ut ante errorum atque heresean quibus ea sigillatim oppugnabantur, originem, nondum satis illustrata et patefacta rei veritate, quædam scriptis suis asperserint, quæ cum orthodoxæ fidei regula minimè consentiant.—*Dion: Petav. in Panar. Epiph. ad Hær.* 69. *quæ est Arian.*

Since therefore they have done thus in other points, what wonder is it if they have likewise done the same in these particular controversies at this day disputed amongst us? and that having lived so long before the greatest part of these controversies arose, they have spoken of them so obscurely, doubtfully, and confusedly? For my part I think it would have been the greater wonder of the two, if they had done otherwise; and shall account it as a very great sign of forgery, in any piece which is attributed to antiquity, whenever I find it treating expressly and clearly of these points, and as they are now-a-days discussed. Only compare the expressions of the most ancient Fathers, on the divinity and eternity of the Son of God, with their expressions on the nature of the Eucharist; and certainly you will find, that the former are not more wide of the truth at this day professed on this last point, than the other were from the doctrine long since declared in the council of Nice. This council expressly and positively declared, "That the Son is consubstantial with the Father." The council of Antioch had before denied this. Whether the Fathers therefore affirm or deny that the Eucharist is really the body of Christ, they will not however therein contradict thy opinion (whosoever thou art, whether Romanist or Protestant) any more than the Fathers of the council of Antioch seem to have contradicted those of the council of Nice.

We may here add, that as the Arians ought not in reason to have adduced, in justification of their opinions, any such passages of the Fathers as had fallen from them inadvertently, and in discoursing on other subjects, without any idea of establishing an opinion thereon; so neither, to say the truth, is there any reason, that either thou or I should produce, as definitive sentences upon our present controversies which have arisen but of late years, any such passages of the Fathers as were written by them, in treating of other matters many ages before the commencement of our differences, of which they never had the least idea; and concerning which they have delivered themselves very diversely and obscurely, and sometimes also seemingly contradicting themselves. And as we find that some of the faithful Christians, who lived after these primitive Fathers, have endeavoured to reconcile their sayings to the truth which they professed; as Athanasius has done in some passages of Dionysius Alexandrinus,* and of the Fathers of the council of Antioch; in like manner ought we to use our utmost endeavour to make a fair interpretation of all such passages in the writings of these men, as seem to clash with the true orthodox belief on the Eucharist and other similar points: not accounting it any great wonder, if we sometimes chance to meet with passages which seem to be utterly inexplicable. For it may so fall out that they may be really so; for it is very possible, that in the points touching the person and the natures of the Son of God, some such expressions may have fallen from them, as is very well known to those who are versed in their writings. Possibly also we may meet with some passages of theirs, which, though they may be explicable in themselves, may notwithstanding appear to us to be inexplicable; by reason perhaps of our wanting some of those circumstances which are necessarily requisite for elucidating and clearing the same: as for example, when we are ignorant of the scope and drift of the author, and of the connection and dependencies of his discourse, and other similar particulars which are requisite for the penetrating into the sense of all kinds of writers. For it is with men's words as it is with pictures: they must have their proper light to show themselves according to the meaning and intention of the author: and according to the

* Athan. ep. de fid. Dionys. Alex. et ep. de Syn. Arim. et Seleuc. ubi supra.

difference of the lights we see them by, they also have a different appearance. As for example, if any one should now urge alone, and barely without reference to the rest of the discourse and history of its author, this short passage of Dionysius Alexandrinus, where he calls the Son of God, *ποιημα του Θεου*, (the workmanship of the Father;) *Ποιημα και γενητον ειναι τον υἱον του Θεου, μητε δε φυσει ἰδιον ἀλλα ξενον κατ' ἰδιαν εἰναι του πατρος, ὡσπερ ἐστιν ὁ γεωργος, προς την ἀμπελον, και ὡς ὁ ναυπηγος προς το σκαφος· και γαρ ὡς ποιημα ων, οὐκ ἠν πριν γενηται*; and adds certain other very strange terms, also touching this particular, (as we daily see the custom of some is, in the business of our present controversies, to produce the like shreds and little short passages severed from the main body of the discourse whereof they are a part;) which of us, how able soever he be, could possibly imagine anything else, but that this is an absolute Arian expression, and such as cannot be interpreted in any other sense? And yet Athanasius, in the places before cited, makes it plainly appear that it is not so; and by the advantage of those lights which he had in the subject there treated of by the author, he demonstrates to us that this expression of Dionysius, how strange soever it appear, has notwithstanding a good and allowable sense in that place.

That we may be enabled more fully to elucidate the subject, we shall in the next place take into consideration some other causes of the obscurity of the Fathers; among which I shall rank, in the first place, their having sometimes purposely, and from design, endeavoured either wholly to conceal their conceptions from us, or at least to lay them down, not clear and open, but as it were with a curtain (and that sometimes a very thick one too) drawn over them, to the end that none but those of the quickest and most piercing eyes should be able to penetrate them: some of their meditations having been such as they themselves accounted either of little use, or else such as it was not so safe to commit to weak vulgar spirits. Whether this practice of theirs was raised upon good grounds or not, I shall not here stay to examine: it is sufficient for me to show that it was usual with them, as may appear, among others in Clemens Alexandrinus, about the beginning of his Stromata, where, giving an account of the design of his book, he says that "He had passed over some things in silence, fearing to write that of which he made some scruple even to speak: not that he envied his readers anything, but fearing rather lest they might haply, from misunderstanding them, fall into error; and thus he might seem to have put a sword into the hand of a child." He adds further, "That he had handled some things clearly, and some others obscurely; laying the one open to our view, but wrapping up the other in riddles." *Τα μεν ἑκων παραπεμπομαι, ἐκλεγων ἐπιστημενως φοβουμενος γραφειν, ἁ και λεγειν ἐφυλαξαμην· οὐ τι που φθονων, οὐ γαρ θεμις· δεδιως δε ἀρα περι των ἐντυγχανοντων, μηπη ἑτερως σφαλειεν, και παιδι μαχαιραν, ἡ φασιν οἱ παροιμιαζομενοι, ὀρεγοντες εὑρεθωμεν, &c. ἐτι δε ἁ και αἰνιξεται μοι γραφη, και τοις μεν παραστησεται, τα δε μονον ἐρει.**

That which tells most to our present purpose is, that they are known to have taken this course particularly in some of those points which are now controverted amongst us; as in that touching the Sacraments of the Church. For as they celebrated their holy mysteries in secret and apart by themselves, not admitting either the Pagans or the Catechumens, nor yet (as some assure us) any person whatsoever, save only the communicants, to the sight of them;† in like manner also in their writings, especially in those that were to be read openly to the people in their public assemblies, they never spoke but very obscurely and

* Clem. Alex. Strom. 1.

† Cassand. in Liturg. c. 26.

darkly, as has been observed on the subject of the Eucharist by cardinal Perron, and by Casaubon, Petavius, and others, and also in the points of baptism, confirmation, and other holy ceremonies of the Christians.* Observe how wary Theodoret, Epiphanius, and other ancient writers are, in adverting to the subject of the Eucharist; describing it in general terms only, and such as they only could understand, who had been formerly partakers of that Holy Sacrament.

I shall not here take upon me to examine the end which they proposed to themselves in so doing, which seems to have been to implant in the minds of the Catechumens, a greater reverence and esteem for the Sacraments, and a more earnest and eager desire to be admitted to partake of them: fearing lest the laying open and discoursing plainly on the matter and manner of celebrating the Sacraments might lessen these feelings for them.

Seeing therefore that not only in this, but in divers other particulars also, they have purposely and from design concealed their meaning and opinions from us; we ought not to account it so strange a matter, if we many times find their expressions to be obscure, (and which is a consequence of obscurity,) if they sometimes also seem to clash, and contradict one another. Indeed, it were more to be wondered at, if these men, who were for the most part able and learned, having a purpose of writing obscurely on these points, should yet have left us their opinions clearly and plainly delivered in their writings. But there is still more in it: for sometimes, even where they had no purpose of being so, they yet are very obscure: and again, the little conversation they have had with those arts, which are requisite for the polishing of language, was the cause of their not expressing themselves so clearly: and sometimes perhaps their genius and natural dispo-

* Casaub. in Baron. exercit. 16.

sition might be the reason; all their study and industry not being able to correct this natural defect in them.

I believe we may very safely reckon Epiphanius in the first rank of this kind of writers, who was indeed a good and holy man, but yet had been very little conversant in the arts, either of Rhetoric or Grammar, as appears sufficiently from his writings; where he is often found failing, not only in the clearness of his expressions, and in the flow and adaptation of his periods, but also even in their order and method, which is the true light of all discourse. These defects must necessarily be the cause of much obscurity in many places; and indeed is much complained of by the interpreters of this Father.

Others perhaps there have been, who have endeavoured to polish their language by art, who yet have not been able to compass their intention; whether it were, because they began too late, or else perhaps through the dulness of their wit, and want of capacity; as we see that all natures are not capable of receiving all forms, whatever pains and industry they take for the making such impressions. In this number you may reckon that Victorinus, of whom Jerome gives this so favourable testimony, saying, that, though indeed he wanted learning, he wanted not a desire and good will to learning.*

Such another also was Ruffinus, whose language and expressions the same great censor of the ancients so sharply reproves, noticing in him many improprieties of speech, and other absurdities: and yet for all this he would not be taken off from his scribbling humour;† and which is more, there were not wanting those who admired him: it being commonly observed, that those who wrote most in any age were not

* Victorino Martyri in libris suis licèt desit eruditio, tamen non deest eruditionis voluntas.—*Hier. ep.* 84, *ad Magn.*

† In Apol. 1, in Ruff. et Apol. 2, et Apol. ad Ruff.

always the ablest men; this mania existing rather in the ignorant than in the other. Photius, in his Bibliotheca, has noticed the like defects in some of his Greek writers.

Yet this obscurity in the Fathers has proceeded, not from their ignorance, but rather from their great learning; for those among them, who were furnished with all kind of secular learning, and had been trained up from their infancy in the eloquence and knowledge of the Greeks, could not but retain this tincture, and sometimes also had their flights, and made show of this their treasury; by this means mixing with the Christian philosophy many exotic words, customs, and discourses: which mixture, though it gives indeed much pleasure to the learned, must necessarily render the sense of these authors the more dark and perplexed.

What can you name more mixed or fuller of variety, than Clemens Alexandrinus's Stromata, as he calls them, and his other works, which are throughout interwoven with historical allusions, opinions, sentences, and proverbs, out of all kinds of writers, both sacred and profane; being here heightened with rich and light colours, there shaded with darkness, to such a degree that it is vain for an ignorant person to hope ever to obtain his meaning?

What shall I say of Tertullian, who, notwithstanding that natural harshness and roughness in which he everywhere abounds, and that Carthaginian spirit and genius which is common to him with the rest of the African writers, has yet shadowed and overcast the brilliancy of his conceptions with so much learning, and with so many new terms and phrases of law, and with such variety of allusions, subtilties, and nice points, that the greatest store of learning and attention you may possess, will be all little enough to give you a perfect understanding of him?

I shall not here speak anything of Hilary, of the

loftiness of his imagination, of the sublimity of his language, and of that *Cothurnus Gallicanus* which Jerome has noticed in him, and in others of his countrymen. Neither shall I here take any notice of the copiousness of the Africans, nor of the subtilty of the Athenians, and of those that had their education among them, the consideration of all which particulars would afford matter for an entire volume. I shall only say in general, that as the manner of the Christian writing and expounding the Scriptures was at first very plain, easy, and brief; in a very short time it began to be changed, and to be clogged with subtilties, and flourishes of secular learning, as testified by Methodius in Epiphanius. "The doctors (says he) no longer regarding an honest, plain, and solid way of teaching, began now to endeavour to please, and to be favourably received by their auditors; just as sophisters are wont to do, who consider their labours rewarded by their auditors applauding their learning; thus selling themselves at so cheap a rate. For as for the ancients, their expositions were always very brief; their utmost ambition in those days being not to please but to profit their hearers." *Των διδασκαλων οὐτε προς το βελτιστον ἁμιλλωμενων ἐτι και σεμνον, ἀλλα προς το ἀρεσαι και εὐημερησαι· καθαπερ οἱ Σοφισται, οἱ μισθον αἱρουνται των λογων ἐπευωνιζομενοι της σοφιας ἐπαινοις. Το μεν οὐν παλαιον βραχυ παντελως το περι την ἐξηγησιν ἠν, φιλοτιμουμενων μη τερπειν, ἀλλα ὠφελειν τους παροντας των τοτε.**

Gregory Nazianzen also very seriously and with his usual eloquence, thus complains:—"There was a time (saith he) when our affairs flourished, and we were in a happy estate, when this vain and loose kind of divinity, which is everywhere now in fashion, together with all its artifices and delicacies of language, was not at all admitted into the sheepfolds of the

* Method. apud Epiph. Hær. 64.

Lord. In those days, to listen to or to vent any novelties or curiosities in divinity, was thought like playing the juggler, and showing tricks of legerdemain, with cunning and nimble shifting of balls under a cup, deceiving the eyes of the spectators; or else by delighting them with the various and effeminate motions and windings of a lascivious dance. On the contrary, rather a plain, masculine, and free way of discourse was then accounted the most pious. But now, since the Pyrrhonians and Sextus's faction, together with the tongue of contradiction, have like a grievous malignant disease, broken in upon our Churches—since babbling is now allowed for learning, and as in the Acts it is said of the Athenians, since we spend our time in nothing else but 'in hearing or telling some new thing'—O for some Jeremiah, to bewail the confusion and darkness we lie under; who might furnish us, as that prophet only was able to do, with lamentations suitable to our calamities!" *Ἠν ὁτε ἠκμαζε τα ἡμετερα, και καλως ἐσχεν, ἡνικα το μεν περιττον τουτο και κατεγλωττισμενον της θεολογιας, και ἐντεχνον, οὐδε παροδον εἰχεν εἰς τας θειας αὐλας· ἀλλα ταυτον ἠν, ψηφοις τε παιζειν την ὀψιν, κλεπτουσαις τω ταχει της μεταθεσεως, ἠ κατορχεισθαι των θεατων παντοιοις και ανδρογυνοις λογισμασι, και περι Θεου λεγειν τι, και ἀκουειν καινοτερον, και περιεργον. Το δε ἁπλουν τε και εὐγενες του λογου εὐσεβεια ἐνομιζετο. Ἀφ' οὑ δε Σεξτοι, και Πυρρωνες, και ἡ ἀντιθετος γλωσσα, ὡσπερ τι νοσημα δεινον και κακοηθες ταις ἐκκλησιαις ἡμων εἰσεφθαρη, και ἡ φλυαρια παιδευσις ἐδοξε, και ὁ φησι περι Αθηναιων ἡ βιβλος των Πραξεων, εἰ ουδεν ἀλλο εὐκαιρουμεν, ἠ λεγειν τι ἠ ἀκουειν καινοτερον· ὠ τις Ἰερεμιας ὀδυρεται την ἡμετεραν συγχυσιν και σκοτομαιναν, ὁ μονος εἰδως ἐξισουν θρηνους παθεσιν.*

Certainly Jerome, in his Epistle to Pammachius,†

* Greg. Naz. Enc. Athan.
† Hieron. ep. 50, ad Pammach. et passim, ibid.

avows, that even for his writings also, it is necessary that the reader be acquainted both with the subtilties of logic, and all the flourishes of rhetoric. This censure of his reaches also to the writings of Origen, Methodius, Eusebius, Apollinaris, Tertullian, Cyprian, Minutius, Victorinus, Lactantius, Hilary, and others, whom he affirms to have all observed the same method in their writings.*

Now although any rational man must willingly grant that the translations of terms and figures, either in word only, or in things themselves, and such other ornaments of rhetoric, with all the subtilties of logic—and, in a word, all the artifices of learning, must necessarily render any discourse the more obscure and dark; yet for the fuller elucidation of this point, I shall here add some proofs and examples. Jerome declares himself sufficiently of this opinion,† where he attributes the cause of the obscurity found in the writings of certain authors to their being too learned and eloquent. Sixtus Senensis observes, that the Fathers have uttered many things in the warmth of feeling, which we are not to take in a strictly literal sense.‡ Petavius has also observed, "that the Fathers have uttered in their homilies many things which cannot be reconciled to good sense, if we examine them by the exact rule of truth.§ We often excuse this in them, by showing that under so many flowers and leaves, wherewith they crown their discourses, they many times convey a different sense from that which their words in appearance seem to bear.

Who has not observed the strange hyperboles of

* Hieron. ep. 50, ad Pammach. et passim, ibid.
† Hier. sup. Ep. 139. ad Cypr.
‡ Sixt. Senens. Biblioth. lib. 6. Annot. 152.
§ Multa sunt à sanctissimis Patribus, præsertimque à Chrysostomo in homiliis aspersa, quæ si ad exactæ veritatis regulam accommodare volueris, boni sensus inania videbuntur.—*Petav. Not. in Epiph.*

Chrysostom, Hilary, Ambrose, and others? But that I may make it plainly and evidently appear how much these ornaments darken the sense of an author, I shall only here lay before you one instance, taken from Jerome; who, writing to Eustochium, gives her an account, how he was brought before the presence of our Lord, for being too much addicted to the study of secular learning, and was there really with stripes chastised for it. "Think not (says he) that this was any of those drowsy fancies or vain dreams which sometimes deceive us. I call to witness hereof, that tribunal before which I then lay; and that said judgment, which I was then in dread of. So may I never hereafter fall into the like danger, as this is true! I do assure you that I found my shoulders to be all over black and blue with the stripes I then received, and which I afterwards felt when I awoke. So that I have ever since had a greater affection to the reading of divine books, than I ever before had to the study of human learning."*

Now hearing Jerome speak thus, who would not believe this to be a true story? and who would not understand this narration in the literal sense? Yet it appears plainly, from what he has elsewhere confessed, that all this was but a mere dream, and a rhetorical piece of artifice, frequently used by the masters in this art; contrived only for the better and more powerful diverting men from their too great affection to the books of the heathens. For Ruffinus, quarreling with him on this account, and objecting against him, that, contrary to the oath which he had before taken, he did notwithstanding still apply himself to

* Nec verò sopor ille fuerat, aut vana somnia, quibus sæpe deludimur. Testis est tribunal illud, ante quod jacui; testis judicium triste quod timui. Ita mihi nunquam contingat in talem incidere quæstionem: liventes fateor habuisse me scapulas, plagas sensisse post somnum, et tanto dehinc studio divina legisse, quanto non ante mortalia legeram.—*Hier. ep.* 21 *ad Eustoch.*

the study of Pagan learning: Jerome, after he had alleged many things to clear himself from this accusation, says, "Thus you see what I could have urged for myself, had I promised any such thing waking. But now do but take notice of this new and unheard of kind of impudence; he objects against me my very dreams."* Then presently he refers him to the words of the prophets, saying, "We must not take heed to dreams; for neither does an adulterous dream cast a man into hell, nor that of martyrdom bring him to heaven."† He at last plainly observes, that this promise of his was made only in a dream; and that therefore consequently it carried no obligation with it.‡

Who knows but that the life of Malchus, which Jerome has so delicately and artificially related to us, and some other similar pieces of his, and of some others, may be the like displays of imagination? We see he does not hesitate to confess, that the life of Paulus Eremita was accounted as such by some of his friends: and it is very probable that his forty-seventh epistle,§ which is so full of learning and eloquence, is but an essay of the same nature; he having there fancied to himself a fit subject only whereon to show his own eloquence, agreeably to the usual manner of orators.

Thus you see, reader, what great darkness is cast over the writings of the ancients by these figures and flourishes of rhetoric, and other artifices of human learning, which they so often and so over licentiously

* Hæc dicerem si quippiam vigilans promisissem. Nunc autem novum impudentiæ genus, objicit mihi somnium meum.—*Hier. Apol. adv. Ruffin.*

† Audiat prophetarum voces, somniis non esse credendum; quia nec adulterii somnium ducit me ad Tartarum, nec corona martyrii in cœlum levat.—*Ibid.*

‡ Tu à me somnii exigis sponsionem. –*Ibid.*

§ Hier. in vit. Hilarion.

use, at least as regards ourselves; who, to our great disadvantage, find that so many ornaments and embellishments rather disguise from us the depth of their conceptions. Who shall assure us that they have not made use of the same arts in their discourses on the Eucharist; to advance the dignity of the divine mysteries, and to increase the people's devotion? and likewise, as regards the power of the prelates, to procure them the greater respect and obedience from their people? What probability is there that they would spare their pencils, their colours, their shadows, and their lights, in those points where this their art might have been employed to such good purpose?

To this place I shall refer those other customs, which are so frequent, of denying and affirming things as it were absolutely; notwithstanding the purpose and intent of their discourse be to deny or affirm them only by way of comparison, and reference to some other things. Who cannot but think that Jerome was tainted with the heresy of Marcion, and of the Encratics, when we hear him so fiercely inveigh against marriage, as he does in his books against Jovinian; and often also in other places to such a degree, that there have sometimes fallen from him such words as these: "Seeing that in the use of the woman there is always some corruption, and that incorruption properly belongs to chastity, marriage cannot be accounted of so high esteem as chastity."* And a little after: "My opinion is, that he that hath a wife, as long as he returns to such a state, that Satan may not tempt him, (that is to say, so long as he makes use of her as a wife,) sows in the flesh, and not in the spirit. Now he that soweth in the flesh, (it is not I

* Si corruptio ad omnem coitum pertinet, incorruptio autem propriè castitatis est: præmia pudicitiæ nuptiæ possidere non possunt.—*Hier. lib.* 1. *adversus Jovin.*

that say it, but the Apostle,) the same shall reap corruption."*

Now the above words, taken literally, condemn marriage and the use thereof, as defiling a man, and depriving him of a blessed immortality. Yet, notwithstanding, in his epistle to Pammachius,† he informs us, that these passages of his, and all other similar ones, are not to be understood as spoken positively and absolutely, but only by way of comparison; that is, he would be understood to say, that the purity and felicity of virgins is such, as that, in comparison with it, the marriage bed is not to be mentioned. This key is very necessary for discovering the sense of the ancients. The Fathers of the seventh council made very good use of this, in giving the sense of two or three passages that were objected against them by the Iconoclasts.

The first passage was out of Chrysostom: "Through the Scriptures we enjoy the presence of the saints, having the images not of their bodies but of their souls: for the things there spoken by them, are the images of their souls." *Ἡμεις δια των γραφων της των ἁγιων ἀπολαυομεν παρουσιας, οὐχι των σωματων αὐτων, ἀλλα των ψυχων τας εἰκονας ἐχοντες· τα γαρ παρ᾽ αὐτων εἰρημενα των ψυχων αὐτων εἰκονες ἐστιν.*‡

The second passage was out of Amphilochius: "Our care is, not to draw in colours on tables the natural faces of the saints, (for we have no need of any such thing;) but rather imitate their life and conversation, by following the examples of their virtue." *Οὐ γαρ τοις πιναξι τα σαρκικα προσωπα των ἁγιων δια χρωματων ἐπιμελες ἡμιν ἐκτυπουν (ὁτι οὐ χρηζομεν*

* Existimo quòd qui uxorem habet, quandiu revertitur ad id ipsum ne tentet eum Satanas, in carne seminet, et non in spiritu. Qui autem in carne seminat, (non ego, sed Apostolus loquitur,) metit corruptionem.—*Hier. lib.* 1. *adversus Jovin.*

† Id. ep. 50, ad Pammachium.

‡ Concil. 7, Act. 6.

τουτων·) ἀλλα την πολιτειαν αὐτων. δὶ ἀρετης ἐκμιμεισθαι.[*]

The third passage was out of Asterius: "Draw not the portrait of Christ on thy garments; but rather bestow upon the poor the price that these expenses would amount to. For as for him, it is sufficient that he once humbled himself, in taking upon him our flesh." *Μη γραφε τον Χριστον ἐν ἱματιοις, ἀλλα μαλλον την των ἀναλωματων τουτων δαπανην πτωχοις προσποριζου· ἀρκει γαρ αὐτω ἡ μια της ἐνσωματωσεως ταπεινωσις.*[†]

Would not any man that hears these words, believe these three Fathers to have been Iconoclasts? I confess I cannot see what could have been said more expressly against images: and yet the second council of Nice pretends, that these Fathers here speak only by way of comparison;[‡] meaning to say no more than that the images of Jesus Christ and of the saints are much less profitable than the reading of their books, or the imitation of their lives, or than charity toward the poor.

I know very well that it is no easy matter suitably to apply this answer to the words of these Fathers: however, we may make this use of it; that seeing that the council of Nice has followed this rule, it is an evident argument to us, that the sayings of the Fathers both may and ought sometimes to be taken in a quite different sense from what they seem to bear: so that it will clearly follow from hence that they are very difficult to be understood.

Consider then, whether or not, among so many passages as are adduced on the one side and the other on the present controversies, there may not be many of them which are to be understood, as just observed, by way of comparison only; that is to say, quite contrary to what they seem to say. Now, as the rhetoric

[*] Concil. 7, Act. 6. [†] Ibid. [‡] Concil. 7. ubi supra.

used by the Fathers has rendered their discourses, which were addresses to the people, full of obscurity; in like manner has their logic sown a thousand thorns and difficulties throughout their polemical writings. For many times, while they are in the heat of their disputations, they have their mind so intent upon the objects they are aiming at, that having regard to nothing else, they let fall such expressions as appear very strange, if they be considered in reference to some other points of Christian religion.

Sometimes also, whilst they use their utmost endeavour to beat down one error, they seem to run into the contrary one: as those who would straighten a crooked plant, are wont to bend it as much the contrary way; that so having been worked out of its former bent, it may at length rest in a middle posture: of which similitude Theodoret also makes use on this very subject.*

In the same manner also did Athanasius explain those words of Dionysius Alexandrinus, which were urged against him by the Arians, as seeming to tell very much in their favour, as we have noticed before. "He wrote not this (answers Athanasius) positively, and with a purpose of giving an account of his belief in these words, but as being led on to utter them, by the occasion and the persons he discoursed with. In like manner (says he) as a gardener orders the same trees in a different manner, according to the difference of the soil where they are. Neither can any blame him for lopping off some and engrafting others; for planting this, and plucking up that by the roots. On the contrary rather, whoever knows the reason of this, will admire the variety and several ways of his industrious proceeding." *'Ουχ ἁπλως, ὡς πιστιν ἐκτιθεμενος.—Καιρου, και προσωπου προφασις εἵλκυσεν αὐτον τοιαυτα γραψαι.—Και γαρ γεωργος των αὐτων*

* Theod. Dial. 3. c. 30. Sic et Bas. de Dion. Alex. ep. 41.

δενδρων ἀλλοτε ἀλλως ἐπιμελειται, δια την ὑποκειμενην της γης ποιοτητα· και οὐ δια τουτο μεμφαιτο ἀν τις αὐτον, ὁτι τουτο μεν τεμνει, ἐκεινο δε ἐγκεντριζει, &c. *ἀλλα και μαλλον μαθων την αἰτιαν, θαυμασει το ποικιλον αὐτου της ἐπιστημης.**

Afterwards Athanasius says, that Dionysius maintained those positions, upon occasion of the error of certain bishops of Pentapolis, who maintained the opinion of Sabellius; and that he did this by dispensation, as he there speaks:—*Τα ὑποπτευθεντα κατ' οἰκονομιαν ἐγραψεν:*† that is to say, not positively and simply, but as in reference to such a certain case only: "Now no man ought (says he) to wrest to the worst sense those things which are either said or done by dispensation; or to interpret them as himself pleases:" *Οὐ δει δε τα κατ' οἰκονομιαν γραφομενα και γινομενα, ταυτα κακοτροπως δεχεσθαι, και εἰς ἰδιαν ἑλκειν ἑκαστου βουλησιν.*‡

In another place Athanasius in the same manner explains the words of the Fathers of the council of Antioch, who had denied the consubstantiality of the Son, showing that their intention was only to overthrow a position which Paulus Samosatenus had laid down; namely, that the Father and the Son were both one and the self-same person, and had not any distinct subsistence.

By this very rule also does Basil interpret that saying of Gregorius Neocæsariensis—"That the Father and the Son are two, according to our apprehension only; but that in hypostasis they are but one:" (*Πατερα και Υἱον ἐπινοιᾳ μεν εἰναι δυο, ὑποστασει δε ἑν;*)§ but alleging "That he spoke this, not dogmatically, but only in the heat of disputation:"—*Τουτο δε ὁτι οὐ δογματικως εἰρηται, ἀλλ' ἀγωνιστικως,* &c.||

* Athan. Ep. de fid. Dion. Alex. † Athan. ibid.
‡ Athan. ibid. § Basil. Ep. 64. || Ibid.

From this it would appear that in all writings of the Fathers, the opinion which they oppugn is the rule and measure of whatsoever they are understood to affirm or deny. This is that which varies their sense and meaning, though oftentimes expressed in the same manner, and with the very same words, with that of the heretics. When they dispute against the Valentinians or the Manichees, a man would then believe them to be Pelagians; and so likewise when they are contesting with the Pelagians, would you then imagine that they defended the opinions of the Manichees. If they dispute against Arius, you would think they favoured Sabellius: and again, when they oppose Sabellius, you would believe that they were Arians: as has been observed by the bishop of Bitonto,* particularly in Augustine.

A system like this we may every day observe in our preachers. When they preach against covetousness, they seem in a manner to cry up prodigality; and if they declaim against prodigality, they then seem to approve covetousness. Thus it is also with the Protestants: when they would overthrow those empty figures, which are fathered by their adversaries upon those they call Sacramentarians, you would suppose that they maintained the real presence in the Eucharist, as the manner of speaking is. And when they dispute against Transubstantiation and the real presence, you would then swear that they defended the opinion of these very Sacramentarians.

There is amongst Athanasius's works a certain very learned, elegant, and acute tract, wherein is debated, as strongly as can be, that point concerning the distinction of the two natures in Jesus Christ. Only read what he there says, in the beginning of that discourse; and you will think that it could not proceed from any but from Nestorius's mouth:—*Προς*

* Corn. Mussus. Episc. Bitont. Comment. in ep. ad Rom. c. 5.

*τους λεγοντας, 'Ιουδαιος ἐστιν, ὁ μη ὁμολογων θεον ἐσταυρωσθαι.** Yet you will perceive plainly, by the last chapter of the said book, that he was not of his opinion. Now if by any misfortune it should so have happened that this last chapter had been lost, Athanasius must necessarily have been taken for a Nestorian, by reason of the dangerous expressions which he has there made use of, being urged thereto through the warmth of the dispute he maintained against the opinions of the Eutychians.

For the same reason also, Julius, bishop of Rome, seems to have favoured the contrary error, namely, that of Eutyches, in that epistle of his cited by Gennadius; which was indeed heretofore of good use, against the opinion of those men who maintained two persons in Christ; but which "is now found to be pernicious (says he) by fomenting the impieties of Eutyches and Timotheus."† This has given occasion to some of the more modern authors, who have written since Gennadius's time,‡ to think that this epistle was not written by Pope Julius, but had been attributed to him by the false dealing of the heretics.

The case was the same with these ancient Fathers, as it is with the pilot of a ship, who is to steer his vessel between two rocks, one only of which he has discovered, the other lying hid underwater. Taking no other care but to avoid the danger which he sees before his eyes, he very easily falls into that other which he never so much as suspected; so that if he split not his vessel upon it, and be utterly cast away, he will with difficulty avoid receiving injury at least. Thus these Fathers saw indeed the rock of Paulus

* T. 2. Oper. Athan. Par. impr. an. 1627.

† Nunc autem perniciosa probatur. Fomentum enim est Eutychianæ et Timotheanæ impietatis.—*Gennad. in Catal. inter op. Hier.*

‡ Facund. Herm. defens. 3 capit. lib. 1. p. 40. quo loco vide Sirmondum.

12*

Samosatenus's doctrine, and that of Nestorius, but did not at all observe that of Arius, or of Eutyches, which lay yet under water and concealed. Thus employing their utmost endeavours to avoid the danger of the two former, which they then only feared, they have scarcely escaped falling into, or at least touching very near upon the two latter, of which they then had no thought at all.

Only imagine then, how warily and carefully it behoves us to walk amidst these disputes of the ancients, which are so beset with thorns; and with what judgment we are to distinguish between what things are principal, and what but accidental only; between the cause and the means; and between the excess and defect in their expressions, and their true sense and meaning: and then tell me whether you think it reasonable or not, that two or three words only, which may perhaps accidentally have fallen from them in their disputations, either against the Valentinians and Marcionites, or against the Nestorians or Eutychists, should be taken as their definitive sentiments upon such points as are now controverted amongst us—whether on free-will, or the properties of the body of Christ, and the nature of the Eucharist.

Before we conclude this matter, however, we should observe that the change of customs, both civil and ecclesiastical, and the variation of words in their signification, do not a little contribute to this difficulty of understanding the writings of the Fathers. Who knows not, and indeed who confesses not, both on the one side and on the other, that the outward face of the world, and even of the Church itself too, is in a manner wholly changed? I speak not here of the doctrine, but only of the upper garment, as I may call it, and the outward part of the Church. Where is the ancient discipline? What is become of the rigid and severe rules of those ancient times? Where are those mysterious ceremonies in baptism, and in the administration of the Eucharist? Where are those customs then used in the ordination of the clergy? All these things are now quite forgotten and buried; the Church by little and little having appareled itself in other colours and in another garb.

The books then of the ancients being full of allusions to these things which we are in a manner now wholly ignorant of, it must necessarily follow from hence, that it will be a difficult matter for us to guess at their meaning in any such passages. But yet there arises much more confusion out of the words they used; which we have still retained, though in a different signification. We have indeed these words, *Pope*, *Patriarch*, *Mass*, *Oblation*, *Station*, *Procession*, *Mortal Sins*, *Penance*, *Confession*, *Satisfaction*, *Merit*, *Indulgence*, as the ancients had, and make use of an infinite number of the like terms; but understand them all in a sense almost as far different from theirs, as our age is removed from theirs; just in like manner as of old, under the Roman Emperors, the names of offices, and of things, for a long time continued the same that had been in use in the time of the old republic; but with a sense quite different from what they had formerly borne. Thus when we light upon any passage in the ancients, where the bishop of Rome is called *Papa*, or *Pope*, we immediately begin to fancy him with all the glory at this day belonging to this name; not disallowing him so much as his guard of Swiss, and his light horse: whereas they that are but indifferently versed in these books, know that the name *Papa*, or *Pope*, was given to every bishop. So likewise, when we meet with the word *Exomologesis*, or *Confession*, we presently fancy a man down upon his knees before his confessor, whispering in his ear all the sins he has committed. The word *Mass* likewise makes us prick up our ears, as if, even from those ancient times, the whole liturgy and all the ceremonies used at the celebration of the Eucharist, had been the very same that they are at this day. Whereas the learned of both parties acknowledge that these names have, since that time, lost very much of their old, and acquired new significations.

But enough, and perhaps too much, has been said, for elucidating the points as regards the obscurities in the writings of the Fathers. We may therefore come to the conclusion, as we stated at the commencement, that it is not so easy a matter, as people may imagine, to discover by their writings what the sense of the ancient Church has been, concerning the points at this day controverted among us.

CHAPTER VI.

REASON VI.—The Fathers frequently conceal their own private opinions, and say what they did not believe; either in reporting the opinions of others, without naming them, as in their commentaries; or in disputing against an adversary, where they make use of whatever they are able; or in accommodating themselves to their auditory, as may be observed in their homilies.

THE writings of the Fathers are, for the most part, of three kinds—Commentaries on the Holy Scriptures; Homilies delivered before the people; and Polemical Discourses and Disputations with the Heretics.

Now we have heretofore seen how much their rhetorical style has darkened and rendered their sense obscure, in their writings of the first and second class; and what their warmth of disputation and logical wranglings have caused in those of the latter. Let us now see if, after having drawn the expressions of the Fathers out of these thick clouds, and attained to a clear and perfect understanding of the sense of them, we may be able at length to rest assured that we have discovered what their opinions were. I confess I could heartily wish that it were so: but considering what they have themselves informed us concerning the nature and manner of their writings, I am much afraid that we neither may, nor indeed ought, to consider ourselves in any certainty, even then, when we are upon these very terms.

With respect to their Commentaries, which we have often occasion to consult, upon sundry passages of Scripture, on the meaning whereof we disagree among ourselves, hear what Jerome says, who was the most learned of all the Latins, and who yields but very little to any of the Greeks in these matters.

"What (says he) is the business of a Commentary? It expounds the words of another man; and declares in plain terms the sense of things obscurely written; it represents the several opinions of others, and says, Some expound this passage thus; and others interpret it thus. These endeavour to prove their sense and meaning by such testimonies and such reasons; to the end that the intelligent reader, having several expositions before him, and reading the judgments of divers men, some bringing what he may, and others perhaps what he cannot admit of; he may judge which among the rest is the truest; and like a wise banker may refuse all adulterated coin. Now I would ask whether he ought to be accounted guilty of diversity in his interpretations, or of contradiction in the senses given, who in one and the same commentary shall deliver the expositions of divers persons?"*

* Commentarii quid operis habent? Alterius dicta edisserunt; quæ obscurè scripta sunt, plano sermone manifestant, multorum sententias replicant, et dicunt: Hunc locum quidam sic edisserunt; alii sic interpretantur; illi sensum suum et intelligentiam his testimoniis, et hàc nituntur ratione firmare; ut prudens lector cùm diversas explanationes legeret, et multorum vel probanda vel im-

And so on, as it there follows in the place afore cited. He speaks likewise to the same sense in various other places throughout his works: "This (says he) is the usual manner of commentaries, and the rule that commentators go by; to set down in their expositions the several opinions they have met with; and to deliver, both what their own and what the judgment of others is upon the passage. And this is the practice not only of the interpreters of the Scriptures, but of the expositors also of all kinds of secular learning, as well in the Greek as in the Latin tongue."*

Now I must needs say, that this seems to be a very strange way of commenting. For what light, or what certainty can a reader be able to gather out of such a rhapsody of different opinions, jumbled together in a heap, without so much as intimating either which is good or bad; probable or necessary; to the purpose or not? But seeing that it has pleased Jerome to follow this course, whatsoever his reason be, you see plainly that we are not to take as his whatsoever he has delivered in his commentaries. And seeing also that he speaks in general terms, as he does, of the nature and manner of a commentary; we are not to doubt, but that the rest of the Fathers have chiefly been of the same judgment; and that consequently they took the same course in those expositions which we have of theirs. So that it will hence follow, that notwithstanding that we should chance to find in this

probanda didicerit, judicet quid verius sit, et quasi bonus trapezita adulterinæ monetæ pecuniam reprobet. Num diversæ interpretationis, et contrariorum inter se sensuum tenebitur reus, qui in uno opere quod edisserit expositiones posuerit plurimorum?—*Hier. ep. ad Pammach. et Marcel. Apol. advers. Ruff.*

* Hic est commentariorum mos, et explanantium regula, ut opiniones in expositione varias persequantur, et quid vel sibi vel aliis videatur edisserant. Et hoc non solùm sanctarum interpretes scripturarum, sed sæcularium quoque literarum explanatores faciunt, tàm Latinæ linguæ, quàm Græcæ.—*Hier. ep. ad Pammach. et Apol. advers. Ruff.*

kind of writings of theirs, an opinion, or an interpretation, clearly delivered; yet may we not from thence conclude that this was the author's own opinion: for perhaps he only delivered it as the opinion of some other man.

Now if the Fathers had been but careful to have taken in water out of wholesome fountains only, filling up their commentaries with no other opinions or interpretations, except only those of persons of known piety, faith, and learning, this mixture would have proved the less dangerous. For, notwithstanding that we should often be at a stand, and doubt whether that which we there find be the true sense and opinion of the Father whose name it bears; yet we might still rest assured, that though it should not perhaps be his, it must certainly be the opinion of some other good author, if not of equal yet of little less authority than he. But the mischief of it is, that they took a quite contrary course, many times filling their commentaries with very strange, senseless expositions, and sometimes too with dangerous ones, and such as were taken out of very suspected authors, who had no very good name in the Church.

Jerome tells us often,* (and who ever shall but diligently and attentively read him, may easily observe as much,) that his commentaries, (which make the greatest and most considerable part of his works,) are interwoven throughout with expositions taken out of Origen, Didymus, Apollinaris, and others, who were at that time ill-spoken of, as men who too presumptuously foisted upon the world their own private opinions, "fashioning the mysteries of the Church out of their own private fancies:"† as Jerome himself sometimes said of Origen.

* Hier. præfat. in Comment. in ep. ad Galat. et Apol. 2. adv. Ruff. et ep. 89. ad August. et alibi sæpe.

† Ingenium suum facit Ecclesiæ sacramenta.—*Hier. Comment.* 5. *in Es. præf. De Origene.*

Now this is strange to me: for no man is more strenuous in crying down these authors than he; being indeed one of the principal heads of that holy league of Theophilus and Epiphanius, against Origen and his party. No man ever reproved any one so sharply as he has done Ruffinus, for offering to present to the view of the Latins the poisonous doctrines of Origen in those books of his which he had translated; and in the meantime he himself crams his own commentaries with the same; many times without using any preparation at all about them, or furnishing his reader with any counter-poison, in case he meets with any of them.* So likewise in his commentaries upon the Prophets, he ever and anon brings in diverse expositions out of the Jews themselves: insomuch that, when you think you are reading and searching after the opinion and sense of Jerome upon such or such a passage, you often read that of a heretic, or of a Jew.

If the Fathers would but have taken the pains to have given us notice every time who the author was, whose opinion they adduced, this manner of commenting upon the Scriptures would have been much more beneficial to us, and less troublesome. For the name would have been useful in directing us what account we were to make of such opinions and expositions. But this they do but very seldom, as you may observe out of the expositions of Hilary, Ambrose, and others; who, robbing poor Origen without any mercy, do not yet do him the honour so much as scarcely to name him.† This is certain, that you shall find in Ambrose many times whole periods and whole pages too, taken out of Basil; but, unless my memory fail me, you shall never find him once named there.

* Vid. Comment. in Nahum.

† Vid. Hieron. Apol. adv. Ruff. ad Pammach. et Marcel. et Ep. 141. ad Marcel.

These men deliver you the opinions and words of other men, just as if they were their own; and yet will not be bound to warrant them for good and sound. Jerome, in his Commentary upon the Epistle to the Galatians, expounds that passage where there is mention made of Paul reproving Peter, by way of dispensation; telling us that Paul did not reprehend him, as if he had indeed accounted him blame-worthy; but only for the better edification, and bringing in of the Gentiles, by this seeming reprehension of his; who did but act this part with Peter, "to the end (says he) that the hypocrisy, or false show of observing the law, which offended those among the Gentiles who had believed, might be corrected by the hypocrisy or false show of reprehension; and that by this means both the one and the other might be saved: whilst the one, who praise circumcision, follow Peter; and those others, who refuse circumcision, applaud Paul's liberty."*

Augustine, utterly disliking this exposition of Jerome, wrote to him in his ordinary grave and meek way, modestly declaring the reasons why he could not assent to it; which epistles of his are yet extant. The other answers him a thousand strange things; but particularly he there protests, that he will not warrant for sound whatever shall be found in that book of his:† and to show that he does not do this without good reason, he sets down a certain passage out of his preface to it, which is very well worth our consideration. For after he has named the writings of Origen, Didymus, Apollinaris, Theodorus of Heraclea, Eusebius of Emesa, Alexander the heretic, and

* Ut hypocrisis observandæ legis, quæ nocebat iis qui ex gentibus crediderant, correptionis hypocrisi emendaretur, et uterque populus salvus fieret; dum et qui circumcisionem laudant, Petrum sequuntur, et qui circumcidi nolunt, Pauli prædicant libertatem.—*Id. Comment. in ep. ad Galat.*

† Hieron. ep. ad August. quæ est 89.

others, he adds; "That I may therefore plainly tell the truth, I confess that I have read all these authors; and collecting together as much as I could in my memory, I presently called for a scribe; to whom I dictated either my own conceptions, or those of other men, without remembering either the order, or the words sometimes, or the sense."* Do but reflect now, whether or not this be not an excellent rare way of commenting upon the Scriptures, and very well worthy to be esteemed and imitated by us! He then turns his address to Augustine, saying, "If therefore thou lightest upon anything in my expositions which was worthy of reprehension, it would have stood better with thy learning to have consulted the Greek authors themselves; and to have seen, whether what I have written be found in them or not; and if not, then to have condemned it as my own private opinion."† And he elsewhere gives the same answer to Ruffinus, who upbraids him for some absurd passages in his Commentaries upon the Prophet Daniel.‡

Now, according to this statement, if we would know whether or not what we meet with in Jerome's commentaries, be his own proper sense or not, we must first turn over the books of all these ancient Greeks; that is to say, we must do that which is now impossible to be done, seeing that the writings of the greatest part of them are utterly lost; and must not attribute anything to him, as his proper opinion, how clearly and expressly soever it be delivered, unless we are first able to make it appear, that it is not to be found in any of those authors, out of whose writings he has

.* Itaque ut simpliciter fatear, legi hæc omnia, et in mente mea plurima coacervans, accito notario, vel mea vel aliena dictavi, nec ordinis, nec verborum interdum, nec sensuum memor.—*Hier. ibid.*

† Si quid igitur reprehensione dignum putaveras in explanatione nostra, eruditionis tuæ fuerat quærere, &c. —*Id. ibid. Vide et Apol. contra Ruff.*

‡ Id. Apol. 2. adv. Ruff.

patched up his commentaries. For if any one of them be found to have delivered anything you here meet with, you are to take notice that it belongs to that author; Jerome in this case having been only his transcriber, or at most but his translator. So that you may be able perhaps, by the reading of books in this manner collected, to judge whether the Fathers have had the skill to make a clever and artificial connection and digestion of those things which they gleaned out of so many several authors or not. Whether or not they believed all that they have set down in their books, you will be no more able to discover, than you can judge what belief any man is of by the books he transcribes; or can guess at the opinions of an interpreter by the books he translates. Whence we may conclude, that testimonies brought out of such books as these are of little or no force at all, either for or against us.

This seems to have been the opinion of cardinal Bellarmine, where to a certain objection brought out of one of Jerome's books, he makes this answer: "that the author in that place speaks according to the opinion of others; as he often does in his commentaries upon the Epistle to the Ephesians, and in other places." The like course has cardinal Perron taken, where the Protestants have urged against the Church of Rome the authority of Hilary, on the canon of the Scriptures of the Old Testament; confidently answering that the notes cited out of that place of Hilary are not his, but Origen's, in his commentary upon the first Psalm; part of whose words he had transcribed and inserted in his own prologue upon the Psalms; and yet Hilary neither so much as names Origen, nor yet gives us any intimation at all, whether we are to receive what is there spoken concerning the Scriptures, as from Origen or from himself. The ground of this answer of his is taken from what Jerome has testified in various places; namely, that Hilary has transcribed the greatest part of his commentaries out of the said Origen.

Now if we but rightly consider the account which Jerome has given, as we showed before, of all commentaries in general, how can we have any assurance whether that which the Fathers deliver in this kind of writings, be their own real opinion, or only some other man's transcribed? and if we can have no assurance hereof, how can we then consider them of any force at all either for or against us? So that it is most evident, that this method which the Fathers have observed in their expositions of the Scriptures, must render the things themselves very doubtful, however clearly and expressly they have delivered themselves.

But has it not behoved them to be more careful in their Homilies, or Sermons; and to deliver nothing there but what has been their own proper opinion and belief? May we not, at least in this particular, rest assured that they have spoken nothing but from their very soul; and that their tongues have expressed here their own opinions only, and not those of other men? Certainly, in all reason, they should not have uttered anything in the sacred place from whence they taught their people, but what they conceived to have been most true. Yet besides what we have heretofore noticed as to this particular, (namely, that they did not always speak out the whole truth, but concealed something of it, as not so fit for the ears either of the Pagans or of the weaker sort of Christians,) cardinal Perron, that great and curious inquirer into all the customs of the ancients, has informed us that, in regard to the aforesaid considerations, they have sometimes gone yet further.* For, in expounding the

* Perron. of the Euchar. l. 1, c. 10. Aut. 24, ch. 15, et passim locis infra citandis.

Scriptures to the people, where the Catechumens were present, if by chance they fell upon any passage where the Sacraments were spoken of, that they might not discover these mysteries, they would then make bold to wrest the text a little, and instead of giving them the true and real interpretation of the place which they themselves knew to be such, they would only present their auditory with an allegorical and symbolical, and (as this cardinal says,) an accidental and collateral one; only to give them some kind of small satisfaction; inasmuch as, if in such cases they should have been utterly silent, it would questionless have much amazed their auditors, and in some degree also have scandalized and given them offence. To satisfy therefore their expectation, and yet to keep these mysteries still concealed from them, they evasively waived the business, laying before them that which they accounted not the best and truest, but the fittest for their purpose and design. Thus do we sometimes please little children with an apple, or some little toy, to take them off the desire they have for something of greater value. Those therefore who take all that the Fathers deliver in the like places for good and solid expositions, and such as they themselves really believed, very much deceive themselves; and believing they have a solid body in their arms, embrace only an empty shadow.

Now we should hardly believe those holy men to have been guilty of any such juggling as this, had we not the word of so eminent a cardinal for our belief; upon whose authority we have, for this once, adventured to propose it to the reader's consideration, and shall withal produce some few examples taken out of the same author.

Augustine being to expound the sixth chapter of the Gospel of John, (where, as he conceives, our Saviour Christ is very copious in his discourse concerning the Eucharist,) presently begins to obumbrate and disguise the mystery with such a number of allegories, riddles, and ambiguities, as that, if you dare believe the cardinal, throughout the whole twenty-sixth tract, there is not one period but has in it some elusion, diversion, or diminution of the true and solid definition of this article. Thus does he interpret the bread which came down from heaven to be the gift of the Holy Ghost: "Our Saviour (says he) purposing to send down the Holy Ghost, saith that it is the bread which descended from heaven."*

You may, if you please, believe, upon the faith of this Father, that this is the true sense and meaning of the passage. But yet the cardinal makes it appear, out of Calvin, that it cannot be so. He likewise contradicts, after the same manner, that which the same Father says a little after, to wit, that the purpose of our Saviour was to let us understand that this meat and drink, whereof he speaks in St. John, is the communion and fellowship, that is between his body and his members, who are the holy Church, in his faithful servants, predestinated, called, justified, and glorified.

Had not the cardinal given us this information, who would ever have imagined that this author (who was so conscientious as to make it a great quarrel with Jerome, only for having laid dissimulation to Paul's charge,) should here himself say that our Saviour Christ would have us to understand his words thus, unless he himself really believed this to be the true sense and meaning of them? The cardinal also applies this very consideration to the greatest portion of those other passages, cited out of this Father by the Protestants; namely, "to believe in Christ is to eat the Bread of Life:" and to this other; "He that believes in him eats of it; and he is invisibly fed by it, because that he is also invisibly born again:" and

* Perron. Tract. de S. August, c. 12, et lib. 2, de Euch. Aut. 22, c. 1.

to this also; "Whosoever eats of this bread, he shall never die; but this is to be understood of him that eats of it, according to the virtue of the sacrament; and not according to the visible sacrament; of him that eats of it internally, and not externally; of him that eats of it with his heart, and not of him that chews it with his teeth."

In all these places the cardinal pretends that Augustine suppresses the true, full, and solid definition of this manducation, or eating of the flesh, and drinking the blood of Christ; and instead thereof presents this allegorical and accidental meditation to the catechumens, only to cast a mist, as it were, before their eyes, and to elude their curiosity.* He makes use of the same course also in answering those passages which are quoted by the Protestants from Theodoret, and Gregory Nazianzen;† who, he says, called the Eucharist "the antitype of the body and blood of Christ,"‡ in the same manner as Abraham, being among infidels, called Sarah his sister; concealing something of what was true, but yet affirming nothing that was false. He likewise explains after the same manner this passage, out of the *Pædagogus* of Clemens Alexandrinus; "The flesh and the blood of Christ is faith and the promise."§ In a word, he is so much pleased with this observation, that he adopts it at every turn: and indeed we may very well say, that this is his main treasury, out of which he produces the greatest part of those subtle and so much admired solutions he gives to the passages objected against them out of the Fathers.||

Those who are disposed to examine these passages

* Perron. Tract. de Euch. l. 2, Aut. 24, c. 15.

† Perron. de Euch. l. 2, Aut. 18, c. 5. ‡ Id. Ibid.

§ Perron. de Euch. l. 2, Aut. 5.

|| Id. de Euch. pages 52, 329, 332, 339, 344, 356, 417, 420, 434, 501, 503, 508, 510, 516; et Trac. de S. August. pp. 55, 57, 95, 145, 191.

of his, may probably find something to retort upon him, in some of those applications he has there made. It is enough for our present purpose, that he admits that the Fathers, in their sermons and discourses made to the people, have often made use of this species of art; from which it clearly follows, that we cannot then possibly have any assurance that they themselves accounted, as solid and full, such expositions and opinions as they have delivered in these writings of theirs.

As the cardinal endeavours by this means to weaken the force of those passages of Augustine, Gregory Nazianzen, Theodoret, and Clemens Alexandrinus, may not the Protestants, when any passages are brought against them out of the homilies of Chrysostom, or Eucherius, which seem to tell strongly against their opinions, be allowed to have the same liberty, and to answer, that these Fathers, speaking before the people, made use of this *dispensation*, speaking that which they thought to be, not the best and truest, but the most proper for the edification of others, and that they had an apprehension that a bare and downright expression of the truth might possibly have abated the warmth of the people's devotion? there being apparently (say they) more cause to doubt, that the people might disesteem and slight the sacrament, than to fear lest they should adore it: indeed the Fathers are much more careful in concealing the matter of the sacrament, the outward appearance whereof is apt to make it disesteemed, than they are in concealing the form, which is of so venerable a nature; saying often, and in express terms, that it is "the body of Christ;" but ordinarily forbearing to say that it is, or that it was, "a piece of bread."

We now enter upon the third class of the writings of the ancients, wherein the Fathers dispute against the adversaries of their faith; namely, the Pagans, Jews, and Heretics.

We have heretofore observed how much obscurity the earnestness and warmth of spirit have caused in the expressions of the Fathers: and this defect arises from mere feeling; and not from any design or purpose that they had of speaking thus rather than otherwise. For seeing that all kind of impassioned feeling disturbs, and in some measure confounds, the judgment; and seeing it is difficult for a man, however holy he be, to go through a disputation, without some alteration in his temper; especially if it be of any importance, as all those on religion are, we are not to wonder, if in these cases we sometimes find the language of the Fathers somewhat confused, and appearing of several colours; just as passion usually tinges both the countenance and language of those it takes possession of.

Besides the confusion which is caused merely by the agitation of the spirits, without the Fathers so much as thinking of it, we are here further to take notice, that the proper design and the law of the method observed in disputations, is the cause of our encountering with so many and great difficulties. For their opinion was, that in this kind of writing it was lawful for them to say and make use of anything that might advance their cause, although it were otherwise but light and trivial, or perhaps also contrary to what themselves believed; and so, on the other side, to conceal and reject whatsoever might prejudice their cause, though otherwise true and allowable.

Now that this observation may not seem strange and incredible, as coming out of my mouth, let us hear what the Fathers themselves say in this particular. And first let us hear Jerome, who was the greatest critic of them all; and who, by often exercising the strength of his admirable wit, both by himself and with others, has observed more respecting the style, method, natural disposition, and opinions of the Fathers, than any other.

"We have learned together, (says he, writing to Pammachius,) that there are divers sorts of discourse; and among the rest, that it is one thing to write *γυμναστικως* (by way of disputation,) and another thing to write *δογματικως* (by way of instruction.) In the former of these the disputes are free and discursive; where, in answering an adversary, and proposing one time one thing, and another time another, a man argues as he pleases; speaking one thing and doing another; showing bread, (as it is in the proverb,) and holding a stone in his hand. Whereas in the second kind, an open front, and, if I may so speak, ingenuousness are required. It is one thing to make inquiries, and another to define: in the one we must fight, in the other we must teach. Thou seest me in a combat, and in peril of my life; and dost thou come with thy grave instructions like some reverend schoolmaster? 'Do not wound by stealth, and from whence thou art least expected: let thy sword strike directly: it is a shame for thee to wound thy enemy by guile and not by strength:' as if it were not a piece of the greatest mastery in fighting to threaten one part, but hit another. I beseech you read Demosthenes, read Tully: and lest perhaps you should refuse orators whose profession it is to propose things rather probable than true, read Plato, Theophrastus, Xenophon, Aristotle, and others; who, springing all from Socrates' fountain, as so many different rivulets, ran several ways: what can you find in them that is clear and open? what word in them but hath its design? and what design, but of victory only? Origen, Methodius, Eusebius, Apollinaris, have written largely against Celsus and Porphyry. Only observe what manner of arguments, and what slippery problems, they made use of, for subverting those works which had been wrought by the spirit of the devil: and how on being sometimes forced to speak, they alleged against the Gentiles, not that which they believed, but that which was most necessary to be said. I shall not here speak anything of the Latin writers, as Tertullian, Cyprian, Minucius, Victorinus, Lactantius, and Hilary, lest I might seem rather to accuse others, than to defend myself."*

Thus Jerome. As for that which he afterwards adds, respecting Paul, whom he believes to have practised the very same arts, this is no proper place to examine either the truth or the use of this opinion of his; as our purpose is here to treat of the Fathers only. Now you see that he testifies clearly, that they were wont, in their disputations, sometimes to say one thing, and believe another; to show us bread, and keep a stone in their hand; to threaten one part, and to hit another; and that they were sometimes constrained to fit their words, not to their own proper thoughts, but to the present necessity. The very same thing is confessed also by Athanasius, speaking of Dionysius Alexandrinus,† as noticed before; namely,

* Simul didicimus plura esse videlicet genera dicendi, et inter cætera aliud esse γυμναστικως scribere, aliud δογματικως. In priori vagam esse disputationem, et adversario respondentem nunc hæc, nunc illa proponere, argumentari ut libet, aliud loqui, aliud agere, panem, (ut dicitur) ostendere, lapidem tenere. In sequenti autem aperta frons, et, ut ita dicam, ingenuitas necessaria est. Aliud est quærere, aliud definire: in altero pugnandum, in altero docendum est. Tu me stantem in prœlio, et de vita periclitantem, studiosus magister doceas? Noli ex obliquo, et unde non putaris, vulnus inferre. Directò percute gladio. Turpe tibi est hostem dolis ferire, non viribus. Quasi non et hæc ars summa pugnantium sit, alibi minari, alibi percutere. Legite obsecro vos Demosthenem, legite Tullium: ac ne forsitan rhetores vobis displiceant, quorum artis est verisimilia magis quàm vera dicere, legite Platonem, Theophrastum, Xenophontem, Aristotelem, et reliquos qui de Socratis fonte manantes diversis cucurrere rivulis; quid in illis apertum, quid simplex est? quæ verba non sensuum? qui sensus non victoriæ? Considerate quibus argumentis, et quàm lubricis problematibus diaboli spiritu contexta subvertant; et quia interdum coguntur loqui, non quod sentiunt, sed quod necesse est, dicunt adversus ea quæ dicunt Gentiles. Taceo de Latinis scriptoribus, Tertulliano, Cypriano, Minucio, Victorino, Lactantio, Hilario, ne non tam me defendisse, quàm alios videar accusasse.

† Athan. ep. de fide Dion. Alex.

that he wrote, not simply and plainly, as giving us an account of his own belief, but that he was moved, and as it were forced, to speak as he did, by reason of the occasion, and of the person he disputed against.

The same account does Basil give of a certain passage of Gregorius Neocæsariensis;* answering for him with this distinction; "That he spake not in that place *dogmatically*, but only by way of *economy* or *dispensation*:" *Τα κατ' οἰκονομιαν γραφομενα.*† By this term is meant, that a man keeps to himself what he believes, and proposes some other thing lying wide of his own opinion, either this way or that way; being induced so to do from some particular considerations.

As we sometimes see that the water ascends, being forced to mount up to fill some space, which otherwise would remain void,—you will not, I hope, conclude from hence, that this is its natural and ordinary motion,—in like manner was it with the Fathers; who, being sometimes harassed and hard driven to it in disputation, in order to avoid, so to speak, some certain vacuum which they were afraid of, sometimes left their natural motion, and their proper sense and opinion, and took up some other contrary one, according to the necessity of tho occasion. Indeed, though Jerome had not noticed it, the fact would evidently enough have appeared from their writings. Otherwise, how could any one possibly have believed that they could have spoken so differently as they have done in many particulars, blowing hot and cold with one and the same mouth? How could they possibly have delivered so many things contrary either to reason, or to the Scriptures, or to the Fathers? "For, (as the same Jerome says) who is so very a blockhead, and so ignorant in the art of writing, as to praise and condemn one and the same thing; pull down what he

* Basil. sup. c. 5.

† Athan. ep. de fide Dion. Alex.

had built; and build what he had pulled down?"* Now the Fathers are often observed to have done this very thing. We are therefore to conclude, that they have been forced to it, out of some special design; and that they did it, as they used to speak, by *economy*, or particular *dispensation;* seeing that it is evident that the greatest part of them were very able men.

Jerome, for example, recommending the going on pilgrimage to Jerusalem, went so far as to say, "that it was a part of our faith to go and worship in those places where the feet of our Saviour once stood, and to have a sight of the tracks, which at this day continue fresh, both of his nativity, cross, and passion."† Now how does this agree with that long discourse which he has made in another place, to a quite contrary sense? namely, in his Epistle to Paulinus, where at last concluding, he gives him this reason of the length of his discourse: "To the end (says he) that thou mayest not think that anything is wanting to the completing of thy faith, because thou hast not visited Jerusalem; or that we are any whit the better for having the opportunity of dwelling in this place."‡ And here he concurs with Gregory Nyssen, who has written a discourse expressly against the opinion of those "who account it to be one of the parts of piety to have visited Jerusalem:"—*Περι των ἀποντων εἰς Ἱεροσολυμα*, &c. *οἷς ἐν μερει εὐσεβειας νενομισται το τους ἐν Ἱεροσολυμοις τοπους ἰδειν*.§

* Quis enim tam hebes, et sic in scribendo rudis est, ut idem laudet et damnet, ædificata destruat, et destructa ædificet?—*Hier. ep.* 50, *ad Pam.*

† Certe adorasse ubi steterunt pedes Domini, pars fidei est, &c. —*Hier. ep. ad Desider. quæ est* 144.

‡ Quorsum (inquies) hæc tam longo repetiti principio? Videlicet ne quidquam fidei tuæ deesse putes, quia Hierosolymam non vidisti, nec nos idcircò meliores existimes quòd hujus loci habitaculo fruimur.—*Id. ep.* 13. *ad Paulin.*

§ Greg. Nyss. in Ep. Tom. 2.

Let any rational man therefore now judge, whether or not this course must not necessarily embroil and enshroud in almost inexplicable difficulties the writings of the Fathers. For how is it possible that we should be able to judge when they speak as they thought, and when not? whether they mean really what they say, or whether they make but a flourish only? whether the bread which they show us be to deceive or to feed us? whether the problems they propose be solid or slippery ones? whether their positions be *dogmatical*, or *economical?* Certainly, if our court judgments were framed after this manner, we should never hope to have an end in any suit of law. As for that which Jerome says, "that an intelligent and favourable reader ought to judge of those things which seem harsh, from the rest of the discourse, and not immediately to condemn an author for having delivered, in one and the same book, contrary opinions;"* I confess that this is very true: but yet it does not remove the difficulty. For however intelligent and discerning a man the reader may be, it will very often be impossible for him to form a right judgment in this particular: as for example, when those other things are wanting, which Jerome would have a man to make the measure of his judgment; or when any one brings us no more of an author than a bare sentence—the chapter and book where these words are, which need to be explained, being quite out of his memory. How many such are adduced every day in our disputations? What can we now do, or which way shall we turn ourselves, if meeting with a passage from any of the Fathers that needs to be explained, we can find no other place in him on the same point; or if there be none found but what is as

* Debuerat prudens et benignus lector etiam ea quæ videntur dura æstimare de cæteris, et non in uno atque eodem libro criminari me diversas sententias protulisse.—*Hier. ep.* 50. *ad Pam.*

doubtful as the other, or that is not controverted in some other book?

Who shall regulate us amidst such contradictions as these? But, what is yet worse, those things which Jerome prescribes us for a rule and direction to our judgment, are now in these days of ours very unseasonable; as being harsh as to the one side, and pleasing to the other, according to men's several affections and interest, agreeably to which they are wont to interpret and judge of the Fathers, whereas we should rather search in them which way we are to direct our judgments. And that favourableness which Jerome requires in us cannot be here of any use, but may possibly besides do very much harm. For the greater the regard we bear to any Father, the greater care and pains shall we take in vindicating his words, and interpreting them in a sense as far different as we can from what we have long since condemned as erroneous and unsound; though possibly this may have been his real sense and opinion. As for example in those passages before cited out of Jerome and Gregory Nyssen, the Protestant accounts that a very harsh piece of doctrine, which however his adversary is well pleased with: the one labours to explain what appears very easy to the other: the one takes that for text, which the other accounts but as a gloss. And thus the greater affection men bear to the name and authority of any one of the Fathers, the more do they labour and use their utmost endeavours to bring him over to speak to their opinion; that is to say, in plain truth, to force him out of his own: it being impossible that he should hold both opinions at once.

We shall here therefore conclude, that however clear and express the words of the Fathers may be, yet nevertheless will it often happen, that we cannot have any assurance that we have their sense expressed in them; whether it be, in their Expositions of the

Scriptures; or in their Homilies and Sermons before the people; or lastly, in their Disputations with their adversaries regarding their Faith.

CHAPTER VII.

REASON VII.—The Fathers have not always held the same doctrine; but have changed some of their opinions, according as their judgment has become matured by study or age.

AMONGST all the ecclesiastical writers, those of the Old and New Testament only have received the knowledge of Divine things by an extraordinary inspiration. The rest have acquired their knowledge by the ordinary means of instruction, reading, and meditation; so that this knowledge came not to them in an instant, as it did to the others, but increased by degrees, ripening by little and little in proportion as they grew in years: whence it is, that their writings are not all of the same weight, or of the same value. For who sees not, that what they, as it were, sportingly wrote in their younger years, is of much less consideration than those other productions which they wrote in their mature age? Who, for instance, would equal the authority of that epistle of Jerome to Heliodorus* (written by him when he had but newly left the schools of Rhetoric, being yet a child, and full of that innocent and inconsiderate heat which usually accompanies those years,) to that of those other graver pieces which he afterwards gave to the Church, when he had arrived at his full strength and ripeness of mind, and to the perfection of his studies?

Augustine has left us a remarkable testimony, that the Fathers profited by age and study in the know-

* Hier. ep. 1. ad Heliodor. Vid. ep. 2, ad Nepot.

ledge of the truth, when, as in his old age, taking pen in hand, he reviewed and corrected all that he had ever written during his whole life; faithfully and ingenuously noting whatsoever he thought worthy of reprehension, and giving us all his animadversions collected together in the Books of his *Retractations*, which in my judgment is the most glorious and most excellent of all those many monuments which he has left to posterity; whether you consider the learning, or the modesty and sincerity of the man.

Jerome reports that Origen also, long before, had in his old age written an epistle to Fabianus, bishop of Rome, wherein he confesses that he repented of many things which he had taught and written.* Neither is there any doubt but that some similar thing may have happened to most of the other Fathers, and that they may have disallowed of that which they had formerly believed as true.

Now from this consideration there arises a new difficulty, which we are to grapple with in this our inquiry into the true and genuine sense of the Fathers respecting our present controversies. For, seeing that the condition and nature of their writings are such, it is most evident that when we would make use of any of their opinions, it will concern us to be very well assured that they have not only sometimes either held or written the same, but that they have moreover persevered in them to the end. Whence Vincentius Lirinensis,† in that passage of his which is so often urged, for making use of the ancient authors in deciding our present controversies, thinks it not fit that we should be bound to receive whatsoever they have said, for certain and undoubted truth, unless they have assured and confirmed it to us by their perseverance in the

* Ipse Origenes in Epistola quam scribit ad Fabianum, Romanæ urbis Episcopum, pœnitentiam agit cur talia scripserit, &c.—*Hier. ep.* 65, *de Erroribus Origenis.*

† Vincent. Lirinens. lib. adv. Novit. seu Common.

same. Cardinal Perron also evidently shows us the same way, by his own practice: for, disputing about the Canon of the Holy Scriptures, (which he pretends to have been always the very same in the Western Church, with that which is delivered to us by the Third Council of Carthage, where the Maccabees are reckoned in among the rest,) and finding himself hardly pressed by some certain passages alleged by the Protestants out of Jerome to the contrary, he answers the objection, by saying, among other things, that this Father, when he wrote the said passages, was not yet come to the ripeness of his judgment, and perfection of his studies;* whereas afterwards, when he was now more fully instructed in the truth of the sense of the Church, he changed his opinion, and retracted (as this cardinal says) both in general and in particular, whatsoever he had before written in those three Prologues, where he had excluded the Maccabees out of the canon.† And so likewise to another objection brought to the same purpose out of the Commentaries of Gregory the Great, he gives the like answer, saying that Gregory, when he wrote that piece, was not yet come to be Pope, but was a plain Deacon only, being at that time employed at Constantinople as the Pope's nuncio to the Greeks.

Now these answers of his are either insufficient, or else it will necessarily follow from hence, that we ought not to rest certainly satisfied in the testimony of any Father; except we first be assured, that not only he never afterwards retracted that opinion of his; but that besides, he wrote it in the strength and ripeness of his judgment. And see now how we are fallen into a new labyrinth. For, first of all, from whence and by what means may we be able to come, truly and certainly, to the knowledge of this secret; since we can hardly meet with any conjectures, tend-

* Perron's Repl. l. 1. c. 50. † Id. Ibid.

ing to the making of this discovery, namely, whether a Father has in his old age changed his opinion on that point for which it is produced against us or not?

If they had all of them been either able or willing to imitate the modesty of Augustine, we should then have had little left to trouble us. But you will hardly find any, either of the ancients, or of those of later times, that have followed this example; unless it be cardinal Bellarmine, who has lately thought good to revive this piece of modesty which had lain dead and buried for the space of so many ages together, by writing a Book of *Retractations*, which is very differently received by the learned of both religions. Yet, if you are fastidious upon it, with cardinal Perron, and will not allow the saying of a Father to be of any value, unless it were written by him after the maturity of his studies, I shall then despair of our ever making any progress, so much as one step forward, by this means, in the business in hand. For both parties will say, on every testimony that shall be produced against them, How do we know whether this Father had arrived at the maturity of his judgment when he wrote this book, or not? Who can tell whether or not, those days of his life that he enjoyed after the writing thereof, might not have bestowed clearness on his understanding, as well as whiteness on his head; and have changed his judgment as well as his hair?

We will here suppose that no such thing appears in any of his other writings. How many authors are there who have changed their opinions, and yet have not retracted what they had formerly written? But suppose now that we should have lost that particular tract wherein the author had given testimony of the changing of his opinion, what should we do in this case? If time should have deprived us of Augustine's Retractations, and some other of his later writings, as it has of an infinite number of other productions, both of his and of the other Fathers, which would have been of as great importance to us, we must certainly have thought that he had believed that the cause of predestination is the *prescience* or foreseeing of the faith of men; if we only read what he says in one of the books which he first wrote, "That God has not elected the works of any man, according to his prescience; seeing that it is he himself that gives the same to a man; but that he has elected his faith by his prescience; that is, he has elected those who he foresaw would believe his word; that is to say, he made choice of them to bestow his Holy Spirit upon; that so by doing good works they might attain everlasting life."*

Now the Pelagians and Semi-Pelagians would have brought this passage as an infallible argument that Augustine was of their opinion, but that his Retractations, and his other books which were written afterwards, clearly make it appear that this argument is of no force at all; forasmuch as this learned Father, having afterwards better considered of this point, wholly altered his opinion: "I had not (says he) as yet diligently enough inquired into, nor found out, what the election of grace was, whereof the Apostle speaks in these words: 'There is a remnant (to be saved) according to the election of grace;' which certainly is not grace, if any merits preceded it; so that what is given should be rendered rather as due to merits, than as given freely by grace."†

Now who knows but that among those Fathers whom we so confidently adduce every day, some of them may have retracted those things which we at

* Non ergo elegit Deus opera cujusquam in præscientiâ, quæ ipse daturus est: sed fidem elegit, &c.—*August. Exposit. quar. prop. ex ep. Rom. proposit.* 60.

† Nondum diligentius quæsiveram nec adhuc inveneram, qualis sit Electio Gratiæ, de quâ idem dicit Apostolus, Reliquiæ, &c.—*Id. Retract.* l. 1, *cap.* 23.

this day read in their works; and that time may have devoured the retractations of their opinions, and may have left us only their errors? Besides, who knows and can truly inform us what date their writings bear? whether they were the fruits of their spring of life, or of their summer, or of their autumn? whether they were gathered green, or were suffered to ripen upon the tree? Doubtless this whole inquiry is very intricate; there being scarcely any mark of their season of life to be found in the greatest part of them. There are indeed some few of them that have some of these marks, but yet they are so doubtful and uncertain, that the most able and distinguished critics are sometimes deceived in their inquiry on this matter.

When all is done, who knows not that there are some trees that bear their summer fruit even in the very beginning of the summer, when the spring time is as yet hardly past? And again, the fruits which are gathered at the end of the later season are not always the ripest: for time, instead of ripening, many times rots them. In like manner is it also with men, and consequently with the Fathers. Sometimes their summer yields much more and better fruit than their autumn. For as for the winter, that is to say, the last part of our age, it is evident that it usually brings forth nothing at all: or if it do chance to force itself beyond nature, the fruits it brings forth are yet worse, and more crude and imperfect, than those even of the spring.

Seeing therefore it is for the most part impossible to give any certain judgment of these things, either by the history of these authors, or by their books themselves: and that again on the other side, without this, we ought not to depend upon anything we find in their writings, by supposing we have discovered what their opinions have been: we may safely conclude in this matter also, as we have done in the former chapter, that it is very difficult to know truly and precisely what the opinions and sense of the ancients have been, as regards the differences at this day existing among Christians.

CHAPTER VIII.

Reason VIII.—It is necessary, but nevertheless difficult, to discover how the Fathers have held all their several opinions; whether as necessary or as probable only; and in what degree of necessity or probability.

Logic teaches us that true propositions are not all equally so: some of them being *contingent* only, as the schools speak, and others being *necessary:* and again, both being more or less either contingent or necessary, according to that admirable division which the philosopher has made into those *three degrees of necessity*, explained by him in the first book of his Demonstrations:—*Κατα παντος, καθ' αὑτο, καθολου πρωτον.**

Hence it comes to pass, that the knowledge or ignorance of these degrees is the more or less important in those sciences whereunto they appertain; there being some of them, as those which they call *principles*, that are so *necessary*, that a man cannot be ignorant of them, without overthrowing the whole science wherein they ought to have place: and there being others again, on the contrary side, that a man may be ignorant of, so far as to hold their contradictories for true, and yet nevertheless not run any great hazard. As, for example, these following are philosophical principles of the first sort: namely, "that there is motion:" and "that everybody occupies some certain place," and the like. For what strange philosophy would it be, that should either be ignorant of or should

* Arist. Poster. Analyt.

deny these principles? But these following are of the second sort: namely, "that there are precisely but five senses in living creatures: and "that the heavens are not of an elementary substance," and the like.

Although these propositions are by most held to be true, yet notwithstanding are they not so *necessary*, but that a man may pass for a philosopher, and yet not only be ignorant of those positions, but may also, if he please, maintain even those things that are contradictory to them. Now if there be any science where this consideration ought carefully to be applied, it is, in my judgment, in that of divinity. For there is a very great difference between the truths of which it consists: some of them being evidently more necessary than others, as Origen proves plainly in his twenty-seventh Homily upon Matthew. Only compare these two propositions together: "Christ is God;" and "Christ suffered death, being of the age of thirty-four, or thirty-five years." Who sees not that though both these propositions are true, yet notwithstanding there is a vast difference between them. For the former of these is necessarily true; that is to say, it is impossible but that Christ should be God; the salvation of mankind, which is the end of our religion, being otherwise not possible to be obtained. But as to the second, notwithstanding that it is true, and is collected clearly enough out of the Scriptures, yet is it not at all necessary. For Christ might, if he had so pleased, have suffered at the fortieth or fiftieth year of his age, without any prejudice at all to our salvation, which was the end of his suffering.

According to this diversity of degrees, the belief or ignorance of these two propositions are also of very different importance. The first of them we may not be ignorant of, and much less deny, without renouncing Christianity. The second we may be ignorant of, and even deny too, as supposing it false, yet without any great danger. To be able therefore to come to a clear and perfect understanding what was the sense of the Fathers, touching the points of religion at this day controverted amongst us, it is necessary that we should know not only whether they believed them or not, but also how they believed or did not believe them: that is to say, whether they held them as propositions necessarily or probably either true or false; and, moreover, in what degree either of necessity or probability they placed them.

That this inquiry is very necessary, cardinal Perron has clearly demonstrated, in that learned epistle of his, written to Casaubon, against king James. The king attributing to himself the name of Catholic, under pretence that he believed, and held all those things that the Fathers of the first four or five centuries did; the cardinal denies his inference; replying, among other things, that to be of the communion of the ancients, a man ought not only to believe what they believed, but also to believe it in the same manner and in the same degree that they did: that is, to believe as necessary to salvation whatever they believed as necessary thereto; and to believe as profitable to salvation what they held for such: and as lawful and not repugnant to salvation, what they held as lawful and not repugnant to salvation. Thus he goes on, and gives us a long and exact division of the different degrees of necessity, which may and ought to be considered in all propositions on religion.

I could sincerely wish that the occasion had carried on this learned prelate so far as to have made an exact application of this doctrine, and to have truly informed us (of what the greatest part of the world is at this day ignorant) in what degree each point of the Christian faith is held, either by the Church of Rome, or by the ancient Fathers; and what things are absolutely necessary in religion, and what are those other things that are necessary under some certain conditions only: which again are necessary by the necessity of the means; and which, by the necessity of the precept, (as he there speaks;) that is to say, which are those things that we ought to observe, either by reason of their profit, as being means which are profitable to salvation; and which we are to observe, by reason of the commandment only, being enjoined us by such an authority as we owe obedience to: and moreover, after these points, which all and every of the faithful are bound to believe expressly; and which are those that it is sufficient to believe in gross only, and by an implicit faith: and lastly, which are those things that we ought actually to do; and which are those that it is sufficient if we approve of them only, though we do them not? So that it appears clear, out of these words of his, that to be able to know what the doctrines of the Fathers have been, especially in the points now in dispute, we ought first to be assured in what degree they believed the same. That this distinction was of very great consideration with the ancient Church, appears sufficiently from the special regard which it always had to it; opening or shutting the door against men, first of all, according to the things which they believed or did not believe; secondly, according to the different manner they believed or did not believe them. For it excommunicated those who rejected the things that it held as necessary; and so likewise those who pressed as things necessary such as it held for things probable only. But it received, with all the suavity imaginable, all those who either were ignorant of, or doubted, or indeed denied, those things which it accounted true, yet not necessarily so. This appears clearly from an epistle written by Irenæus to Victor, bishop of Rome, cited by Eusebius, in his Ecclesiastical History:* where this holy man testifies, that although

* Hist. Eccles. Euseb. lib. 5, cap. 24, Codicis Græci, cap. 26.

there had been, before Victor's time, the same difference between the Asiatic and the Romish Church, touching the celebration of Easter; yet notwithstanding they lived in peace and mutual amity together; neither were any of the Asiatic bishops ever excommunicated at Rome, for their dissenting from them, either in this or in any other point; but rather the contrary; for on Polycarpus coming to Rome, in the time of Pope Anicetus, after they had a conference on the differences between them, and each of them continued still firm in his former opinion; they still did not forbear holding fair correspondence with each other, and to communicate together; Anicetus also, out of the respect he bore to Polycarpus, allowing him the use of his own church, to celebrate the Eucharist in.

Tertullian, in his book "De Præscriptionibus adversus Hæreticos," requires only that the rule of faith, (as he calls it) should continue in its proper form and order; allowing every man, in all other particulars, to make what inquiries and discourses he pleased, and to exercise his curiosity to the utmost liberty;* which is an evident argument, that he admitted into his communion all those who, not contradicting the rule of faith, broached any other opinions; that is, if they held them as probable only, and proposed not anything which was contrary to the rule of faith.

The author of the Apology of Origen,† published by Ruffinus, under the name of Pamphilus, was of the same opinion. For having confessed that Origen, if he held not, yet published certain very strange opinions on the state of the soul before the birth of man, and on the nature of the stars, he maintains that

* Cæterûm manente formâ ejus in suo ordine, quantumlibet quæras, et tractes, et omnem libidinem curiositatis effundas, &c. *Tertul. de Præscript. advers. Hæret. Vid. l. de Virg. vel. l.* 1.

† Apol. Orig. inter opera Origen.

these opinions do not presently make a man a heretic; and that even among the doctors of the Church there was diversity of opinion on the same.

Besides all this, it is evident that this difference of judgment is even at this day to be found in the Church of Rome; where you shall find the Dominicans and the Franciscans maintaining opinions entirely contradictory to each other, on the conception of the Virgin Mary; the one maintaining that she was conceived without sin, whereas the other utterly deny it. And that which makes me wonder the more is, that they suffer such contradictory opinions as these to be held amongst them, in such particulars as, considered barely in themselves, seem yet to be of very great importance. As for example, a man may either believe that we ought to yield to the cross the adoration of *Latria;* or, if he please, he may believe the contrary; without losing, either by reason of the one or the other, the communion of the Church and salvation. Yet notwithstanding, if you but consider the thing in itself, it will appear to be a matter of no such indifference as people imagine. For if the former of these opinions be indeed true, then must those that are of the other opinion sin very grievously, in not worshipping an object that is so worthy of adoration. But if it be false, then are those men that maintain the same, guilty of a much greater sin, by committing such horrible idolatry.

What point is there in religion, that seems to be of greater importance than that concerning the foundation and head of all ecclesiastical power, upon the authority of which the whole faith and state of the Church depends? And yet on this particular also, which is of such great consequence, do they suffer men to maintain contradictory opinions; some attributing this dignity to the Pope, and others to a general council.

If the opinion of the first of these be true, then is

the faith of the latter built upon a very erroneous ground:* but if the opinion of the latter be true, then does the faith of the former depend upon a cause which is not infallible; and consequently is null. Now these different opinions are reconciled, by saying that the Church accounting neither of these doctrines as necessary to faith, a man is not at once a heretic for holding the false opinion of the two, nor yet is he to be accounted orthodox, merely for holding the true one.

Seeing therefore that this particular concerns the communion of the Church, and our salvation also, which depends thereon, it will behove us to know certainly in what degree the ancients placed those articles which are at this day so eagerly pressed upon the Protestants; and whether they held them in the same, or in a higher, or else in a lower degree of necessity than they are now maintained by the Church of Rome. For unless this be made very clear, the Protestants, though they should confess (which yet they do not) that the Fathers did indeed really believe the same, might yet allege for themselves, that, notwithstanding all this, they are not bound to believe the same; inasmuch as all opinions in religion are not at once obligatory, and such as all men are bound to believe; seeing that there are some that are indeed necessary, but some others that are not so. They will answer likewise, that these opinions are similar to those at this day controverted between the Dominicans and the Franciscans; or to those other points debated between the Sorbonnists and the Regulars; wherein every one is permitted to hold what opinions he pleases. They will urge for themselves the determination of the council of Trent;† which in express terms distinguishes between the opinions of the Fa-

* Perron. Repl. l. 4, in Præfat.

† Conc. Trident. Sess. 21, cap. 5, extr. et Càn. 4.

thers: where having thundered out an anathema against all those that should maintain that the administering of the Eucharist was necessary for little infants, they further declare that this thunderbolt extended not to those ancient Fathers who gave the communion to infants; inasmuch as they maintained and practised this from being moved thereunto upon probable reasons only, and not accounting it necessary to salvation.

Seeing therefore that some errors which have been condemned by councils, may be maintained in such a certain degree, without incurring thereby the danger of their thunderbolts; for the same reason a man may be ignorant of, and even deny some truths also, without running the hazard of being anathematized. Who can assure us (the Protestants may further add) that the articles which we reject are not of this kind, and such as, though perhaps they may be true, it is nevertheless lawful for us to disbelieve? My opinion therefore is, that there is no man now that sees not that it concerns the doctors of the Romish Church, if they mean to convince their adversaries out of the Fathers, first to make it appear to them that the ancients held the said points, not only as true but as necessary also, and in the very same degree of necessity that they now hold them. Now this must prove a matter of extreme difficulty, and much greater here than in any of the other points before proposed. And I shall adduce no other argument for the proof of this than that very decree we cited before, where the council of Trent has declared that the Fathers did not administer the Communion to infants, "out of any opinion that it was necessary to salvation, but did it upon some other probable reason only."* For we have

* Ut enim sanctissimi illi Patres sui facti probabilem causam pro illius temporis ratione habuerunt; ita certè eos nullâ salutis necessitate id fecisse, sine controversiâ tenendum est.—*Concil. Trident. Sess.* 21. c. 4.

not only very good reason to doubt, whether the Fathers held this opinion and followed this practice as *probable* only; but it seems besides (with all reverence to that council be it spoken) to appear evidently enough out of their writings, that they did hold it as *necessary*.

Only hear the Fathers themselves, and Augustine in the first place, who says, "that the Churches of Christ hold by an ancient, and as I conceive an apostolical tradition, that without Baptism and the Communion of the Lord's Table, no man can come either into the kingdom of God, or unto salvation or eternal life."* Afterwards having, as he conceives, proved this out of the Scriptures, he adds further: "seeing therefore that no man can hope either for eternal life or salvation without Baptism and the body and blood of Christ," (thus does he call the Sacrament of the Eucharist, according to the language of his time;) "as has been proved by so many divine testimonies; in vain is it promised to infants without the participating of these."† Three chapters before, treating of those words of our Saviour in John, "Except you eat my flesh, and drink my blood, you can have no life in you," (which words Augustine understands, both there and elsewhere, of the Communion of the Eucharist,) he makes a long discourse to prove that they extend as well to infants as to people of maturer age. "Is there any man (says he) that dares affirm that this speech belongs not to infants also; or that they may have life in them, without participating of this body,

* Ex antiqua, ut existimo, et apostolica traditione Ecclesiæ Christi insitum tenent, præter Baptismum et participationem Dominicæ mensæ, non solùm ad regnum Dei, sed nec ad salutem, et vitam æternam posse quenquam hominum pervenire. Hoc enim et Scriptura testatur, &c.—*Aug. l.* 1, *de Peccat. Mor. et Remiss.*

† Si ergo, ut tot et tanta divina testimonia concinunt, nec salus, nec vita æterna sine Baptismo, et corpore et sanguine Domini cuiquam spectanda est; frustra sine his promittitur parvulis.—*Ibid.*

and of this blood?"* And this is his constant manner of speaking, in eight or ten other passages in his works, which are too long to be here inserted.†

Pope Innocent I., Augustine's contemporary, speaks also after the same manner; proving against the Pelagians that Baptism is necessary for infants, to render them capable of eternal life; inasmuch as without Baptism they cannot communicate of the Eucharist, which is necessary to salvation.‡

Cyprian also,§ long before them, spake to the very same sense: and this Maldonate affirms to have been the opinion of the first six centuries.||

These things being considered, we must infer either that the council of Trent, by its declaration, has made that which has been, to be as if it had never been, which is a power that the poet Agatho in Aristotle would not allow to God himself: *Μονου γαρ αὐτου και θεος στερισκεται, Αγεννητα ποιειν ὁσσ' ἀν ᾖ πεπραγμενα*:¶ or else that the Fathers of this council, either out of forgetfulness or otherwise, mistook themselves in this account of theirs respecting the opinion of the ancient Church in this particular: which in my judg-

* An verò quisquam etiam hoc dicere audebit, quòd ad parvulos hæc sententia non pertineat; possintque sine participatione corporis hujus et sanguinis in se habere vitam, &c.—*Id. ibid.* c. 20.

† Id. t. 2, ep. 106, ep. 107, ep. poster. ib. Mar. l. 2, contr. Pel. et Celest c. 18, l. 1. contr. 2. ep. Pelag. ad Bon. cap. 22, et l. 4, c. 4, l. 1, contr. Jul. et l. 3, c. 1, et c. 12, lib. de Prædest. Sanct. ad Prosp. c. 13, Hypomn. l. 5 et 6, Tract. 120, in Job. Serm. 32, de verb. Ap.

‡ Illud verò quod eos vestra fraternitas asserit prædicare, parvulos æternæ vitæ præmiis, etiam siae baptismatis gratia posse donari, perfatuum est. Nisi enim manducaverint carnem filii hominis, et biberint sanguinem ejus, non habebunt vitam æternam in semetipsis. (*Innoc. in ep. ad. Milevit. Synod. quæ est inter ep. Aug.* 15.)—Vid. Aug. l. 2, contr. 2 ap. Pelag. c. 5, et lib. 1, contr. Jul. c. 2.

§ Cyprian. lib. 3, Test. ad Qui. c. 25.

|| Missam facio Augustini et Innocentii I. sententiam, quæ sexcentos circiter annos viguit in Ecclesia, Eucharistiam etiam infantibus necessariam.—*Maldon. in Joan.* c. 6. *num.* 116.

¶ Agatho apud Aristot. Eth. ad Nicom. l. 7. c. 2.

ment is the more favourable and the more probable conceit of the two: and if so, I shall then desire no more. For if these great personages, who were chosen with so much care and circumspection out of all parts of Christendom, and sent to Trent, to deliberate upon and determine a matter of the greatest importance in the world; and were directed by the legates of such supereminent wisdom, and digested their decrees with a judgment so mature and deliberate, that there is scarcely one word in them without its design—if after all this, I say, these men should be found to have erred in this inquiry, in affirming that the Fathers held only as *probable* that which they evidently appear to have held as *necessary*, if Pope Pius IV., with his whole consistory, consisting of so many eminent and wise men, has approved and confirmed this mistake of theirs, not perceiving it at all—what can we, or indeed what ought we, to expect from any other hands, whosesoever they be, as regards the points now controverted between us; in comparison with which, a man may very well say, that all the difficulty which this matter now presents is nothing at all; wherein, notwithstanding, this whole council mistook itself? Where shall we find a man, that after this failing of theirs, can have the courage to adventure upon so difficult and so intricate an undertaking? Who can promise himself success there, where so great a council has failed? The very hope of effecting so weighty a matter can hardly be excused from the guilt of high presumption. For, first of all, the Fathers tell us very seldom in what degree, either of necessity or probability, they held their opinions: and even when they do tell us, their expressions being such as we have observed of them, we ought not at once to conclude anything from them, without first examining them thoroughly. For many times, when they would recommend to us such things as they accounted profitable for us, they would speak of them as if they had been necessary: and so again, to take off our belief of and to divert our affections from such things as they conceived either to be simply false, or otherwise unprofitable for us, they represented them as the most detestable and pernicious things. "Whosoever (said Ignatius) fasts upon the Lord's day, or upon any Saturday (meaning Easter-eve,) he is a murderer of Christ:"—*Εἰ τις Κυριακην, ἡ σαββατον νηστευει, πλην ἑνος σαββατου, οὗτος Χριστοκτονος ἐστι.**

Who would not think, hearing these tragical expressions of his, that certainly he was speaking of the very foundation of the whole Christian religion? And yet the business he there speaks of was only the observation of a certain part of a positive law, and which yet (as most are of opinion) was at that time received but by a part only of the Church; the belief and observation whereof was so far from being classed among those things that were necessary, that it was scarcely placed in the first degree of probability; and is now at length utterly abolished.

This manner of discoursing is very frequently used by Tertullian, Ambrose, and especially by Jerome; who are all so enthusiastic for the side they espouse, that you would think, in reading them, that all those whom they commend were really angels; and all those whom they speak against were arrant devils; that whatsoever they maintain, is the very foundation and ground-work of the Christian religion; and whatsoever they refute is mere atheism, and the highest impiety.

Certainly Jerome, writing to a certain Roman matron, named Furia, who was a widow, and dissuading her from marrying again,† discourses of this matter in the very same manner as he would have done in dissuading her from the committing of murder.

Here we are to call to mind again the various rea-

* Ignat. ep. 4, ad Phil. † Hieron. ep. 10, ad Furiam, tom. 1.

sons for the obscurity of the Fathers, and particularly that of their rhetoric, all which have place in this particular rather than in any other. So that there seems to be but one only certain way left us to discover in what degree they placed the propositions of Christian doctrine; namely, their creeds and expositions of their faith, whether they were general, or particular ones; and the determinations of their councils and ecclesiastical assemblies. For we may very well believe that they held as necessary all such points as they made profession of; anathematizing all such as should deny the same. By this rule we may indeed assure ourselves that they held as necessary the greatest part of all those points wherein we at this day agree among ourselves. Some of these we have already noticed in our preface: for they are most of them either delivered expressly in their creeds, or else positively determined in their councils; and the deniers of them are there expressly condemned. But yet this rule will scarcely be of any use in the decision of our present controversies. For some of them appear not at all, either in that Rule of Faith so often mentioned by Tertullian, or in the Nicene creed, or in that of Constantinople, or in the determinations of the council of Ephesus, or in those of Chalcedon. The first of these councils anathematized Arius; the second Macedonius; the third Nestorius; and the fourth Eutyches: and yet nevertheless are the several tenets of these very men at this day received, and maintained by one side or other. Nay, what is more, the aforesaid articles do not appear at all in the two following councils; namely, the second council of Constantinople, which condemned certain writings of Theodorus, Theodoretus, and Ibas, as we have noticed before: nor yet in the third council of Constantinople, which anathematized the Monothelites, and was held about the year of our Lord 681. Yet have these first six councils (if you believe the

Fathers of the seventh) "established and confirmed all those things which had been taught in the Roman Catholic Church from the primitive times, whether by writing or by unwritten tradition." *Παντα τα παραδοθεντα ἐν τῃ καθολικῃ ἐκκλησιᾳ, και ἐγγραφως, και ἀγραφως, ἐκ των ἀρχηθεν χρονων, αὗται (Sex Synodi Oecumenicæ) και ἐβεβαιωσαν, και ἐστηριξαν.** It will hence follow, that these points, which appear not here in the said first six councils at all, were not taught from the beginning, either in writing or otherwise.

About the eighth century however, and for a good while afterwards, we find mention of one of those points now controverted among us, namely, that relating to images; which was diversely and contrarily determined in the councils of Constantinople, of Nicæa, and of Frankfort; the second of these councils enjoining the use and adoration of images; whereas the first had utterly forbidden it: and the last of these councils taking off, and correcting, as it were, the excesses of the other two. What can you say to this, that even in the writings of particular men, which yet are usually more copious than the determinations of councils are, there is no mention made of the said points?

Epiphanius,† in the conclusion of his Treatise on Heresies, gives us two discourses; in the one of which he notes down the order, customs, and discipline of the Church in his time: wherein I must say, that there are many things which much differ from the customs that are at this day observed by us on both sides. In the other is contained an exposition of the faith of the Church set down at large, which he calls "the pillar of the truth, the hope and assurance of

* Synod. 7, Act. 6, Refut. Synod. Iconocl.

† Epiphan. in Panar. l. 3, et in Anacephal.

immortality:"—*Τουτο το ἐρεισμα της ἀληθειας, ἡ ἐλπις και ἡ βεβαιωσις της ἀφθαρσιας.**

Yet of all those controversies which are at this day disputed amongst us, you will there meet with one only; and that is the local descent of our Saviour Christ into hell: which yet is an article of very small importance, as every one knows. In the acts of the sixth council we have a synodical epistle of Sophronius, patriarch of Jerusalem;† wherein, as the usual custom was, he explains the faith, in a very ample and particular manner: and yet, notwithstanding, you will not there meet with any of those points which are now controverted amongst us.

Those that search more closely into the business, will be apt positively to conclude from this their silence, that these points were not at that time any part of the doctrine of the Church: and certainly this kind of argument seems not to want reason. But as regards myself, it is sufficient that the truth of my assertion is confirmed; that it is, if not impossible, at least a very difficult thing to discover in what degree, either of *necessity* or *probability*, the ancient Fathers held each of those points, which are now disputed amongst us; seeing that they appear not at all, either in the expositions of their faith, or in the determinations of their councils, which are, as it were, the catalogues of those points of doctrine, which they accounted *necessary*.

* Epiphan. in Panar. l. 3, et in Anacephal.
† Concil. vi. Act. 2.

CHAPTER IX.

REASON IX.—We ought to know what have been the opinions, not of one or more of the Fathers, but of the whole ancient Church: which is a very difficult matter to discover.

THOSE who make the most account of the writings of the Fathers, and who urge them the oftenest in their disputations, inform us, that the value of their sentiments in these matters arises from the fact, that they are so many testimonies of the general sense and judgment of the Church; to which alone these men attribute the supreme power of judging in controversies of religion. For if we should consider them severally, each by himself, and as they stand by their own strength only, they confess that they may chance to err; so that it will hence follow, that in order to make use of the testimonies of the Fathers, it is not sufficient for us to know whether such or such sentiments be truly theirs, and if so, what the meaning of them is; but we ought further also to be very well assured that they are conformable to the belief of the Church in their time: in the same manner as in a court of judicature, the opinion of any single person on the bench is of no weight at all, as to the passing of judgment, unless it be conformable to the opinion of all the rest, or at least of the major part of those present.

Now observe how we are fallen again into new difficulties. Whence and by what means can we learn whether the whole Church, in the time of Justin Martyr, or of Augustine, or of Jerome, maintained the same opinions in every particular that these men severally did, or not? I confess that the charity of these men was very great; and that they very heartily and constantly embraced the body and substance of the belief of the Church, in all particulars, that they saw apparently to be such. But where the Church did not at all express itself, and clearly declare what its sense was, they could not possibly, however great their desire of so doing, follow its authority as the rule of their opinions. Wheresoever therefore they treat of points which were long since decided, believed, and received, expressly and positively, by the whole Christian Church, either of their own age, or of any of the preceding ages, it is very probable that they conformed to what was believed by the Church: so that, in these cases, their sentiments may very well pass for a testimony of the judgment and sense of the Church: it being very improbable, that they could be either ignorant what was the public doctrine of the Church; or that knowing the same, they would not follow it. As for example, when Athanasius, Ambrose, Jerome, Augustine, and others, discourse on the Son of God, they speak nothing but what is conformable to the belief of the Church in general, because the belief of the Church had then been clearly and expressly delivered upon this point; so that whatsoever they say, as to this particular, may safely be received as a testimony of the Church's belief. The same may be done in all the other points which have either been positively determined in any of the general councils, or delivered in any of the creeds, or that any other way appear to have been the public belief of the Church.

If the Fathers had but contained themselves within these bounds, and had not taken the liberty to treat of anything, save what the Church had clearly delivered its judgment upon, this rule might then have been received as a general one; and, whatever opinion we found in them, we might safely have concluded it to have been the sense of the Church as existing in their time. But the curiosity of man's nature, together with the impudence of the heretics, and the tenderness of conscience, whether of their own, or of others, and divers other reasons perhaps, having partly made them willingly, and partly forced, and as it were, constrained them to go on further, and to proceed to the search of the truth of several points, which had not as yet been established by the universal and public consent of all Christians; it could not be avoided, but that necessarily they must in these inquiries make use of their own proper light, and must deliver upon the same their own private opinions, which the Church, that came after them, has since either embraced or rejected.

I shall not here stand to prove my opinion, since it is a thing that is confessed on all hands, and whereof the Romanists make special use upon all occasions, in answering several objections brought against them out of the Fathers. As, for example, where cardinal Bellarmine excuses the error of Pope John XXII. on the state of departed souls before the Resurrection;* by saying, that the Church, in his time, had not as yet determined anything as to this particular. So likewise, where he applies the same salvo to that (in his judgment) unsound opinion of Pope Nicolas I., who maintained that Baptism, administered in the name of Jesus Christ only, without expressing the other persons of the Holy Trinity, was, notwithstanding, valid and effectual.† "This is a point (says Bellarmine) on which we find not the Church to have determined any thing." And however dangerous and almost heretical the opinion of those men seems to him, who hold that the Pope of Rome may fall into heresy; yet does he permit Pope Adrian to hold the same, not daring to rank him among the heretics, because the Church had not as yet clearly and definitively expressed itself on this point.

* Bellarm. de Rom. Pont. l. 4, c. 14. Sect. Respondeo in primis, &c.

† Non invenitur ulla certa definitio Ecclesiæ de hac re.—*Id. ibid. Sect. ult. ex his.*

The same Bellarmine, in another controversy of great importance, regarding the Canonical Books of the Old Testament, (finding himself closely put to it, by his adversary's urging against him the authority of Jerome, who casts Tobit, the Book of Wisdom, Ecclesiasticus, and the Maccabees, out of the Canon, contrary to the judgment of the Church of Rome, which receives them now,) gets over this objection after the same manner. "I confess (says he) that Jerome held this opinion, because no general council had as yet ordained anything regarding these books."

Seeing therefore that it is most clear, both from the confession of our adversaries, and from the consideration of the thing itself, that the Fathers have in their writings circulated many of their own particular opinions, digested out of their own private meditations, and which they had not learnt in the school of the Church—who sees not, that before we give any certain credit to their sentiments, we ought first to be assured of what nature they are? Whether they were their own particular opinions only, or the public sense of their age: since it is confessed by all, that those of the former kind are not always necessarily obligatory, but are such as oftentimes may, and sometimes ought to be rejected, without any scruple at all.

You may urge perhaps to a Protestant, that Jerome worshipped the relics of departed saints. How shall I know, (will he reply upon you again) whether this was his private opinion only, or not? If the authority of this Father, for want of being grounded upon some public declaration of the Church, could not bind Bellarmine to receive his opinion on the Canon of the Old Testament, why should this opinion of his, which is not any whit better grounded than the other, persuade me to the worship of relics? The same reply will he make, and many times with much more appearance of reason, concerning divers other testimonies produced out of the Fathers. So that, whether you would confirm your own faith, or whether you would wrest out of your adversary's hand this manner of reply, and make good all such allegations, it will behove you to make it clear, concerning any passage whatever that you shall urge out of a Father, that it is not his own private opinion, but was that of the Church itself wherein he lived: which, in my judgment, is a thing that is more difficult to be demonstrated, than any of those matters we have yet discoursed upon. For those means by which we might easily attain to this knowledge are wanting, and those which we have left us are very feeble, and very inconclusive.

If the Fathers themselves had but taken so much pains, as to have distinguished betwixt these two sorts of opinions, informing us, in every particular case, which were their own private ones only, and which were taught by the whole Church; or, at least, had but proposed some of them as *doubtful*, and others again as *assured* truths, in the same manner as Origen has sometimes done, they would indeed have aided us very much; though, to say the truth, they would not have wholly cured us of our grief: forasmuch as sometimes (as we shall hereafter make it appear,*) they attribute to the Church those things which it is most evident it never held. Yet they very seldom make any such distinction, but commonly express their own private opinions in the same manner as they do those publicly received; and sometimes also, by reason of the partial feelings to which these authors might chance naturally to have been subject, we have them recommending to us with much more eagerness that which they have conceived, and brought forth themselves, than that which they have received from any other hand; so that we shall meet with very little in them that may afford us any light in this particular.

* Infra, l. II. c. 1.

There would be left us yet another aid in this business, by comparing that which they say here and there throughout their writings, with the public opinions of the Church, which would be rather a safe and certain rule to go by, had we anywhere else, besides their books, any clear and certain evidence what the belief of the Church has been, in each distinct age, on all points of religion: and if this were so, we should not then need to trouble ourselves with studying the writings of the Fathers, seeing that we read them for no other purpose, but only to discover out of them what the doctrine of Christendom has been on those points which are at this day controverted among us. Yet there is no man but knows that this aid is wanting to us. For, setting aside the creeds, and the determinations of the first six General Councils, and of some few of the Provincial, you will not meet with any work of this nature throughout the whole stock of antiquity.

Now (as we have already made it appear in the preceding chapter,) the ancient Church has not any where declared, either in its creeds or in the aforesaid councils, what the opinion and sense of it has been, on the greatest part of those points which are now in dispute amongst us; it followeth therefore, that by this means we shall never be able to distinguish, in the writings of the Fathers, which were their own private opinions, and which they held in common with the rest of the Church.

If we could indeed learn, from any creditable author, that the present controversies had ever been decided by the ancient Church, we should then readily believe that the Fathers would have followed this their decision: and then, although the *Constitutions* themselves would not perhaps have come down to our hands, yet notwithstanding should we be in some sort obliged to believe, that the Fathers, who had both seen and assented to the same, would also have delivered over the sense of them unto us in their writings. But we meet with no such thing in any author: for it rather appears evidently to the contrary, through the whole course of ecclesiastical history, that these matters were never so much as started in the first ages of Christianity; so far are they from having been then decided. So that it manifestly appears from hence, that if the Fathers of those primitive times have by chance said anything of them, they took not what they said from the determinations of the Church, which had not as yet declared itself on the same, but expressed rather their own private thoughts and opinions.

Neither will it be to any purpose to object here, that the testimonies of many Fathers together do represent to us the sense of the Church, although the voice of one or two single persons only is not sufficient to do the same. For, not to answer that what has happened to one may have happened to many others, and that, if some particular persons chance to have fallen into some particular opinions, possibly others may either have accompanied or else have followed them in the same—I say further, that this objection is of no force at all in this particular. For, seeing that the Church had not as yet declared its opinion publicly on the points at this day controverted, it is as impossible that many together, that lived in the same time, should represent it to us, as that one single person should. How could they possibly have seen that which lay as yet concealed? How could they possibly measure their belief by such a rule, as was not yet visible to the world?

The Chiliasts* adduce the testimonies, not of one, or of two, but of a very great number of the most eminent and the most ancient among the Fathers, who were all of their opinion, as we shall see hereafter.

* Millennarians.—EDITOR.

The answer that is ordinarily made to this objection, is, that the Church having not as yet declared its sense on this point, the testimonies of these men bind us not to believe the same; which is an evident argument, that a great number, in this case, signifies no more than a small one, in representing to us what the belief of the Church has been; and that it is necessary, that either by some General Council, or else by some other public way, it must have declared its judgment on any question in dispute; in order that we may know whether the Fathers have been of the same opinion or not. So that, according to this account, we are to raise up again the whole ancient Church, and to call it to account on every one of these particular points now discussed, on which the testimonies of the Fathers are adduced; it being impossible otherwise to give any certain judgment, whether what they say is their own private opinion, or that of the public; that is to say, whether it be fit to be believed or not.

Thus any man, even of the meanest judgment, may easily perceive that it is not only difficult, but almost impossible, to draw from the writings of the Fathers such information as is necessary for our satisfaction in matters of so great importance.

CHAPTER X.

Reason X.—It is very difficult to ascertain whether the opinions of the Fathers, as to the controversies of the present day, were received by the Church universal, or only by some portion of it; this being necessary to be known, before their sentiments can be adopted.

Suppose that one of the Fathers, relieving us in this difficult or rather impossible business, should tell us, in express terms, that what he proposes is the sense and opinion of the Church in his time; yet this would not quite extricate us from the doubtful condition we are in. For, besides that their words are many times, in such cases as these, liable to exception, suppose that it were certainly and undoubtedly so; .yet it would concern us then to examine what that Church was, of which he speaks; whether it was the Church universal, or only some particular Church; and whether it was that of the whole world, or that of some city, province, or country only.

Now that this is a matter of no small importance is evident, because the opinions of the Church universal in points of faith are accounted infallible, and necessarily true; whereas those of particular Churches are not so, but are confessed to be subject to error. So that the question being here about the faith, which ought not to be grounded upon anything save what is infallibly true, it will concern us to know what the judgment of the Church universal has been; seeing the opinion of no particular Church can do us any service in this case. And that this distinction is also otherwise very necessary, appears evident by this; because the opinions and customs which have been commonly received by the greatest part of Christendom, have not always immediately taken place in each particular Church; and again, those which have been received in certain particular Churches have not been entertained by all the rest. Thus we find in history, that the churches in Asia Minor kept the feast of Easter upon a different day from all the other parts of Christendom: and although the matter itself seems to be of no very great importance, yet nevertheless it caused a great sensation in the Church; Victor, bishop of Rome, by reason of this little difference, excommunicating all Asia Minor.*

Now each party here alleged their reasons, and

* Euseb. Hist. Eccles. l. 5, c. 23, 24, p. 55, Cod. Græc.

apostolical tradition also, for what they did; speaking with such great confidence in the justification of their own opinion, that on hearing them individually a man would really believe that each of their opinions was the very sense of the whole Church; which notwithstanding was only the opinion of one portion of it.

The greatest part of Christendom held the baptism of heretics to be good and effectual:* and received all those, who, forsaking their heresy, desired to be admitted into the communion of the Church, without rebaptizing them; as appears out of Cyprian, who confesses that this had also been the custom formerly, even in the African Churches themselves. Yet notwithstanding Firmilianus, archbishop of Cæsarea in Cappadocia, testifies that the Churches of Cappadocia had immemorially believed and practised the contrary.† They had also, in his time, so declared and ordained, together with the Churches of Galatia and Cilicia, in a full synod, held at the city of Iconium. About the same time also Cyprian and the bishop of Africa entered on the same affair, and embraced this opinion of rebaptization of heretics. The acts of the council held at Carthage are yet extant; where you have eighty-seven bishops, who with one unanimous consent established the same.

The custom at Rome, in Tertullian's time, was to receive into the communion of the Church all fornicators and adulterers, after some certain penances which they enjoined them. Tertullian, who was a Montanist, exclaimed fearfully against this custom, and wrote a book expressly against it; which is also extant among his works at this day. Who now, that should read this work of his, would not believe that

* Cypr. ep. 71, et ep. 75, quæ est Firmil.

† Cæterum nos veritati et consuetudinem jungimus: et consuetudini Romanorum consuetudinem veritatis opponimus; ab initio hoc tenentes quod à Christo et ab Apostolis traditum est.—*Firmil. ep. ad Cypr. quæ est* 75 *inter ep. Cypr.*

it was the general opinion of all Catholics, that such sinners were not to be excluded from penance and the communion of the Church? Yet for all this, it is evident, out of a certain epistle of Cyprian,* that even some of the Catholic bishops of Africa were of the contrary persuasion: and the Jesuit Petavius is further of opinion, that this indulgence was not allowed nor practised in the Churches of Spain, till a long time after; and that the ancient rigour, which excluded for ever such offenders from the communion of the Church, was in practice among them, till the time of Pacianus, bishop of Barcelona, who left not any hopes of ecclesiastical absolution, either to idolaters, murderers, or adulterers; as may be seen in his Exhortation to Repentance.†

In the year of our Lord 364, the council of Laodicea ordained,‡ that none but the canonical books of the Old and New Testament should be read in churches, giving us moreover a catalogue of the said books, which amount in all, in the Old Testament, to the number of twenty-two only; without making any mention at all of those other books which cardinal Perron calls posthumous, namely, Ecclesiasticus, the Book of Wisdom, the Maccabees, Judith, and Tobit. All the canons of this council were afterwards inserted in the code of the Church universal, where you have this very canon also, Num. 163; that is as much as to say, they were received as rules of the Catholic Church.

Who would believe now, but that this declaration of the canon of the Scriptures was at that time received by all Christian Churches? And yet, notwithstanding, you have the Churches of Africa meeting together in the Synod at Carthage,§ about the year

* Cypr. ep. ad Anton.
† Pacian. Paræn. ad Pœnit. t. 3, Bibl. PP. p. 71.
‡ Concil. Laodic. can. 59, in Cod. Eccles. Univers. 163.
§ Concil. Carthag. iii. can. 47.

of our Lord 397, and ordaining quite contrary to the former resolution of Laodicea, that among those books which were allowed to be read in churches, the Maccabees, Judith, Tobit, Ecclesiasticus, and the Book of Wisdom, (which two last they also reckon among the books written by Solomon,) should be taken into the number.

Who knows not the difference there was in the first ages of Christianity, between the Eastern and the Western Churches, respecting the fasting on Saturdays;* the Church of Rome maintaining it as lawful, and all the rest of the world accounting it unlawful? Whence it was that we had that bold canon passed in the council at Constantinople, in Trullo, in these words: "Understanding that in the city of Rome, in the time of the holy fast of Lent, they fast on Saturdays, contrary to the custom and tradition of the Church, it seems good to this holy council, that in the Roman Church they inviolably also observe that canon, which says, that whosoever shall be found to fast either upon the Lord's day, or upon the Saturday, (excepting only that one Saturday) if he be a clergyman, he shall be deposed; but if he be of the laity, he shall be excommunicated."†

Who knows not in how many different ways the fast of Lent was anciently observed in various Churches, an account of which is given by Irenæus, in that pious epistle of his which he wrote to Victor; part whereof Eusebius inserts in his Ecclesiastical History?‡ Who knows not also, that the opinions and expressions of the Greek Church, on Free-will and Predestination, are very different from what the Church believed and taught in Augustine's time, and afterwards?

As to the *Discipline* of the Church, only hear

* Vid. Petav. in Epiph. p. 359.
† Can. Synod. Quininsext. Can. iv.
‡ Iren. ap. Euseb. Hist. Eccles. l. 5, cap. 26.

Anastasius Bibliothecarius, upon the sixth Canon of the Seventh General Council, which enjoins all Metropolitans to hold provincial synods once a year: "Neither let it at all trouble thee (says he) that we have not this decree; seeing that there are some others found among the canons, whose authority nevertheless we do not admit of. For some of them are in force, and are observed in the Greek Church only; and others again only in certain other provinces. As for example, the sixteenth and seventeenth canons of the council of Laodicea are observed only among the Greeks; and the sixth and the eighth canons of the council of Africa are received by none but the Africans."*

I could here produce various other examples; but these may suffice to show that the opinions and customs which have been received in one part of the Church, have not always been entertained in all the rest. Whence it evidently follows that all that is acknowledged as the opinion or observation of the Church, ought not therefore at once to pass for a universal law.

The Protestant alleges, for justifying his canon of the Scriptures, the council of Laodicea, before mentioned. You answer him perhaps that this indeed was the opinion of the Churches; but it was only of some particular Churches. I shall not here enter into an examination, whether this answer be well grounded or not: it is sufficient for me that I can then safely conclude from hence, that according to this account, before you can make use of any opinion or tes-

* Nec te moveat, si hanc definitionem minimè nos habemus: cùm et earum nonnullas, quas inter canones habemus, in auctoritatem non recipiamus; sicut quasdam ex conciliis. Aliæ namque apud Græcos tantùm, aliæ verò apud certas tantùm provincias in observantiam Ecclesiarum assumuntur: sicut Laodicensis concilii 16 et 17 regulæ apud Græcos tantùm servantur: et Africani concilii 6 et 8 capitula, quæ nulla provincia servare, nisi Africana, dignoscitur. —*Anastas. Biblioth. ad Can.* 6, *Conc.* 7 *Gener.*

timony out of any of the Fathers, it is necessary that you first make it appear, not only that it was the opinion of the Church at that time; but you must further also clearly demonstrate to us, what Church's opinion it was; whether of the Church universal, or else of some particular Church only. It is objected against the Protestants, that Epiphanius* testifies that the Church admitted not into the higher orders of the ministry, any save those that were virgins, or professed continency. Now to make good this allegation, it is necessary that it be first proved, that the Church he there speaks of was the Church universal. For (the Protestant will reply) as Laodicea had, it seems, a particular opinion on the canon of the Scriptures; possibly also Cyprus may in like manner have had its particular resolutions as to the ordination of the clergy. The same may be said of the greatest part of those other allegations and opinions of the ancient Church.

Now how difficult a business it will be to clear these matters, which are so full of perplexity; and to distinguish the writings of antiquity at this great distance of time, separating that which was *public* from what was *particular*, and that which was *provincial* from what was *national*, and what was national from that which was *universal*—any man may be able to imagine; but none can thoroughly understand, except he who has made the trial. Only conceive to yourselves a city, that has lain in ruins a thousand years, nothing of which remains but the ruins of houses, lying all along confusedly here and there; all the rest being covered over with thorns and bushes. Imagine then that you have met with one that will undertake to show you precisely where the public buildings of the city stood, and where the private ones: which were the stones that belonged to the one, and which

* Epipha. Hær. 59, tom. 1.

belonged to the other; and, in a word, who will in these confused heaps, where the whole lies all together, separate for you, notwithstanding, the one from the other. The very same task in a manner does he undertake, who thus endeavours truly and precisely to distinguish the opinions of the ancient Church.

This antiquity is now of eleven or twelve hundred years' standing: and the ruins of it are now only left us in the books of the writers of that period; which have indeed met with none of the best treatment in their passage through the several ages down to our time; as we have before shown. How then can we entertain the least hope that, amidst this so great confusion, we should be able yet to distinguish the remains, and to tell which of them honoured the public temple, and which went to the furnishing of private chapels only? especially considering that the private ones have each of them ambitiously endeavoured to make their own pass for public. For where is the province, or the city, or the doctor, that has not boasted of his own opinions and observations as apostolical, and not used his utmost endeavours to gain them the repute of being universal? Jerome allows every particular province full liberty to do herein as it pleases. "Let every province (says he) abound in its own sense, and hold the ordinances of their ancestors as apostolical laws."*

It is true indeed, that Jerome speaks in this place only of certain observations of things which are in themselves indifferent. But yet, that which he has permitted them in these matters, they have practised in all others. I shall not here trouble myself to produce any other reasons, to prove the difficulty of this inquiry, because I should then be forced to repeat a great part of that which has been already noticed.

* Unaquæque provincia abundet in sensu suo, et præcepta majorum leges apostolicas arbitretur.—*Hieron. ep.* 28 *ad Lucinum.*

If it be a very difficult matter to attain to any certain knowledge what the sense of the writings of the Fathers is, as we have proved before, how much more difficult a thing will it be, to discover whether their opinions were those of the particular Churches wherein they lived, or else were the opinions of the Church universal in their age; the same things which cause obscurity in the one having as much or rather more reason for doing the like in the other. And if you would fully understand how painful an undertaking this is, only read the disputations of the learned of both parties on this point; where you will meet with so many doubts and contradictions, and such diversity of opinions, that you will easily conclude, that this is one of the greatest difficulties to be met with throughout the whole study of antiquity.

CHAPTER XI.

Reason XI.—It is impossible to know exactly what has been the belief of the ancient Church, either universal or particular, as to any of those points which are at this day controverted amongst us.

Before we proceed to the Second Part of this treatise, it may not be irrelevant to give the reader this last advice, and let him know that, though all these difficulties before represented were removed, it would still be impossible for us to know certainly, out of the Fathers, what the judgment of the whole ancient Church, whether the Church universal, or only a considerable portion of it, has been, as regards the differences which are now agitated in religion.

Now that we may be able to make the truth of this proposition appear, it is necessary that we should first of all explain the terms.

We understand commonly by the *Church*, (especially in these disputations) either all those persons in general who profess themselves to be of the said Church, of what condition or quality soever they be; or else, in a stricter sense, the collective body of all those who are set over, and who are representatives of the Church; that is to say, the *clergy*. So that whether you speak of the Church universal, or of some particular Church—as, for example, that of Spain, or of Carthage—this term may be taken in either of these two senses. By the Church universal we understand either all those persons in general, who live in the communion of the Christian Church, whether they be of the laity or of the clergy; or else those persons only who are *Ecclesiastici*, or churchmen, as we now call them. For in the primitive times, all Christians that lived in the communion of the Catholics were called *Ecclesiastici*. In like manner, by the Church of Carthage is meant, either generally, all the faithful that lived in the particular communion of the Christian Church of Carthage; or else particularly, and in a stricter sense, the bishop of Carthage, with his whole clergy.

Now I do not believe that there is any man, but will easily grant me, that if we take the Church in the first sense, it is impossible to know, by way of testimony given of the same, what the sense and judgment of it have been in each distinct age, as to all the points of the Christian religion. We may indeed collect, by way of discourse, what has been the belief of the true members of the Church. For there being some certain articles, the belief of which is necessarily requisite for the rendering a man such; whosoever rightly understands which these articles are, may certainly conclude that the true Church, whether universal or particular, has believed the same. But now, in the first place, this does not extend to all the points of the Christian religion, but only to those which are necessary: besides which there are various others, concerning which we may have not only different but even contrary judgments; and yet not thereby hazard the loss either of the communion of the Church, or of our inheritance of everlasting salvation. But this reasoning applies only to those who are the true members of the Church. As for those who make but an outward profession of the truth, it being not at all necessary that they should be saved, there is in like manner no more necessity for their embracing those beliefs which are requisite for that end. They may, under this mask, hide all kind of opinions, however impious they are. Lastly, that which makes most for our purpose is, that this knowledge is acquired by discourse; whereas we speak here of such a knowledge as is collected by the hearing of several witnesses, who give in their testimonies as to the thing which we would ascertain. Now the Fathers having written with a purpose of informing us, not what each particular man believed in their time, but rather what they thought fit that all men should have believed, we must needs conclude that certainly they have not told us all that they knew on this particular. And therefore partly their charity and partly their prudence may have caused them to pass by in silence all such opinions, either of whole companies, or of particular persons, as they conceived to be not so consonant to the truth. But supposing that they had not any of these considerations, and that they had taken upon them to give us a just account, each man of the opinions of his particular church wherein he lived; it is evident, however, that they could never have been able to have attained to the end of their design. For how is it possible that they should have been able to have learnt what the opinion of every single person was, amongst so vast a multitude, which consisted of so many several persons, who were of such different capacities and dispositions? Who will believe that Cyprian, for example, knew all the several opinions of each particular person in his diocese, so as to be able to give us an account of the same? Who can imagine, but that among such a multitude of people as lived in the communion of his church, there must needs have been very many who differed in opinion from him, on divers points of religion? Even at this very day, that we may not trouble ourselves to look so high, we see by experience, that there is scarcely that parish to be found, however small, where there are not particular persons that maintain, in many points of religion, opinions different from those of their minister. But if we take a whole diocese together, and pass by all those who trouble themselves not at all with the difference of opinions in religion, whether it be by reason of their want of years, or their weakness of judgment, or their malice; and take notice only of the rest, dividing them according to the difference of their opinions; I am persuaded that that part which shall agree in all points with the bishop of that diocese, will many times be found to be the least. Let a bishop preach or write what he will, on the points which are now in controversy, he will scarcely represent to you the opinions of half the people of his diocese.

Now we must conceive that the temper of the world of old was no other than what it is at this present day; and therefore, for this very reason, the liberty of embracing what opinions a man pleased was much greater then than it is now; inasmuch as the Church of Rome did not exercise its power then throughout Christendom so absolutely as it does now-a-days:* neither did the pastors or the princes use that severity and rigour which is now everywhere practised in our times, for the repressing this diversity

* That is, at the commencement of the sixteenth century.—Ed.

of opinions. We must therefore necessarily believe, that the opinions of the faithful were in those days altogether as different, if not much more than they are now. Whence it will also follow, that even the doctors themselves, who lived in those times, could not know all the different opinions of men, much less could they represent them to us in their writings.

We shall not dwell any longer upon what no man can deny; but shall rather proceed to the consideration of that which every one no doubt will be here ready to retort on us, respecting this particular; namely, that it is not necessary that we should know the opinions, in points of religion, of all individual persons, which are almost infinite in number, and for the most part very ill grounded and uncertain: but that it is sufficient, if we know what the belief has been of the pastors, and those who have been set over the Church: that is to say, of the Church taken in the latter sense. Yet I confess I do not see that this rule is so absolutely right, that we ought to adhere to it. For if we are to take the Church for the rule and foundation of our faith (as the authors of this reply pretend we ought to do,) the people, in my judgment, ought not then to be here excluded and passed by, as being of no consideration. I confess, the opinions of particular persons are very different, one from the other; and the knowledge of some of them is very confined, and sometimes none at all. But yet possibly this reason may chance to exclude even a good part of the clergy also from the authority to which they lay claim in this particular; as it cannot be denied that both ignorance and malice have oftentimes as great a share here, proportionably, as they have among the very people themselves. Who sees not, that if we must have regard to the capacity of men, there are sometimes found, even among the plain ordinary sort of Christians in a Church, those that are more considerable, both for their learning and piety, than the pastors themselves? One of those Fathers, of whom we now discourse, has informed us, "That many times have the clergy erred; the bishop has wavered in his opinion; the rich men have adhered in their judgment to the earthly princes of the world; meanwhile the people alone preserved the faith entire."*

Seeing therefore that it may sometimes happen, and that it has also many times happened, that the clergy have held erroneous opinions, while the people held the true, it is very evident, in my judgment, that the opinion of the people in these cases ought not wholly to be neglected. Truly Cyprian tells us in divers places, that the Church in his time had the people in very great esteem; no business of any importance being then transacted without communicating the same to the people; as may be seen in the epistles of this Father: insomuch that "the greatest part of the people also were present at the council of Carthage,"† where the question on the baptism of heretics was debated; whereof we have already spoken somewhat a little before. But because this point is controverted, I shall pass it over this time. Let us therefore grant, (since our adversaries will needs have it so,) that it is sufficient in this case to know what the belief was of the Church, taken in the latter and stricter sense; that is to say, of the clergy: for even this way it is evident enough that it is a very hard, if not an impossible thing, truly to discover what it has been in each distinct age. For there is no less diversity of opinion among the clergy, than there is among the people; and many times too there is much more: being conversant in books usually reducing things into nicer subtilties, and giving occasion for raising divers opinions on the same.

*Plerumque clerus erravit; sacerdotum nutavit sententia; divites cum sæculi istius terreno rege senserunt; populus fidem propriam reservavit.—*Ambros. Ser.* 17, t. 4. p. 725.

† Præsente etiam plebis maximâ parte.—*Cypr. in Conc. Carthag.* p. 397.

Who is he that will undertake to give us an account what the opinion is of all the clergy of one city only, (I do not say of a kingdom, or of all Christendom) concerning all the articles of religion? Who would be able to perform this, if he should undertake it? Never was there more exact care taken, for the conservation of uniformity in judgment among Christians, than is now at this day; when there is use made, not only of the censures and thunderbolts of the Church, but even also of the fire and the sword of the secular powers. Yet notwithstanding all this, how many ecclesiastical persons are there to be found, even in those very places where these rigorous measures are observed with the greatest strictness, even at Rome itself, and as it were in the Pope's own bosom, who differ very much in judgment respecting points of religion, both from their equals and from their superiors? In France, where, by the blessing of God, the liberty of conscience is much greater than in other places, it would be a wonder, if, where four clergymen of the more learned and polite sort had met together, two of them should not, upon some point or other of the faith, differ in judgment from the main body of their Church.

Here I have to entreat all those who follow Cassander in great numbers (who adore the monuments of the Fathers, and take whatsoever they find in him for the general sense of the ancient Christians,) only to turn their eyes back a little upon themselves, and to consider how many opinions they themselves hold, which are not only different, but even quite contrary to the Church, in the communion of which they live, and of which they profess themselves to be members, and by which indeed they subsist. The difference is here so great, that it seems to be, as it were, one state within another state, and one church within another church. Yet notwithstanding, when any of the doctors of that party to which they adhere, deliver unto us, either in their definitions, or in their sermons, or in their books, the common sense and judgment of their Church, this intermixture of opinions quite disappears. They speak only of the opinions of others, passing by those of Cassander, which are contrary to them, in silence, as if they did not at all concern the Church of Rome. Yet it is very well known, even to us who live at this very day, that they are favoured and maintained by very many of the most eminent persons of the Roman clergy. And if this senseless sect, who forsooth think themselves much more refined in their opinions than the rest of the body whereof they are a part, should chance in time either to fall of itself, or be suppressed by force, the memory of them would so utterly come to nothing, that posterity would know nothing of their doctrines, except by conjecture. Every one will then suppose that the Church of Rome at this time held precisely to the doctrine and opinions that he reads in the decrees of Trent, and in other similar books: and yet notwithstanding we both know and see that among those very persons who have been anointed, consecrated, and preferred also by the said Church, there is a party that dissents from it in judgment on divers important articles of faith. We may therefore conclude that the ancient Church had also its Cassanders, and very many even among the clergy itself, who held opinions different from those which were the common belief of the Church, and which it hath at length by little and little sunk, as it were, under water, and wholly swallowed up; so that now there is not any trace of them left.

Christianity was either different in the ancient times from what it is now, or else it was the same. If it was different, it is then a piece of mere sophistry, to endeavour to make it seem to be the same; and a very great abuse to produce us, for this purpose, so many different testimonies from antiquity. If it were the same, it must then without all doubt have produced the same accidents, and have sown the same seeds of diversity of opinion, in the spirits of its clergy. Those opinions and observations, which now give offence to the Cassandrists, would then also have offended some persons or other, that were endued with the like moderation. For we are not to conceive but that those first ages of Christianity brought forth spirits that were as much, and more refined and delicate than ours.

But that we may insist upon this particular no longer, it is sufficient for me, that I have thus clearly made it appear, that in the ancient Church the whole clergy of a city, or of a nation, much less of the whole world, had not necessarily one and the same sense and opinion on points of religion. So that it will follow from hence, that we cannot know with certainty, whether those opinions with which we meet in the Fathers, were received or not by all and each of the pastors of the Church at that time. All that you can gather thence is but this at the most; that they themselves, and some others perhaps of the most eminent amongst them (if you please,) maintained such or such opinions: in like manner, as that which Bellarmine and others have written on the Sacrament of the Eucharist, will inform posterity, that these men, and many others of our time, held these opinions in the Church of Rome. But as those who shall conclude, from the books of these authors, that there is at this day no other opinion maintained among the clergy themselves of the Church of Rome, on this particular, would very much mislead themselves; so is it much to be feared that we in like manner deceive ourselves, when, from what we find in two or three of the Fathers, we conclude that there was at that time no other opinion held in the Christian Church on those points whereof they treat, except that which they have delivered. It is a very hazardous business to take eight or ten men, however holy and learned they may have been, as sureties for all doctors of the Church universal that lived in their age. This is too little security for so great a sum.

Now, there are two things which may be objected against that which we have before delivered. The first is, that if there had been in antiquity any other opinions on the points now in debate, which had been different from those we now meet with in the books, either of all the Fathers, or at least of some of them, they would have mentioned and refuted them. But we have already heretofore answered this objection, by saying that the Fathers forbare to speak anything of this diversity of opinion, partly out of prudence, lest they might provoke the authors of the said opinions, which were contrary to their own, and so increase the difference, instead of appeasing it; and partly also out of charity; mildly bearing with that which they accounted not dangerous.

I only speak here of those differences in opinions which they knew of: for there might be a great number of others of which they knew not. Who can oblige you to believe that a monk, for example, that had retired into a corner, and as it were forsaken the world, professing only to instruct a small number of men and women in the rules of devotion, must needs have known what the opinions in points of religion of all the prelates of his age were? Who will pass his word to us in his behalf, that he does not sometimes reprove that in some men, which yet the Church allowed in an infinite number of others? Who will warrant us that all Christendom in his time embraced all his opinions, and had no other of their own?

Possevine, answering an objection relative to the works of Dionysius the Areopagite, which Jerome has made no mention of, says, that it is no great wonder that a man who lay hid in a corner of the world should not have seen this book, which the

Arians endeavoured to suppress.* May not a man with as much reason say, that it is no great wonder if Jerome or Epiphanius, or any other authors who were all of them engaged with their particular charges and employments, did not know of some opinions of the prelates of their age; or that either their modesty, or their charity, or the little eloquence and repute they had, might have made them conceal the same?

The other objection is drawn from the fact that these doctors of the ancient Church, who held some opinions different from those which we read at this day in the Fathers, did not publish them at all. But I answer first of all, that every man is not able to do so. In the next place, those who were able were not always willing. Various other considerations may perhaps also have hindered them from so doing; and if they are wise and pious men, they are never moved till the necessity arises. And hence it is, that oftentimes those opinions which have less truth in them do yet prevail; because prudence, which maintains the true opinion, is mild and patient; whereas rashness, which defends the false, is of a froward, eager, and ambitious nature.

Now let us but imagine how many of the evidences of this diversity of opinion may have been lost by the various ways before represented, having been devoured by time, or suppressed by malicious men, for fear they should let the world see the traces of the truth which they would have concealed. But that I may not be thought to adduce bare conjectures without any proof, I shall produce some examples for the confirming and elucidating my assertions.

Epiphanius maintains against Aërius,† whom he ranks among the Heresiarchs, that a bishop, according to the Apostle Paul, and the original institution of the office itself, is more than a priest: and this he

* Possevine in Appar. † Epiph. in Panar. Hær. 75.

proves in many words, answering all the objections that are made to the contrary. If you only read the passage, I am confident that when you have done, you would not hesitate to swear that what he has there delivered, was the general opinion of all the doctors of the Church; it being very unlikely that so great and so renowned a prelate would so positively have denied the opinion which he disputed against, if any one of his own familiar friends had also maintained the same. Yet for all this, Jerome, who was one of the principal lights of our western Church, and who lived at the same time with Epiphanius, who was his intimate friend, and a great admirer of his piety, says expressly, "that among the ancients, bishops and priests were the same; the one being a name of dignity, and the other of age."* That it may not be thought that this fell from him in discourse only, he there undertakes to prove the same at large, alleging several passages of Scripture on this subject;† and he also repeats the same thing, in two or three several places of his work; whereby it evidently appears that even positions quite contradictory to the opinions which have been delivered and maintained by some of the Fathers, and proposed in whatever terms, have notwithstanding been sometimes either maintained, or at least tolerated, by some others of no less authority.

Jerome himself has severely criticised Ruffinus, and condemned many of his opinions as most pernicious and deadly; yet we do not anywhere find that he was ever accounted a heretic by the rest of the Fathers. But we shall have occasion hereafter to consider more

* Quanquam apud veteres iidem episcopi et presbyteri fuerint: quia illud nomen dignitatis est, hoc ætatis.—(*Hieron. Ep.* 83. *ad Ocean. tom.* 2.)—Cùm Apostolus perspicuè doceat eosdem esse presbyteros, quos et episcopos, &c.—*Id. ep.* 85. *ad Evagr. tom.* 2.

† Id. Com. in Agg. tom. 5. p. 512. Et Com. in Tit. tom. 6. p. 443.

at large similar examples; and shall only at present observe, that if those books of Jerome, which we mentioned a little before, should have chanced to be lost, every man would then assuredly have concluded from Epiphanius, that no doctor of the ancient Church ever held, that a bishop and a priest were one and the same thing in their institution.

Who now, after all this, will assure us, that among so many other opinions as have been rejected here and there by the Fathers, and that too in as plain terms as those of Epiphanius, none of them have ever been defended by some of the learned of those times? Or, is it not possible, that they may have held them, though they did not write in defence of the same? Or may they not perhaps have written also in defence of them, and their books have been since lost? How small is the number of those in the Church, who had the ability, or at least the will, to write! And how much smaller is the number of those whose writings have been able to secure themselves against either the injury of time or the malice of men!

It is objected against the Protestants, as we have observed before, that Jerome commends and maintains the adoration of relics: but yet he himself testifies, that there were some bishops, who defended Vigilantius, who held the contrary opinion; whom he, according to his ordinary rhetoric, calls "accomplices in his wickedness."*

Who knows now what these bishops were, and whether they deserved any such usage at Jerome's hands or no? For the expressions which he uses against them, and against their opinions, are so full of gall and enmity, that they utterly take away all credit from his testimony. But we have insisted long enough upon this particular, and shall therefore forbear to instance any further in others.

* Proh! nefas, episcopos sui sceleris dicitur habere consortes.—*Hier. in Vigil.* 2, *p.* 159.

As it is therefore impossible to discover exactly, out of the Fathers, what have been the sense and judgment of the ancient Church,—whether taken universally or particularly, or whether the Church is taken for the whole body of believers, or for the prelates and inferior clergy only,—I shall here conclude as heretofore, that the writings of the ancients are altogether insufficient for proving the truth of any of those points which are at this day controverted amongst us.

BOOK THE SECOND.

THE FATHERS ARE NOT OF SUFFICIENT AUTHORITY FOR DECIDING CONTROVERSIES IN RELIGION.

CHAPTER I.

REASON I.—That the Testimonies given by the Fathers, on the doctrines of the Church, are not always true and certain.

WE have before shown how difficult it is to discover what the sense of the Fathers has been, as respects the points at this day controverted in religion; owing to the small number of books of the Fathers of the first centuries that have come down to us; and those which we have, moreover, treating of things of a very different nature from our present disputes; and of which besides we cannot be very well assured, by reason of the many forgeries and monstrous corruptions, which they have for so long a time been subject to; also by reason of the obscurity and ambiguity in their expressions; and their often representing to us the opinions rather of others than of their authors: besides those imperfections which are found in them; as for instance their not informing us in what degree of faith we are to hold each particular point of doctrine; and their leaving us in doubt, whether what they teach be the judgment of the Church, or their own private opinion; and whether, if it be the judgment of the Church, it be of the Church universal, or of some particular Church only.

Now the least of these objections is sufficient to render their testimony invalid; and that this testimony may be of force, it is necessary that it be clearly and evidently free from all these defects; forasmuch as the question is here touching the Christian faith, which ought to be grounded on nothing but what is sure and certain. Whosoever therefore would make use of any passage out of a Father, he is bound first to make it appear that the author, out of whom he cites the said passage, lived and wrote in the first ages of Christianity; and moreover, that the said person is well known to be the author of the book out of which the passage is quoted: and also that the passage cited is no way corrupted nor altered: and likewise, that the sense which he gives of it, is the true genuine sense of the passage; and that it was the opinion of the author, when he had arrived at ripeness of judgment, and which he changed not, nor retracted afterwards. He must also make it appear in what degree he held it; and whether he maintained it as his own private opinion only, or as the opinion of the Church: and lastly, whether it was the opinion of the Church universal, or of some particular Church only: which inquiry is of such vast and almost infinite labour, that it makes me very much doubt whether or not we can be ever able to attain a full and certain assurance what the positive sense of the ancients has been, on the whole body of controversies now debated in this age. Hence therefore our principal question seems to be decided; whether adducing the Fathers be a sufficient and proper means for demonstrating the truth of all those articles which are at this day maintained by the Church of Rome, and rejected by the Protestants. For who does not now see that this kind of proof has as much or more difficulty in it than the question itself? and that such testimonies are as obscure as the controverted opinions themselves? Notwithstanding, that we may not be thought too hasty, and upon too light grounds to reject this way of proceeding, we will pass by all the obscurity that is found, as regards the opinions of the ancients; and supposing it to be no difficult matter to discover what was the opinion and sense of the Fathers on the aforesaid points, we will now, in this Second Book, consider whether or not their authority be such, as that we ought or may, without further examination, believe, on their authority, what we know to a certainty was their belief, and hold it in the same degree as they did.

There are two sorts of passages to be observed in the writings of the Fathers: in the one you have them speaking only as witnesses, and testifying what the belief of the Church was in their time: in the other, they propose to you, like doctors, their own private opinions. Now there is a world of difference betwixt these two things: for in a witness, there is required only faithfulness and truth; but in a doctor, learning and knowledge. The one persuades us by the opinion we have of his veracity; the other, by the strength of his arguments. The Fathers are *witnesses* only when they barely tell us that the Church in their times held such or such opinions: and they are *doctors*, when, mounting as it were the dictatorial chair, they propose to us their own opinions; making them good either by Scripture or by reason.

Now as it concerns the testimonies they give on the faith held by the Church in their time, I know not whether we ought to receive all they bring for certain truths or not: but of this I am sure, that though they should deserve to be received by us for such, yet nevertheless would they answer little purpose as to the business now in hand. The reason which induces me to doubt of the former of these, is, because I observe that those very men, who are the greatest admirers of the Fathers, do yet confess, that although they err very little, or not at all, in matter of right, yet nevertheless they often err, and have their failings, in matter of fact: because right is a universal thing, which is every way uniform, and all of one kind; whereas matter of fact is a thing which is mixed, and as it were enchased with divers particular circumstances, which may very easily escape the knowledge of, or at least be not so rightly understood by, the most clear and penetrating minds. Now the condition of the Church's belief in every particular age, is matter of fact and not of right; a point of history, and not an article of faith: so that it follows hence, that possibly the Fathers may have erred in giving us an account hereof; and that therefore their testimonies in such cases ought not to be received by us as infallibly true; neither yet may we be thought hereby to accuse the Fathers of falsehood. For how often do the most honest persons innocently testify to such things as they thought they had seen, which it afterwards appears that they saw not at all! for goodness renders not men infallible. The Fathers therefore being but men, might both be deceived themselves in such things, and might consequently also deceive those who have confided in them, though innocently, and without any design of doing so. But besides all this, it is very evident that they have not been wholly free from passion either: and there is no man but knows that passion very often disguises things, and makes them appear, even to the most honest men, much otherwise than they are; insomuch that sometimes they are affectionately carried away with one opinion, and do as much abhor another. This secret passion might easily make them believe that the Church held that opinion with which they themselves were most captivated; and that it rejected that which they themselves disliked, especially if there were but the least appearance or shadow of reason to incline them to this belief. For men are very easily persuaded to believe what they desire.

I conceive we may here adduce the testimony of Jerome, where he affirms, "that the Churches of Christ held that the souls of men were immediately created by God, at the instant of their entrance into the body."* And yet, that doubt, which Augustine was in, in this particular, and his evidently inclining to the contrary opinion; which was, that the soul was propagated together with the body, and descended from the father to the son; manifestly proves that the Church had not at that time embraced or determined on the former of these opinions; it being utterly improbable, that so modest a man as Augustine would have rejected the general opinion of the Church, and have taken up a particular fancy of his own. But the feeling wherewith Jerome was at that time carried away against Ruffinus, a great part of the learned men of his time being also of the same opinion, easily brought him to a belief that it was the common judgment and opinion of the whole Christian Church.† From the same root also sprang that error of John, bishop of Thessalonica, (if at least it be an error) who affirmed, "that the opinion of the Church was, that angels are not wholly incorporeal and invisible; but that they have bodies, though of a very rare and thin substance; not much unlike those of the fire or the air." *Νοερους μεν αὐτους ἡ καθολικη ἐκκλησια γινωσκει, οὐ μην ἀσωματους παντη και ἀορατους, λεπτοσωματους δε και ἀερωδεις, ἡ πυρωδεις.*‡ For those who

* Omne deinceps humanum genus quibus animarum censetur exordiis? utrum ex traduce, juxta bruta animalia, &c.; an rationabiles creaturæ desiderio corporum, &c.; an certè, quod ecclesiasticum est, quotidiè Deus fabricetur animas: cujus velle fecisse est, et conditor esse non cessat?—*Hier. ep.* 61, *de Error. Jo. Hier.*

† Miraris si contra te fratrum scandala concitentur; cum id nescire te jures, quod Christi Ecclesiæ se scire fatentur?—*Id. Apol.* 2, *contra Ruff.*

‡ Joan. Thessal. in Concil. 7, Act. 5.

published the general councils at Rome conceive this to have been his own private opinion only.* If this be so (and we need not at present examine the truth of the assertion,) you then plainly see, that the affection this author bore to his own opinion carried him so far away, as to make him father upon the whole Church what was indeed but his own particular opinion; though otherwise he was a man who was highly esteemed by the seventh council;† which not only cites him among the Fathers, but honours him also with the title of a Father.

Epiphanius must also be excused in the same manner, where he assures us that the Church held by apostolical tradition the custom which it had of meeting together thrice a week, for the celebration of the holy Eucharist; but which Petavius makes appear not to have been of apostolical institution.‡

The mistakes of the venerable Bede, noted and censured elsewhere by Petavius,§ are of the same nature also: "the belief of the Church, if I mistake not, (says he,) is, that our Saviour Christ lived in the flesh thirty-three years, or thereabouts, till the time of the passion:" and he says moreover, "that the Church of Rome testifies that this is its belief, by the marks which they yearly set upon their tapers on Good Friday; whereon they always inscribe a number of years, which is less by thirty-three than the common æra of the Christians." He likewise says, in the same place, "that it is not lawful for any Catholic to doubt whether Jesus Christ suffered on the cross the 15th day of the moon, or not."||

* Loquitur ex propria sententia.—*Ibid. in Marg.*

† Concil. 7, Act. 5. ‡ Petav. in Epiphan. pag. 354.

§ Petav. in Epiphan. p. 113. 143. 145.

|| Habet enim, nisi fallor, ecclesiæ fides, Dominum in carne paulo plus minus quam xxxiii annis, usque ad suæ tempora passionis vixisse. *Mox;* Sancta si quidem Romana et apostolica ecclesia hanc se fidem tenere, et ipsis testatur indiculis, quæ suis in cereis annuatim inscribere solet, ubi tempus Dominicæ passionis in me-

Petavius has proved at large, that both these opinions which Bede delivers as the Church's belief, are nothing less than what he would have them.*

The curious reader may observe many similar traits in the writings of the Fathers: but those already noticed, in my judgment, sufficiently justify the doubt which I have offered; that we ought not to receive, as certain truths, the testimony which the Fathers give, as regards the doctrine of the Church in their time. Nevertheless, that we may not seem to make a breach upon the honour and reputation of the Fathers, I say, that though we should grant, that all their depositions and testimonies in this particular were certainly and undoubtedly true; yet notwithstanding they would be of little use to us in our present purpose. For, in the first place, there are but very few passages wherein they testify plainly, and in direct terms, what the doctrine of the Church in their time was, as regards the points now controverted amongst us. This is the business of an historian rather than of a doctor of the Church; whose office is to teach, to prove, and to exhort the people committed to his charge, and to correct their vices and errors; telling them what they ought to do or believe, rather than troubling them with discourses of what is done or believed by others. Yet when they do give their testimony as to what were the doctrine and discipline of the Church in their time, it ought to extend only to what was evidently such, and which moreover was apparent to themselves also.

Now, as we have formerly proved, they could not possibly know the sense and opinions of every par-

moriam populis revocans, numerum annorum triginta semper et tribus annis minorem quàm ab ejus incarnatione Dionysius ponat, annotat. (*Id. ibid.*) Nam quod Dominus xv. Luna, feria vi. crucem ascenderit, &c. nulli licet dubitare Catholico.—*Beda, lib. de Temp. ratione. c.* 45.

* Petav. in. Epiphan. p. 113. 143.

ticular Christian that lived in their time; nor yet of all the pastors and ministers who were set over them: but of some particular Christians only. As therefore it is confessed, even by those very men who have the Church in greatest esteem, that the belief of particular Churches is not infallible, we may very easily perceive that such testimonies of the Fathers as these can be of little avail; seeing that they represent to us such opinions as are not always certainly and undoubtedly true, and which consequently are so far from confirming and proving ours, that they rather stand in need of being examined and proved themselves. But suppose that the Church of Rome did hold that the beliefs of particular Churches were infallible (which however it does not,) yet this would not at all militate against the Protestants, as they are of a quite contrary opinion.

Now it is taken for granted on all hands that proofs ought to be taken from such things as are confessed and acknowledged by your adversary, whom you endeavour to convince; otherwise you will never be able to change him, or induce him to quit his former opinion. Seeing therefore that the testimonies of the Fathers, as to the state of the faith and ecclesiastical discipline of their times, are of this nature, it remains for us now to consider their other discourses, wherein they have delivered themselves, not as witnesses deposing what they had seen, but as doctors instructing us in what they believed: and certainly, however holy and able they were, it cannot be denied but that they were still men; and consequently were subject to error, especially in points of faith, so much transcending human apprehension. The Spirit of God alone was able to direct their understandings and their pens in the truth, and to withhold them from falling into any error: in like manner as it directed the holy prophets and apostles, while they wrote the books of the Old and New Testament. Now we cannot be any way assured that the Spirit of God was present always with them, to enlighten their understandings, and to make them see the truth of all those things of which they wrote. They pretend not to this themselves, nor yet does any one that I know attribute to them this assistance, unless it be perhaps the author of the "Gloss upon the Decrees," who is of opinion that we ought to stand to all that the Fathers have written, even to the least tittle:* but he is very justly called to account for this, by Alphonsus à Castro,† and Melchior Canus,‡ two Spanish doctors.

Since, therefore, we are not bound to believe any thing but what is true; it is most evident that we neither may nor ought to believe the opinions of the Fathers, till such times as they appear to us to have been certainly true. Now we cannot be certainly assured of this by their single authority; seeing that they were but men, who were not always inspired by the Holy Spirit from above: and therefore it is necessary that we make use of some other guides in this our inquiry; namely, either of the Holy Scriptures, or of reason, or tradition, or the doctrine of the present Church, or of some other means, such as they themselves have made use of. It hence follows that their bare assertions are no sufficient ground for us to build any of our opinions on; as they only serve to incline us beforehand to the belief of the same; the great opinion which we have of them causing us to conclude that they would never have embraced such an opinion, except it had been true. This manner of argumentation, however, is at the best but probable, so long as the persons we have here to do with are only men and no more; and in this particular case,

* Hodie jubentur omnia teneri, usque ad ultimum iota.—*Gloss. in Decr. D.* 9. *c.* 3.

† Alphons. à Castr. l. 1. advers. Hær. c. 7.

‡ Melch. Canus. l. 7, loc. Theol. c. 3. Num. 4.

where the question is on points of faith, it is by no means to be allowed; since faith is to be grounded, not upon probabilities, but upon necessary truths. The Fathers are like other great masters in this point, and their opinions are more or less valid, in proportion to the reason and authority on which they are grounded: they have, however, this advantage, that their very names beget in us a readiness and inclination to receive whatever emanates from them; while we think it very improbable that such excellent men as they were, should ever believe anything that was false.

Thus, in human sciences, the saying of an Aristotle is of far different value from that of any other philosopher of less account; because all men are beforehand possessed with an opinion, that this great philosopher would not maintain anything that was not consonant to reason. But this is prejudice only; for, if, upon better examination, it should be found to be otherwise, his bare authority would then no longer prevail with us; what he himself had once wisely said, would then here take place—"that it is a sacred thing always to prefer the truth before friendship;" *Ἀμφοιν ὀντοιν φιλοιν, ὁσιον προτιμαν την ἀληθειαν.**

Let the Fathers, therefore, if you please, be the Aristotles in Christian philosophy, and let us have a reverent esteem of them and their writings as they deserve; and not be too rash in concluding that persons so eminent for learning and sanctity should maintain any erroneous or vain opinions, especially in a matter of so great importance: yet notwithstanding are we bound to remember, that they were but men, and that their memory, understanding, or judgment, might sometimes fail them, and therefore, consequently, that we are to examine their writings by those principles from whence they draw their conclusions,

* Arist. in Ethic. l. 1, c. 6.

and not to rest satisfied with their bare assertions, until we have discovered them to be true.

If I were to speak of any other persons than of the Fathers, I should not add anything more to what has been now said; sufficient having been, in my judgment, already adduced, to prove that they are not of themselves of sufficient authority to oblige us necessarily to follow their opinions. But seeing that the question is relative to those great names, who are so highly honoured in the Church; in order that no man may accuse us of endeavouring to rob them of any of the respect which is due to them, I conceive it necessary to examine this matter a little more rigidly, and to make it appear, on due consideration, that they are of no more authority, either in themselves or in regard to us, than we have already attributed to them.

CHAPTER II.

Reason II.—The Fathers testify themselves that they are not to be believed absolutely, and upon their own bare assertion, in what they declare in matters of religion.

There are none so fit to inform us what the authority of the writings of the ancients is, as the ancients themselves, who in all reason must necessarily know this better than we. Let us therefore now hear what they testify in this particular; and if we do indeed hold them in such high esteem, as we profess, let us allow of their judgment in this particular, attributing neither more nor less to the ancients, than they themselves require at our hands.

Augustine, who was the principal light of the Latin Church, having entered into a contest with Jerome, on the interpretation before-mentioned, of the second chapter of the Epistle of Paul to the Galatians; and finding himself hardly pressed by the authority of six or seven Greek writers, which are urged against him by the other; to extricate himself, states in what account he held that kind of writers:—"I confess," says he, "to thy charity, that I have learned to pay to those books of Scripture alone which are now called canonical, such reverence and honour, as to believe steadfastly that none of their authors ever committed any error in writing them. And if by chance I there meet with anything, which seems to contradict the truth, I immediately think that either my copy is imperfect, and not so correct as it should be; or else, that the interpreter did not so well understand the words of the original: or lastly, that I myself have not so rightly understood him. But as for all other writers, however eminent they are, either for sanctity or learning, I read them in such manner as not instantly to conclude that whatever I there find is true, because they have said it; but rather, because they convince me, either out of the said canonical books of Scripture, or else by some probable reason, that what they say is true. Neither do I think, brother, that thou thyself art of any other opinion: that is to say, I do not believe that thou expectest that we should read thy books, as we do those of the Prophets or Apostles; of the truth of whose writings, as being exempt from all error, we may not in anywise doubt."*

* Ego enim fateor caritati tuæ solis eis Scripturarum libris, qui jam canonici appellantur, didici hunc timorem, honoremque deferre, ut nullum eorum auctorem scribendo aliquid errasse firmissimè credam. Ac si aliquid in eis offendero litteris, quod videatur contrarium veritati, nihil aliud quàm mendosum esse codicem, vel interpretem non assequutum esse quod dictum est, vel me minimè intellexisse, non ambigam. Alios autem ita lego, ut quantalibet sanctitate, doctrinaque præpolleant, non ideo verum putem, quia ipsi ita senserunt, sed quia mihi, vel per illos authores canonicos, vel probabili ratione, quod à vero non abhorreat, persuadere potuerunt. Nec te, mi frater, sentire aliquid aliter existimo: prorsus inquam, non te arbitror sic legi libros tuos velle tanquam Prophe-

Having afterwards opposed some other similar authorities against those alleged by Jerome, he adds, "that he had done so, notwithstanding that, to say the truth, he accounted the canonical Scriptures only to be the books to which (as he said before) he owed that ingenuous duty, as to be fully persuaded that the authors of them never erred, or deceived the reader in anything."*

This holy man accounted this advice to be of such great importance, that he thought fit to repeat it again in another place; and I must entreat my reader to give me leave to extract here the whole passage at length.

"As for this kind of books," (says he, speaking of those which we write, not with the authority of commanding, but only from the design of exercising ourselves to benefit others,) "we are so to read them, as not bound necessarily to believe them, but having the liberty left us of judging of what we read. Yet notwithstanding, that we may not quite exclude these books, and deprive posterity of the most profitable labour of exercising their language and style, in the handling and treating of difficult questions, we make a distinction between these books of later writers, and the excellency of the canonical authority of the Old and New Testament; which having been confirmed in the Apostles' time, has since, by the bishops who succeeded them, and the churches which have been propagated throughout the world, been placed as it were upon a high throne, to which every faithful and godly understanding must be subject. And if we chance here to meet with anything that troubles us,

tarum vel Apostolorum, de quorum scriptis, quod omni errore careant, dubitare nefarium est.—*August. ep. ad Hier. quæ est* 19. *t.* 2. *fol.* 14. *ed. Paris.* 1579, *et inter Hier. Op.* 97. *t.* 2. *p.* 551.

* Quanquam, sicut paulò antè dixi, tantummodo Scripturis canonicis hanc ingenuam debeam servitutem, qua eas solas ita sequar, ut conscriptores earum nihil in eis omninò errasse, nihil fallaciter posuisse non dubitem.—*Id. ibid.*

and seems absurd, we must not say that the author of the book was ignorant of the truth, but rather that either our copy is false, or the interpreter is mistaken in the sense of the place, or else that we do not understand him aright.

"As for the writings of those other authors who have come after them, the number whereof is almost infinite, though coming very far short of this most sacred excellency of the canonical Scriptures, a man may sometimes find in them the very same truth, though not of equal authority. Therefore if by chance we here meet with such things as seem contrary to the truth, only, perhaps, because we do not understand them, we have our liberty, either in reading or hearing the same, to approve of what we like, and to reject that which we conceive not to be right. So that unless all such passages be made good, either by some certain reason, or else by the canonical authority of the Scriptures; and it be made to appear, that what is asserted either really is, or else at least might have been, he that shall reject or not assent to the same, ought not in any wise to be reprehended."*

* Quod genus literarum, non cum credendi necessitate, sed cum judicandi libertate legendum est. Cui tamen ne intercluderetur locus, et adimeretur posteris ad difficiles quæstiones tractandas atque versandas, linguæ ac styli saluberrimus labor, distincta est à posteriorum libris excellentia canonicæ auctoritatis Veteris et Novi Testamenti; quæ Apostolorum confirmata temporibus, per successiones episcoporum, et propagationes ecclesiarum, tanquam in sede quadam sublimiter constituta est, cui serviat omnis fidelis et pius intellectus. Ibi si quid velut absurdum moverit, non licet dicere, auctor hujus libri non tenuit veritatem: sed, aut codex mendosus est, aut interpres erravit, aut tu non intelligis. In opusculis autem posteriorum, quæ libris innumerabilibus continentur, sed nullo modo illi sacratissimæ canonicarum Scripturarum excellentiæ coæquantur, etiam in quibuscumque eorum invenitur eadem veritas, longe tamen est impar auctoritas. Itaque in eis, si qua forte propterea dissonare putantur à vero, quia non ut dicta sunt, intelliguntur, tamen liberum ibi habet lector auditorve judicium quo vel approbet quod placuerit, vel improbet quod offenderit: et ideo cuncta ejusmodi, nisi vel certa ratione, vel ex illa canonica aucto-

Thus far have we Augustine testifying on our side, (as well here, as in many other places, which would be too long to be inserted here,)* that those opinions which we find delivered by the Fathers in their writings, are grounded not upon their bare authority but upon their reasons; and that they bind not our belief otherwise than so far as they are consonant to Scripture or reason; and that they ought to be examined by both, as proceeding from persons that are not infallible.

Hence it appears, that the course which is at this day pursued is not sufficient for the demonstration of the truth. For suppose we are in doubt what is the sense and meaning of a certain passage in Scripture. You will immediately have the judgment of a Father brought upon the said passage, quite contrary to the rule which Augustine gives us, who would have us examine the Fathers by the Scriptures, and not the Scriptures by the Fathers. Certainly, according to the judgment of this Father, the Protestant, though a passage is clear and express as any of the canons of the council of Trent, should be brought against him, out of any of the Fathers, ought not to be blamed, if he should answer, that he cannot by any means assent to it unless the truth of it be first proved, either by some certain reason, or else by the authority of the canonical Scriptures; and that then, and not till then, would he be ready to assent to it.

Thus, according to this account, we are to allege, not the names of, but the reasons given in, books; to

ritate defendantur, ut demonstretur sive omnino ita esse, sive fieri potuisse, quod vel disputatur ibi, vel narratum est, si cui displicuerit, aut credere noluerit, non reprehenditur.—*August. Ep. ad Hier. l.* 11 *contr. Faust. c.* 5.

* August. ep. ad Hier. t. 2. Epist. 48, ep. 111, t. 3, l. 1, 3, de Trinit. c. 2, l. 3, præfat. l. 5, c. 1. t. 7, l. 2, contr. Crescon. Gram. c. 31, et c. 32, l. 2, de Bapt. contr. Don. c. 3, l. 3, de Peccat. mer. et rem. c. 7, c. 1, de Nat. et grat. c. 61, l. 4, contr. du. ep. Pelag. c. 8, l. 1, contr. Julian. c. 2, l. de bon. persever. c. 21.

take notice, not of the quality of their authors, but of the solidity of their proofs; to consider what it is they give us, and not the face or hand of him that gives it us; and, in a word, to reduce the dispute from persons to things.

Jerome also seems to commend to us this method of proceeding, where, in the preface to his second Commentary upon Hosea, he has these words: "Then (that is, after the authors of books are once departed this life) we judge of their worth and parts only, not considering at all the dignity of their name: and the reader has regard only to what he reads, and not to the author of the work. So that whether he were a bishop or a layman, a general and a lord, or a common soldier and a servant; whether he lie in purple and silk, or in the vilest and coarsest rags, he shall be judged, not according to his degree of honour, but according to the merit and worth of his works."* Now he here speaks either of matter of right or of fact; and his meaning is, that either we ought to take this course in our judgments, or else it is a plain affirmation, that it is the practice of the world so to do. If his words are to be taken in the first sense, he then clearly takes away all authority from the bare names of writers, and so would have us to consider the quality only, and weight of their writings; that is to say, their reasons, and the force of the arguments they use. If we understand him in the second sense, he seems not to speak the truth; it being evident, that the ordinary course of the world is, to be more led by the titles and names of books, than by the matter therein contained. Suppose, however, that this was

* Tunc sine nominum dignitate, sola judicantur ingenia; nec considerat, qui lecturus est, cujus, sed quale sit quod lecturus est, sive sit episcopus, sive sit laicus, imperator et dominus, miles et servus, aut in purpura et serico, aut vilissimo panno jaceat, non honorum diversitate, sed operum merito judicabitur.—*Hier. Com.* 2, *in Oseam, Præfat.*

Jerome's meaning; we may notwithstanding very safely believe, that he approves of the said course; forasmuch as having this occasion of speaking of it, he does not at all reprehend it. If therefore, reader, thou hast any wish to rely on his judgment, lay aside the names of Augustine and of Jerome, of Chrysostom and of Cyril; and forget for this once the rochet of the first, and the chair of the second, together with the patriarchal robe of the two last: and observe what they say, and not what they were; the ground and reason of their opinions, and not the dignity of their persons.

But that which excites my wonder is, that some of those who have been the most conversant in antiquity should trouble themselves with filling their books with declamatory expressions in praise of the authors they produce,* not forbearing to recount the nobleness of their extraction, the choiceness of their education, the splendour of their talents, the eminency of their see, and the greatness of their state. This manner of writing may perhaps suit well enough with the rules of rhetoric: but certain I am that it ill agrees with Jerome's advice, which we gave a little before.

Let us now observe, out of some other more clear and express passages of his, what the judgment of this great Aristarchus, and censor of antiquity, was on this point. "I know (says he, writing to Theophilus, patriarch of Alexandria) that I place the Apostles in a distinct rank from all other writers: for as for them, they always speak truth: but as for those other, they err sometimes, like men, as they were."†

What could he have said more expressly, in confirmation of our assertion before laid down? "There are others, (says he,) both Greeks and Latins, who

* Card. Perron, of the Eucharist. Aut. 20.

† Scio me aliter habere Apostolos; aliter reliquos tractatores: illos semper vera dicere; istos in quibusdam, ut homines, errare.—*Hier. ep.* 62. *ad Theoph. Alex.*

have erred also in points of faith; whose names I need not here notice, lest it might seem to defend Origen by the errors of others rather than by his own worth."*

How then can we confide in them, unless we examine their opinions by their reasons? "I shall (says the same author) read Origen as I read others; because I find he has erred in like manner as they have done."†

In another place, speaking in general of ecclesiastical writers; that is, of those whom we now call Fathers, and of the faults and errors that are found in their books, he says: "It may be that they have erred out of mere ignorance, or else that they wrote in some other sense than we understand them; or that their writings have been gradually corrupted, through the ignorance of the transcribers; or else before the appearing of that southern devil Arius, in Alexandria, they let some things fall from them innocently, and not so warily as they might have done; and such as can hardly escape the cavils of wrangling spirits."‡ Which passage of his, is a very excellent and remarkable one; and contains in it a brief yet clear and full justification of the greatest part of what we have hitherto advanced in this discourse.

Do but think therefore with how much circumspection we are to read and to weigh these authors; and how careful we ought to be in examining in their

* Erraverunt in fide alii, tam Græci quàm Latini, quorum non necesse est proferre nomina, ne videamur eum, non sui merito sed aliorum errore, defendere.—*Hier. ep.* 65. *ad Pamm. et Oceanum.*

† Sic eum legam, ut cæteros; quia sic erravit, ut ceteri.—*Id. ibid.*

‡ Fieri enim potest, ut vel simpliciter erraverint, vel alio sensu scripserint, vel à librariis imperitis eorum paulatim scripta corrupta sint: vel certè antequàm in Alexandrià quasi dæmonium meridianum Arius nasceretur, innocenter quædam, et minùs cautè loquuti sint, et quæ non possint perversorum hominum calumniam declinare.—*Hier. l.* 2. *Apol. contra Ruff.*

books, whether there be not either some fault committed by the transcriber, or some obscurity in the expression, or some negligence in the conception, or lastly, some error in the proposition.

In another place, having set down the opinions of several authors, respecting a certain question that had been proposed to him, that thus the reader might make choice of the best, Jerome gives this reason for so doing; "because (says he) we ought not, according to the example of Pythagoras's scholars, to have an eye to the prejudged opinion of the proposer, but rather the reason of the thing proposed:"* which words of his sufficiently confirm the sense we have formerly given of that passage of his in the Preface to his second commentary upon Hosea. He presently afterwards adds; "my purpose is to read the ancients; to prove all things, and to hold fast that which is good; and not to depart from the faith of the Catholic Church:"† according to the rule which he has commended to us, in his seventy-sixth epistle, where he advises us "to read Origen, Tertullian, Novatus, Arnobius, Apollinarius, and others of the ecclesiastical writers: but with this caution, that we should make choice of that which is good, but take heed of embracing that which is not so; according to the apostle, who bids us prove all things, but hold fast only that which is good."‡

This is the course Jerome constantly takes, censuring with the greatest liberty the opinions and exposi-

*Nec juxta Pythagoræ discipulos, prejudicata doctoris opinio, sed doctrinæ ratio ponderanda est.—*Hier. Ep.* 15. 2.

† Meum propositum est, antiquos legere, probare singula, retinere quæ bona sunt, et à fide Ecclesiæ Catholicæ non recedere.—*Id. ibid.*

‡ Ego Origenem propter eruditionem sic interdum legendum arbitror, quomodo Tertullianum, Novatum, Arnobium, Apollinarium, et nonnullos ecclesiasticos scriptores, Græcos pariter, et Latinos, ut bona eorum eligamus, vitemusque contraria; juxta apostolum dicentem, Omnia probate; quod bonum est tenete.—*Id. Ep.* 76. *ad Tranquil*

tions of all those who went before him. He gives you freely his judgment of every one of them; affirming "that Cyprian scarcely touched the Scripture at all: that Victorinus was not able to express his own conceptions; that Lactantius is not so happy in his endeavours to prove our religion, as he is in overthrowing that of others; that Arnobius is very uneven and confused, and too luxuriant; that Hilary is too swelling, and encumbered with too long periods."*

I shall not here lay before you what he says of Origen, Theodorus, Apollinaris, and of the Chiliasts; whose professed enemy he has declared himself, and whom he reproves very sharply upon all occasions, whenever they come in his way: and yet he confesses them all to have been men of very great parts; giving even Origen himself, who is the most dangerous writer of them all, this testimony, "that none but the ignorant can deny but that, next to the Apostles, he was one of the greatest masters of the Church."†

But to speak only of those whose names have never been cried down in the Church, do but mark how he deals with Rheticius of Autun, an ecclesiastical author: "There are (says he) an infinite number of things in his Commentaries, which in my judgment appear very mean and poor:"‡ and a little after; "He seems to have had so ill an opinion of others, as to have a conceit that no man was able to judge of

* Cyprianus de scripturis divinis nequaquam disseruit. Inclyto Victorinus martyrio coronatus, quod intelligit eloqui non potest. Lactantius utinam tam nostra confirmare potuisset, quàm facile aliena destruxit. Arnobius inæqualis et nimius est, et absque operis sui partitione confusus. Sanctus Hilarius Gallicano cothurno attollitur, et longis interdum periodis involvitur et à lectione simpliciorum fratrum procul est.—*Hier. ep.* 13. *ad Paulin.*

† Quem (Origenem) post apostolos ecclesiarum magistrum nemo nisi imperitus negat.—*Hier. Præfat. in lib. de Nom. Hebr.*

‡ Innumerabilia sunt, quæ in illius mihi Commentariis sordere visa sunt.—*Id. ep.* 133, *ad Marcel.*

20

his faults."* He takes the same liberty also, in rejecting their opinions and expositions; and sometimes not without passing upon them some smart ridicule. He maintains the truth of the Hebrew text of the Old Testament, and finds an infinite number of faults in the translation of the Seventy, against almost the general consent, not only of the more ancient writers, but also of those too who lived in his own time, who all esteemed it as a divine production. He scoffs at the conceit of those men, who believed that the seventy interpreters, being placed separately in seventy distinct cells, were inspired from above, in the translation of the Bible.† "Let them keep, (says he, speaking of his own backbiters by way of scorn,) with all my heart, in the seventy cells of the Alexandrian Pharos, for fear they should lose the sails of their ships, and be forced to bewail the loss of their cordage."‡

As for their expositions, he refuses them openly whenever they do not please him. Thus does he find fault with the exposition which is given by the greatest part of the Fathers, of the word *Israel;* which they will have to signify, *a man seeing God:* "notwithstanding that those who interpret it thus, are persons of very great authority and eloquence, and whose very shadow is sufficient to bear us down: yet (says he) we cannot but choose to follow the authority of the Scriptures; and of the angel, and of God, who gave this name of Israel, rather than the power of any secular eloquence, however great it may be."§ And in

* Sed tam malè videtur existimasse de cæteris, ut nemo possit de ejus erroribus judicare.—*Hier. ep.* 133, *ad Marcel.*

† Nescio quis primus auctor septuaginta cellulas Alexandriæ mendacio suo extruxerit.—*Hier. Præfat. in Pentateuc. ad Desid.*

‡ Habitentque in septuaginta cellulis Alexandrini Phari, ne vela perdant de navibus, et funium detrimenta suspirent.—*Id. Comm.* 10. *in Ezech.*

§ Quamvis igitur grandis auctoritatis sint, et eloquentiæ, et ipsorum umbra nos opprimat, qui, Israel, virum, sive mentem viden-

his 146th epistle, written to Pope Damasus, he says: "that there are some who, not considering the text, conceive superstitiously rather than truly, that these words in the beginning of the 44th Psalm, '*Eructavit cor meum verbum bonum*,' are spoken in the person of the Father."* Yet the greatest part of those who lived in the time of Arius, and a little after him, understood these words in the same sense.

It was likewise their opinion, almost without exception, that Adam was buried upon Mount Calvary, and in the very same place where our Saviour Christ was crucified. Yet Jerome rejects this opinion:† and which is more, he makes himself merry with it, without any scruple at all. So likewise there were some among the aforenamed ancient Fathers, who out of a pious affection which they bore to Peter, maintained that he denied not God, but man,‡ and that the sense of the words of his denial, is, "I know him not to be a man, for I know that he is God." "The intelligent reader (says the same Jerome) will easily perceive how idle and frivolous a thing this is, to accuse our Saviour as guilty of falsehood, by excusing his Apostle. For if Peter did not deny him, our Saviour must then necessarily have spoken falsely, when he said unto him, 'verily, I say unto thee,'" &c.§ He takes the same liberty also in reprehending Ambrose, who understands by *Gog*, spoken of in the Prophet Ezekiel, the nation of the *Goths*.‖ Neither do those other

tem Deum, transtulerunt; nos magis Scripturæ, et angeli et Dei, qui ipsum Israel vocavit, auctoritate ducimur, quàm cujuslibet eloquentiæ sæcularis.—*Hier. Tradit. Hebr.*

* Licet quidam superstitiosè magis, quàm verè, considerantes textum psalmi, ex Patris persona arbitrentur hæc intelligi.—*Id. ep.* 146, *ad Damas.*

† Hier. in loc. Hebr. Euseb. et Com. 4. in Matth.

‡ Hilar. in Matth. Can. 31.

§ Hoc quàm frivolum sit, prudens lector intelligit. Sic defendunt Apostolum, ut Deum mendacii reum faciant, &c.—*Hier. Com.* 4. *in Mat. in* c. 26.

‖ Id. Com. xi. in Ezech. in Præfat. Ambros. l. 2, de fid. ad Grat.

Fathers, escape his lash, who indulging too much in allegories, take *Bosra* in Isaiah for *the flesh;* whereas it signifies *a fortress.**

I might here produce many similar passages, but these few may suffice: for who sees not by this time that these holy men considered not the Fathers, who went before them, as judges or arbitrators on the opinions of the Church; and that they did not receive their testimonies and depositions as oracles, but reserved the right which Augustine allows to every man, of examining them by reason, and the Scripture? Neither are we to take any notice at all of Jerome, when he seems to except out of this number the writings of Athanasius, and of Hilary; writing to Læta, and telling her, that her daughter Paula might walk securely, and with firm footing, by the epistles of the one, and the books of the other; and therefore he counsels her "to take delight in these men's writings; inasmuch as in their books the piety of faith wavers not: and as for all other authors, she may read them; but rather to pass her judgment upon them, than to follow them."† For first of all, though perhaps there should be some work of a Father that should have no error in it, (as questionless there are many such,) yet this would not render the authority of the same infallible. How many such books are there, even of the moderns, wherein neither the one party nor the other has been able to discover the least error in matter of faith? And yet I suppose no man will at once conclude from hence, that we ought to admit of these authors as judges of our faith. A man may there find perhaps the same truth, (as Augustine says a little before:) but it will not be of equal authority with that of the canonical books. Besides, as Cardinal Baro-

* Hier. in Esai. Comm. x.

† Illorum tractatibus, illorum delectetur ingeniis, in quorum libris pietas fidei non vacillat. Cæteros sic legat, ut magis judicet, quàm sequatur.—*Hier. Ep.* 7. *ad Læt.*

nius* has observed, this last passage of Jerome ought to be understood only in the point touching the Holy Trinity; concerning which there were at that time great disputes between the Catholics and the Arians; for otherwise, if his words be taken in a general sense, they will be found to be false, as to Hilary, who had his failings in some certain things, as we shall see hereafter. In a word, although Jerome were to be understood as speaking in a general sense, (as his words indeed seem to bear,) yet might the same thing possibly happen to him here, which he has observed has oftentimes befallen others; namely, to be mistaken in his judgment. For we are not to imagine, that he would have us entertain a greater opinion of him, than he himself has of other men. Augustine told him, as we have before shown, that he did not believe he expected that men should judge otherwise of him; and I suppose we may very safely adhere to Augustine's judgment, and believe with him that Jerome had never any intention that we should receive all his positions as infallible truths: but rather that he would have us to read and examine his writings with the same freedom that we do those of other men.

If we have no wish to take Augustine's word in these particulars, let us yet receive Jerome's; who in his second commentary upon the prophet Habakkuk says: "and thus have I briefly delivered to you my opinion; but if any one produce that which is more exact and true, take his exposition rather than mine."† So likewise upon the prophet Zephaniah he says, "we have now done our utmost endeavour, in giving an allegorical exposition of the text; but if any other can bring that which is more probable and agreeable to reason than that which we have delivered, let the reader be guided by his authority rather than by

* Baron. Annal. an. 369, Sect. 24.

† Si quis autem his sagaciora et veriora repererit, illi magis explanationi probete consensum.—*Hier. Com.* 2. *in Abac.*

ours."* And in another place he speaks to the same purpose in these words: "this we have written according to the utmost of our poor ability, and have given a short sketch of the divers opinions, both of our own men and of the Jews; yet if any man can give me a better and truer account of these things, I shall be very ready to embrace them."†

Is this now, I would fain ask, to bind up our tongues and our belief, so that we should have no further liberty of refusing what he has once laid down before us, or of searching into the reasons and grounds of his opinions? No, let us rather make use of that liberty which they all allow us; let us hearken to them, only (as they themselves advise us) when what they deliver is grounded upon reason, and upon the Scriptures. If they had not made use of this caution, in the reading of those authors who went before them, the Christian faith had now been altogether replete with the dreams of an Origen, or an Apollinaris, or some other similar authors. But neither the fame of their learning, nor yet the resplendency of their holy life, which no man can deny to have shone forth in these primitive Fathers, was able so to dazzle the eyes of those that came after them, that they could not distinguish between what was sound and true in their writings, and what was trivial and false. Let not therefore the excellency of those who came after them hinder us, either from passing by, or even rejecting their opinions, when we find them ill founded.

They confess themselves that this may very possi-

* Si quis autem magis verisimilia, et habentia rationem, quàm à nobis sunt disserta, repererit, illius magis lector auctoritate ducatur.—*Id. in Sophon.*

† Hæc ut quivimus, ut vires ingenioli nostri ferre potuerunt, loquuti sumus, et Hebræorum et nostrorum varias opiniones breviter perstringentes. Si quis meliùs, imo verìùs dixerit, et nos libenter melioribus acquiescemus. —*Hier. Com. in Zach.*

bly be: we should therefore be left utterly inexcusable, if after this their so charitable admonition, we should still believe all they say, without examining anything. "I take it for a favour, (says Ambrose) when any one that reads my writings, gives me an account of what doubts he there meets with. First of all, because I may be deceived in those very things which I know. And besides, many things escape us; and some things sound otherwise to some than perhaps they do to me."*

I shall here further desire the reader to take notice, how careful the ancients were in advising those who lived in their own time to take a strict examination of their words: as for example, where Origen advises, "that his auditors should prove whatever he delivered, and that they should be attentive, and receive the grace of the Spirit from whom proceeds the discerning of spirits, that thus, as good bankers, they might diligently observe when their pastor deceives them; and when he preaches to them that which is pious and true."† Cyril likewise, in his fourth catechesis, has these words: "Believe me not (says he) in whatsoever I shall simply deliver, unless thou find the things which I shall speak demonstrated out of the Holy Scriptures. For the conservation and establishment of our faith, is not grounded upon the eloquence of language, but rather upon the proofs that are brought out of the Divine Scriptures." *Μηδε ἐμοι τῳ ταυτα σοι λεγοντι ἁπλως πιστευσης, ἐαν την ἀποδειξιν των καταγγελλομενων ἀπο των θειων μη*

* Ego enim beneficio annumero, siquis mea legens scripta dicat mihi, quo videatur moveri. Primùm, quia et in iis quæ scio, falli possum. Multa autem prætereunt, multa quibusdam aliter sonant. —*Ambros. l.* 7, *Ep.* 47.

† Quæso audientes, ut diligenter attendant, et accipiant gratiam Spiritus, de qua dictum est discretio spirituum; ut probati trapezitæ facti, diligenter observent, quando falsus sim magister, quando verò prædicem, quæ sunt pietatis ac veritatis.—*Orig. Hom.* 2, *in Ezech.*

*λαβης γραφων· ἡ σωτηρια γαρ αὐτη της πιστεως ἡμων οὐκ ἐξ εὑρεσιλογιας, ἀλλα ἐξ ἀποδειξεων των θειων ἐστι γραφων.**

If therefore they would not have those who heard them speak *viva voce*, to believe them in anything, unless they had demonstrated the truth of it out of the Scriptures, how much less would they have us now receive, without this demonstration, those opinions which we meet with in their books, which are not only mute, but corrupted also, and altered so much, as we have formerly shown?

Certainly, when I see these holy men on one side declaring that they are men subject to errors; and that therefore we ought to consider and examine what they deliver, and not take it all as oracular: and then on the other side, bring before my eyes these worthy maxims of the ages following: viz. "that their doctrine is the law of the Church universal;" and "that we are bound to follow it, not only according to the sense, but according to the bare words also: and that we are bound to hold all that they have written, even to the least tittle;"—*Ὡν (πατερων) τα δογματα νομος τῃ καθολικῃ καθεστηκεν Ἐκκλησιᾳ. Tum; Πασα γαρ ἀναγκη μη μονον κατ' ἐννοιαν τοις των ἁγιων πατερων ἑπεσθαι δογμασιν, ἀλλα και ταις αὐταις ἐκειναις κεχρησθαι φωναις;*†—this representation, I say, makes me call to mind the history of Paul and Barnabas, to whom the Lycaonians would needs render divine honour, notwithstanding all the resistance these holy men were able to make; who could not forbear to rend their garments, through indignation, at seeing that service paid to themselves which was due to the Divine Majesty alone; running in amongst them, and crying out aloud—"Sirs, why do ye these things? we also are

* Cyril. Hieros. Catechès. 4.
† Serg. Patr. Constant. Mon. in ep. ad Cyr. Concil. VI.

men of like passions with you." For seeing that there is none but God, whose word is certainly and necessarily true; and seeing that, on the other side, the word, whereon we ground and build our faith, ought to be such; who sees not, that it is the same as investing man with the glory which is due to God alone, and placing him in a manner in his seat, if we make his word the rule and foundation of our faith, and the judge of our differences concerning it?

I am therefore firmly of opinion, that if these holy men could now behold from their blessed mansions, where they now live in bliss on high with their Lord and Saviour, what things are acted here below, they would be very much offended at this false honour, which men confer upon them much against their wills; and would take it as a very great injury offered them; seeing that they cannot receive this honour, but to the prejudice and diminution of the glory of their Redeemer, whom they love a thousands times more than themselves. Or if, from out of their sepulchres, where their mortal remains are now laid up, they could but make us hear their sacred voice, they would (I am very confident) most sharply reprove us for this abuse, and would cry out, in the words of Paul, "Sirs, why do ye these things? we also were men of like passions with you."

Yet what need is there, either of ransacking their sepulchres, or of calling down their spirits from heaven; seeing that their voice resoundeth loud enough, and is heard so plainly in those very books of theirs, which we imprudently place in that seat, which is only due to the word of God? We have heard what the judgment was of Augustine and of Jerome, (the two most eminent persons in the western Church,) on this particular: let us not then be afraid, having such examples to follow, to speak freely our opinions. But now, before we go any further, I conceive it will be necessary, that we answer an objection that may be brought against us, which is, that Athanasius, Cyril, and Augustine himself also, frequently cite the Fathers.

Besides what some have observed, that the Fathers seldom entered into these lists, but when they were provoked by their adversaries: I add further, that when we maintain that the authority of the Fathers is not a sufficient medium to prove an article of faith by, we do not thereby forbid either the reading or the citing of them. The Fathers often quote the writings of the learned Heathens, the oracles of the Sibyls, and passages out of the Apocryphal books. Did they therefore think that these books were of sufficient authority to ground an article of faith upon? God forbid we should entertain so ill an opinion of them. Their faith was grounded upon the word of God: yet to evidence the truth more fully, they searched into human records, and by this inquiry made it appear that the light of the truth, revealed unto them, had in some degree shot its beams even into the schools of men, dark and obscure as they were. If they had produced no other but human authority, they would never have been able to have brought over any one person to the faith. But after they had derived from divine revelation the matter of our faith, it was very wisely done of them, in the next place, to prove, not the truth, but the clearness of it, by these little sparks which shot forth their light in the spirits of men. For the like reason did Augustine, Athanasius, Cyril, and many others of them, make use of allegations out of the Fathers. For after they had grounded, upon the authority of divine revelation, the necessity and efficacy of grace, the consubstantiality of the Son with the Father, and the union of the two natures in Christ; they then began to produce several passages out of those learned men who had lived before them; to evince to the world that this truth was so clear in the word of God, that all who preceded them had both seen and acknowledged the same: a plan both pleasing and profitable. For what can more delight a faithful heart, than to find that the most eminent persons in the Church, celebrated for their holiness and learning, had long since held the same opinions as regards our Saviour Jesus Christ and his grace, that we hold at this day?

Yet it does not hence follow, that if these holy men had met with these articles of our faith only in the writings of their predecessors, without finding any foundation for them in the canonical Scriptures, they would notwithstanding firmly have believed and embraced them, thus contenting themselves with the bare authority of their predecessors. Augustine professes plainly, that in such a case they might better have rejected them, and not be blamed for so doing, than have received them, unless they would incur the imputation of being credulous. For to believe any thing without reason is mere credulity: and he further affirms, that where men speak without either Scripture or reason, their bare authority is not sufficient to oblige us to believe what they propose to us. Hence it thus appears, that human testimonies are adduced, not to prove the truth of the faith, but only to show the evidence of it after it is once well grounded.

Now the question is not concerning the evidence of the articles believed and taught by the Church of Rome; it lies upon them to prove even the very ground and foundation of them. Show me, therefore, (will a Protestant here say,) either out of some text of Scripture, or else by some evident reason, that there is any such place as Purgatory, and that the Eucharist is not bread; and that the Pope is the monarch and head of the Church universal; and then I shall be very glad to try, if for our greater comfort we may be able to find, in the authors of the third or fourth century, these truths embraced by the Fathers of those times.

But to begin with these, is to invert the natural order of things. We ought first to be assured that the thing is, before we make inquiry whether it has been believed or not. For to what purpose is it to find that the ancients believed it, unless we find withal in their writings some reason of this their belief? And again, on the other side, what harm is it to us to be ignorant whether antiquity believed it or not, so long as we know that the thing is? And whereas there are some who, to establish the supreme authority of the Fathers, allege the counsel which Sisinnius, a Novatian, and Agellius his bishop, gave of old to Nectarius, archbishop of Constantinople,* and by him to Theodosius the emperor, which was, that they should demand of the Arians, whether or not they would stand to what the Fathers who died before the breaking forth of their heresy, had delivered on the point disputed between them, this is hardly worth our consideration; for, this was a trick only, devised by a subtle head, and, which is worse, by a schismatic, and consequently to be suspected as a captious proposal, purposely made to entrap the adverse party; rather than any free and ingenuous way of proceeding.

If this manner of proceeding had been right and proper, how came it to pass, that so many Catholic Bishops never thought of it? How came it to pass, that they were so ignorant of the weapons wherewith the enemies of the Church were to be encountered? How happened it that it should be proposed only by a young man, and he a schismatic too? And if it were approved of, as right and good counsel, why did Gregory Nazianzen, Basil, and so many others of the Fathers who wrote in that age against the Arians, deal with them almost entirely by arguments from the Scriptures? Certainly those holy men, indepen-

* Sozomen. l. 7. c. 12. Hist. Eccles.

dent of their Christian candour, which obliged them to this mode of proceeding, took a very wise course in so doing. For if this controversy had been to be decided by the authority of human writers, I know not how any man should have been able to make good what this conceited trifler so confidently affirms in the place just cited; namely, "that none of the ancients ever said that the co-eternal Son of God had any beginning of his generation;" *Εὐ γαρ ἤδει ὡς οἱ παλαιοι συναΐδιον τω πατρι τον υἱον εὑροντες, οὐκ ἐτολμησαν εἰπειν ἐκ τινος ἀρχης την γενεσιν αὐτον ἐχειν;** considering those many harsh expressions that we yet at this day meet with on this particular, in the books of the first Fathers: which is the reason also why the Arians alleged their testimonies, as we see they do in the books of Athanasius, Hilary, and others of the ancients who wrote against them. But why need we insist so long upon a story which is rejected by cardinal Baronius, as being an idle tale devised by Sozomen, who was a Novatian, in support of his own schism?†

The counsel of one Vincentius of Lerins, which he gives us in a certain little discourse of his, very highly praised by Gennadius,‡ is accounted by many men much more worthy of our consideration. For—having first told us, that he speaks not of any authors, "save only of such who, having piously, wisely, and constantly lived, taught, and persevered in the Catholic faith and communion, obtained the favour at length, either to die faithfully in Christ, or else to suffer martyrdom happily for Christ's sake;"—he further adds, "that we are to receive, as certain and definitive, whatsoever all the aforesaid authors or at least the greatest part of them, have clearly, frequently, and constantly affirmed, with an unanimous

* Sozomen. loc. citat. † Baron. Annal. Ann. 383.
‡ Gennad. in Catal. inter. Op. Hieron.

consent, receiving, retaining, and delivering it over to others, making up all of them, as it were, but one common and unanimous council of doctors."*

But this passage is so far from establishing the supreme authority, which some would attribute to the Fathers in matters of faith, that, on the contrary, I meet with something in it that makes me doubt more of their authority than I did before. For I find, by this man's discourse, that whatsoever his reason was, whether good or bad, he clearly appears to have had a very great desire to bring all differences in religion before the judgment seat of the Fathers; and for this purpose, he labours to prove, with the same eagerness and feeling, that their judgment is infallible in these cases. But in the meantime I find him so perplexed and troubled in bringing out that which he would have, that it appears evident he saw well enough that what he desired was not agreeable to truth. For he has so qualified his proposition, and bound it in with so many limitations, that it is very probable, if all these conditions which he here requires were anywhere to be found, we might then safely, perhaps, rely upon the writing of the Fathers. But then, on the other side, it is so very difficult a matter to meet with such a conjunction of so many several qualifications, that we can never be sure of finding them all together.

* Sed eorum duntaxat Patrum sententiæ conferendæ sunt, qui in fide et communione Catholica sanctè, sapienter, constanter viventes, docentes, et permanentes, vel mori in Christo fideliter, vel occidi pro Christo feliciter meruerunt. Quibus tamen hac lege credendum est, ut quicquid vel omnes, vel plures, uno eodemque sensu manifestè, frequenter, perseveranter, velut quodam consentiente sibi magistrorum concilio, accipiendo, tenendo, tradendo firmaverint, id pro indubitato, certo, ratoque habeatur: quicquid verò quamvis ille sanctus et doctus, quamvis episcopus, quamvis confessor, et martyr, præter omnes, aut etiam contra omnes senserit, id inter proprias, et occultas et privatas opiniunculas à communis, publicæ, et generalis sententiæ authoritate secretum sit.—*Vincent. Lirin. Comm. c.* 39.—*T.* 4. *Bibl. PP.*

First of all, for the persons of those men whose testimonies we allege, he requires that they should be such as not only *lived*, but also *taught*, and which is more, *persevered* too, not only in the faith but in the communion also of the Catholic Church. And then, for fear of being surprised, he qualifies his words with a restriction of three adverbs, and tells us, that they must have lived and taught *piously*, *wisely*, and *constantly*. But yet this is not all; for besides this, they must have either *died in Christ* or *for Christ*. So that if they lived but did not teach; or if they both lived and taught, but did not persevere; or if they lived, taught, and also persevered in the faith, but not in the communion; or else in the communion, but not in the faith of the Catholic Church; or if they yet lived and taught in it piously but not wisely; or, on the contrary, wisely but not piously; and if, in the last place, after all this, having performed all the particulars before set down, they did not at last die either in Christ or for Christ; they ought not, according to this man's rule, to be admitted as witnesses in this case. Certainly he might have stopped here, and not have gone on still with his modifications as he does, limiting the number and the words of these witnesses. For what Christian ever made scruple of receiving the opinions of such a one as had piously, wisely, and constantly lived, and taught in the faith and communion of the Catholic Church? For you might hence very well rest assured, that whatsoever he had delivered was true; and consequently fit to be believed: for how could he have taught wisely and constantly if he had taught any false doctrine? All that he here promises us therefore is no more but this; that we shall be sure not to be deceived, provided that we believe no other doctrines but those which are holy and true. This promise of his is like that which little children are wont to make, when they tell you, that you shall never die, if you but eat always. Nor do I believe that there is any man in the world so perverse and wilful, as not readily to submit his faith to such a man, as he assuredly knew to be so qualified, as Vincentius here describes.

But seeing that it is necessary that we should first know the qualifications of a witness before we hear him; it follows, in my judgment, that before we do so much as hear any of the Fathers, we ought to be first assured, that he was so qualified in every particular, according to Vincentius's rule before laid down. Now I would wish to be informed how it is possible for us to know this. Who will assure us, that Athanasius, Cyril, or what other Father you please, "lived, taught, persevered, and died piously, wisely, and constantly in the faith and communion of the Catholic Church?" This can never be done without a most exact inquiry made, both into their life and doctrines, which is an impossible thing, considering the many ages that have passed from their times down to ours. But yet supposing that this were a possible thing, it would nevertheless be of no use at all as to this author's purpose. For he will have us hear the Fathers, to the end that we may be by them instructed in the truth. Now that we may be rightly informed, whether or not they were so qualified as is before required, we ought necessarily to know first of all what the truth is. For how is it otherwise possible that we should be able to judge whether they have "taught piously and wisely?" And if you were beforehand instructed in the truth, what need have you then to hear them, and to desire to be instructed in it by them? You may indeed make use of them for the illustration and confirmation of that which you knew before; but you cannot learn any truth from them which you knew not before. If you understand the maxim before alleged in another sense, and take this wisdom and piety, this faith and communion of the Catholic Church therein mentioned for a shadow only, and the superficies and outward appearance of those things, and for a common and empty opinion, grounded merely upon the public voice, and not upon an exact knowledge of the thing itself, it will then prove to be manifestly false; those persons who have but the outward appearance only, and not the reality of these qualities, being no way fit to be admitted as witnesses, much less to be received as the supreme judges of the articles of the Christian faith. Thus this proposition is either impossible, if you understand it as the words seem to sound, or else it is false, if you take it in a looser sense. The like exceptions may be made against those other conditions, which he there further requires, on the *number* and the *words* of these witnesses. For he allows not the force of a law to anything, but what has been delivered either by *all*, or else by the greatest part of them. If by *all*, he here means all the Fathers that have ever been, or but the greatest part of them only, he then puts us upon an impossibility. For taking the whole number of Fathers that have ever been, the greatest and perhaps too the best part of them have not written anything at all: and among those that have written, how many has time devoured? and how many have the false dealings of men either wholly suppressed or else corrupted? It is therefore evidently impossible to know, what the opinions have been, either of all, or of the greatest part of the Fathers in this sense. And if he restrains this *all*, and this *greatest part*, to those who appear at this day, either in their own books, or in histories and the writings of other men, it will concern us then to inquire, whether or not, by *all*, he means all promiscuously, without distinguishing them by the several ages in which they lived: or else, whether he would have us distinguish them into several *classes*, putting together in the same rank all those that lived in one and the same age; and receiving for truth whatsoever we find to have been held and confirmed by the greatest part of them. Now both these ways agree in one thing, that they render the judgment of the Christian faith wholly casual, and make it depend upon divers and sundry accidents, which have been the cause of the writings of the Fathers being either preserved or lost. Suppose that Vincentius had established, by this excellent course of his, some point or other which had been controverted: he must have thanked the fire, the water, the moths, or the worms for having spared those authors which he made use of, and for having consumed all those others that wrote in favour of the adverse party: for otherwise he would have been a heretic. And if we should decide our differences in matters of faith after this manner, we should do in a measure as he did, who gave judgment upon the suits of law that came before him, by the chances he threw with three dice.

Do but conceive what an endless labour it would be, for a man either to go and heap together, and run over promiscuously all the authors that ever have written; or else to distinguish them into the several ages in which they wrote, and to examine them by companies. And do but imagine again, what satisfaction a man should be able to obtain from hence; and where we should be, in case we should find, (as it is possible it may sometimes so happen, as we shall show hereafter,) that the sense and judgment of this greatest part should prove to be either contrary to, or perhaps besides, the sense and meaning either of the Scriptures or of the Church. And again, how senseless a thing were it, to make the suffrages of equal authority, of persons that are so unequal, in respect of their merit, learning, holy life, and integrity: and that a Rheticius, whom Jerome censured so sharply a little before, should be reckoned equal to Augustine: or a Philastrius be as good a man as Jerome? There is perhaps among the Fathers one, whose judgment is of more weight than a hundred others; and yet forsooth will this man have us to make our farthings and our pence pass for as much as our shillings and pounds.

Lastly, what reason in the world is there, that although perhaps the persons themselves were equal in other respects, we should yet make their words also of equal force, which are often of very different and unequal authority; some of them having been uttered, as it were, before the bar, the books having been produced, both parties heard, and the whole cause thoroughly examined; and the other perhaps having been thrown out by their authors at hap-hazard as it were; either in their chamber, or else in discourse walking abroad; or else perhaps by the by, while they were treating of some other matter? But our author here, to prevent in some degree this latter inconvenience, requires, that the word of this *greatest part*, which he will allow to be authoritative, must have been uttered by them "clearly, often, and constantly;" and then, and not till then, does he allow them for certain and undoubted truth. And now you see he is got into another hold. For I wish to be informed, how it is possible for us to know whether these Fathers whom we thus have called out of their graves to give us their judgment on the controversies in religion, affirmed those things which we find in their writings, clearly, often, and constantly, or not? If in this his pretended council of doctors, you will not allow the right of suffrage to those, of whom it may be doubted that they either expressed themselves obscurely, or gave in their testimonies but seldom, or but weakly maintained their own opinion; I pray you tell me, whom shall we have left at last to be the judges in the decision of our present controversies?

As for the Apostles' creed, and the determinations of the first four general councils, (which are assented to, and approved by all the Protestant party,) I confess we may, by this way of trial, allow them as competent judges in these matters. But as for all the rest, it is evident, from what has been stated in the First Part of this treatise, that we can never admit of them, if they are thus to be qualified, and to have all the afore-mentioned conditions. We may therefore very safely conclude, that the expedient here proposed by this author is either impossible, or not safe to be reduced to practice; and I shall therefore rather approve of Augustine's judgment, as regards the authority of the Fathers.

I should not have insisted so long upon the examination of this proposal, had I not seen it to have been in such high esteem with many men, and even with some of the learned.* For after Augustine and Jerome have delivered their judgments, it matters not much what this man shall have believed to the contrary. Yet before we finish this point, let us a little examine this author, both by Augustine's and by his own rule before laid down.

Augustine considers us not bound to believe the saying of any author, except he can prove to us the truth of it, either by the canonical Scriptures, or by some probable reason. What text of Scripture, or what reason has this man alleged to prove the truth of what he has proposed? So that whatever his opinion be, he must not take it amiss, if, according to the advice and practice of Augustine, we take leave to dissent from him: especially considering we have so many reasons to reject that which he, without any reason given, would have us to receive.

Thus you see that, according to the judgment of Augustine, the saying of this Vincentius of Lerins, although you should class him among the most eminent of the Fathers, does not at all oblige us to give our assent to it. And yet you will find that this tes-

* Perron, Cassander, &c.

timony would be yet of much less force and weight, if you but examine the man by his own rule. For according to him, we are not to hearken to the Fathers, except they both lived and taught piously and wisely, even to the hour of their death. Who is there now that will pass his word for him, that he himself was one of this number? Who shall assure us, that he was not either a heretic himself, or at least a favourer of heretics? For is it not evident enough that he favoured the Semi-Pelagians, who at that time in Gaul, railed against the memory of Augustine, and who were condemned by the whole Church? Who cannot easily see this, by his manner of discourse in his Commonitorium tending this way;* where he seems to intimate to us underhand, that Prosper and Hilary had unjustly slandered them; and that Pope Celestine, who also wrote against them, had been misinformed?† May not he also be strongly suspected of having been the author of those "Objections" made against Augustine, and refuted by Prosper, which are called *Objectiones Vincentianæ*, (Vincent's Objections.)‡ The great commendations also which are given him by Gennadius, very much confirm this suspicion;§ it being clear that this author was of the same sect, as appears plainly by the great account he makes of Ruffinus, a priest of Aquileia, who was the Grand Patriarch of the Pelagians, saying, "that he was not the least part of the doctors of the Church;" tacitly reproaching Jerome his adversary, and calling him, "a malicious slanderer:" and also by the judgment which he gives of Augustine, who was *flagellum Pelagianorum*, (the scourge of the Pelagians;)‖ passing this insolent censure upon him, "that in

* Vincent. Lirin. in Comm. 2. c. 43.

† Celestinus apud Aug. l. 2, Contr. Pelag. et Celest. c. 3.

‡ Prosper. Resp. ad Object. Vincent.

§ Gennad. in Catal. in Ruff. inter Op. Hieron.

‖ Gennad. ubi supra.

speaking so much, it had happened to him, what the Holy Ghost has said by Solomon, That in the multitude of words there wanteth not sin."*

Thus I cannot sufficiently wonder at the boldness of Cardinal du Perron, who when he has any occasion for quoting this author, usually calls him "St. Vincent of Lerins;" thus by a very bad example canonizing a person who was strongly suspected to have been a heretic.† Since therefore he was such, why should any one think it strange that he should so much laud the judgment and opinions of the Fathers, as every one knows that the Pelagians and Semi-Pelagians had the better of it, by citing their authorities, and laboured by this means to run down Augustine's name; and all this forsooth, only because the greatest part of the Fathers, who lived before Pelagius's time, had delivered themselves with less caution than they might have done, on those points which were by him afterwards brought into question; and many times too in such strange expressions, as will scarcely be reconciled to any orthodox sense?

Notwithstanding, should we allow this Vincentius to have been a person who was thus qualified, and to have had all those conditions, which he requires in a man, to render him capable of being attended to in this particular, what weight, I would ask, ought this proposal of his to carry with it, which yet is not found anywhere in the mouth of any of those Fathers who preceded him; which is also strongly contradicted both by Augustine and Jerome, as we have seen in those passages before adduced from them: and which besides, is full of obscurities and inexplicable ambiguities?

Thus, "however learned and holy a man he might be; whether he were a bishop, confessor, or martyr, (which he was not,) this proposal of his (according to

* Proverbs x. 19.

† Du Perron, en la Repliq. au Roy de la Grande Bret. passim.

his own maxims) ought to be excluded from the authority of public determinations, and to be accounted only as his own particular private opinion."* Let us therefore in this business rather follow the judgment of Augustine, which is grounded upon evident reason—a person whose authority (whenever it shall be questioned) will be found to be incomparably greater than that of Vincentius of Lerins: and let us not henceforth give credit to any sayings or opinions of the Fathers, save only those, the truth of which they shall have made evident to us, either by the canonical books of Scripture, or by some probable reason.

CHAPTER III.

REASON III.—That the Fathers have written in such a manner, as to make it clear that when they wrote they had no intention of being our authorities in matters of religion; as evinced by examples of their mistakes and oversights.

WHOEVER takes the pains diligently to consider the manner of writing by the Fathers, will not require any other testimony for the proof of the above truth. For the very form of their writings witnesses clear enough, that in the greatest part of them they had no intention of delivering such definitive sentences, as were to be binding, merely by the single authority of the mouth which uttered them: but their purpose was rather to communicate to us their own meditations on divers points of our religion; leaving us free to examine them, and to approve or reject the same, according as we saw proper. Thus has Jerome expressly delivered his mind, as we showed before, where he speaks of the nature and manner of com-

* Vincent. Lirin. Common. l. c. 39, ubi supra.

mentaries on the Holy Scriptures. And certainly if they had had any other design or intention, they would never have troubled themselves, as they usually do, in gathering together the several opinions of other men. This diligence, I confess, is laudable in a teacher, but it would be very ridiculous in a judge. Their style also should be entirely of another kind: and those obscurities which we have observed in the former part of this treatise, proceeding either from the rhetorical ornaments or the logical subtilties which they adopt, should have no place here. For who could tolerate any such thing in pronouncing a sentence of judgment, or indeed in giving one's bare testimony only to anything? But that which makes the truth of this our assertion more clearly to appear than all the rest, is the little care and diligence that they took, in composing the greatest part of these writings of theirs, which we would now wish to be the rules of our faith. If these men, who were endued with such sanctity, had had any intention of prescribing to posterity a true and perfect rule of faith, is it probable that they would have gone carelessly to work, in a business of such great importance? Would they not rather have gone to it with their eyes opened, their judgments settled, their thoughts fixed, and every faculty of their soul attentively bent upon the business in hand; for fear that, in a business of so great weight as this, something might chance to fall from them, not so becoming their own wisdom, or so suitable to the people's advantage? A judge, that had but ever so little conscience, would not otherwise give sentence concerning the oxen, the field, and the gutters of Titius and Mævius. How much more is the same gravity and deliberation requisite here, where the question is on the faith, the souls, and the eternal salvation of all mankind? It were clearly therefore the greatest injury that could be offered to these holy persons, to imagine that they would have taken upon them to have passed judgment in so weighty a cause as this, but with the greatest care and attention that could be. Now it is evident, on the other side, that in very many of those writings of theirs, which have come down to our hands, there seems to be very much negligence; or, to speak a little more tenderly of the business, want of care at least, both in the invention, method, and elocution. If therefore we tender the reputation either of their honesty or wisdom, we ought rather to say, that their design in these books of theirs, was not to pronounce definitively upon this particular, neither are their writings judiciary sentences or final judgments, but rather discourses of different kinds, occasioned by divers emergencies; and are more or less elaborate, according to the time, judgment, age, and disposition they were of, when they wrote them. Now although this want of diligence and of deliberation, appears of itself evident enough to any one that reads the Fathers with the least attention, yet, that I may not leave this assertion of mine unproved, I shall here give you some few instances merely as a sample.

First of all, there are many pieces among the works of the Fathers, which were written in haste; and some too, which were mere extemporary discourses, and such as, in all probability, their authors themselves would have found many things therein which would have required correction, had they had but leisure to review the same.

Jerome, in a prologue to certain Homilies of Origen, translated by him into Latin, says that Origen composed and delivered them in the Church extempore.* As to these, therefore, we are well satisfied by Jerome; but how many, in the meantime, may there be of the like nature, among those numerous Homilies of Chrysostom, Augustine, and others; all which we

* Hier. Prol. in Hom. Orig. in Ies. Nau.

perhaps imagine to have been leisurely and deliberately studied, digested, and composed, which yet some sudden occasion might perhaps have put forth into the world on the instant, and which were as soon born as conceived, and as soon published as made?

Jerome often tells us, that he dictated what he wrote in haste. Thus at the end of that long epistle which he wrote to Fabiola, he says, "that he had despatched it in one short evening, when he was about to set sail on a voyage."* And (which is a matter of much more importance) he says in another place, "that he had allotted himself but three days for the translating of the three books of Solomon;" namely, the Proverbs, Ecclesiastes, and the Canticles;† which yet a man will hardly be able to read over well and exactly in a month, by reason of the great difficulties he will there meet with, as well in the words and phrases, as in the sense. Yet for all this (if, what the Church of Rome pretends, be true) this little three-days' work of Jerome has proved so fortunate, as to deserve, not only to be approved and highly esteemed, but even canonized also by the Council of Trent.

Now whether the will of our Lord be, that we should receive this translation as his pure word or not, I leave to those who have a desire and ability to examine. However I dare confidently affirm that Jerome himself never had the least thought or hope that this piece of his should one day come to this honour; it being a thing not to be imagined, but that he would have taken both more time and more pains in the matter, if ever he had desired or foreseen this. Thus it sometimes happens, that men have better fortune than ever they wished for. The same author

* Hier. Ep. 128, ad Fabiol. t. 3, vid. et in Epitaph. Marcel. Epist. 16, extr.

† Itaque, &c. tridui opus nomini vestro consecravi, interpretationem videlicet trium Salomonis voluminum.—*Id. Præf. in Prov.*

says, at the end of another production of his, "that it was an extemporary piece, and poured out so fast, that his tongue outran the hands of his amanuenses, and by its volubility and swiftness, in a manner, confounded them and their ciphers and abbreviations."* He elsewhere excuses in like manner another work of his, of no small importance (his commentary upon the Gospel of Matthew,) telling us, that as he had been straitened in time, he was constrained to dictate it in very great haste. So likewise in the preface to his second commentary upon the Epistle of Paul to the Ephesians, he confesses that he wrote it in such great haste, that he many times made as much of it as came to a thousand lines in a day. In a word, that I may not weary the reader with producing all the instances of the same kind, that I could here adduce, it is his ordinary way of excusing himself, either in prefaces, or else at the closing up of all his discourses, to say that either the messenger was in haste, or some design called him away; or else some other similar cause was alleged. So that he scarcely did anything but in haste, and at full speed. Sometimes again, either sickness had broken his spirit, or else the study of the Hebrew had made his tongue grow rusty, or his pen was not able to exert its wonted power.

Now, if he would have us receive all his sayings as oracles, and did not indeed desire us rather to excuse some things in him, and to forgive him in others, why should he use these speeches? Who ever heard a judge excuse himself on account of the shortness of the time? Would not this be rather to accuse than to excuse himself, by making such an apology as this for himself; forasmuch as giving an over hasty judgment in any cause, is a very great fault? In my opinion the Fathers could not more clearly have de-

* Extemporalis est dictatio, et tanta ad lumen lucernulæ facilitate profusa, ut notariorum manus lingua præcurreret, et signa ac furta verborum volubilitas sermonum obrueret.—*Id. Ep.* 47.

prived themselves of this dignity of being our judges, with which we would invest them, whether they will or not, than by writing and speaking after this manner. But yet, although Jerome had not given us these advertisements, which yet ought to make us look well also to the rest of the Fathers, it appears evidently enough, out of their very writings themselves, how little both time and diligence they bestowed, in composing the greatest part of them. For otherwise how could so many trifling faults, in history, grammar, philosophy, and the like, have escaped such great and eminent persons, who were so well furnished with all sorts of literature? How happened it, that they thus either forgot or else mistook themselves, as they have sometimes done?

I shall here give the reader some few examples of this kind, not to detract from the praises due to these learned persons, as if we thought them really to have committed these errors out of ignorance, but rather to let the world see, that they did not always make use of their whole store of worth and learning; and that sometimes they either could not, or else would not, make use but of some part only of their knowledge, and of their time; which is a most certain argument, that they had never any intention of being received by us as judges in points of faith.

I shall not say much of their errors in matters of time, which are both very notorious and very frequent with them: as, for example, where Justin Martyr says that, "David lived fifteen hundred years before the crucifixion of Christ;"—*Δαβιδ ἐτεσι χιλιοις και πεντακοσιοις πριν ἢ Χριστον ἀνθρωπον γενομενον σταυρωθηναι, τα προειρημενα ἐφη*:* it being very apparent, by observing the course of times, derived through history both sacred and profane, that from the death of David to the birth of our Saviour Christ,

* Just. Apol.

there elapsed no more than a thousand and twenty-five or thirty years, or thereabouts. So likewise, when Epiphanius writes, "that Moses was but thirty years old when he brought forth the children of Israel out of Egypt:"—*Ὁ δε Μωυσης εν τω λ' αὐτου ἐτει πατει την ἐρυθραν θαλασσαν, ἅμα Ἰσραηλιταις ἐξ Αἰγυπτου ἐξιων:** whereas the Scriptures clearly testify, that he was eighty years of age. And also where he affirms, "that the taking of the city of Jerusalem happened sixty-five years after the passion of our Saviour Christ:—*Γεγονεν ἡ ἐρημωσις Ἱεροσολυμων μετα ἑξηκοστον πεμπτον ἐτος της Χριστου σταυρωσεως και ἡμερας τινας.*†

Chrysostom says that Jerusalem was destroyed by Titus five hundred years before his own time. In another place, he reckons the period at four hundred years. Now it is well known that only three hundred and thirty-three or four years elapsed between that event and the banishment of Chrysostom. He also states that Hezekiah lived one thousand years after the death of David; whereas the interval was not as much as four hundred years.

Truly the chronology of the ancients is generally very strange, and for the most part very far wide of the truth, as has been observed, and also proved at large, by all the moderns; as Scaliger, Petavius, and others. But these matters are so very difficult, that oftentimes the most diligent inquiries into them may chance to mistake. I shall therefore forbear to insist any longer upon this particular; and shall now lay before you some examples of another nature, and such as shall most evidently discover the carelessness and negligence of these authors.

Justin Martyr, speaking of the translation of the Seventy Interpreters, says "that Ptolemy king of

* Epiphan. in Ancor. num. 112.

† Epiphan. l. de. Ponder. et Mens. Num. 12.

Egypt sent his ambassadors to Herod king of Judea,"—(*'Οτε δε Πτολεμαιος ὁ Αἰγυπτιων βασιλευς βιβλιοθηκην κατεσκευασε,* &c. *προσεπεμψε τῳ των Ιουδαιων τοτε βασιλευοντι 'Ηρωδῃ αξιων, διαπεμφθηναι αὐτω τας βιβλους των προφητειων;*)* whereas the truth of the story is, that he sent to Eleazar the high priest, two hundred forty and odd years before Herod was king of Judea.

Epiphanius tells us, in two or three places, that the Peripatetics and Pythagoreans were one and the same sect of heathen philosophers;† which yet were as much different one from the other, as the Stoics and Epicureans were; as every child knows. The same author also confidently affirms, though contrary to the faith of all ancient history, that the several sects and opinions in philosophy sprang from some certain mysteries brought to Athens by Orpheus and others;‡ and that the Stoics believed the immortality and transmigration of souls;§ both of which are false: and likewise that Nabuchadonosor sent a colony into the country about Samaria, after the taking of Jerusalem;|| whereas, in truth, it was Shalmaneser who had so done, long before the other's time. What can you think of him, when you find him mistaken in such things, as happened not many years before he was born; as when he says that Arius died before the council of Nice;¶ and when he relates the story of Meletius and his schism altogether contrary to the truth?

Justin Martyr likewises assures us, as a certain truth, that in the reign of the Emperor Claudius, there was erected at Rome a statue to Simon Magus, in the river Tiber, between the two bridges, with this inscription: "TO THE HOLY GOD SIMON:"—*'Ος (Σιμων)*

* Justin. Mart. Apol. 2.
† Epiphan. in Panar. lib. 1, et Anaceph. p. 127, 129, 133.
‡ Id. contr. Hæres. l. 1.
§ Id. Hær. 5.
|| Id. Panar. l. 1.
¶ Id. Hær. Arian. 69. num. 10, 11.

ἐν τῃ πολει βασιλιδι Ῥωμῃ θεος ἐνομισθη, και ἀνδριαντι παρ' ὑμων ὡς θεος τετιμηται· ὁς ἀνδριας ἀνεγηγερται ἐν τω Τιβερι ποταμω, μεταξυ των δυο γεφυρων, ἐχων ἐπιγραφην Ῥωμαϊκην ταυτην Σιμωνι δεω σαγκτω:* whereas, as our learned critics now inform us, it was only an inscription to one of the Pagan demigods, in those words, "SEMONI DEO SANCO:† which this good Father mistook; instead of Semoni, reading Simoni; and for sanco reading sancto.

Eusebius says,‡ and Jerome frequently repeats it after him,§ that Josephus, the Jewish historian, reports, that at the time of our Saviour's passion the heavenly powers forsook the temple of Jerusalem; and that there was a great noise heard, and a voice saying, *Μεταβαινωμεν ἐντευθεν*, "Let us depart hence;" and yet nevertheless the truth of the story is, that Josephus reported this to have happened at the time the city was besieged; that is to say, above thirty-five years after the death of our Saviour.

The same authors, and in a manner all others after them,‖ have constantly delivered, as a certain truth, that Philo the Jew, in that book of his entitled "*De Vita Contemplativa*," describes to us the manner of life of the Christian *Ασκηται*, or Monks; and yet that book of Philo, which is still extant, proclaims loud enough, that he there speaks not of the Christians but of the Essenes, who were one of the three sects among the Jews; as has been observed by Scaliger, and various others after him.¶ We have noticed how Ambrose,** without giving us any account of his reasons why he does so, understands by *Gog* and

* Just. Mart. Apol. 2. † Desider. Herald. in Apol. Tertul.

‡ Euseb. in Chron. et 'Αποδειξ. 8. p. 250.

§ Hier. ep. 150, Hedibiæ Comment. 4. in Matth. ep. 17, quæ est Paul. et Eustoch. T. i. p. 153.

‖ Euseb. Hist. Eccles. l. 2. c. 15, 16. Hier. lib. de Script. Eccles.

¶ Scalig. de Emend. Temp. l. 6. c. 1.

** Ambros. l. 2. de fide ad Gratian.

Magog mentioned in Ezekiel, the nations of the *Goths*, who in his time overran all Christendom. He tells us in another place, with the very same confidence, that Zacharias,* the father of John the Baptist, was high priest of the Jews; which yet Baronius has clearly proved to be false.†

Epiphanius affirms that *Pison*, which was one of the four rivers that watered the terrestrial Paradise, mentioned by Moses, "was the same that the Indians and Ethiopians call *Ganges*, and the Greeks *Indus:* which river passing at length through Ethiopia, discharges itself at last into the ocean at Cadiz! *Και Φεισων μεν ἐστιν ὁ Γαγγης παρα τοις 'Ινδοις καλουμενος και Αἰθιοφιν· 'Ελληνες και τουτον καλουσιν Ινδον ποταμον*, &c. *διαπερα δε την μεγαλην Αἰθιοπιαν, και δυει ἐσωθεν Γαδειραν εἰς τον μεγαν ὠκεανον.*‡ What wonderful geography have we here, (if at least we may call it by this name,) which jumbles together the east and the west, and confounds places which are nearly a whole hemisphere distant from each other!

Basil also, who is otherwise an excellent author, has mistaken likewise, though not so much, the source of the river Danube; for he only makes it rise out of the Pyrenean mountains:—*'Απο δε δυσμων των θερινων ὑπο το Πυρρηναιον ὀρος Ταρτησος τε, και 'Ιστρος.*§

Speaking of those rivers reminds me, that all the Fathers‖ unanimously understand by *Gihon* (one of the rivers of Paradise,) the river *Nile*, which has so deceived cardinal Perron also,¶ that he delivers it to us as the express text of the Scripture; by this means making it guilty of a manifest absurdity, however innocent in itself it be, and free from intending any

* Ambros. Comment. in Luc. † Baron. in Apparat. num. 69.
‡ Epiphan. in Ancor. § Basil. Hom. 3. in Isa.
‖ Theoph. Antioch. l. 2. Ambros. l. de Parad. c. 3. Epiph. Panar. hær. 66. Hieron. de locis Hebr. voc. *Geon.* Alii.
¶ Du Perron en sa Repr. p. 950.

such thing; since neither in the Hebrew, Greek, nor Latin text, is it ever said that the river Nile watered the land of Paradise; it being only a dream of the Fathers, that one of those rivers of Paradise must needs have been the Nile; though this fancy of theirs (as Scaliger makes it appear,* and as it is confessed by Petavius also,†) is built upon no ground or reason at all.

Neither has their philosophy been less wonderful than their geography: as for example, when Tertullian maintains,‡ that plants are endued both with feeling and understanding. So likewise where Epiphanius holds,§ that it is impossible for a dead man to return to life again, without the reunion of the soul to the body. As also where Ambrose says that the sun, to the end he may allay his extreme heat, refreshes himself with the nourishment which he draws up from the waters; and that from hence it is, that we sometimes see him appear as it were all over wet, and dropping with dew.||

Again, you have some of them treating the doctrine of the spherical figure of the heavens with very great scorn; and maintaining, that it is only, as it were, an arch which is built upon the waters as on its base.¶ Others of them you have, who will not endure to hear of the earth being of a spherical figure, or of the Antipodes; and account those men little less than infidels, who shall offer to maintain any such opinions.** But these are not bare mistakes and oversights only; but are rather errors which proceeded from the want of a due examination and a

* Scalig. de Emend. Temp. † Peta. in Epiph. p. 371.

‡ Tertul. l. de An. c. 19.

§ Epiphan. in Ancor. num. 90.

|| Frequenter solem videmus madidum, atque rorantem, in quo evidens dat indicium quod alimentum sibi aquarum ad temperiem sui sumpserit.—*Ambrose Hexaem. l. 2. c. 3.*

¶ Justin. Quæst. et Respons. Qu. 130. ad Autolyc.

** Lactant. Instit. l. 3. c. 34. August. de Civit. Dei, l. 16. c. 9.

right apprehension of things. As for their grammatical errors, they are more frequent and usual with them than any other: and the reason of their so often mistaking here, is the little knowledge they had of the Hebrew tongue: as, for instance, when Optatus, and some others of them, deduce the name *Cephas* from the Greek κεφαλη, which signifies *a head:** whereas *Cepha* is a Syriac word, and signifies *a stone*, as the Evangelist expressly testifies.† Ambrose is in the like manner mistaken, where he derives the word *Pascha*, which is of Hebrew extraction, and which signifies properly *a passing*, from a Greek word signifying *to suffer;*‡ in which etymology he is faithfully followed by Pope Innocent III., in an oration of his, which he made at the opening of the council of Lateran.§

We have heretofore noticed some errors of theirs of this nature, observed by Jerome, to whom the Church is very much obliged, both for the great pains that he took to attain so deep a knowledge of the Hebrew tongue; and also for the great courage he had in freely noting all such impertinences, whenever he met with them; who or however great the authors of them were. All the rest of the Fathers, a very few only excepted, do here as it were only grope their way in the dark: and hence it is that we have so many wild etymologies given by them of the proper names we meet with in the Scriptures. Who can read without amazement, what Irenæus has delivered on the derivation of the name of *Jesus;* which he will have to be composed of two letters and a half;|| add-

* Omnium Apostolorum caput Petrus, unde et Cephas appellatus est.—*Optat. l. contr. Don.*

† John i. 42.

‡ Quod quidem sacrum nomen ab ipsius Domini passione descendit.—*Ambros.* 1. *de Pasch. c.* I.

§ Innoc. III. Ser. I. in Concil. Later.

|| Jesus autem nomen secundum propriam Hebræorum linguam, literarum est duarum et dimidiæ, &c.—*Iren. contr. Hær. l.* 2. *c.* 41.

ing moreover, that in the ancient language of the Hebrews it signifies *heaven*, notwithstanding that the angel expressly testified at the very beginning of Matthew's gospel, that our Saviour Christ was called Jesus, because "he was to save his people from their sins."*

Of the like nature is his assertion, "That the name of God, *Adonai*, signifies *wonderful:* or if you write thus, *Addhonei*, it then signifies Him that bounds and separates the earth from the water." He gives similar etymologies of the words *Sabaoth*, and *Jaoth*. Similar to these are those mysteries of which he informs us, in the afore-cited treatise of his, which no author else, either ancient or modern, ever heard of;† telling us that *Barneth* is the name of *God* in Hebrew; and that the first and most ancient Hebrew letters, which were called *Sacerdotal*, were only ten in number, and were written fifteen different ways.

Out of the same storehouse has Clemens Alexandrinus produced us that precious etymology which he has given of the name of *Abraham*, saying, "It is, by interpretation, *The elect Father of a sound.*" Ἑρμηνευεται μεν γαρ, πατηρ ἐκλεκτος ἠχους:‡ and that other of the name *Rebecca*, which he will have to signify, *The glory of God*, Ῥεβεκκα δε ἑρμηνευεται, θεου δοξα.§

Hilary says, that *Zion* signifies *a fruitless tree.*‖ But Jerome informs us,¶ that Hilary, understanding nothing of the Hebrew, and being not so very excellent in Greek either, was glad to make use of a certain priest, named Heliodorus, to interpret to him out of Origen whatever he himself understood not; who, not discharging his trust sometimes so faithfully as he should have done, was the cause of this Father's

* Matth. i. 12. Iren. l. 2. c. 66.
† Id. ibid.
‡ Clem. Alex. Strom. l. 4.
§ Id. p. 222.
‖ Seon infructuosæ arboris interpretatio est.—*Hilar. Ps.* 132.
¶ Hieron. Ep. 141, ad Marcell.

committing certain errors of this nature, in his Commentaries.

Theophilus of Antioch says, that before Melchisedec's time, the city of Jerusalem was called *Hierosolyma;** but that afterwards it was called *Hierusalem*, from him; which is a very strange fancy of his, and such a one as it is no very easy matter to guess what ground he should have for it.

What strange dreams does Ambrose entertain his readers with,† when he expounds the names of *Chorat*, and of *Oreb:* the one whereof with him signifies *the understanding*, and the other, *the whole heart*, or, *as the heart:* and thus likewise in his exposition of the 118th Psalm,‡ where he gives us the meaning of each of the Hebrew letters with which the first verses begin, of every one of the twenty-two Octonaries, whereof the said 118th Psalm, according to the Hebrew reckoning, consists. But he is by no means to be pardoned,§ where he is so much out in the Greek tongue, which he understood, in deriving the word *οὐσια*, *essence*, from *ἀει always*, and *οὐσά being:* which is such a gross mistake as would not have been pardoned to a schoolboy at a grammar school.

As for Jerome, it is true that he is sometimes guilty of the same fault; though I should think he does it on purpose, and to make himself merry only, rather than any way mistaking himself: as for example, when he derives the Latin word *Nugæ* from the Hebrew נדגי *Nogè*,|| which you read in the prophet Zephaniah, iii. 8. And so likewise when he searches in the Hebrew, for the signification of Paul,¶ Philemon, Onesimus, Timothy, and other words which are purely Greek.

Even in the very Scriptures themselves, which they were both better acquainted with, and which

* Theoph. Antioch. l. 2. ad Autol. † Ambros. Ep. l. 10. Ep. 82.
‡ Ambros. in Psal. 118.
§ Id. lib. de Incarn. Dom. Sacr. c. 9.
|| Hier. in Sophon. c. 3. ver. 8. ¶ Id. Comm. in ep. ad Philem.

they also had in greater veneration than any other books whatever, they often mistake themselves in citing them. As, for example, when Justin Martyr adduces a passage out of the prophet Zephaniah,* which is not found anywhere but in Zechariah; and in another place where he names Jeremiah instead of Daniel.† Thus likewise when Hilary tells us that Paul, in the thirteenth chapter of the Acts, adduces a certain passage out of the first Psalm, which yet is found only in the second;‡ whereas Paul in that place speaks not one syllable of the first Psalm, but expressly names the second. So also when Epiphanius says, out of the twenty-seventh chapter, verse thirty-seven, of the Acts of the Apostles,§ that the number of those who were in the ship with Paul, when he suffered shipwreck, was one while seventy, and by and by eighty souls; whereas the text says expressly, that they were in all two hundred and seventy-six. Thus likewise when in another place he affirms, out of the Gospel, that our Saviour Christ said to his mother, "Touch me not;"—*Οὕτω και ὁ κυριος διεταξεν ἐν τω εὐαγγελιω*, &c. *φησας τῃ μητρι αὐτου, Μη μου ἁπτου*:|| whereas it appears plainly out of the text, that these words were spoken only to Mary Magdalene. So where Jerome takes great pains to reconcile a certain passage alleged by him out of Habakkuk,¶ with the original, telling us that Paul had cited it in these words, "the just shall live by my faith:" whereas it is most evident that the Apostle, both in the first chapter of the epistle to the Romans, and in the epistle to the Galatians, has it only thus: "the just shall live by faith," and not "the just shall live by my faith."

Athanasius in his Synopsis, (or whoever else was

* Just. Mart, Apol. 2.
† Id. ibid.
‡ Hilar. in Psal. 2.
§ Epiphan. in Ancor.
|| Id. in Panar. l. 3, Hær. 80.
¶ Hieron. Comm. 1, in Abac.

the author of that piece) reckoning up the several books of Scriptures, evidently takes the third book of Esdras, which has been always accounted apocryphal by the consent of all Christendom, for the first, which is received by all Christians and Jews into the canon of the Scriptures. We might class in this number (if at least so foolish a piece deserves to have any place among the writings of the Fathers) that gross mistake which we meet with in an epistle of Pope Gregory II., who rails fiercely against Uzziah for breaking the brazen serpent; calling him, for this act, "the brother of the Emperor Leo the Iconoclast:"* which, as he thought, was the same as to reckon him among the most mischievous and wretched princes that ever had been; and yet all this while the Scripture tells us, that this was the act, not of Uzziah, but of the good king Hezekiah; and that he deserved to be rather commended for the same than blamed.

As for their slips of memory, he had need of a very happy one himself, who should undertake to enumerate them all. For example, Ambrose tells us somewhere, that the *eagle* on dying is revived again out of her own ashes.† Who sees not, that in this place he would have said the *phœnix?* In another place, however, giving us an account of the story of the phœnix, as it is commonly delivered, he says that "this we have learned from the authority of the Scriptures."‡ By a like mistake it was that he affirmed, that these words, "for this very purpose have I raised thee up, that I might show my power in thee,"§ were spoken to Moses; to whom, notwith-

* Greg. II. in Ep. ad Leon. Isaur. de col. Imag.

† Quod etiam aquila, cum fuerit mortua, ex suis reliquiis renascatur. —*Ambros. l.* 2. *de Pœnit. c.* 2.

‡ Atqui hoc relatione crebra, et Scripturarum authoritate cognovimus, memoratam avem, &c.—*Id. lib. de fid. Resur.*

§ Denique iterum Moysi dicit, Quia in hoc ipsum te suscitavi, ut ostendam in te virtutem meam.—*Ambros. ser.* 10.

standing, the Lord never said any such word, but rather to Pharaoh. In like manner does he attribute to the Jews those words in the ninth chapter of John, which were indeed spoken by Christ's disciples, who asked him, saying, "Master, who did sin, this man or his parents, that he was born blind?"* I impute that other mistake of his to the heat of his rhetoric, where he brings in one of the seven brethren in the Maccabees,† who suffered under king Antiochus; and makes him quote the example of John and of James, "the sons of thunder," two of our Saviour's Apostles, who came not into the world, as every one knows, till a long time after this.

It was a slip of memory also in Tertullian, where he tells us, "that the Lord said to Moses, They have not rejected thee, but they have rejected me:"‡ which words were indeed spoken to Samuel, and not to Moses.§

Jerome also was misled in like manner, when he tells us, "that none of the Fathers ever understood the word *knew*, in the last verse of the first chapter of Matthew, otherwise than of the conjugal act;‖ not remembering, that his own dear friend Epiphanius takes the word in a quite different sense, and will have the meaning of the place to be, "that Joseph, before the miraculous birth of our Saviour Christ, knew not what glory and excellency was to befall the blessed virgin;" knowing nothing else of her before, save only that she was the daughter of Joachim, and of Anna, and cousin to Elizabeth, who was of the house of David: *'Αλλ' ὁμως ἐγνω την Μαριαμ ὁ Ιωσηφ, οὐ*

* Quam stolidi autem Judæi qui interrogant, Hic peccavit, an parentes?—*Ambros. Ep. l.* 9, *Ep.* 75.

† Id. l. 2, de Sanct. Jacob. c.11.

‡ Tertul. contr. Marc. l. 4, c. 24.

§ 1 Sam. 8.

‖ In quo primùm adversarius superfluo labore desudat, cognoscendi verbum ad coitum magis quam ad scientiam esse referendum, quasi hoc quisquam negaverit.—*Hieron. l. contr. Helvid.*

*κατα γνωσιν τινα χρησεως, οὐ κατα γνωσιν κοινωνιας, ἀλλ' ἐγνω αὐτην, τιμων την ἐκ του θεου τετιμημενην· οὐ γαρ ᾔδει αὐτην, τοιαυτης δοξης οὖσαν;** whereas he at that time knew clearly that God had done her that honour of sending his angel to her, and of choosing her to receive that great and wonderful benefit.

But we intend not here to give an inventory of all the errors of this nature, which are to be found in the writings of the ancients; these specimens may sufficiently serve to show what their whole productions are. I shall only add here, that besides this carelessness which is so common with them, in writing thus confidently whatsoever came into mind, or whatever others had delivered to them for sound and good, without ever examining it thoroughly; they yet had another kind of custom, which seems not to suit so well with the character of judges, which we attribute to them. And this is, that in their writings they sometimes amuse themselves with presenting us such rare allegorical observations, as have scarcely any more solidity or body, than those castles of cards that little children are wont to make. These Cardinal Perron calls *des gaiétés joyeuses*.†

I know very well that allegories are useful, and many times also necessary, if they be but sound, clear, and well grounded. But I speak here only of such as wrest the text, and, as it were, drag it along by the hair, and make the sense of the Scripture evaporate in empty fumes. Of these are the writings of the Fathers full. Jerome often complains of the strange liberty that Origen and his disciples took herein. Certainly he himself often indulges in this way; and whoever has a mind to see it, may read his 146th Epistle, where he expounds the parable of the Prodigal Son:‡ or let him but turn to the discourse which

* Epiphan. in Panar. Hær. 78. Antidicom.
† Perron's Repl. p. 743.
‡ Hier. in ep. 146, ad Damas. pæne tot.

he has made on the genealogy of the prophet Zephaniah, and concerning the city of Damascus,* and also upon the history of Abishag the Shunamite,† and upon the five-and-twenty men and the two princes spoken of in Ezekiel, chap. xi.‡ and upon the destruction of Tyre, of Egypt,§ and of Assyria,|| foretold by the same prophet: as also his subtle obversations upon the Numbers, and upon king Darius,¶ and upon that command of our Saviour Christ,** where he bids us turn the left cheek to him that hath smitten us on the right: and many other the like discourses of his.

Hilary is so much taken with this manner of writing, that his expositions upon the Scripture are half full of these allegories,†† and to make himself the more work, he sometimes frames certain impossibilities and absurdities which he would make the Scripture seem to be guilty of, which yet it is not; only that he may have some pretence to have recourse to his allegories.‡‡ As for example, in the 136th Psalm, he will needs have the letter of the text to be utterly inexplicable, where it says, that the Jews sat down by the rivers of Babylon, and hanged up their harps upon the willows: as if in this country that was watered by the Tigris and Euphrates, there had been neither river, nor willow, nor any aquatic tree. He also demands,§§ (as if it had been a most indissoluble question, if taken in the literal sense,) who the "daughter of Babylon" is; and why she is called "miserable;" which is so easy a question, that any child almost might very easily resolve it, without torturing the text with allegories. So likewise, in his exposition of the 146th

* Hier. Com. in Soph.
† Id. ep. ad Nepot.
‡ Hier. Comm. 3. in Ezech.
§ Id. Comm. 8. in Ezech.
|| Id. Comm. 9. in eundem.
¶ Id. Comm. 10. in eund.
** Id. Comm. in Agg.
†† Id. Comm. 1. in Matth.
‡‡ Hilar. in Ps. 136.
§§ Id. ibid. fol. 108.

Psalm, he understands by the clouds, wherewith God is said to cover the heavens, the writings of the prophets; and by the rain, which he prepares for the earth, the evangelical doctrine; by the mountains which bring forth grass, the Prophets and Apostles; by the beasts, he understands men; and by the young ravens, the Gentiles; assuring us withal, that it would not only be erroneous, but rather very irreligious to take these words in a literal sense.* May not this be called rather trifling with than expounding the Scriptures? So likewise in another place, speaking of the fowls of the air, which our Saviour said neither reaped nor gathered into barns, he understands, by these, the devils; and by the lilies of the field, which spin not, the angels.†

I should much abuse the reader's patience, if I should set down the strange discourses he has upon the story of the two possessed with devils, who were healed by our Saviour, in the country of the Gergesenes; and upon the leap which the devils made the neighbouring herd of swine take into the sea;‡ and of the swine-herds running away into the city, and of the citizens coming forth, and entreating our Saviour to depart out of their coasts: or if I should but give you the whole exposition which he has made of these words of Matthew x. 29: "are not two sparrows sold for a farthing?" &c.§ where, by the two sparrows he understands sinners, whose souls and bodies, which were created to fly upward and to mount on high, sell themselves to sin for mere trifles and things of no value; by this means becoming both as one, the soul by sin thickening as it were into a body; with such other wild fancies, the reading of which would astonish a man of any judgment rather than edify him.

* Hæc ita intelligere, non dicam erroris, sed irreligiositatis est. —*Hilar. in Psal.* 146. *fol.* 128.

† Id. Can. 5. in Matth. vi. 26. fol. 7.

‡ Id. Can. 8. in Matth. viii. 28. fol. 10.

§ Id. Can. 10. fol. 13.

Neither is Ambrose a whit more serious, when expounding those words of our Saviour, Matth. xvii. 20: "If ye have faith as a grain of mustard seed, ye shall say to this mountain, Remove hence to yonder place," &c.* "By this mountain (saith Ambrose) is meant the devil." It would be too tedious a business to set down here at length all that might be collected of this nature out of Ambrose: he that has a mind to see more examples of this kind, may read but his homilies upon the 118th Psalm; which will indeed be otherwise very well worth any man's reading, as being a very excellent one, and full of eloquence and sound doctrine. Yet a man would find it a troublesome business to make any defence for him, where he ventures sometimes to use the sacred words of the Scripture in his own sportive fancies: as where he applies to Valentinian and Gratian that which is spoken of Christ and the Church in the Canticles: "O that thou wert as my brother that sucked the breasts of my mother! When I should find thee without, I would kiss thee, &c. I would lead thee, and bring thee into my mother's house, &c. I would cause thee to drink of spiced wine, and of the juice of my pomegranates. His left hand should be under my head, and his right hand should embrace me." "In this place," says he, "is meant the emperor Gratian, of renowned memory, who tells his brother that he is furnished with the fruits of divers virtues."† To the same purpose does he make application of divers other passages of this sacred Canticle; and with such great license, as, to say the truth, no poet ever launched out with more liberty and freedom than he has done in that book.

* Si habueritis fidem sicut granum sinapis, dicetis huic monti, Tollere et jactare in mare. Huic; Cui? Dæmonio inquit, a quo iste invasus fuerat, &c.—*Ambros. in Ps.* 36. *p.* 503. *Matth.* xvii. 20.

‡ Promittit fratri augustæ memoriæ Gratianus, præsto sibi fructus diversarum esse virtutum.—*Id. tract. de Obit. Valent. p.* 11, 12.

I shall here purposely pass by what I might produce of this nature, out of Gregory Nazianzen, Augustine, and almost all the rest of the Fathers: for what we have already brought is enough, and indeed more than we needed for our present purpose. Let the reader therefore now judge whether or not the Fathers, by this their manner of writing, have not clearly enough attested against themselves, that their intention, when they wrote these their books, never was either to bound and determine our faith, or to decide our differences about the same. I must needs confess, that they were persons who were endued with very large gifts of the Spirit; and with a most lively and clear understanding for diving into the truth. Yet those who have the greatest share of those gifts, have it to very little purpose, if they employ it not to the utmost of their power, when the business they are to treat of is of such great difficulty, and importance; and such as to the deciding and discussing of which we can never bring enough attention or diligence.

Now that the Fathers have not observed this course in their writings, appears clearly enough by what has been formerly said. Their books therefore are not to be received by us, either as definitive sentences, or final judgments upon our present controversies.

I confess that these trivial errors ought not to lessen the opinion we have of the greatness and power of their minds. I believe they might very easily have avoided falling into them, if they would but have taken a little pains. And I am of opinion that they fell into them merely by inadvertency only; which may also sometimes happen even to the greatest masters in any sciences whatever. I shall as willingly also yield to you, (if you desire it,) that they have sometimes done these things purposely; letting fall here and there throughout their writings such little slips from their pen, sportively and by way of recreation; or else from a design of exercising our ingenuity. But certainly, whatever the reason was, seeing that they had no intention to use any more care or diligence in the composing of their books, we may very well, and indeed we ought to conclude from hence, that they had never any intention that these books of theirs should be our judges.

These venial faults, these mistakes, these oversights, these inadvertencies, and these sportings of theirs, do sufficiently evidence, that we are to make our references to others; and that they have not so seriously delivered their opinions as if they had sat on the seat of judgment, but rather have spoken as in their chamber, delivering their own private opinions only, and not in the capacity of judges.

These considerations, joined to what has been said in this particular, by some of the chief and most eminent among themselves, as we have formerly shown, make it appear in my judgment evident enough, that their own will and desire is, that we should not embrace their opinions as oracles, or receive them as definitive decisions; but that we should rather examine them by the Scriptures and by reason: as being the opinions of doctors, who were indeed very able and excellent men; but yet, were still men, subject to error, and who were not always able to see what was true and sound: and who peradventure, even in this very case in hand, have not always done what they might, by reason of their employing either less time, or less care and diligence, than they would have done, if they had had any serious purpose of doing their utmost endeavour in this particular.

CHAPTER IV.

Reason IV.—That the Fathers have erred in divers points of religion; not only singly, but also many of them together.

I conceive that what has been stated in the two preceding chapters is sufficient to make it appear to any moderate man, that the authority of the Fathers in matters of religion is not so great as people commonly imagine it to be. Thou therefore, whosoever thou art, if thou be but an indifferent and impartial reader, mayest omit the reading of this and the following chapter; both which I must add, though much against my will, to answer all objections that may yet be made by perverse and obstinate persons. For the prejudice wherewith they are beforehand possessed, may hinder them perhaps from seeing the clearness of reason, and from hearing the voice of the Fathers themselves; whose words they perhaps will be ready to impute to their modesty, rather than consent to yield to them no more honour than they themselves require. The pertinacity therefore of these men, and not any need that thou hast of my doing so, has constrained me to lay aside some of that respect that I bear towards antiquity; and has obliged me to expose to view some errors of the Fathers, which are of much more importance than the former, if by this means at least I may be able to overcome their opposition. For when they shall but see that the Fathers have erred in many considerable points, I hope they will at length confess, that they had very good reason gravely to advise us, not to believe, or take upon trust, any of their opinions, unless we find that they are grounded either upon the Scriptures, or else upon some other truth.

I confess, I enter upon this inquiry very unwillingly, as taking very little pleasure in discovering and exposing the infirmities and failings of any men, especially of such as are otherwise worthy of such great esteem and honour: yet there is nothing in the world, however precious or dear it be, that we ought not to disregard, if compared with truth and the edification of men. And I am verily persuaded that even these holy men themselves, were they now alive, would give us thanks for the pains we have taken, in endeavouring to make the world see that they were but men; and would account themselves beholden to us, for having boldly undertaken the business of discovering those imperfections and failings of theirs, which Divine Providence has suffered them to leave behind them in their writings, to the end only that they might serve as so many arguments to us of their humanity. If there be any, notwithstanding, that shall take offence at it, I must entreat them once again to consider that the perverseness only of those men with whom I have to deal, has forced me to this irreverence, (if we are to call it so) together with the desire I have to manifest to the world so important a truth as this is.

If I wished to defend myself by precedents, I could here make use of that of cardinal Perron;* who, to justify the Church of Rome's interdicting the reading of the Bible to any of the laity, except only such as should have express permission, scruples not to expose to the view of the world, not all the *faults*, for there are none; but all the *false appearances of faults* that are found in the Bible, writing a whole chapter expressly on the subject. How much more lawfully then may we adventure here to expose to public view some few of the failings of the Fathers, to whom we owe infinitely less respect than to God; if it be only to moderate a little that excessive devotion which

* Du Perron, Repliq. l. 6, c. 6, p. 949.

most men bear towards their writings; that so the one party may be persuaded to seek out for some other weapons, than the authority of these men, for the defence of their opinions; and that the other party may not so easily be induced to regard the bare testimony of antiquity?

It was the saying of a great prince long ago, that the vilest and most shameful necessities of his nature, were the things that most clearly convinced him that he was a man, and no God, as his flattering courtiers would needs have made him believe he was. Seeing therefore that it behoves us so much to know that the Fathers were but men, let us not be afraid to produce here this argument so clear and evident of their humanity. Let us boldly enter into their most hidden secrets, and let us see whatever marks of their humanity they have left us in their writings, that we may no longer adore their authority, as if it were divine.

Yet I protest here before I begin, that I will not take any advantage of the many proofs of their human passions which we meet with, partly in their own writings, and partly in the histories of their life. I wish rather, that all of this kind might be buried in an eternal oblivion, and that we would speak of them as of persons that were most accomplished for purity and innocence of life, as far, at least, as the frail condition of human nature can bear. I shall only touch upon the errors of their belief, and those things wherein they have failed, not in living but in writing.

The most ancient of them all is Justin Martyr; a man renowned in all ancient histories for his great knowledge, both in religion and philosophy; and also for the fervency of his zeal, which he so evidently manifested, by his suffering a glorious martyrdom for our Saviour Jesus Christ. Yet for all this, how many opinions do we meet with in his books, which are either very trivial, or else manifestly false? Only hear how he speaks of the last times immediately preceding the day of judgment and the end of the world:—"As for me (says he) and the rest of us that are true Christians, we know that there shall be a resurrection of the flesh, and that the saints shall spend a thousand years in Jerusalem, which shall be rebuilt, enriched, and enlarged, as the prophets Ezekiel, Isaiah, and others assure us. *Ἐγω δε και εἰ τινες εἰσιν ὀρθογνωμονες κατα παντα Χριστιανοι, και σαρκος αναστασιν γενησεσθαι ἐπισταμεθα και χιλια ἐτη ἐν Ἱερουσαλημ οἰκοδομηθειση, και κοσμηθειση και πλατυνθειση*, &c.*

To this purpose he cites what is written, Isaiah lxv., and besides, that other passage in the Revelation, where it is said, "That those which had believed in Christ, should live and reign with him a thousand years in Jerusalem; and that after this there should be a general and final resurrection and judgment." *Χιλια ἐτη ποιησειν ἐν Ἱερουσαλημ τους τω ἡμετερω Χριστω πιστευσαντας*, &c.; *και μετα ταυτα, την καθολικην, και συνελοντι φαναι, αιωνιαν ὁμοθυμαδον ἁμα παντων ἀναστασιν γενησεσθαι, και κρισιν.*† In these words you see plainly that he holds with the Millennarians, that the saints shall reign a thousand years in Jerusalem, before the resurrection be perfectly accomplished: which is an opinion that is at this day condemned as erroneous, by the whole Western Church, both on the one side and on the other. He seems, in another place, to have held that the essence of God was finite, and was not present in all places; where he endeavours to prove against a Jew that it was not the Father who rained fire and brimstone upon Sodom, because that he could not then have been at that time in heaven. *Ἐπει ἐαν μη οὑτω νοησωμεν τας γραφας συμβησεται τον πατερα και κυριον*

* Justin. contr. Tryph. p. 307. † Id. p. 307.

των ὁλων μη γεγενησθαι τοτε ἐν τοις οὐρανοις, ὁτε δια Μωσεως λελεκται, και Κυριος ἐβρεξεν ἐπι Σοδομα, &c.*

That which he has delivered concerning the angels is altogether as senseless, though not so dangerous; namely, "That God having in the beginning committed to them the care and providence over men, and all sublunary things, they had broken this order, by suffering themselves to be overcome by the love of women, by associating with whom had been also born children, which are those we now call *demons*, or *devils*." *Την μεν των ἀνθρωπων, και των ὑπο τον οὐρανον προνοιαν ἀγγελοις, οὑς ἐπι τουτοις ἐταξε, παρεδωκεν· Οἱ δε ἀγγελοι παραβαντες τηνδε την ταξιν, γυναικων μιξισιν ἡττηθησαν, και παιδας ἐτεκνωσαν, οἱ εἰσιν οἱ λεγομενοι Δαιμονες.*†

I know not either whether Justin will be able easily to convert any one to that other opinion of his, where he says that "all the souls of the saints, and of the prophets, had fallen under the power of evil spirits, such as were the spirits of *Python;* and that this was the reason why our Saviour Christ, being ready to give up the ghost, recommended his spirit to God:" *Φαινεται δε και ὁτι πασαι αἱ ψυχαι των οὑτως δικαιων, και προφητων, ὑπο ἐξουσιαν ἐπιπτον των τοιουτων δυναμεων*, &c. . . . . *Και γαρ ἀποδιδους το πνευμα ἐπι τω σταυρω, εἰπε, Πατερ, εἰς χειρας σου παρατιθεμαι το πνευμα μου:*‡ I pray you tell me, out of what part of God's word he learned this doctrine, which he delivers in his second Apology; where he says, "that all those who lived according to the rule of reason were Christians, notwithstanding that they might have been accounted as Atheists; such as among the Greeks were Socrates, Heraclitus, and the like; and among the Barbarians, Abraham and Azarias." *Καί οἱ μετα λογου βιωσαντες Χριστιανοι*

* Justin contr. Tryph. p. 283 et 357.
† Id. in Apol. pro Christ. ad Senat. p. 44.
‡ Id. contr. Tryph. p. 333.

εισιν κἂν ἄθεοι ἐνομισθησαν· οἷον ἐν Ἑλλησι μεν Σωκρατης, και Ἡρακλειτος και οἱ ὁμοιοι αὐτοις· ἐν βαρβαροις δε Ἀβρααμ, &c.* He repeats the same doctrine within a few lines afterwards, and says that "all those who lived, or do now live, according to the rule of reason, are Christians, and are in an assured, quiet condition." *Οἱ δε μετα λογου βιωσαντες και βιουντες, Χριστιανοι, και ἀφοβοι, και ἀταραχοι ὑπαρχουσι.*†

Irenæus, bishop of Lyons, who lived very near Justin's time, was also of the same opinion with him, as to the state of the soul after it was once departed from the body, till the hour of judgment. For, towards the conclusion of that excellent book of his, which he wrote against Heresies, after he has told us that our Saviour Christ had descended into hell, or the place of departed spirits, which place he opposes to the light of this world, he further adds, that "It is evident that the souls of the disciples of our Saviour, for the love of whom he did all these things, shall go also into a certain invisible place, which is provided for them by God, there to expect the resurrection; and shall afterwards resume their bodies, and be raised up again in all perfection; that is to say, corporeally, in the same manner as our Saviour was raised up again, and so shall they come into the presence of God."§ This opinion he opposes against that of the Valentinians and Gnostics, which he had before produced in the beginnng of that chapter of his, who held that the souls of men, immediately after they had departed out of the body, were carried up above the heavens and the Creator of the world; and went to that Mother or that Father which these here-

* Justin. Apol. 2, p. 83. † Idem.

§ Manifestum est, quia et discipulorum ejus, propter quos et hæc operatus èst Dominus, animæ abibunt in invisibilem locum, definitum eis à Deo, et ibi usque ad resurrectionem commorabuntur, sustinentes resurrectionem, &c.—*Iren. l.* 5, *contr. Hæres c.* 26.

tics had fancied to themselves. This opinion of theirs is in like manner rejected by Justin Martyr, in the passage a little before quoted out of his book against Tryphon.* Whence it plainly appears (that we may not trouble ourselves to produce any other proofs) that Justin and Irenæus were both of the same belief as to the state of the soul after death.

But to return to Irenæus. In his second book against Heretics, he maintains very strongly, that "our Saviour Christ was above forty years of age, when he suffered death for us:"† alleging in defence of this opinion of his, which so manifestly contradicts the evangelical history, certain probabilities only; as, "that our Saviour passed through all ages, as having come to the world to sanctify and save people of all ages;" urging also those words of the Jews to our Saviour, "thou art not yet fifty years old, and hast thou seen Abraham?"‡ In conclusion he says that "St. John had delivered it by tradition, to the priests of Asia, that Christ was somewhat aged when he began to preach, being then about the age of forty or fifty years." This fancy of his appeared so ridiculous to cardinal Baronius, that (nothwithstanding the faith of all the copies of his Father, and the context, which appears evidently to be his, together with the vein and marks of his fancy and style,) he has had the confidence to say, that this whole passage had been foisted into the text of Irenæus, either by some ignorant or some malicious person, and that it was not Irenæus's own.§ But it seems he had no great reason for his suspicion; as the Jesuit Petavius has clearly made it appear in his notes upon Epiphanius.||

However, you may hence perceive that Baronius thinks that very possible which we have endeavoured

* Justin. contra Tryph. p. 307.
† Iren. cont. Hær. l. 2. c. 39.
‡ John viii. 57.
§ Baron. Annal. t. 1. an. 34. num. 137.
|| Petav. in Epiphan. p. 145.

to prove in the former part of this treatise; namely, that there may possibly have been very many and great alterations and corruptions in the books of the writers of the first ages, by many passages and clauses having been either inserted in them, or else maliciously erased out of them.

Irenæus holds and endeavours to prove in the same book, "that the souls of men, after death, retain the character (that is to say, the figure) of the bodies to which they were formerly united, and that they represent the shape of the said bodies, so that they can be recognized."*

I shall here pass by that which Irenæus seems to mean in the forty-ninth chapter of the same book, that our Saviour Christ did not at all know when the day of judgment should be, according to either of his natures; although these words of his look as if they would very hardly be reconciled to any good meaning. Nor shall I yet take notice of what both he and Justin Martyr have in divers places so rashly averred, as regards the strength of human nature, in the business of salvation;† because I conceive with Cassander,‡ that all those passages may, and indeed ought to be understood, with respect to the scope and drift of these authors; whose business was to confute those heretics of their time, who maintained that there was a fatal necessity in the actions of men, by this means depriving them of all manner of election or judgment.

The great learning of Clemens Alexandrinus has not prevented him from falling into many errors: as for instance, where in divers places he says plainly, "that the heathen, who lived before the coming of

* Animas, &c. characterem corporis, in quo etiam adaptantur custodire eundem; et animas hominis habere figuram ut etiam cognoscantur.—*Iren. l.* 2. *contra Hær. c.* 62, 63.

† Iren. contr. Hær. l. 2. c. 49.

‡ Cassand. in defens. libelli de Offic. Pii Viri.

our Saviour Christ, were *justified* by philosophy, which was then necessary for them, whereas it is now only useful to them; and that this philosophy was the schoolmaster of the Gentiles, which brought them to Christ, or served to guide them till the time of his coming, in like manner as the law did the Jews; and that the Greeks were justified by it alone; and that it was given to them as their covenant, being a step to, and as it were a foundation laid for, Christian philosophy. *Ἠν μεν οὐν προ της του Κυριου παρουσιας εἰς δικαιοσυνην Ἑλλησιν ἀναγκαια φιλοσοφια, νυν δε χρησιμη προς θεοσεβειαν γινεται. . . . Ἐπαιδαγωγει γαρ και αὐτη το Ἑλληνικον, ὡς ὁ νομος τους Ἑβραιους εἰς Χριστον.* Clem. Alex. Strom. lib. 1. *Καθ' ἑαυτην ἐδικαιου ποτε και ἡ φιλοσοφια τους Ἑλληνας.* Ibid. p. 117. *Την δε φιλοσοφιαν και μαλλον Ἑλλησιν οἱον διαθηκην οἰκειαν, αὐτοις δεδοσθαι, ὑποβαθριαν οὐσαν της κατα Χριστον φιλοσοφιας.*—Id. lib. 6, Strom. p. 279.

Clemens was of opinion also, "that our Saviour went down into hell, to preach the gospel to the departed souls;" and that he saved many of them; that is, all that believed: "and that the Apostles also, after their death, descended likewise into the same place, and for the same purpose;" conceiving that God otherwise would have been unjust and an acceptor of persons, if he had condemned all those who died before the coming of his Son. "For (says he) if he preached to the living to the end they might not be condemned unjustly; why should he not, for the same reason, preach also to those who were departed this life before his coming? *Καθαπερ Ἰουδαιους σωζεσθαι ἐβουλετο ὁ θεος, τους προφητας διδους, οὑτως και Ἑλληνων τους δοκιμωτατους, οἰκειους αὐτων τῃ διαλεκτῳ προφητας ἀναστησας.* Id. p. 268. *Ὁ Κυριος εὐηγγελισατο και τοις εν ἀδου,* &c. Id. Strom. lib. 6, p. 269. *Και οἱ Αποστολοι καθαπερ ἐνταυθα, οὑτως κἀκει* (*in inferis*) *τους των ἐθνων ἐπιτηδειους εἰς ἐπιστροφην εὐηγγελισαντο.* Clem. Alex. Strom. lib. 6, p. 267. *Ἰησους δε τοινυν τους ἐν σαρκι δια τουτο εὐηγγελισατο, ἱνα μη καταδικασθωσιν ἀδικως· πως οὐν τους προεξεληλυθοτας της παρουσιας αὐτου δια την αὐτην ἐυηγγελισατο αἰτιαν.*—Ibid. p. 271.

From these and the like considerations, Clemens concludes, that it was necessary that the souls of all the departed, Gentiles as well as Jews, should have heard the preaching of our Saviour, "and should have had the benefit of the same dispensation, which he used towards others upon earth, in order either to their salvation, through repentance, or their just condemnation for their impenitency." *Τι οὐν οὐχι και ἐν ἁδου ἡ αὐτη γεγονεν οἰκονομια, ἱνα κἀκει πασαι αἱ ψυχαι ἀκουσασαι αὐτου κηρυγματος, ἡ την μετανοιαν ἐνδειξωνται, ἡ την κολασιν δικαιαν εἰναι, δἰ ὡν οὐκ ἐπιστευσαν, ὁμολογησωσιν.**

He plainly maintains also, in several places of his works, that all the punishments, which God inflicts upon men tend to their salvation, and are sent them for their instruction and amendment; comprehending also within this number even those very pains which the damned endure in hell. Hence it is, that he somewhere also affirms that wicked men are to be purged by fire; and to this does he refer the conflagration, spoken of by the Stoics; alleging also to this purpose divers passages out of Plato, and out of a certain philosopher of Ephesus, which I conceive to be Heraclitus;† from all of which it clearly appears that he had the same belief as to the pains in hell that his scholar Origen had, who maintains, in an infinite number of places in his works, that the pains of hell are purgative only, and consequently are not eternal, but are to have an end, when the souls of the damned are once thoroughly cleansed and purified by this fire. He believes also, with Justin Martyr, that the angels

* Clem. Alex. Strom. lib. 6, p. 270. † Id. Strom. l. 5, p. 227.

fell in love with the first women, and that this love of theirs transported them so far, as to make them indiscreetly to discover to them many secrets which they ought to have concealed:—*Οἱ ἀγγελοι ἐκεινοι οἱ την ἀνω κληρον εἰληχοτες, καθολισθησαντες εἰς ἡδονας, ἐξειπον τα ἀπορρητα ταις γυναιξιν*, &c.*

Clemens, quite contrary to Irenæus, who maintains that our Saviour Christ lived upon the earth to the age of fifty† years, will have him to have preached in the flesh but one year only, and to have died in the thirty-first year of his age—*Οὑτω πληρουται τα τριακοντα ἐτη ἑως οὑ ἐπαθε.*‡

But since it is confessed by both parties, that there are many absurd tenets in this author, I shall not dwell any longer upon him.

As for Tertullian, I confess the fact of his turning *Montanist* has taken away very much of the repute which he before had in the Church, both for the fervency of his piety and for his incomparable learning. But besides that a part of his works were written while he was yet a Catholic, we are also to notice, that his *Montanism* put no separation between him and other Christians, except in point of discipline, which he, according to the austerity of his nature, chose to be most harsh and rigorous. As for his doctrine, he often declares that he constantly kept to the very same rule, and the same faith that the Catholics did:§ whence proceeded that tart speech of his, "That people rejected Montanus, Maximilla, and Priscilla, not because they had anywhat departed from the rule of faith, but rather because they would have us to fast oftener than to marry."|| And this is

* Clem. Alex. Strom. lib. 5. p. 227.

† [The Latin copy of Daillé has *forty*, the French *fifty*.—Am. Ed.]

‡ Clem. Alex. Strom. p. 127.

§ Vid. lib. de Mon. cap. 2, &c. et l. contr. Psych. cap. 1.

|| Si paracleto controversiam faciunt propter hoc, prophetiæ novæ recusantur, non quòd alium Deum prædicant Montanus, et Pris-

evident enough, from all those books which were written by him, during the time of his being a Montanist; wherein he never disputes or contends about anything, except about discipline. This is ingenuously confessed also, by the learned Rigault, in his preface to those nine books which he has lately published.*

Now, notwithstanding the great repute which this Father had in the Church, and his not departing from it in anything, in point of faith; yet how many wild opinions and fancies do we meet with in his books! I shall here speak only of some of the principal of them, passing by his dangerous expressions on the person of the Son of God, as having touched upon this particular before. But how strange is his manner of discourse on the nature of God,† whom he seems to render subject to the like passions with us; as to anger, hatred, and grief! He attributes also to him a corporeal substance, and "does not believe (as he says) that any man will deny that God is a body;"‡ so that we need wonder the less that he so confidently affirms, "that there is no substance which is not corporeal:"§ or that, with Justin Martyr and Clemens Alexandrinus, he attributes to the evangelical nature the carnal love of women:|| which occasioned those words in that book of his, "*De Virginibus Velandis*,"—where he says, "that it is necessary that so

cilla, et Maximilla, &c., sed quòd planè doceant sæpiùs jejunare, quàm nubere.—*Id. contr. Psych.* c. 10.

* Nicol. Rigaltius Prolog. in animad. ad Tertul. 9. Tract. Lutet. 1628.

† Tertul. l. 1, adv. Marc. c. 25, et l. 2, c. 16.

‡ Quis negabit, Deum corpus esse, etsi spiritus est?—*Id. adv. Orig. cap.* 7, *et l.* 2, *contra. Marc. c.* 16.

§ Cùm ipsa substantia corpus sit cujusque.—*Ib. lib. adv. Hermog. c.* 35.

|| Angelos esse illos desertores Dei, amatores fœminarum.—*Id. l. de Idol. cap.* 9.

dangerous a face should be veiled, which had scandalized even heaven itself."*

We need not, after this, wonder at his doctrine on the nature of man's soul, which he will have to be corporeal, and endued with form and figure, and to be propagated, and derived from the substance of the father, to the body of the son, and sowed and engendered with the body, increasing and extending itself together with it;† and many other the like dreams; in the maintaining of which he uses so much subtlety, force, and eloquence, that you will through the whole range of antiquity, scarce meet with a more excellent and more elegant piece than this book of his, *De Anima.* He also, with Irenæus, shuts up the souls of men, after they are departed this life, in a certain subterraneous place, where they are to remain till the day of judgment; the heavens not being to be opened to any of the faithful till the end of the world: only he allows the martyrs their entrance into Paradise, which he fancies to be some place beneath the heavens; and here he will have them continue till the last day. "It is thy blood (says he) which is the only key of Paradise."‡ And this place, whither the souls of the departed go, is, according to him, to continue shut up till the end of the world. He is besides of a contrary opinion to that of Justin Martyr, spoken of before; and maintains that all apparitions of the deceased are mere illusions and deceits of the devil; and that this inclosure of the souls of men shall continue till such time as the city of the New Jerusalem, which is to be all of precious stones, shall descend

* Debet et adumbrari facies tam periculosa, quæ usque ad cœlum scandala jaculata est.—*Id. de Virg. Veland. cap.* 7.

† Definimus animum dici statu naturam immortalem, corporalem, effigiatam, &c., et unà redundantem, &c.—*Ibid. lib. de. Anim. passim: nominatim c.* 22.

‡ Quo (in inferis) spes omnis sequestratur, tota Paradisi clavis sanguis tuus est. Nulli patet cœlum, terrâ adhuc salvâ, ne dixerim clausâ.—*Id. lib. de an. c.* 55, 56, 57, 58.

miraculously from heaven upon the earth, and shall there continue a thousand years, the saints long living therein in very great glory; and that during this space the resurrection of the faithful is to be accomplished by degrees; some of them rising up sooner, and some later, according to the difference of their merits.* Hence we are to interpret what he says in another place, "that small sins shall be punished in men by the lateness of their resurrection:"† and, "that when the thousand years are expired, and the destruction of the world, and the conflagration of the day of judgment is passed, we shall all be changed in a moment into the nature of angels."‡

I pass by his invectives against second marriages, and also his opinion against all marriage in general; these fancies being a part of the discipline of Montanus's Paraclete. But as to his opinions on the *baptism of heretics*, he has many fellows among the Catholic Fathers, who held the same; namely, that their baptism signified nothing: and therefore he never received any heretic into the communion of the Catholic Church, without first rebaptizing him—"cleansing him (says he) both in the one and in the other man; that is to say, both in body and soul, by the baptism of the truth, accounting an heretic to be in the same, or rather in a worse, condition than any pagan."§ As to others, he is so far from pressing

* Nam et confitemur in terra nobis regnum repromissum post resurrectionem in mille annos in civitate divini operis, Hierusalem cœlo delata, &c. inter quam ætatem (1000 annorum) concluditur sanctorum resurrectio, pro meritis maturius, vel tardius resurgentium.—*Id. lib. adv. Marc. c.* 24.

† Modicum quoque delictum morâ resurrectionis illic luendum. —*Id. l. de. An. c.* 58.

‡ Post cujus mille annos, &c., tunc et mundi destructione, et judicii conflagratione commissâ, demutari in atomo in angelicam substantiam; scilicet per illud incorruptionis superindumentum transferemur in cœleste regnum, &c.—*Id. lib. adv. Marc. c.* 29.

§ Apud nos ut ethnico par, imo et super ethnicum hæreticus etiam per baptisma veritatis utroque homine purgatus admittitur.—*Tertul. l. de Bapt. adv. Quint. c.* 15.: *et de Pudic. c.* 19.

men to the baptizing of their children while they are young, which yet is the custom of these times; that he allows, and indeed persuades to the contrary; not only in children, but even in persons of riper years; counselling them to defer it, every man according to his condition, disposition, and age.* And as his opinion, in this particular, is not much different from that of the Anabaptists of our time; so does he not much dissent from them in some other matters. For he will not allow, no more than they do, that a Christian should take upon him or execute any office of judicature, or "that he should condemn, or bind, or imprison, or torture any man;" or that he should make war upon any, or serve in war under any other; saying expressly, "that our Saviour Christ, by disarming Peter, hath from henceforth taken off every soldier's belt:"† which is as much as to say, that the discipline of Christ allows not of the profession of soldiery. From which I cannot but wonder at the confidence (or rather the inadvertency) of some who would persuade us, from a certain passage of this author,‡ which themselves have very much mistaken, that this innocent and peaceable Father maintained, that heretics are to be punished, and to be suppressed by inflicting on them temporal punishments: which rigorous proceeding was as far from his thoughts as heaven is from earth.

I shall add here, before I proceed further, that Tertullian held that our Saviour Christ suffered death in

* Itaque pro cujusque personæ conditione, ac dispositione, etiam ætate cunctatio baptismi utilior est, &c.—*Id. l. de Baptism. cap.* 18.

† Jam verò quæ sunt potestatis, neque judicet de capite alicujus, vel pudore, (feras enim de pecunia,) neque damnet, neque prædamnet, neminem vinciat, neminem recludat, aut torqueat, &c. omnem postea militem Dominus in Petro exarmando discinxit.—*Id. lib. de Idol. c.* 17. *et* 19, *&c. et lib.* 1, *de Cor. Mil. c.* 11.

‡ Pamel, in Scap. Tertul. c. 2. num. 15. et in l. ad Scap. c. 2, num. 7.

the thirtieth year of his age,"* which is manifestly contrary to the Gospel. He thought also that the heavenly grace and prophecy ceased in John the Baptist,† after the fulness of the Spirit was transferred to our Saviour Christ.

Cyprian, who was Tertullian's very great admirer, calling him absolutely, *the master*, and who never let any day pass over his head without reading something of him,‡ has confidently maintained some of the aforesaid opinions; among others that of the nullity of baptism by heretics, which he defends everywhere very strongly, having also the most eminent men of his time consenting with him in this point; as Firmilianus, metropolitan of Cappadocia,§ Dionysius, bishop of Alexandria,|| together with the councils of Africa, Cappadocia, Pamphilia, and Bithynia, notwithstanding all the anger and the excommunication also of Stephen, bishop of Rome, who for his own part held a particular opinion of his own, allowing the baptism of all kinds of heretics, without re-baptizing any of them; as it appears by the beginning of the 74th epistle of St. Cyprian;¶ whereas the Church, about sixty-five years after, at the council of Nice declared null the baptism of the Samosatenians, permitting, as it seems, all other heretics whatsoever to be received into the Church without being re-baptized. *Περι των Παυλιανισαντων, και προσφυγοντων τη καθολικη*

* Christus annos habens quasi triginta cùm pateretur, &c.—*Tertul. lib. adv. Jud. Cap.* 8.

† Id. de Bapt. adver. Quint. cap. 10.

‡ Vidi ego quondam Paulum, &c. qui se B. Cypriani, &c. Notarium, &c. Romæ vidisse diceret, referrique sibi solitum, nunquam Cyprianum absque Tertulliani lectione unum diem præterisse, ac sibi crebro dicere, Da magistrum, Tertullianum videlicet significans.—*Hiero. l. de Script. Eccles. in Tertul.*

§ Cypr. Ep. 74. ad Steph. et alibi passim.

|| Firmil. Ep. 75. inter. Ep. Cypr.

¶ Hieron. lib. de Script. Eccles.

*ἐκκλησια· ὁρος ἐκτιθηται ἀναβαπτιζεσθαι αυτυς ἐξαπαντος.**

The Fathers of the second general council went yet further, re-baptizing all those just as they would have done Pagans, who came in from the communion either of the Eunomians, Montanists, Phrygians, or Sabellians; or indeed any other heretics whatsoever, except the Arians, Macedonians, Sabbatians, Novatians, Quartodecimani, and Apollinarians; all which they received without re-baptization, as you may see in the Greek copies of the said council, canon seventh; which canon also appears in the Greek code of the Church Universal, Num. 170.

Thus you see that Stephen and Cyprian maintained each of them their own particular opinion in this point; the one of them admitting, and the other utterly rejecting the baptism of all kinds of heretics: whereas the two aforenamed general councils neither admitted nor rejected, save only the baptism of certain heretics only. Cyprian however seems to have dealt herein much more fairly than his adversary; seeing that he patiently endured those who were of the contrary opinion;† as it appears clearly by the Synod of Carthage, and as it is also proved by Jerome:‡ whereas Stephen, according to his own hot choleric temper, declared publicly against Firmilianus's opinion,§ and excommunicated all those that differed from himself.||

The same blessed martyr of our Saviour Jesus Christ was also carried away with that error of his time, on the necessity of administering the sacrament

* Con. Nic. Can. 19.—Si quis ergo a quacunque hæresi venerit ad nos, nihil innovetur, nisi quod traditum est, ut manus illi imponatur ad pœnitentiam, &c.—*Cypr. ep.* 74. *init. ubi referuntur hæc Stephani verba.*

† Neminem judicantes, aut a jure communionis aliquem, si diversum senserit, amoventes.—*Cypr. Præ. Conc. Carth.*

‡ Hier. contra Lucifer. t. 2, p. 197, &c.

§ Firmil. ep. ad Cypr. quæ est 75, inter. ep. Cypr. p. 204.

|| Cypr. ep. 74, p. 194, et ep. 75, quæ est Firmil.

of the holy eucharist to all persons when they were baptized, and even to infants also; as appears by his 59th epistle,* where, by the suffrages of sixty-five other bishops, he admits infants to baptism and the Lord's Supper, as soon as they were born; contrary to the opinion of one Fidus, who would not admit them to these sacraments till the eighth day after they were born:—and also by that story of his which he tells us of a certain young girl, who being not as yet of years to speak, by a remarkable miracle put back the liquor which had been consecrated for the blood of our Saviour, and was presented to her by a deacon to drink in the church; as judging herself unworthy to receive it, by reason that not long before she had been carried to the celebration of some certain pagan sacrifices.

Now the original of this error of theirs was the belief they had, that the eucharist was as necessary to salvation as baptism; as may easily be collected out of the words of the said author. Having first laid it down as the groundwork, "that no man can come into the kingdom of God, unless he be baptized and regenerated:"† he produces for a proof hereof, first that passage out of the third chapter of John, where it is said, "except a man be born of water and of the Spirit, he cannot enter into the kingdom of God," &c.: and again, "except ye eat the flesh of the Son of man, and drink his blood, ye have no life in you:" urging the first of these texts to prove the necessity of baptism, and the other, of the eucharist; accounting each of them necessary to regeneration. Hence, it is that we find him speaking so often of being "born again, by virtue of the one and of the other sacra-

* Ut intra octavum diem eum qui natus est baptizandum, et sacrificandum non putares.—*Cypr. ep.* 59, *p.* 137.

† Ad regnum Dei nisi baptizatus, et renatus quis fuerit, pervenire non posse; *in Evang. secundum Joan.—Id. l.* 30. *Quæst. ad Quir.*

ment," by which words he does not mean baptism and confirmation (as some would persuade us,) but rather baptism and the Lord's supper, as is evident from the following words; "It is to very little purpose to be baptized, and to partake of the holy eucharist, unless a man proceed in the good works," &c.*

I shall here pass by some words, which he has sometimes let fall on the baptism of heretics,† from which he seems to make the efficacy of the sacrament depend upon the integrity and sanctity of the person who administers it.

We shall proceed, in the next place, to speak of Origen; but since there have been some since his time, who have very much decried both him and his doctrine, and others again on the other side who have as strongly defended him, we shall forbear to say any thing of him that may engage us in a tedious discussion: we shall only observe, from this example of his, that neither the antiquity, nor the learning or holy life of any man necessarily prevents him falling into very strange and gross errors. For Origen was one of the most ancient among the Fathers, having lived about the middle of the third century; and having been so eminent for those two other excellencies of virtue and learning, that his fiercest adversaries cannot deny that he possessed them both in a very high degree. Neither ought the story of his fall, related by Epiphanius,‡ to disparage the reputation of his virtue; for though perhaps it might have been true, yet has it frequently happened to others of the faithful to fall into great temptations, as appears evidently enough from the example of the apostle Peter himself.

* Parum esse baptizari et eucharistiam accipere, nisi quis factis et opere proficiat, *al.* perficiat.—*Cypr. l.* 30. *c.* 26.

† Quando nec oblatio sanctificare illic possit, ubi Spiritus Sanctus non sit, nec cuiquam Dominus per ejus orationes et preces prosit, qui Dominum ipse violavit.—*Id. ep.* 63.

‡ Epiphan. 64. Hær. quæ est Orig.

But that I may not dissemble, I profess myself much inclined to be of cardinal Baronius's opinion;* who thinks this story to be an arrant fable, maliciously devised by those who envied the fame of this great and admirable man, and that it was foisted into Epiphanius by some such hand; or else (as I rather believe,) was accredited by himself, and foisted into that book of his without any further examination, as many other things have been; in the relating of which this Father has shown himself a little over-credulous, as is truly observed by his last interpreter.†

Yet Origen, notwithstanding all those excellent gifts of his, has not hesitated to broach very many opinions, which by reason of their absurdity have been utterly rejected (and very deservedly so) by the Church in all succeeding ages: which is an evident argument, that however ancient, learned, and holy an author may have been, we ought not at once to believe him, and to urge him as infallible: since there is no reason in the world why the same thing which has befallen Origen in so many points, may not in some or other have also happened to any other author. But of this I am very well assured that those very men who have written against Origen, have not been so thoroughly happy in their undertaking; but while opposing some error of his, have sometimes fallen into as great a one of their own. One of them for example, Methodius by name, as he is cited by Epiphanius, maintains, that after the resurrection and final judgment, we shall dwell for ever upon earth, leading there a holy, blessed, and everlasting life, exercising ourselves in all good things, as the angels do in heaven. He also, as well as the rest, represents the angels as addicted to the love of women; and he will have God's providence to extend itself

* Baron. Annal. ad An. 253, num. 120, 122.
† Petav. Not. ad Hær. 55, p. 217.

only to universal causes, affirming that he has committed the care of particular things to the angels. *Ταραχθησεσθαι μεν γαρ την κτισιν, οὐ μην ἀπολεισθαι προσδοκητεον, ὁπως ἀνακαινοποιηθεντες ἐν ἀνακαινοποιηθεντι κοσμῳ ἀγευστοι λυπης κατοικησωμεν. . . . Ὡσπερ και οἱ μετα ταυτα σαρκων ἐρασθεντες, και ταις των ἀνθρωπων εἰς φιλοκοιτιαν ὁμιλησαντες θυγατρασιν. . . . Ἱνα την μεν παντελικην και γενετικην ἐχων ὁ θεος των ὁλων προνοιαν, την δε δια μερους οἱ ἐπι τουτῳ ταχθεντες ἀγγελοι.**

These opinions of Methodius, if they be thoroughly examined, will be found to be not much less dangerous, and contrary to the Scriptures, than some of those which he reproves in Origen.

For the same reason just assigned, I shall also pass by Eusebius, Didymus, Apollinaris, and others, who though they are ancient authors, yet there is usually little account made of them, by reason of the indifferent opinion the greatest part of the Church had of them. The most ancient Fathers, (although perhaps their faith may not have been much freer from stains than that of others,) have yet been more favourably dealt with by posterity than their brethren; whether it were because, the time they lived in being so far distant from tho ages of our censors of other men, they have so much the less excited their envy and passion; or else because they were willing to spare them, by reason of the high opinion that the Church in general had of them.

Lactantius Firmianus, whose repute was scarcely questioned among the ancients, had, notwithstanding, his errors. For it is long since Jerome observed a very strange one in him, in an epistle that he wrote to Demetrianus; where he denies "that the Holy Ghost is a distinct person in the Godhead, subsisting

* Method. apud Epiphan. in Panar. Hær. 54, quæ est Orig. p. 555.

together with the Father and the Son."* His other errors are not so dangerous, and are indeed common to him, with some other of the Fathers: as where he says, that the angels defiled themselves with women; and that from this their communion with them were born demons, or devils;† as likewise where he teaches, "that the souls of men, after this life, are all shut up together in one common prison, where they are to continue till the day of judgment:"‡ and, "that our Saviour Christ shall come again upon the earth, before the last and final resurrection; and that those who shall then be found alive shall not die at all, but shall be preserved alive, and shall beget an infinite number of children, during the space of a thousand years; living all of them peaceably together, in a most happy city, which shall abound with all good things, under the reign of our Saviour Jesus Christ, and of some of the saints, who shall be raised from the dead."§

But what will you say, if Hilary also himself, who flourished about the middle of the fourth century, has his tares also; which are the more observable in him, in proportion as his estimation was greater among the ancients. The principal and most dangerous of all is that strange opinion which he held on the nature of Christ's body, which he maintained had no sense or feeling of those stripes and torments he suffered:

* Lactantius in libris suis, ut maximè in epistolis ad Demetrianum Spiritus Sancti omninò negat substantiam, et errore Judaico dicit, eum vel ad Patrem referri, vel ad Filium, et sanctificationem utriusque personæ sub ejus nomine demonstrari.—*Hieron. ep.* 65, *ad Pam. et Octav.*

† Lact. Firm. lib. 2. divin. Instit. cap. 15.

‡ Omnes (animæ) in una communique custodia detinentur, donec tempus adveniat, quo maximus Judex meritorum faciat examen.—*Id. lib.* 7, *cap.* 21, *extr.*

§ Tum qui erunt in corporibus vivi, non morientur, sed per eosdem mille annos infinitam multitudinem generabunt, &c., qui autem ab inferis suscitabuntur, ii præibunt viventibus velut Judices.—*Id. lib.* 7, *c.* 24.

"but that he really suffered indeed at that time when he was beaten, and when he was hanged upon the cross, and fastened to it, and died upon it: but that this passion falling wholly upon his body, notwithstanding that it was a real passion, yet did not show upon him the nature of a passion; and that while the furious strokes were dealt upon him, the strength and vigour of his body received the force of the strokes upon it, yet without any sense of pain. I shall confess (says he) that the body of our Saviour had a nature susceptible of our griefs, if the nature of our body be such, as that it is able to tread upon the water, and to walk upon the floods without sinking, or without the waters yielding to our footsteps, when we stand thereon: if it can penetrate solid bodies, or can pass with ease through doors that are shut."* And within two or three lines after he says, "Such is the man sent from God, having a body capable of suffering, (for he really suffered,) but not having a nature capable of pain. When the blows (said he, a little before) fell upon him, or a stripe pierced his skin, it brought indeed with it the violence and impetuosity of passion, but yet it wrought no pain in him; in like manner as when a sword is thrust through and through the water, or through and through the fire, it goes through indeed, and pierces the water or the fire, but it wounds it not; these things having not a nature that may be wounded or hurt, notwithstanding that the nature of the sword be to work the said

* Passus quidem Dominus Jesus Christus dum cæditur, dum suspenditur, dum crucifigitur, dum moritur: sed in corpus irruens passio, nec non fuit passio, nec tamen naturam passionis exercuit, dum et pænali ministerio illa desævit, et virtus corporis sine sensu pœnæ vim pœnæ in se desævientis excepit; habuit sanè illud Domini corpus doloris nostri naturam, si corpus nostrum id naturæ habet, ut calcet undas, et super fluctus eat, et non deprimatur ingressu, neque aquæ insistentis vestigiis cedant: penetret etiam solida, nec clausæ domus obstaculis arceatur.—*Hilar. de Trinit. l.* 10.

effect."* In conclusion, that you may not think this to be a sudden fancy, that he fell on by chance, before he was aware, you must know that he repeats the same thing in divers other places: as in his comment on the fifty-third Psalm: "the passion of Christ (says he) was undergone by him voluntarily, to make an acknowledgment that pains were due; not that he that suffered was at all pained by them."† And again, in another place: "Christ is thought to have felt pain, because he suffered; but he was really free from all pain, because he is God."‡

Only think now, to what all this tends, and what will become of our salvation, if the passion of our Saviour Christ, which is the only foundation whereon it is built, were but a mere imaginary passion, without any sense of pain at all. And, as one absurdity being granted, there will necessarily others always follow upon it, so has this strange peculiar fancy of his made him corrupt and spoil the whole story of our Saviour's passion. For he supposes that in that dismal night, wherein Christ was delivered up for our sins, all his anguish, his distress, and drops of bloody sweat, proceeded not from the consideration of the torments, and the death which he was now going to suffer, (and

* Et homo ille de Deo est, habens ad patiendum quidem corpus, ut passus est; sed naturam non habens ad dolendum. Naturæ enim propriæ ac suæ corpus illud est, quod in cœlestem gloriam transformatur in morte.....In quo quamvis aut ictus inciderit, aut vulnus descenderit, aut nodi concurrerint aut suspensio elevarit, afferunt quidem hæc impetum passionis, non tamen dolorem passionis inferunt: ut telum aliquod, aut aquam perforans, aut ignem compungens, aut aëra vulnerans, omnes quidem has passiones naturæ suæ infert, ut perforet, ut compungat, ut vulneret, sed naturam suam in hæc passio illata non retinet, dum in natura non est vel aquam forari, vel pungi ignem, vel aëra vulnerari, quamvis natura teli sit vulnerare, compungere, et forare.—*Hilar. de Trin. l.* 10.

† Suscepta voluntariè est, (passio) officio quidem ipsa satisfactura pœnali, non tamen pœnæ sensu læsura patientem, &c.—*Hilar. in Ps.* 53.

‡ Putatur dolere, quia patitur; caret verò doloribus ipse, quia Deus est.—*Id. in Ps.* 138.

indeed according to his account, since he will not allow him to have felt any pain, he ought not to be, nor indeed could be, in any agony,) but rather from the fear he was under lest his disciples, being scandalized at these sad sights, might possibly sin against the Holy Ghost, by denying his Godhead; and that from hence it was, that Peter, in his denial of his Master, used these words: "*Non novi hominem;*" (I know him not as a man,) because that whatsoever is spoken against the Son of man may be forgiven.* So likewise in these words of our Saviour, "O my Father, if it be possible, let this cup pass from me," his opinion is, that our Saviour did not here desire that he himself might be delivered from his passion, but rather that after he had suffered, his disciples might also suffer in like manner;"† that this cup might not rest at him, but that it might pass on to his disciples also; that is to say, that it might be drunk by them in the same manner as he himself was now going to taste of it; to wit, without any touch of despair or distrust, and without any sense of pain, or fear of death.

What could have been written more coldly, or more disagreeing with the truth and simplicity of the gospel? Yet I cannot sufficiently wonder at him, that having thus rarefied the flesh of our Saviour Christ into a spirit, he should in another place condense our spirits into bodies. "There is nothing (says he) which is not corporeal in its substance and creation, &c. For the species of our souls themselves, whether they be united to the body, or are separated from

* Scribit exterrendos, fugandos, negaturos; sed quia spiritus blasphemiæ nec hic, nec in æternum remittitur, metuit ne se Deum abnegent, quem cæsum, et consputum, et crucifixum essent contemplaturi; quæ ratio servata est in Petro; qui cùm negaturus esset, ita negavit, Non novi hominem: quia dictum aliquod in filium hominis remittitur.—*Hilar. in Matth. can.* 31.

† Transeat calix a me, id est, quomodo a me bibitur, ita ab iis bibatur, sine spei diffidentia, sine sensu doloris, sine metu mortis, &c.—*Id. ibid.*

them, have still a nature whose substance is corporeal."* He believes also, that baptism does not cleanse us from all our sins; and therefore he holds that all men must at the last day pass through the fire.† "We are then (says he) to endure an indefatigable fire. Then is the time that we are to undergo those grievous torments for the expiation of our sins, and purging our souls. A sword shall pierce through the soul of the blessed Virgin Mary, to the end that the thoughts of many hearts may be revealed. Seeing, therefore that that Virgin, who was capable of receiving God, shall taste of so severe a judgment, where is he that dares desire to be judged of God?"‡

I know not whether he might heretofore have persuaded any number of people to embrace this doctrine of his or not; but sure I am, that were he alive at this day, he would take but a useless piece of labour in hand, if he should go about to win the Franciscan friars over to this belief.

Ambrose, one of the most firm pillars of the Church in his time, is not more free than the rest from the like failings. For first of all, he agrees with Hilary in this last point, and maintains that all in general shall be proved by fire at the last day; and that the just shall pass through it, but that the unbelievers shall continue in it: "After the end of the world, (says he) the angels being sent forth to sever the good from the bad, shall that baptism be performed; when

* Nihil est quod non in substantia sua, et creatione corporeum sit, &c. Nam et animarum species sive obtinentium corpora sive corporibus exulantium, corpoream tamen naturæ suæ substantiam sortiuntur.—*Ser. in Matth. can.* 5.

† Est ergo quantum licet existimare, perfectæ illius emundatio puritatis, etiam post baptismi aquas reposita, &c.—*Id. in Ps.* 118, *tit. Gimel.*

‡ In quo (*die judicii*) nobis est ille indefessus ignis obeundus, in quo subeunda sunt gravia illa expiandæ à peccatis animæ supplicia. Beatæ Mariæ animam gladius pertransibit, ut revelentur multorum cordium cogitationes. Si in judicii severitatem capax illa Dei Virgo ventura est, desiderare quis audebit a Deo judicari?—*Id. ibid.*

all iniquity shall be consumed in a furnace of fire, that so the just may shine like the sun in the kingdom of God their Father. And although a man be such a one as Peter, or as John, yet nevertheless shall he be baptized with this fire. For the great baptizer shall come, (for so I call him, as the angel Gabriel did, saying, 'he shall be great,') and shall see a multitude of people standing before the gate of Paradise, and shall brandish the fiery sword, and shall say unto those who are on his right hand, who are not guilty of any grievous sins, 'enter ye in,'" &c.*

Ambrose says the same also in another place, where he exempts none from this fiery trial, except our Saviour Christ alone: "It is necessary (says he) that all that desire to return into Paradise should be proved by this fire. For it is not without some mystery that it is written, that God having driven Adam and Eve out of Paradise, placed at the entrance of Paradise a flaming sword which turned every way. All must pass through the flames, whether he be John the Evangelist, whom our Saviour loved so much, that he said, concerning him, to Peter, &c. Or whether it be Peter himself, who had the keys of heaven committed to him, and who walked upon the sea; he must be able to say, 'we have passed through the fire,' &c. But as for John, this brandishing of the flaming sword will soon be dispatched for him, because there is no iniquity found in him, who was so beloved of the truth, &c. But the other (that is Peter) shall be tried as silver is, and I shall be tried like lead: I shall burn till all the lead is quite melted down, and if there be no

* Si quidem post consummationem sœculi missis angelis qui segregent bonos et malos, hoc futurum est baptisma, quando per caminum ignis iniquitas exuretur, ut in regno Dei fulgeant justi sicut sol, in regno Patris sui. Et si aliquis ut Petrus sit, ut Johannes, baptizatur hoc igne. Veniet ergo Baptista Magnus, (sic enim eum nomino, quo modo Gabriel, &c.)—*Ambros. in Ps.* 118, *Ser.* 5.

silver at all found in me, (wretched man that I am) I shall be cast into the lowest pit of hell."*

As for the resurrection of the dead, Ambrose's opinion is, that all shall not be raised at once, but by degrees one after another, in a long yet certain order;† those who were believers rising first, according to the degrees of their merits: to which we are to refer that which he has elsewhere delivered, saying, that "those who are raised up in the first resurrection, shall come to grace, without judgment; but as for the rest, who are reserved for the second resurrection, they shall burn with fire till they have fulfilled the full space of time between the first and the second resurrection; or if they do not finish this time, they shall continue very long in their torments."‡

I shall leave the reader to take the pains in examining whether or not that passage of his can be reconciled to any good sense, where he says, that before the publication of the law of Moses, adultery was not an unlawful thing: "we are to take notice in the first place (says he) that Abraham living before the giving of the law by Moses, and before the Gospel, in all

* Omnes oportet per ignem probari, quicunque ad Paradisum redire desiderant. Non enim otiosè scriptum est, quòd ejectis Adam et Eva posuit Deus in exitu Paradisi gladium igneum versatilem. Omnes oportet transire per flammas, sive Joannes Evangelista sit, quem ita dilexit Dominus, ut de eo diceret ad Petrum, &c. Sive ille sit Petrus qui claves accepit regni cœlorum, qui supra mare ambulavit, oportet dicat, Transivimus per ignem, &c. Sed Joanni citò versabitur igneus gladius, quia non invenitur in eo iniquitas, quem dilexit æquitas, &c. Sed ille (Petrus) examinabitur ut argentum; ego examinabor ut plumbum, donec plumbum tabescat ardebo, si nihil argenti in me inventum fuerit, (heu me) in ultima inferni detrudar.—*Id. in Ps. eund. ser.* 20.

† Licet in momento resuscitentur omnes, omnes tamen meritorum ordine suscitantur.—1. *l. de Fid. Resurrectionis.*

‡ Beati qui habent partem in prima resurrectione; isti enim sine judicio veniunt ad gratiam. Qui autem non veniunt ad primam resurrectionem, sed ad secundam reservantur, isti urentur donec impleant tempora inter primam et secundam resurrectionem: aut si non impleverint, diutiùs in supplicio permanebunt.—*Id. in Ps.* 1.

probability, adultery was not as yet forbidden: the crime is punished after the time of the law made which forbids it; for things are not condemned before the law, but by the law;* and whether those discourses of his, which you meet with in his books, "*De Instit. Virg. et ad Virg. et de Virg.*" and in other places, do not much reflect upon the honourable state of marriage. I shall also leave to the consideration of the judicious reader whether there be more of solidity or of subtlety in that exposition which he gives us of the promise made by God to Noah after the flood; telling him that he had set his *bow* in the clouds, to be a token of a covenant between him and the whole earth. On these words Ambrose utterly and positively denies that by this *bow* is meant the *rainbow;* but will have it to be I know not what strange allegorical bow. "Far be it from us (says he) that we should call this God's bow; for this bow, which is called *Iris*, is seen indeed in the day-time, but never appears at all in the night."† And therefore he understands by this bow, the invisible power of God, by which he keeps all things in one certain measure, enlarging and abating it as he sees cause. Neither do I know whether that opinion of his, which you have in his first book "*De Spiritu Sancto*," is at all more justifiable, where he affirms that "baptism is available and legitimate, although a man should baptize in the name either of the Son or of the Holy Ghost only, without mentioning the other two persons of the Trinity."‡

Epiphanius, as he was a man of a very good, hon-

* Sed consideremus primùm, quia Abràham ante legem Moysis et ante Evangelium fuit, nondum interdictum adulterium videbatur. Pœna criminis ex tempore legis est, quæ crimen inhibuit, nec ante legem ulla rei damnatio est, sed ex lege.—*Ambros. l.* 1. *de. Abr. Patr. c.* 4.

† Absit ut hunc arcum Dei dicamus; hic enim arcus, qui Iris dicitur, per diem videri solet, per noctem non apparet, &c. Est ergo virtus invisibilis Dei, &c.—*Id. lib. de Noe, et Arca, c.* 27.

‡ Id. lib. 1. de Spir. Sanct. cap. 3.

est, and plain nature, and (if I may be permitted to speak my own opinion) a little too credulous, and moreover very sanguine and fierce in maintaining whatever he thought was right and true; so has he the more easily been induced to deliver and to receive things for sound which yet were not so; and pertinaciously to defend them, after he had once embraced them. It would take up both too much time and paper, if I were to enumerate all those things wherein he failed: if you choose you may have an account of a number of them in the notes of the Jesuit Petavius, his interpreter; who takes the liberty to correct him frequently, and sometimes also very rudely. Thus first of all he accuses him of obscurity, and of falsehood also, in the opinion he held on the year and day of our Saviour's nativity;* saying that some of his expressions regarding this point, are more obscure and dark than the riddles of the Sphinx. Truly he has reason enough to say so, of what he has delivered on the year of our Saviour's nativity; but as for the day of that year, whether it were the sixth of January, as Epiphanius held, with the Church of Egypt;† or else it were the twenty-fifth of December, which is the general opinion at this day; I think it very great rashness for any man to affirm either the one or the other; neither of these opinions having any better ground than the other. He likewise in plain terms gives him the lie, upon that place where he says that "in the beginning of the Church the Apostles had ordained that the Christains should celebrate the Passover at the same time and in the same manner as those of the Circumcision did; and that those who were then made bishops at Jerusalem being of the Circumcision, it was necessary that all the world should follow them, and should likewise keep the

* Petav. in Epiphan. p. 127, 132.

† Epiphan. Hær. 51, quæ est Alog. T. 1. p. 446.

Passover as they did."* Neither do I see whereon he could ground that fancy of his, which he proposes to us as a certain truth: "that the devil, before the coming of Christ, was in hopes of grace and pardon; and that out of this persuasion of his, he never showed himself all that while refractory towards God; but that having understood, by the manifestation of our Saviour, that there was left him no hope of salvation, he from thenceforth had grown exceedingly enraged, doing as much mischief as he possibly could against Christ and his Church." *'Ηκουε γαρ ἀει των προφητων καταγγελλοντων του Χριστου παρουσιαν λυτρωσιν ἐσομενην των ἁμαρτησαντων, και δια Χριστου μετανοουντων, ἐνομιζε τε τευξεσθαι τινος ἐλεους. Ὁτε δε εἰδεν ὁ ταλας τον Χριστον μη δεξαμενον αὐτου την περι σωτηριας ἐπιστροφην*, &c.†

Jerome, the boldest and most judicious censurer of the ancients, has also left to posterity something, whereon they may exercise the same sacred criticism that he has so happily employed upon others. For how should a man be able to make good that which he has affirmed so positively, respecting God's providence, where he says, that it takes care of all men indeed in general, and also of each particular man; but not of other things, whether they be inanimate or irrational? "It is an absurd thing (says he) so to abase the majesty of God, as to make him take particular notice how many gnats are bred, or die every hour; and how many bugs, fleas, and flies there are through the whole earth: and how many fishes swim in the water; and which among the smaller fishes are to be a prey to the greater. Let us not be such foolish flatterers of God, as, by making his power descend even to the lowest things, to disparage ourselves; while we say, that his providence in like

* Petav. Ibid. ad Hær. 70, num. 10.
† Epiphan. in Pan. cap. 1. Hær. 39.

manner extends both to rational and irrational creatures."*

I shall not examine here whether this opinion be justifiable or not: but this I am sure of, that you will hardly be able to make it good out of these words of our Saviour Christ—"are not two sparrows sold for a farthing? and yet one of them shall not fall on the ground without your Father." Yet supposing that this opinion might be defended, it is however evident that this Father has dashed out a little too much, when he derides all those as fools and absurd people, who choose rather to adore the knowledge of God as infinite, than to bound it and make it finite: and for my part I should rather fear that there would be much more rashness in the one, than folly in the other.

This same man, who here limits the knowledge and providence of God, in another place extends to infinity the presence of the souls of departed saints; not by any means suffering them to be confined and shut up in any certain place. The reason which he gives of this his opinion is indeed very wonderful: for "they always follow the Lamb (says he) wherever he goes; forasmuch therefore as the Lamb is present everywhere, we ought to believe that they also who are with the Lamb are present everywhere."†

Where is the school of logic, however loose and remiss it may be, that would not give a scholar the

* Cæterùm absurdum est ad hoc Dei deducere majestatem, ut sciat per singula momenta quot nascantur culices, quotve moriantur, quot cimicum et pulicum et muscarum sit in terra multitudo, quanti pisces in aqua natent, et qui de minoribus majorum prædæ cedere debeant. Non simus tam fatui adulatores Dei, ut dum potentiam ejus ad ima detrahimus, in nos ipsos injuriosi simus, eandem rationabilium quam irrationabilium providentiam esse dicentes.—*Hier. Hom.* 1, *in Abac.*

† Sequuntur Agnum quocumque vadit: si Agnus ubique, &c. et sic qui cum Agno sunt, ubique esse credendi sunt.—*Hier. contra Vigil. tom.* 2, *p.* 161.

ferula, if he should but offer to argue thus, confounding the divinity and the humanity of our Saviour together; and from that which is spoken in respect of the one, concluding that which is proper to the other? So in another place, in order to accommodate all the parts of an allegory to his purpose, he makes the souls of the blessed saints, and of the angels themselves, subject to sin.*

I shall pass by what he has spoken so reproachfully, both against marriage in general, and against second marriages in particular; where he uses such harsh expressions, that though we should, in explaining them, follow those very rules which he himself has laid down in an epistle of his written to Pammachius on this very subject—it seems notwithstanding an impossible thing to acquit him of holding the same opinion on marriage as Tertullian did, which was condemned by the Church as being contrary to the honour of marriage and the authority of the Scripture. As for example, how much honey or sugar would be sufficient to sweeten that which he says, writing to a certain widow, named Furia, where he tells her, "that she was not so worthy to be commended, if she continued a widow, as she would be to be cursed if she married again: seeing she was not able, being a Christian, to preserve that which many women of her family had done, being but Pagans."† These expressions of his he repeats again in the following epistle, where he dissuades Ageruchia from marrying again;‡ and for this purpose makes use of

* Nulli periculosum, nulli videatur esse blasphemum, quod et in apostolos invidiæ venenum diximus potuisse subrepere, cum etiam de angelis hoc dictum putamus, &c.—*Id. ep.* 164, *ad Pam. t.* 3. *p.* 210.

† Ut non tam laudanda si vidua perseveres, quàm execranda, si id Christiana non serves, quod per tanta sæcula Gentiles fœminæ custodierunt.—*Mox* p. 90; Canis revertens ad vomitum, et sus lota ad volutabrum luti.—*Id. ep.* 10. *ad Fur. t.* 1, *p.* 89 & 101.

‡ Hæc brevi sermone perstrinxi, ut ostendam adolescentulam

very unseemly comparisons; applying to those women who marry again, that proverb which Peter made use of in another sense—"the dog is turned to his own vomit again, and the sow that was washed to her wallowing in the mire." Is not this the same as if he in plain terms ranked second marriages among unclean and polluted things? Not unlike this is that which he says in another place in these words: "I do not at all condemn those who marry the second, third, or (if any such thing may be) the eighth time: nay, more than this, I receive also even a penitent harlot."* Thus he places those women that marry a second time, in the same rank as those that submit to prostitution. And he is so full of such expressions as these, that the whole Canary islands themselves would hardly be sufficient to sweeten them.

Certainly if Jerome had not believed that there was some uncleanness in marriage, he would never have been so unwilling as he was to speak out, and confess in plain terms that Adam should nevertheless have had carnal knowledge of Eve his wife, though they had both of them continued in their state of innocence:† which thing is evident enough to any one that considers the second chapter of Genesis, from verse 18, to the end. Nevertheless this Father durst not positively affirm any such thing, fearing lest he might thus impose some uncleanness upon the state of innocence, in case he should have allowed them the use of marriage. Nor is his opinion more sound, on the eating of flesh, which being unknown to the world

meam non præstare monogamiam generi suo, sed reddere; nec tam laudandam esse si tribuit, quàm omnibus execrandam si negare tentaverit.—*Id. ep.* 11. *ad Ageruch. t.* 1, *p.* 101.

* Non damno digamos, imò nec trigamos, et si dici potest octogamos; Plus aliquid inferam, etiam scortantem recipio pœnitentem. —*Id. l.* 1. *adv. Jovin. p.* 4.

† Quod si objeceris, antequam peccarent, sexum viri et fœminæ fuisse divisum, et absque peccato eos potuisse conjungi, quid futurum fuerit incertum est, &c.—*Id. lib.* 1. *adv. Jovin. p.* 51.

before the flood, was afterwards permitted to mankind; but (as he believes) in the very same manner as divorce was heretofore permitted to the Jews, only from the hardness of their hearts; whence it follows (as he also says in express terms) that it was abolished by our Saviour Christ, in the same manner as divorce and circumcision were. "And whereas it is objected against us by Jovinian, that God, in the second benediction, permitted the eating of flesh, which he did not in the first; let him know, that as the liberty to put away a man's wife, according to the words of our Saviour, was not granted from the beginning, but was afterwards permitted to mankind, for the hardness of their heart; in like manner was the eating of flesh unknown until the flood: but after the flood, the sinews and poisonous juices of flesh were thrust into our mouths, as the quails were given to the people of Israel murmuring in the wilderness."* Certainly divorce is a thing which is evil in itself, and is contrary to the creation of the man and woman, and to marriage also, which was instituted by God in Paradise; as is divinely proved by our Saviour, when disputing with the Jews on this point. If therefore the eating of flesh be like it, this also is evil and unlawful in itself. Marcion and the Manichees could hardly have said more than this.

In another place Jerome seems to be of opinion that our Saviour has utterly forbidden the use of an oath to Christians,† which doctrine is evidently con-

* Quod autem nobis objicit in secunda Dei benedictione comedendarum carnium licentiam datam, quæ in prima concessa non fuerat; sciat, quomodo repudium juxta eloquium Salvatoris ab initio non dabatur, sed propter duritiem cordis nostri per Moysem humano generi concessum est, sic et esum carnium usque ad diluvium ignotum fuisse; post diluvium verò quasi in eremo murmuranti populo coturnices, ita dentibus nostris nervos, et virulentias carnis ingestas.—*Hieron. lib.* 1. *adv. Jovin.*

† Hoc quasi parvulis Judæis fuerat lege concessum, ut quo modo victimas immolabant Deo, ne eas idolis immolarent, sic et jurare

trary both to the Scripture and to reason. It will be a difficult matter also to clear him from the suspicion of that error, some traces of which, we have observed before, are apparent in Cyprian, respecting the efficacy of the sacraments. For only hear what he says. "The priests also, (says he) who serve at the Eucharist, and distribute the blood of our Saviour to his people, commit a great impiety against the law of Christ, in thinking that the Eucharist is made by the words and not by the life of the person who consecrates it; and that the solemn prayers only of the priests are necessary, and not their merits also."*

On the state of the blessed after the resurrection, he says, though very faintly, that they shall live without eating. "What then, will you say (these are his own words,) shall we eat after the resurrection? I know not that, I confess; for we find no such thing written: yet if I were to speak my opinion, I do not think we shall eat."†

To give a judgment in general of this author, I do not know whether we may allow as being good, and perfectly conformable to the discipline of our Saviour Christ, the course which he usually observes in his disputations, wresting the words of his adversaries from the authors' intention; and framing to himself such a sense as is not to be found in them; and then fiercely encountering this giant of his own making, mixing with it abusive language and sarcasms, and

permitterentur in Deum; non quòd rectè hoc facerent, sed quòd melius esset Deo id exhibere, quàm dæmonibus. Evangelica autem veritas non recipt juramentum, &c.—*Hier. Com. in Matth. t.* 6. *p.* 15.

* Sacordotes quoque qui Eucharistiæ serviunt, et sanguinem Domini populis ejus dividunt, impie agunt in legem Christi, putantes Eucharistiam imprecantis facere verba, non vitam; et necessariam esse tantùm solennem orationem, et non sacerdotum merita.—*Id. Com. in Soph. tom.* 5, *p.* 489.

† Ergo, inquies, et nos post resurrectionem comesuri sumus? Nescio; non enim scriptum est; et tamen si quæritur, non puto comesuros.—*Id. ep.* 61, *ad Pammach. t.* 2, *p.* 252.

tart expressions borrowed from profane authors; in which kind of learning he was indeed very eminent.

Augustine, in the contest he had with him,* said that the holy ceremonies of the Jews, though they were abolished by Jesus Christ, might yet notwithstanding in the beginning of Christianity, be observed by those who had been brought up in them from their infancy, even after they had believed in Jesus Christ, provided they did not put their trust in them: because that salvation which was signified by these holy ceremonies, was imparted to us by Jesus Christ; which doctrine of his is both godly and consonant also to what is urged by Paul, in the first epistle to the Corinthians, and elsewhere, respecting Christian liberty, which both permits and commands us to use or abstain from such things as are in themselves indifferent, according as shall be requisite for the edification of our neighbour. Now Jerome here would make us believe, that his meaning is, that all those who believed, among the Jews, were subject to the law, and that the Gentiles were the only people whom the faith in Christ had exempted from this yoke.† Then presently he takes occasion to pass as tart and cutting a sarcasm upon him as he could; saying, that since it was so that all the believers among the Jews were bound to observe the law, Augustine himself, who was the most eminent bishop in the whole world, ought to publish this his opinion, and to endeavour to bring over all his fellow bishops to be of his mind. But he had then to deal with an able adversary, and one that knew well enough how to clear his words from that interpretation which the other had put upon them, and to retort upon him whatever he had impertinently

* Aug. Ep. ad Hier. quæ est 87, inter Ep. Hier. tom. 2. p. 518.

† Hoc si placet, imò quia placet, ut quicunque credunt ex Judæis debitores sint legis faciendæ; tu, ut Episcopus in toto orbe notissimus, debes hanc promulgare sententiam, et in assensum tuum omnes coepiscopos trahere.—*Hier. Ep.* 89, *ad Aug. t.* 2, *p.* 525.

urged against him; as any man may perceive in that excellent and divine answer of his to Jerome, on this point, and the whole substance of his letters.* The case was otherwise between him and Ruffinus: for there he grappled with one much below his match, and dealt his blows upon a mere wooden statue; one that had scarcely any reason in what he said, and yet much less dexterity in defending himself. But the sport of it is, to see that after he has handsomely belaboured and goaded this pitiful thing, from head to foot, and sometimes till the blood followed, he at length protests, at the end of his first book, "that he had spared him for the love of God, and that he had not afforded words to his troubled breast, and had set a watch before his mouth; according to the example of the Psalmist."†

In another place he reads him a long lecture,‡ telling him that they were not to use railing language in their disputations, nor to leave the question in hand; and to labour to bring in what accusations they could against each other, which are more proper at the bar than in the church, and fitter to fill a lawyer's bill than a churchman's papers.

'Tis true indeed, that those who have been galled by him, are themselves to blame; forasmuch as he, out of his own candid disposition, courteously gave them warning himself; telling them beforehand, "that those that meddled with him had to do with a horned beast."§ Yet some perhaps may still very much wonder how it should come to pass, that all those watch-

* Aug. Ep. ad Hier. quæ est 97, inter Ep. Hier. tom. 2. p. 550.

† Sentisne quid taceam, quod æstuanti pectori verba non commodem? et cum Psalmista loquar, Pone Domine custodiam ori meo, &c.—*Hier. lib.* 1, *contra Ruff. t.* 2, *p.* 311.

‡ Quis omissà causa in superflua criminum objectione versatus est? quæ non chartæ ecclesiasticæ, sed libelli debent Judicum continere.—*Id. in Apol. adv. Ruff. tom.* 2, *p.* 373.

§ Hoc unum denuncio, et repetens iterum iterumque monebo, cornutam bestiam petis. —*Id. Apol.* 1, *contra Ruff. t.* 2, *p.* 311.

ings and that strict discipline which he endured in Bethlehem and the Desert of Arabia, should not have mortified these horns: to which I have no more to say than this; that God by a certain secret and wise judgment, has suffered these holy men, notwithstanding all those excellent gifts of charity, patience, and meekness, wherewith they were abundantly endued, sometimes to let fall such slips as these on particular occasions; to let us understand, that there is nothing absolutely perfect but God alone; all men, however accomplished, carrying about them some relics of human infirmity.

However it be, this course of Jerome's makes me doubt whether he has dealt any better with others than he has with Augustine, wresting their words much further than he ought to have done. But sometimes he goes further yet, and speaks even of the penmen of the Old and New Testament in such a disrespectful manner, that I am very dissatisfied with his proceedings. As for example, where he says, in plain terms, without any circumlocution, that "the inscription of the altar at Athens was not expressed in those very words which were delivered by Paul, in Acts xvii. TO THE UNKNOWN GOD; but in other terms thus; TO THE GODS OF EUROPE, ASIA AND AFRICA; UNKNOWN AND FOREIGN GODS.* So likewise where he tells us, and repeats the same too in many several places, that Paul knew not how to speak, nor to make a discourse hang together:† and "that he makes solecisms sometimes; and that he knew not how to render a hyberbaton, nor to conclude a sentence:"‡ and "that he

* Inscriptio autem aræ non ita erat, ut Paulus asseruit, IGNOTO DEO; sed ita: DEIS EUROPÆ, ASIÆ, ET AFRICÆ, DEIS IGNOTIS ET PEREGRINIS.—*Hier. Com. in Ep. ad Tit. t.* 6. *p.* 450.

† Hebræus ex Hebræis profundos sensus aliena lingua exprimere non valebat.—*Hier. Com.* 3, *in Ep. ad Gal.* p. 348, *t.* 6.

‡ Iste qui solœcismos in verbis facit, qui non potest hyperbaton reddere, sententiamque concludere, audacter sibi vendicat sapientiam, &c.—*Id. Comm.* 2, *in Ep. ad Ephes. t.* 6. *p.* 384.

was not able to express his own deep conceptions in the Greek tongue: and that he had no good utterance, but had much ado to deliver his mind."* Again, in another place he tells us, that "it was not out of modesty, but it was the plain, naked truth that he told us, when the apostle said of himself, that he was *imperitus sermone*, (rude in speech;) because the truth is, he could not deliver his mind to others in clear language."†

He says moreover, (which is yet much worse than all the rest) that "the apostle, disputing with the Galatians, became a fool, as knowing them to be a dull, heavy people; and that he had let fall some such expressions as might possibly have offended the more intelligent sort of people, had he not beforehand told them, that he spake after the manner of men."‡ Whosoever shall have had but the least taste of the force and vigour, and of the candour of the spirit and discourse of this holy apostle, can never see him thus used, without being extremely astonished at it: especially if he but consider, that this kind of speeches, although they had perhaps some ground (which yet they have not,) must needs give offence to the weaker sort of people; and therefore ought not to have been

* Qui non juxta humilitatem, ut plerique æstimant, sed verè dixerit, imperitus sermone, non tamen scientia, Hebræus ex Hebræis, &c., profundos sensus Græco sermone non explicat, et quid cogitat, in verba vix promit.—*Com. in Ep. ad Tit. t.* 6. *p.* 440.

† Illud, &c. etsi imperitus sermone, &c. nequaquam Paulum de humilitate sed de conscientiæ veritate, dixisse; profundos enim et reconditos sensus lingua non explicat, et cùm ipse sentiat, quid loquatur, in alienas aures puro non potest transferre sermone.—*Ep.* 15, *ad Algas. Q.* 10, *t.* 3. *p.* 167.

‡ Apostolus Galatis quoque, quos paulò ante stultos dixerat, factus est stultus; non enim ad eos his usus est argumentis, quibus ad Romanos, sed simplicioribus, et quæ stulti possent intelligere, et penè de trivio. . . . . . . Unde manifestum est id fecisse Apostolum quod promisit nec reconditis ad Galatas usum esse sensibus, sed quotidianis, et vilibus, et quæ possent, nisi præmisisset, "secundum hominem dico," prudentibus displicere.—*Id. Com.* 1. *Ep. ad Gal. t.* 6. *p.* 304, 305.

uttered, without some qualification and softening down.

Augustine, I confess, is much more discreet in this particular, everywhere testifying (as there is very great reason he should) the great respect he bare to the authors of the books of the Holy Scriptures, and never speaking of any of them, whether of their style or sense, without singular admiration. But as to his private opinions, and those of other men which he embraces, he is not without his errors also. Such is that harsh sentence of his, which he has pronounced upon all infants that die before baptism; whom he will have not only to be deprived of the vision of God, which is the punishment to which the ordinary opinion condemns them; but he will further have them to be tormented in hell.* In this he is also followed by Gregorius Ariminensis, a famous doctor in the schools,† where he is called, by reason of this rigour of his, *Tormentum infantium*. Augustine maintains also, that the Eucharist is necessary for infants, as we have formerly noted to another purpose. To which we must also add that opinion to which he evidently inclines, that the soul is derived from father to son,‡ and is engendered of his substance as well as the body, and is not immediately created by God, which is the common opinion at this day. There is no man but knows that he everywhere attributes to the angels a corporeal nature;§ and also that he conceives, against all sense and reason, that the whole world was created all in an instant of time;|| and refers the six days' space of time, wherein the creation is said to have been perfected, to the differ-

* Aug. t. 10. Ser. 14. de verb. Apostoli.

† Greg. Arim. in 2, sent. d. 33. q. 3.

‡ Aug. t. 2. Ep. 28. tot. mox F. 21. M. T. 3. de Gen. ad lit. lib. 10. c. 11. t. 7. c. 2, de An. et ejus Orig. c. 14.

§ See also toward the latter end of this chapter.—*Id. t.* 1. *l.* 1. *contr. Acad. c.* 7.

|| Id. t. 3. 1. imperf. de Gen. ad lit. c. 7. et lib. 4. de Gen. ad lit. c. 31—34, et l. 5. c. 11.

ent degrees of the knowledge of the angels. He believed also, with most of the ancient Fathers, that the souls of men departed are shut into I know not what secret dark receptacles, where they are to remain from the hour of their departure till the resurrection.*

We need not trouble ourselves any further in proving that he also might err in matters of religion, seeing that himself has made so clear and so authentic a confession thereof, in his *Retractations*, where he corrects many things which he had formerly written either foreign to or against the truth.

I must here confess also, that in my opinion it would have added very much to the great and high esteem which we generally have of his learning and worth, if he had been more positive and more resolved in the decision of matters which he has treated, for the most part after the manner of the Academics, doubtingly, and waveringly all the way; insomuch that he leaves undecided not only whether the sun and the other stars be endued with reason, but also whether the world itself be a living creature or not.†

He that will but critically and carefully read the rest of the Fathers, may very easily observe in their writings various errors of a similar nature; and a man will scarcely meet with any one Father of repute, from whom something of this kind has not escaped. As for my own part, who have taken upon me this troublesome subject very unwillingly, I shall content myself with these few instances already set down, seeing they do, in my judgment, make this business very clear; the discovery whereof I have

* Tempus quod inter hominis mortem et ultimam resurrectionem interpositum est, animas abditis receptaculis continet, &c.—*Id. t.* 5. *Ench. ad Laur. cap.* 109. *Vide et t.* 4. *c. de curâ pro mortuis. c.* 2. *l.* 1. *de Civit. Dei, c.* 12. *t.* 9. *Trac.* 49. *in Joan. fol.* 74.

† Id. t. 3. Enchir. ad Laur. c. 58. de Gen. ad lit. l. 2. c. 18. Id. l. 1. Retract. c. 11.

been obliged to undertake, though I wish rather they had been concealed. For seeing that these so eminent persons, who were of the greatest repute amongst all the ancients, have through human infirmity fallen into such errors in point of faith; what ought we to expect from others who come much behind these in antiquity, learning, and holiness of life? Since Justin Martyr, Irenæus, Clemens Alexandrinus, Tertullian, Cyprian, Lactantius, Hilary, Ambrose, Jerome, Augustine, and Epiphanius, (that is to say, the most eminent and most approved persons that ever were,) have yet stumbled in many places, and utterly failed in others; what are we to expect of Cyril, Leo, Gregorius Romanus, and Damascene, who have come after them, and in whom has appeared both much less talent and sanctity, than in the former? Besides, if these holy men have been mistaken in matters of such great importance; (some of them, for instance, on the nature of God; some on the humanity of our Saviour Christ; others on the quality of our souls; and some on the state and condition thereof after death, and on the resurrection;) why must they needs be infallible, when they speak of the points now disputed amongst us? Why may not the same thing have happened to them in the one case that has so manifestly befallen them in the other? It is not probable (as we have said before) that they so much as ever thought of our differences: and it is much more improbable, that ever they had any intention of being our judges in the decision of them, as we have before proved.

But now suppose, that they were acquainted with the business, and that they did intend to clear our doubts, and to give us their positive determination, regarding the same in their books; who shall assure us that they have had better success here than they had in so many other things, wherein we have before heard them give their verdict so utterly against all justice and reason? He that has erred on the subject of the resurrection, is it not possible that he should be in an error on the state of the soul after this life? He that could be ignorant of the nature of Christ's body, must he necessarily have a right judgment on the eucharist? I do not see what solid reason of this difference can possibly be given. It cannot proceed but from one of these two causes, neither of which has yet any place here. For it happens sometimes that he who has failed on one subject, has succeeded better on another; by reason perhaps of his taking more heed to, and using more attention in the consideration of the latter than he did in the former; or else because one of the points is easier to be understood than the other. For in this case, though his attention be as great in the one as in the other, yet notwithstanding he may perhaps be able to understand the easy one, but shall not be able to master the difficult one. But now, neither of these reasons can be alleged here: for why should the ancients have used less care and attention in the examination of those points wherein they have erred? Or why should they have used more in those points, which are at this day controverted amongst us? Are not those ancient points of religion of as great importance as these latter? Is there less danger in being ignorant of the nature of God, than of the authority of the Pope? or of the state of the faithful in the resurrection, than of the punishment of souls in purgatory; the real qualities of the body of Christ, than the nature of the eucharist; the cup of his passion, than the cup of his communion? Is it more necessary to salvation to know him sacrificed upon the altar, than really suffering upon the cross? Who sees not that these matters are of equal importance? or if there be any difference betwixt them, that those points wherein the Fathers have erred, are in some sort more important than those which we now dispute about?

We shall therefore conclude, that if they had both before their eyes, they would questionless have used as much diligence at least, and attention in the study of the one as of the other; and consequently in all probability would have been either as successful, or else have erred as much in the one as in the other.

Neither may it be here objected, that those points wherein they have failed, are of more difficulty than those others wherein these men will needs have them to have been certainly in the right: for whosoever shall only consider them more narrowly, will find that they are equally easy and difficult: or if there be any difference betwixt them in this particular, those which they have erred in, were the easier of the two to have been known. For I pray, is it not as easy to judge by reason, and by the Scripture, whether or not the saints shall dwell upon earth after the resurrection, as it is to determine whether, after they are departed this life, they shall go into purgatory or not? Is it a harder matter to know whether the angels are capable of carnal love, than it is to judge whether the Pope, as he is Pope, be infallible or not? And if it be answered here, that the Church having already determined these latter points, and having not declared itself at all touching the other, has taken away all the difficulty of the one, but has left the other in their former doubtful state, this is to beg the question; or rather it is manifestly false: the Church in the first ages having not, to our knowledge, passed any public or authentic judgment on the points now controverted, as we have already proved.

As therefore these holy men, if they had any thought at all of our present disputes, had an equally clear insight in these things, and according to all reason and all probability, applied to them an equal attention and affection; I believe that there is no man but sees, that if they might err in the decision of the one, it is altogether as possible that they might be mistaken also in their judgment upon the other. Now those books of theirs, which are left us, proclaim aloud and openly, (as we have seen by those few testimonies, which we have but just now produced out of them,) that they have erred, and sometimes also very grievously, on those first questions: it remains therefore to say, that their judgment is not a whit more infallible in our present controversies. Should you therefore demonstrate to any Protestant, by clear and undeniable reasons, that Hilary, in those passages which are produced out of his works for this purpose, has positively taught the real presence of Christ in the eucharist; and should he even grant you the same; which yet perhaps he will never do; after all, he has this still to remind you of, that this is the selfsame Hilary, who in the same book maintains, that the body of Christ felt no pain upon the cross. And if he was in error in this particular, why must he necessarily be right in the other? The question on the body of Christ is of as great importance as that of the eucharist: and it is besides much more clearly decided in the Scriptures; where there is nothing that obliges us in the least degree to fancy any such thing of the body of Christ, as Hilary has done: but where, on the contrary, there seems to be some kind of ground for the opinion which he is pretended to have had on the eucharist. Since therefore, (will the Protestant say) in a thing which is of equal importance, and of much less difficulty, he has manifestly erred, who can assure me, that in this point, which is both less necessary and more difficult, he may not also be mistaken? The same has he to reply upon you, on those other allegations, which you produce from the rest of the Fathers; every one of whom has either really erred, or else possibly might have erred, in matters of religion. Neither can you hope that any solid answer should be given to these things; especially if you but consider that the practice, both of the Fathers, and also of our adversaries themselves, has clearly confirmed this our position. For Augustine,* in that dispute of his which he maintained against Jerome, seeing him produce the testimonies of seven authors (taking no notice at all of the words of the first four of them) answers no more than that some of them were guilty of heresy, and the rest of error: which answer is very insufficient, unless you allow that the testimony of a man who has erred in any one particular point of faith is null and void.

The Fathers of the second council of Nice took the very same course in answering an objection brought against them by the Iconoclasts, who alleged a certain passage for themselves out of Eusebius, bishop of Cæsarea; answering them nothing more than that the author they cited was an Arian.† We need not examine whether this answer of theirs be true or not: and if so, whether it be to the purpose or not: it is sufficient for us that it appears by their making use of this kind of answer, that they took it for granted that he that had failed in one point was not to be trusted in any other. Cardinal Perron, and the rest of the learned of that party, make use of the same manœuvre, rejecting the testimonies brought against them out of Socrates or Sozomen, two ecclesiastical historians, because they say they were Novatians. Those who published the general councils at Rome disauthorize Gelasius Cyzicenus, who was the compiler of the acts of the council of Nice, by producing many gross oversights committed by him in that piece of his.‡

* Aug. Ep. ad Hier. inter Ep. Hier. 47. t. 2, p. 551. & inter Epist. Aug. 19. t. 2.

† Conc. VII. Act. 6. tom. 3. Conc. Gen. p. 627.

‡ In Præfat. præfixa Act. Conc. Niceni, Gelas. Cyzic. in edit. Rom. Conc. Gen. tom. 1.

As therefore we are not to build upon the authority of any author who may justly be accused of error, it is most evident that the authority of the greatest part, and indeed in a manner, of all the Fathers, may very well be called in question: seeing that you will hardly find any one of them that is not liable to this exception.

But it will here be objected perhaps, that although it be confessed that the opinion of one single Father possibly may be, and many times is, really false; yet it is very improbable, or indeed impossible, that what has been delivered unanimously by many of them together, should be otherwise than true. But we have answered something already to this objection, where we took occasion to examine that maxim of Vincentius Lirinensis, on this particular. And in short, this is as if, having confessed that every particular person of a company is sick of some disease, we should notwithstanding still deny that the whole company, taken altogether, can possibly fall into any common distemper of body. It is not indeed, altogether so probable, that many should be sick of any disease, as that one single person should: yet neither is the thing altogether impossible, especially when the disease is contagious, and besides not so well known; as for the most part the errors of great persons are, whose very name bears them out, and makes them easily received by the ordinary sort, who run after them, and receive them without the least suspicion.

Yet if reason be insufficient, let experience persuade us to receive the truth. For it is most evident that some of those errors before specified have been maintained, not by one, nor by two, nor by three of the Fathers only, but by many, by the major part, and sometimes also by all the Fathers of the same age; at least of all those whose names and writings have come to our hands. We have heard how Justin Martyr maintained the opinion of the Millennarians, which is manifestly false in itself, and very dangerous in its consequences. Now this opinion he did not maintain alone; the rest of the learned of his time were in a manner all of the same persuasion, as it appears by his own words. For, writing against Tryphon, and the Jews that agreed with him, he says, "If you by chance meet with some who bear the name of Christians, but do not believe this article of faith, but dare to blaspheme the God of Abraham, of Isaac, and of Jacob, and say that there is no resurrection of the dead, but that the souls, immediately after death, are transported up to heaven, do not suppose these persons to be Christians, no more than, in speaking truly and precisely, the Samaritans, or any other sect of Judaism, are to be called Jews." *Εἰ γαρ και συνεβαλετε ὑμεις τισι λεγομενοις Χριστιανοις, καί τουτο μη ὁμολογουσιν, ἀλλα και βλασφημειν τολμωσι τον θεον Ἀβρααμ, και τον θεον Ἰσαακ, και τον θεον Ἰακωβ, οἵ και λεγουσι μη εἶναι νεκρων ἀναστασιν, ἀλλα ἁμα τω ἀποθνησκειν τας ψυχας αὐτων ἀναλαμβανεσθαι εἰς τον οὐρανον· μη ὑπολαβητε αὐτους Χριστιανους*, &c.*

The false Christians, of whom he here speaks, were the Valentinians, and others of the Gnostics. He shortly proceeds, and says, "As for me, and the rest of us, who are perfectly orthodox Christians, we know that there shall be a resurrection of the flesh, and that the saints shall afterwards spend a thousand years in Jerusalem, which shall be rebuilt, beautified, and enlarged." *'Εγὼ δε, και εἰ τινες εἰσιν ὀρθογνωμονες κατα παντα Χριστιανοι, και σαρκος ἀναστασιν γενησεσθαι ἐπισταμεθα, και χιλια ἐτη ἐν Ἱερουσαλημ οἰκοδομηθειση, και κοσμηθειση, και πλατυνθειση*, &c.† By which words he seems to testify that all the Catholics in his time maintained this erroneous opinion, and that the heretics only rejected it. I know very well that he confesses before, "that there were many who were per-

* Just. contr. Tryph. p. 306. † Id. ibid. p. 307.

fect and religious Christians, who yet did embrace the said opinion:" but let any man that can, reconcile these two contrary sayings: "that all orthodox Christians held this opinion;" and "that there were some of the orthodox party that did not receive the same:"—*Πολλους δ' αὖ και των της καθαρας και εὐσεβους ὀντων Χριστιανων γνωμης, τουτο μη γνωριζειν ἐσημανα σοι.**

Let any man that will, search also into Justin's works, and see whether this contradiction has not been foisted in, by the zeal of the following ages; who probably might take offence at seeing such an opinion fathered upon all the true Christians by so great a martyr. It is sufficient for us that it is clear from this passage, that a very great part of the doctors, and of the faithful people of those times, maintained this error. We see that Irenæus, who lived in the same time, and also Tertullian, who followed not long after him, were both of the same persuasion; no one, all this while, of whom we hear, offering to contradict them. Eusebius, and Jerome, and various other authors, inform us, that Papias, bishop of Hierapolis, who flourished about the year of our Lord 110, was the author of this opinion.†

It follows then from hence, that the consent of all the Fathers that are now extant, who lived in the same age, and maintained all the same opinion, is no necessary argument of the truth. But if you go down lower, you will find that the very same error was defended by several doctors of very great repute in the Church.

Jerome, who in divers places of his commentaries has excellently and solidly refuted this foolish fancy, says,‡ that many among the learned Christians had maintained the same; and to those whom we have

* Just. contr. Tryph. p. 306.

† Euseb. Hist. Eccl. l. 3, c. 39. Hieron. l. de Scrip. Eccles. in Papia. Tom. 1. p. 356.

‡ Id. Comm. 11. in Ezech. t. 4, p. 984.

already mentioned, he adds Lactantius, Victorinus, Severus, and Apollinarius, "who is followed in this point (says he in another place) by great multitudes of Christians about us, insomuch that I already foresee and presage to myself, how many men's anger I shall hereby incur;"* that is, because he everywhere spoke against this opinion.

Whence it plainly appears, that in Jerome's time (that is to say, about the beginning of the fifth century) this opinion generally prevailed in the Church. And indeed however fierce he seems to be in his onset, yet he dares not condemn this opinion absolutely. "Although we embrace not this opinion, (says he) yet can we not condemn it; forasmuch as there have been various eminent personages and martyrs in the Church, who have maintained the same. Let every man abound in his own sense, and let us leave the judgment of all things to God."† Whence you see, by the way, that the Fathers have not always held an opinion in the same degree that we do. For Jerome conceived this to be a *pardonable error*, of which we at this day will not endure to hear.

If it be here answered, that the Church in the ages following condemned this opinion as erroneous, this is no more than to say, that the Church in the ages following acknowledged that the joint consent of many Fathers together on one and the same opinion, is no solid proof of the truth of the same. If Dionysius Alexandrinus had been of any other judgment, he would never have written against Irenæus as he did; as Jerome also testifies‡ in one of his books of Com-

* Quem (Apollinarium) nostrorum in hac parte duntaxat plurima sequitur multitudo, ut præsaga mente jam cernam, quantorum in me rabies concitanda sit.—*Id. Com.* 18. *in Esa. in Præfat.*

† Quæ licet non sequamur, tamen damnare non possumus, quia multi ecclesiasticorum virorum, et martyres ista dixerunt: et unusquisque in suo sensu abundet, et Domini cuncta judicio reserventur. —*Hier. Com.* 4. *in Hierem. t.* 4, *p.* 598.

‡ Id. Com. 18, in Es. in Præfat.

mentaries before cited. And if we are to have regard to authority only, the judgment of the succeeding church cannot then serve us, as a certain guide in this question, to inform us on which side the truth is: for to allege it in this case were rather to oppose one authority against another, than to decide the controversy.

As Dionysius Alexandrinus, Jerome, Gregory Nazianzen, and others, conceived not themselves bound to submit to the authority of Justin Martyr, Irenæus, Lactantius, Victorinus, Severus, and others; so neither are we any more bound to submit to theirs: for their posterity owes them no more respect than they themselves owed to their ancestors. It seems rather that in reason they should owe them less; because the further they are distant in time from the Apostles, who are as it were the spring and original of all ecclesiastical authority, so much do the credit and authority of the Doctors of the Church decrease. If antiquity (as we said) be the mark of truth, then certainly that which is the most ancient is also the most venerable and the most considerable. And if there were no other instance but this, against the authority of many Fathers unanimously consenting in any opinion, yet would it clearly serve to lessen the same; but there are yet behind many others, some of which we shall here produce. We have before seen Justin Martyr, Irenæus, Tertullian, and Augustine, affirming all of them that heaven shall not be opened till the day of judgment; and that, in the interval, the souls of all the faithful are shut up in some subterraneous place, except some small number of those who had the privilege of going immediately to heaven. The author of those *Questions and Answers*, that go under the name of Justin Martyr, maintains the same opinion, as you may see in the answers to the 60th and 74th questions.

That I may not unprofitably spend both time and

paper in citing all the particular passages, I say in general, that both the major part, and also the most eminent persons among the ancient Fathers, held this opinion, either absolutely, or at least in part. For besides Justin Martyr, Irenæus, Tertullian, Augustine, and the author of those Questions and Answers we before mentioned, which is a very ancient production indeed, though falsely fathered upon Justin Martyr, it is clear that Origen, Lactantius, Victorinus, Ambrose, Chrysostom, Theodoret, Œcumenius, Aretas, Prudentius, Theophylact, Bernard, and, among the Popes, Clemens Romanus, and John XXII., were all of this opinion, as is confessed by all; neither was this so admirable and general consent of theirs contradicted by any declaration of the Church, for the space of fourteen hundred years; neither yet did any one of the Fathers, so far as we can discover, take upon him to refute this error, as Dionysius Alexandrinus and Jerome did to refute the Millennarians; all the rest of the Fathers being either utterly silent as to this particular, and so by this their silence going over in a manner into the opinion of the major part, or else contenting themselves with declaring sometimes here and there in their books, that they believed that the souls of the saints should enjoy the sight of God till the resurrection; never formally denying the other opinion.

But that which further shows that this opinion is both very ancient, and was also very common among the Christians, is, that even at this day it is believed, and defended by the whole Greek Church: neither is there any of all those who profess to follow the writings of the Fathers, as the rule of their faith, who have rejected it, save only the Latins who have expressly established the contrary at the council of Florence, held in the year of our Lord 1439.*

* Diffinimus insuper, &c., illorum animas qui post susceptum baptisma nullam omnino maculam incurrerunt, illas etiam quæ post

Do but imagine now to yourselves a Vincentius Lirinensis, standing in the midst of this council, and laying before them his own oracle before mentioned; which is, "that we ought to hold as most certainly and undoubtedly true, whatever has been delivered by the ancients unanimously and by a common consent:" would he not have been hissed out by these reverend Fathers, as one that made the truth, which is holy and immutable, to depend upon the authority of men? For these men regarded not either the multitude, or the antiquity, or the learning, or the sanctity of the authors of this foolish opinion; but finding it to be false, without any ceremony rejected it, as they thought they had good reason to do, and at once ordained the contrary.

Now I am verily persuaded, that there are very few points of faith, among all those which the Church of Rome would have the Protestants receive, for which there can be alleged as many *specious* testimonies, as there can be *undoubted* ones for this. Since then, after all this, it has not only been called in question, but has been also even utterly condemned, who sees not, that the consent of many Fathers together, although any such might be found upon all the points now in debate, would yet be no sufficient argument of the truth of the same? But I shall pass on to the rest.

We have before heard that Tertullian, Cyprian, (who was both a bishop and a martyr,) Firmilianus, (metropolitan of Cappadocia,) Dionysius, (patriarch of Alexandria,) together with the synods of bishops of Africa, Cappadocia, Cilicia, and Bithynia, all held that the baptism of heretics was invalid and null. Basil,* who was one of the most eminent bishops of

contractam peccati maculam vel in suis corporibus, vel eisdem exutæ corporibus, prout superiùs dictum est, sunt purgatæ, in cœlum mox recipi, et intueri clarè ipsum Deum, trinum et unum.—*Conc. Flo. in defin. t.* 4, *p.* 584.

* Basil. ep. Amphiloch. tom. 2. p. 758, 759.

the whole Eastern Church, held also, in a manner, the very same opinion, and that a long time too after the determination of the council of Nice; as it appears by the epistle which he wrote to Amphilochius; which is also put in among the public decrees of the Church, by the Greek Canonists. And yet this opinion is now confessed by all to be erroneous.

Many in like manner of the Fathers, as Tertullian,* Clemens Alexandrinus,† Lactantius,‡ and Africanus,§ believed that our Saviour Christ kept the Feast of the Passover, but once only, after his baptism. Yet, notwithstanding this assent of theirs, the opinion is known to be very erroneous, as Petavius|| also testifies; and besides it is expressly contrary to the text of the Gospel.

I shall not here say anything of the opinion of Chrysostom,¶ Jerome,** Basil,†† and the Fathers of the council held at Constantinople, *Αλλα και ἐντεταλται ἡμιν παρα του σωτηρος Χριστου, μη ὀμοσαι*, &c.,‡‡ under the patriarch Flavian; who seem all to have held, that an oath was utterly unlawful for Christians, under the New Testament. Neither shall I take any notice in this place of that conceit of Athanasius, Basil, and Methodius, who, according to John, bishop of Thessalonica,§§ believed that the angels had bodies: to whom we may also add, (as we have shown before,) Hilary, Justin Martyr, Tertullian, and very many more of the Fathers, who all thought the nature of angels to be capable of carnal love; of which number

* Tertul. lib. contr. Jud. cap. 8.
† Clem. Alex. Strom, 1, 6.
‡ Lactant. Firmian. l. 4. cap. 10.
§ African. apud Hieron. Com. in Dan. cap. 10, tom. 4. pag. 1147.
|| Petav. Not. in Epiphan. p. 203.
¶ Chrysost. Hom. in statuas, *et passim.*
** St. Hieron. Com. 1, in Matth. t. 6, p. 15.
†† Basil. Hom. in Ps. 14, t. 1, p. 154 et 155.
‡‡ Act. Conc. Const. act. 1, t. 2, p. 129.
§§ T. 3. Conc. p. 547, in act. Conc. vii. act 5.

is even Augustine* also. Whosoever should now conclude from hence, that this fancy of theirs (which yet is of no small importance) is a truth; would he not be as sharply reproved for it by the Romanists, as by those of Geneva? But I must not forget, that besides Cyprian, Augustine, and Pope Innocent I. whose testimonies we have given before,† all the rest of the Doctors, in a manner, of the first ages maintained, that the eucharist was necessary for infants; if at least you will take Maldonat's word,‡ who affirms that this opinion was in great request in the Church, during the first six centuries after our Saviour Christ.

Cassander also testifies§ that he has often observed this practice in the ancients; and Charlemagne and Louis the Pious, who lived a long time after the sixth century, testify that this custom continued in the West, even in their time, according to Cardinal Perron:|| and the traces of this custom remain to this day among those Christians who are not of the Communion of the Latin Church. For Nicolaus de Lyra, who lived above three hundred years since, observed, "That the Greeks accounted the holy eucharist so necessary, that they administered it to little children also, as well as baptism."¶ Even in our fathers' time, the Patriarch Jeremiah,** speaking in the name of the whole Greek Church, said, "We do not only

* Aug. t. 1, lib. 1. contr. Acad. c. 7, t. 2, ep. 111, et ep. 115, et t. 3, Enchir. ad Laur. c. 59, de Trin. l. 2, c. 7, et l. 3, cap. 1, et. l. 8, cap. 2, et de Gen. ad lit. l. 3, cap. 10, et l. 11, cap. 22, et de divin. Dæm. cap. 3, 4, 5, et t. 4, l. 93, quæst. 9, 47, t. 5, l. 11, de Civ. Dei. cap. 25, et. l. 15, cap. 23, et ibi Vives, et l. 21, cap. 23, et cap. 10.

† Supr. l. 1, c. 8.

‡ Maldon. in Joh. vi. 53,

§ Cassand. Cònsult. ad Fer. et Max. p. 936, et lib. de Bapt. Int. p. 747.

|| Du Perron. traict. de St. August. pag. 1001.

¶ Notandum quod ex hoc quod dicitur hic, Nisi manducaveritis, &c., dicunt Græci, quod hoc sacramentum est tantæ necessitatis, quod pueris debet dari, sicut baptismus—*Nicol. de Lyra in Joh.*

** Hierem. Patr. Const. Doctr. Exh. ad Germ.

baptize little children, but we make them partakers of the Lord's Supper." And a little after, "we account both sacraments to be necessary to salvation for all persons, namely, Baptism and the Holy Communion." The Abyssinians also make their children in like manner communicate of the holy eucharist, as soon as they are baptized.*

These are most evident arguments, that this false opinion on the necessity of the eucharist, was of old maintained, not by three or four of the Fathers only, but by the major part, and in a degree by all of them. For we do not hear even of one among all the ancient Fathers, who rejected it in express terms, as the council of Trent has done in these later times.

To conclude, the Jesuit Pererius has informed us† (and indeed the observation is obvious enough to any man, who is ever so little conversant in the writings of those authors, who lived before Augustine's time) that the Greek Fathers, and a considerable part also of the Latins, were of opinion that the cause of predestination was the foresight which God had, either of men's good works, or else of their faith; either of which opinions, he assures us, is manifestly contrary both to the authority of the Scriptures, and also to the doctrine of Paul. Therefore I conceive we may, without troubling ourselves any further in making this invidious inquiry into the errors of the Fathers, conclude, from what has been already produced, that seeing the Fathers have erred in so many particulars, not only singly, but also many of them together, neither the private opinions of each particular Father, nor yet the unanimous consent of the major part of them, is a sufficient argument to prove with certainty the truth of those points which are at this day controverted amongst us.

* Alvarez, in his Voyage to Ethiopia.
† Perer. in Rom. c. 8, disp. 22, et 23.

CHAPTER V.

REASON V.—That the Fathers have strongly contradicted one another, and have maintained different opinions in matters of importance.

BESSARIO, a Greek, (who was honoured with the dignity of Cardinal by Pope Eugenius IV., as a reward of his earnest desire and the great pains he took in endeavouring to effect a reconciliation between the Eastern and the Western Churches,) in a book which he wrote upon this subject to the council of Florence, will have the whole difference between the Greek and Latin Churches to be brought before the judgment seat of the Fathers.* And forasmuch as he knew, that unless the judges all agreed, the cause, (especially in matters of religion) necessarily remains undecided, he strongly labours to prove, that not only is each Father consistent with himself, but (which is yet much harder to prove) that they are all of the same opinion one with another: insomuch that he commands us, whenever there appears any contrariety in their writings, that we should accuse our own ignorance, rather than blame them for contradicting each other.

We may conclude therefore, from what is here laid down by this author, who was both as acute and as learned a man as any at this council, that to render the Fathers capable of being the judges of our controversies, it is necessary that they should be all of the same judgment and opinion in point of religion. And certainly this is a most clear truth; for if there be any contradiction amongst them, or dissension in opinion, they will leave our controversies more perplexed, and instead of uniting, will rather distract

* Bessar. Orat. Περὶ ἑνώσεως, c. 2. p. 520, et 521, t. 4, Conç.

us. That we may therefore be able to come to the knowledge of the truth in this particular, it will behove us first of all to examine the truth of Bessario's assertion, that the opinions of the Fathers never clash, on points of religion.

Now, although this were so, it would not necessarily follow that their judgment is infallible; since even an error may, either by conceit, or by accident, or by some other similar means, happen to meet with unanimous accordance by various persons. But if this should prove to be false, then certainly we may make this infallible conclusion, that we ought to seek out for other judges of our controversies than the writings of the Fathers. We shall therefore show, by way of addition to the rest of our proofs, that this assertion of his is more bold than true; and, that there are many real differences to be found among the ancient Fathers in matters of religion. We have already noticed some of them incidentally, when speaking of other matters, and therefore we shall only lightly advert to them; and first of all as to that disagreement in opinion of the most ancient among the Fathers, Justin Martyr, Irenæus, and Tertullian, on one side; and Dionysius Alexandrinus, Gregory Nazianzen, and Jerome, on the other: the first of these promising us very seriously the delights and pleasures of a thousand years, and the diamonds and the sapphires of a new earthly Jerusalem, with all its glory and prosperity; but the other very coarsely, and in downright terms, reproving this their conceit, as being an idle fancy, fit to be entertained by little children and old women only; and which seems to have been derived rather from the dreams of the Jews than from the doctrine of the Apostles.

Similar to this was that difference between the bishops of Asia and Pope Victor, about the observation of Easter-day: and of Cyprian and Stephen, about the baptism of heretics: in all which differences the heat was so high, that it proceeded so far as to excommunicate each other. If Bessario now could but make it appear to us, that these were not real but seeming contradictions only, I should then make no question but that he would easily reconcile fire and water, or whatever things else in nature are the most contrary to one another.

We have heard that Tertullian maintained, that the soul was *ex traduce*, and was propagated from the father to the son, by the natural course of generation; and that Augustine likewise inclined to the same opinion; to whom, if we will believe Jerome, we must add a very considerable number of the Western Church also, who were all of the same persuasion.* But Jerome rejects them all, and their opinion,† and says that the soul is created immediately by God, at the very instant that it is united to the body; adding moreover (as we have formerly noticed) that this is the belief of the Church in this point.

Jerome, and his adherents, held that all that reprehension used by Paul to Peter, which we find mentioned in the epistle to the Galatians, was only a feigned business, purposely acted between the two Apostles, by an agreement made between themselves. Augustine, and several others, maintain the contrary, and say that the thing was real, and was meant heartily and seriously, and as it is related by Paul; and that there was no cunning or underhand dealing in the business between Peter and him. And Jerome pursued this dispute with so much earnestness, that besides those epistles of his, which are full of gall and choler, on this particular, he yet, in his Commentaries,‡ which he wrote in his quieter temper, many

* An certè ex traduce, ut Tertullianus, Apollinarius, et maxima pars occidentalium autumant.—*Hieron. Ep.* 82. *t.* 2.

† Id. Com. in Eccles. c. 12, t. 5. et Ep. 61, ad Pamm. t. 2. p. 242, et alibi passim.

‡ Vid. Com. 14, in Es. t. 4, p. 378, et Com. 18, in eund. p. 485.

times takes occasion to point underhand at Augustine, upon this old quarrel between them. So that certainly he must be quite out of his wits, whoever shall seriously maintain, that these two Fathers were perfectly of one opinion, and agreed upon these points.

Justin Martyr is of opinion that it was the real ghost of Samuel that appeared to Saul; *Την Σαμουηλ ψυχην κληθηναι ὑπο της ἐγγαστριμυθου;** being raised up by the enchantments of the witch at Endor. Others say it was but a phantom: *Του θεου του δεδωκοτος τω δαιμονι, ἐν τω σχηματι του Σαμουηλ ὀφθηναι τη ἐγγαστριμυθω;*† some of them hold that the meeting together of the faithful at the eucharist thrice a week, is an apostolical tradition:‡ others believe the contrary.§ Some enjoin us to fast on Saturdays;|| others forbid the same, under the penalty of being accounted no less than the murderers of Christ.¶ Some of them conceive that our Saviour Christ suffered death in the fortieth or fiftieth year of his age.** Others again would persuade us, that he died in the thirtieth or thirty-first year of his age:†† both which opinions are manifestly contrary to the text of the gospel, which tells us clearly that after his baptism, that is to say, after the thirtieth year of his age, he conversed above three, and under five years, upon the earth. Some of them (as we are informed by these Latinized Greeks‡‡) allow of these terms, *cause* and *effect*, in the doctrine of the Trinity; but some others again do not so. Some

* Justin. cont. Tryph. p. 333.

† Pseudo Just. l. Q. et R. Resp. ad q. 52.

‡ Epiphan. in Panar. Expos. fid. p. 1104.

§ August. in Ep. 118, ad Jan. t. 3, vid. Petav. in Epiph. p. 354.

|| Vid. Petav. p. 359, in Epiph. Eccl. Rom. ap. Socr. l. 5, c. 22. August. Ep. 86, et 118. Innoc. I. Ep. 1, c. 4.

¶ Ignat. Ep. 4, ad Philip. Can. Apost. c. 68, Constit. Apost. l. 7, c. 24, Syn. Trull. can. 55.

** Iren. l. 2, c. 39.

†† Tertull. Clem. Alex. Lactant. Afric. ubi supr.

‡‡ Scholarius, Orat. 3, t. 4, Concil. Gen. p. 658, 659.

of them are of opinion, that there is a certain order or distinction of priority in the persons of the Trinity. Others again there are, who will not endure to hear of this expression.

Those of the Western Church call the Son only, The Image of the Father; but the Greek Church makes this name extend to the Holy Ghost also. Basil will not allow of the word γεννημα, *offspring*, in discoursing of the Son. Others again make use of it without any scruple at all.

I doubt very much whether Bessario had ever read the Apologies and Invectives of Jerome and of Ruffinus, who were yet both of them Fathers, and of good, though not of equal repute in the Church, both of their own time and of the ages following; nor do I believe he remembered the quarrel there was between Theophilus and Epiphanius on the one part, and Chrysostom on the other. For certainly their conduct toward each other, does not show them to have been very well agreed. But now to overthrow this bold assertion of his at once, we need go no further than to the very point on which he proposed it. For whom will he ever be able to persuade that all the Fathers have written and said the very same things on the Procession of the Holy Ghost? It is evident that sometimes they will have him to proceed from the Son also, as Basil has expressed himself, in that passage of his which is alleged by the Latins, out of his book against Eunomius, (which poduction however the Greeks say is forged,) and as the Fathers of the Western Church have most expressly declared themselves in many places.* But yet I cannot possibly see how we can say that they have all been of this opinion.

I shall not here interfere with those other authorities produced by the Greeks out of the Fathers which

* Con. Flor. Act. 20, t. 4, Conc. p. 454.

their adversaries put by as well as they can; oftentimes most miserably wresting, and torturing the words and meaning of the Fathers. But that passage of Theodoret, in his refutation of Cyril's Anathemas, is so clear and express, that nothing can be more so.

Cyril had said, in his 9th Anathema, that the Holy Ghost proceeds properly from the Son: *'Ιδιον αὐτου (Χριστου) το πνευμα.** Theodoret answers, that it is both impious and blasphemous to say that the Holy Ghost has his subsistence from the Son, or by the Son. "If he means (says he) that the Holy Ghost proceeds properly from the Son, as being of the same nature with him, and as proceeding from the Father, we shall willingly agree with him, and receive his doctrine as sound and pious; but if he mean that the Holy Ghost has its subsistence from the Son, or by the Son, we will reject it as impious and blasphemous." *'Ιδιον δε το πνευμα του υἱου, εἰ μεν ὡς ὁμοφυες, και εκ πατρος ἐκπορευομενον ἐφη, συνομολογησομεν, και ὡς εὐσεβη δεξομεθα την φωνην· εἰ δ' ὡς ἐξ υἱου, ἢ δἰ υἱου την ὑπαρξιν ἐχον, ὡς βλασφημον τουτο, και ὡς δυσεβες ἀπορριψομεν.*†

He could not have thrown by this proposition of Cyril more bluntly, or in coarser terms; and yet to so direct a charge of falsehood, and to so insolent a rejection of a doctrine then received by the Church, as the Latins pretend, Cyril replies no more than this: "that the Holy Ghost, although he proceeds from the Father, nevertheless is not a stranger to the Son; since he has all things common with the Father!" *'Εκπορευεται μεν γαρ ἐκ του θεου και πατρος το πνευμα το ἁγιον, κατα την του Σωτηρος φωνην, ἀλλ' οὐκ ἀλλοτριον ἐστι του υἱου· παντα γαρ ἐχει μετα του πατρος.*‡

* Cyril. Anath. 9.
† Theodor. Refut. Anath. 9, Cyril. Act. Conc. Eph.
‡ Cyril. Resp. ad Ref. Theod. Anath. 9, ibid.

Why did he not cry out against Theodoret as a heretic, as he many times elsewhere does, with much less reason; if at least, as you assert the Church at that time held that the Holy Ghost proceeded from the Son? Why did he not take it very ill at his hands, that he should in so insolent a manner reject, as impious and blasphemous, a proposition that was so holy and so true? Why did he not call the whole Church in, to be his warrant for what he had said, if it had really been the general belief of the Church at that time? And how comes it to pass that, instead of all this, he rather returns so tame an answer, that he seems rather to betray his own cause, and to incline to the opinion of his adversary? For it is evident that neither Theodoret, nor yet any of the modern Greeks, ever held that the Holy Ghost was a stranger to, or was unconcerned in, the Son: seeing that they all confess, that these three, to wit, the Father, the Son, and the Holy Ghost, are one and the same God, who is blessed for ever.

Whosoever shall but diligently consider these things, (for we cannot enter further into the examination of them,) cannot, in my judgment, but confess that the Church has not as yet declared itself, or determined anything on this point; and that these doctors spake herein each man his private opinion only, and according as the present occasion of disputation led him to speak; contradicting one another, in the manner usual in speaking of things not as yet thoroughly examined, or expressly determined: insomuch that it would grieve a man to see how the Greeks and the Latins toil to no purpose, each of them labouring to bring over the Fathers to speak to their side, and wresting their words, whenever they seem to be but ever so little ambiguous; and repeatedly accusing one another of having corrupted the writings of the ancients, whenever they are found to speak expressly against them; and when all is done, giving very little satisfaction to unprejudiced readers; whereas it had been much easier to have honestly confessed at first, what is but too apparent, that the Fathers, in this, as in many other points of religion, have not all been of one and the same persuasion. And whereas Bessario, that he may elude this testimony of Theodoret, affirms that he was cast out of the Church, for having denied that the Holy Ghost proceeded from the Son;* and that he afterwards publicly confessed his error at the council of Chalcedon, where he was received into the Church again; all this, I say, is only a piece of Grecian assurance; which shows more clearly than all the rest how much this man was carried away by his zeal on this subject. For, I pray, in what ancient author, had he ever read, that Theodoret was, I do not say condemned or excommunicated, but so much as reproved, or accused only, for having maintained any erroneous opinion on the procession of the Holy Ghost? We have the acts of the council of Ephesus, where he was excommunicated. We have the letters of Cyril, wherein he again received into the communion of the Church, John, Patriarch of Antioch, and all his followers, of which number Theodoret was the chief. We have the council of Chalcedon; where Theodoret, after some certain accusations of his adversaries against him, was at length received by the whole assembly as a Catholic bishop, and was admitted to sit amongst them. In which of all these authentic pieces is there so much as one word spoken on this opinion of his, concerning the point of the proceeding of the Holy Ghost? Cyril himself, that is to say, those of his party, did not at all condemn what he said on this particular; but he rather contented himself with excusing, or, if you please, in defending only his own opinion. The busi-

* Bessar. in Orat. Dogmat. sive de Unione Extra. cap. 9, in Act. Conc. Flor. Sess. 20, t. 4, Conc. p. 551.

ness for which Theodoret was questioned in the councils of Ephesus and Chalcedon, had nothing in the world to do with this, touching the procession of the Holy Ghost; for the question was only there on the two natures of our Saviour Christ, whom Nestorius would needs divide into two persons; John, Patriarch of Antioch, Theodoret, and divers other Eastern bishops, favouring in some sort his person, or being indeed offended rather at the proceeding of the council of Ephesus against him; and withal rejecting several things that were contained in the anathemas of Cyril.

Now with what conscience could this man tell us, after all this, that Theodoret had been deposed from his bishopric for having maintained an erroneous opinion on the procession of the Holy Ghost? But enough of this.

I would, in the next place, wish to know how this reconciler of differences could compose that debate between the six hundred and thirty Fathers of the council at Chalcedon, and Leo bishop of Rome; and how he can reconcile the twenty-eighth canon of the one, with those many epistles written by the other on this point, to Anatolius, Patriarch of Constantinople, to the emperor Marcianus and his empress, to the prelates who were met together in that council, and to the Patriarch of Antioch: the Fathers of this council advancing the throne of the Patriarch of Constantinople above those of Alexandria and of Antioch, and making it equal even with that of Rome itself: Pope Leo on the contrary sending out his thunderbolts against this decree of theirs, as a most insufferable error. And when this our conciliator shall have done his business at Chalcedon, if he please he may pass over into Africa, and there also reconcile the Fathers of that country to the bishops of Rome; the former of these forbidding their clergy to make any appeals to Rome, and the other in the meantime to their utmost endeavouring to prove, that it is their proper right to have such appeals brought before them. And when he has finished this work, our Greek may then in the next place try to remove all misunderstanding between the Fathers of the council of Francfort, and those of the second council of Nice, on the point of the use of images; the latter of these ordaining, "that we ought to pay them salutations and adoration of honour; and that we ought to honour them with incense and lights;" *Και ταυταις ἀσπασμον και τιμητικην προσκυνησιν ἀπονεμειν. . . . Και θυμιαματων και φωτων προσαγωγην προς την τουτων τιμην ποιεισθαι ;** and the other, as every man knows, having not only rejected this Greek Council, but having written also expressly against it, by the command of the emperor Charlemagne.

Certainly he that shall but read the Fathers themselves will readily perceive that they contradict each other in most plain and irreconcilable terms; and that there is no other way of bringing them fairly together, but by receiving every one of them with his own private opinions; imitating herein the marvellous wisdom of the council of Constantinople in Trullo;† which receives and allows all in gross without distinction, both the canons of the Apostles, and the whole code of the Church universal, together with those of Sardica, Carthage and Laodicea; amongst which notwithstanding there are found strong contradictions. As, for example, the council of Sardica will have the right of receiving the appeals of all bishops to belong to the see of Rome,‡ whereas Chalcedon gives this privilege to that of Constantinople.§ The council of Laodicea leaves out of the canon of the

* Conc. 7, Act. 7, in defin. t. 3, Conc. p. 661.

† Synod. Quinisexta Can. 2, t. 3. [Trullus, a hall in the palace at Constantinople, so called from Trullium, a bowl, which it resembled in form.—Ed. Bd. of Pub.]

‡ Synod. Sard. Can. 3 et 7.

§ Synod. Chalced. c. 9 et 17.

Scriptures the Maccabees, Ecclesiasticus, the book of Wisdom, Tobit and Judith:* that of Carthage puts them in expressly.† But now these honest Fathers of Constantinople, that they may satisfy all, take no notice whatever of these their differences; but receive each of them with their own particular canons and opinions, without obliging them to any one common rule; doing this, I believe, on condition that they themselves may not be required by those whom they thus admit to receive any more from them than they shall think convenient. I know no man that would not at this rate readily admit as canonical, all the writings of the Fathers: provided that he might but have liberty to adopt or reject what he pleased. Thus we may very well from henceforth rest satisfied, that, notwithstanding Bessario's decision to the contrary, the Fathers have not always been of the same judgment in matters of religion: and that consequently they ought not to be received by us as our judges on the matter. For seeing that I find them contradicting each other in so many important points, how shall I be assured that they are unanimously agreed on those points which are now debated amongst us? Why may they not have had the same diversity of opinion on the eucharist, the authority of the Church, the power of the Pope, freewill or purgatory, that they had in those other points which we have before presented to the reader's view; which were of as great importance as these, and no less easy to be determined, as we have proved in the preceding chapter?

Epiphanius and Jerome are as opposite in their judgments, on the ancient condition of priests and bishops, as Theodoret and Cyril are, on the procession of the Holy Ghost. Neither are some opinions of Tertullian and of Damascene, of Theodoret and Eusebius of Emesa; of Eusebius of Cæsarea and

* Synod. Laod. Can. 59. † Synod. Carthag. iii. c. 47.

the Seventh Council, on the point of the eucharist, less opposite to each other, than are those of Cyprian and of Stephen on the baptism of heretics; and so likewise in many other particulars. Why then should we take so much pains in reconciling these men, and making them speak all the same thing? Why should we so cruelly torture them as we do, to make them all of one opinion, and to say the same things, whether they will or no; and sometimes too against our own conscience; but certainly, for the most part, without any satisfaction to the reader? Why should we not rather honestly confess that their opinions were also different, as well as their words?

We make no scruple in affirming that they have been of contrary opinions, on those other points of religion, which are not at all now controverted amongst us. What great harm would it do, if we should confess that they were not any better agreed on these points now in debate? But we need not press this matter any further; it is sufficient for us that we have proved that they were of different opinions in point of religion; so that it clearly follows from hence, that we ought not to admit of their writings, as the proper judges of our controversies.

I have heretofore adverted, though very lightly, to their diversity of opinion and contrariety in their expositions of the Scriptures; which is, however, a business of no trifling consideration. For if we take them for our judges, we shall then necessarily be obliged every minute to have recourse to them, for the sense of those passages of Scripture on which we disagree among ourselves. If there be now as great difference in judgment on these things among them as there is amongst ourselves, what have we then left us to trust to? This passage, for example, in the Gospel according to John, "I and my Father are One,"* is of very great importance in the dis-

* Ego et Pater unum sumus.—*John* x. 30.

putes against both Sabellius and Arius. Would you now know the true sense and meaning of these words, lest otherwise, by misinterpreting the same, you might chance to fall over the one or the other of these two precipices? If you have recourse to the Fathers in this case, you shall have some of them referring it to the union of the affection and of the will,* and others again, to the unity of essence and of nature.†

So likewise this other passage in the same Evangelist: "My Father is greater than I,"‡ is very considerable also in the question on the divinity of Jesus Christ: and yet there are some among the Fathers§ who understand the words as spoken indefinitely of the Son of God, although the rest of them ordinarily restrict them to his humanity. These words also of John, "the word was made flesh,"‖ are of no small consideration in the disputes against Nestorius and Eutyches. Now if you bring the business before the Fathers, you shall have some of them expounding these words,¶ by comparing them with those passages in Paul, where it is said that Christ was made sin** and a curse for us:†† but Cyril says, that we must take heed how we thus interpret the words.‡‡

It would be an endless task if I should here attempt to enumerate all the differences and contrarieties of judgment to be found in the Fathers. Those who have a mind to see any more of them may have recourse to some of our late commentators,

* Unum non pertinet ad singularitatem, sed ad unitatem, ad similitudinem, ad conjunctionem, ad dilectionem Patris, qui Filium diligit, et ad obsequium Filii, qui voluntati Patris obsequitur.—*Tertul. contr. Prax. c.* 22.—*Autor libri de Trin.* c. 22. *Orig. contra Celsum, lib.* 8, *p.* 396.

† Athanas. Greg. Nazianz. alii penè omnes passim.

‡ John xiv. 28. § Epiphan. Ancor. p. 23. ‖ John i. 14.

¶ Ambros. l. de Incar. Sacr. c. 6. t. 2. p. 183. Athan. Ep. ad Epict. t. 1. p. 587. & t. 2. p. 298.

** 2 Cor. v. 21. †† Gal. iii. 13.

‡‡ Cyril. Apol. Athan. 1. t. 1. Conc. Gener. p. 515.

whose usual course is, to bring in all together the several interpretations of the Fathers upon those books which they comment upon: as Maldonate has done upon the Gospels; Cardinal Tolet upon John; Justinianus, upon the epistles of Paul, and others: where they will find that there is scarcely any one verse that all the ancients understood in the same sense. What is yet worse than this, besides this contrariety and difference of interpretation, you will often meet with many frigid and vapid expositions: and it is very seldom that you shall find there that solid simplicity which we ought to expect from all those who take upon them the interpretation of the Holy Scriptures.

Thus, therefore, as we often meet with contrariety of judgment, as well in their expositions of the Scriptures as in their opinions, we may safely conclude that they are not of sufficient authority to be admitted as supreme judges of our controversies: that contradiction which is often found amongst them, evidently showing that they are not *infallible* judges, such as it is requisite that they should be, for establishing all those points which are at this day maintained by the Church of Rome against the Protestants.

CHAPTER VI.

Reason VI.—Neither the Church of Rome nor the Protestants acknowledge the Fathers for their judges in points of religion; both of them rejecting such of their opinions and practices as are not suited to their taste. An answer to two objections that may be made against what is delivered in this discourse.

Thus far have we laboured to prove that the writings of the Fathers have not authority enough in themselves to be received as *definitive judgments* upon our differences in religion. Let us now, in the last place, see *what* claim they have to our regard. For although a sentence of judgment should be good and valid in itself, as being pronounced by a competent judge, duly and according to the forms of law; yet this would not serve to determine the controversy, if the authority of this judge be denied by either of the parties, unless, as it is in worldly affairs, the law be armed with such a power, as to be able to force those who are obstinate to submit to reason. As the question is here concerning religion, which is a holy and divine thing, to the embracing whereof men ought to be persuaded and not compelled, force has no place here. For although, perhaps, they could compel men outwardly to render some such respect to the writings of the Fathers, this would not serve to make any impression of the belief of the same, in the heart of any one. The same divisions would still remain in the minds of men, which you are first of all to pluck up by the roots, if ever you intend to make men agree in points of religion. For the certain determination therefore of all differences of this nature, it is necessary that both parties be persuaded that the judge who is to pronounce sentence upon the same, has as much authority as is requisite for that purpose. Though the Fathers had clearly and positively pronounced what they thought on the point in hand, (which yet they have not done, as we have proved before,) and though they had been endued with all these qualities which are requisite for rendering a man fit to be a supreme judge, from whom there can be no appeal, (which yet is not so, as we have already clearly proved,) yet all this would be to no purpose, unless this authority were acknowledged by both parties.

The Old Testament is a book which was written by divine inspiration, and is endued with supreme authority, so that every part of it ought to be believed. Yet this has not any influence with a Pagan; because he does not acknowledge any such excellent worth to be in it. In like manner the New Testament cannot decide the differences between the Jews and us; not because it is not of sufficient authority in itself, but because it is not so to the Jew. And indeed he who should adduce, in disputing against the Pagans, the authority of the Old Testament, or that of the New, for bringing over a Jew to our belief, would be worthy of ridicule.

Suppose therefore, that the writings of the Fathers were clear upon our questions; nay, let it be granted moreover that they were written by Divine inspiration, and are of themselves of a full and undeniable authority; I say still that they cannot decide our debates, if either of the parties shall refuse to acknowledge this great and admirable dignity to be in them; much less if both parties shall refuse to allow them to have this advantage. Let us therefore see, in what account the several parties hold the Fathers, and whether they acknowledge them as the supreme judges of their religion; or at least as arbitrators, whose definitive judgment ought to stand firm and inviolable.

As for Protestants, whom their adversaries would fain persuade, if they could, to receive the Fathers for judges in religion; and to whom consequently they ought not, according to the laws of legitimate controversy, to adduce for the proof of any point in debate, any other principles than what they admit: it is evident that they attribute to the Fathers any thing but such an authority. For in their Confession of Faith* they declare, in the very beginning of it, that they hold the Scriptures to be the rule of their faith: and as for all other ecclesiastical writings, although they consider them useful, yet do they not

* Confess. de Foi des Eglis. Ref. de Fran. Art. 4. [With this agree all the Protestant Confessions.—Ed. Bd. of Pub.]

conceive that a man may safely build any article of faith upon them. And indeed, since they believe (as they tell you immediately afterwards,) that the Scripture contains all things necessary, both for the service of God, and the salvation of men, they have no need of any other judge, and should in vain have recourse to the writings of the ancients; the authority whereof, however great it be, is still much less, both in itself and also in respect of us, than that of the Bible.

In the next place, they seriously profess that their intent is to reform the Christian doctrine according to this rule, and to retain firmly whatever articles of faith are therein delivered, and to reject constantly all those that are not there found laid down, however high and eminent the authority be, that shall rescind the one or establish the other in the belief of men: "It is not lawful (say they) for men, nor yet for the angels themselves, either to add to, or diminish from, or to alter it; neither may antiquity, nor customs, nor multitude, nor judgments, nor human wisdom, nor definitive sentences, nor edicts, nor decrees, nor councils, nor visions, nor miracles, be brought in opposition to it: but on the contrary, rather all other things ought to be examined, regulated, and reformed by it."* These are their own words. If therefore they will not depart from this their belief, which is, as it were, the foundation and key of their whole reformation; they cannot receive the Fathers who lived in the second, third, and fourth, and in the following centuries, as judges, nor yet absolutely and simply as witnesses, in the points of faith. For they all hold that that pure, simple, and holy doctrine which was taught and preached by the Apostles at the beginning of Christianity, and delivered over to us by themselves in the New Testament, has been by little and little altered and corrupted; time, which changes all things, con-

* Confess. de Foi des Eglis. Ref. de Fran. Art. 5.

tinually mixing with it some corruption or other: sometimes a Jewish or a Heathenish opinion, and sometimes again some peculiar observation; other times some superstitious ceremony or other; whilst one building upon the foundation with stubble, another with hay, a third with wood, the body seems at length by little and little, to have become quite different from what it anciently was; we having, instead of a palace of gold and of silver, a house built of plaster, stone, wood, and mud, and the like poor materials. In like manner (say they) as we see that brooks of water, the further distant they are from their springs, the more filth they contract, and the more does their water lose its first purity. As a man, the more he grows in years, the more does that native simplicity which appeared in him in his infancy decay; his body and his mind are changed, and he is so much altered by little and little, through study and art, that at length he seems to be entirely another man. In like manner (say they) has it fared with Christianity. And here they urge that notable passage out of Paul, in his second epistle to the Thessalonians, where he speaks of a great falling away, which then in his time began already to work secretly and insensibly, but was not to break forth till a long time after; as you see it is in all great things, whether in nature, or in the affairs and occurrences that happen to mankind, which are all conceived and hatched slowly, and by degrees, and are sometimes a whole age before they are brought forth.

Now according to this hypothesis, which, as I conceive, is equally common to all Protestants, the doctrine of the Church must necessarily have suffered some alteration in the second age of Christianity, by admitting the mixture of some new matter into its faith and discipline: and so likewise in the third age some other corruption must necessarily have crept in: and so in the fourth, fifth, and the rest that follow;

the Christian religion continually losing something of its original purity and simplicity, and on the other side still contracting all along some new impurities, till at length it came to the highest degree of corruption: in which condition, they say, they found it; and have now at last, by the guidance of the Scriptures, restored it to the self-same state wherein it was at the beginning; and have, as it were, fixed it again upon its true and proper hinge, from whence, partly by the ignorance and partly by the fraud of men, during the space of so many ages together, it had by little and little been removed. This therefore being their opinion, they cannot recognize, as the rule of all their doctrine, the writings of any of the Fathers who lived from the Apostles' time down to ours, without betraying and contradicting themselves. For according to what they maintain, on the progress of corruption in religion, there has been some alteration in the Christian doctrine, both in the second, third, and all following ages. And then again, according to what they conceive and believe of their own reformation, their doctrine is the very same that was in the time of the Apostles, as being taken immediately out of their books. If therefore they should examine it by what the Fathers of the second century believed, there must necessarily be something found in the doctrine of the Fathers which is not in theirs: and the difference will be much greater, if the comparison be made between it and the doctrine of the third, fourth, and the following ages; in all which, according to their hypothesis, the corruption has continually increased. For if their doctrines were in every respect conformable to each other, and the one had neither more nor less than the other, there must necessarily then follow one of these two things; namely, that either this corruption, which they presuppose to be in the faith and discipline of the Church, is not that mystery which worked in St. Paul's time; or else, that their reformation is not the pure and simple doctrine of the Apostles: the members of which division are contradictory to those two positions, which, as we have said, they unanimously maintain. Therefore, to avoid this contradiction, it concerns them constantly to persevere in that which they profess is their belief, in their confession of faith: to wit, that there are no ecclesiastical writings whatsoever, that are of sufficient authority to be safely built upon, and made the judges of faith; and that the Holy Scripture is the only rule by which all these things are to be examined. And this is that which they all agree upon (as far as I have either read or known,) as any one may see in the books of Calvin, Bucer, Melancthon, Luther, Beza, and the rest; who all rely upon the authority of the Scriptures only; and in no case admit the authority of the Fathers, as a sufficient ground whereon to build any article of their belief.

It is true, I confess, that some of their first authors, as Bucer, Peter Martyr, and Jewel of Salisbury, and in a manner all the later writers also, allege the testimonies of the Fathers; but (if you but mark it) it is only by way of confutation, and not of establishing anything: they do it only to overthrow the opinions of the Church of Rome, and not to strengthen their own. For though they hold that the doctrine of the Fathers is not so pure as that of the Apostles; yet do they withal believe that it is much purer than that which is at this day taught by the Church of Rome; the purity of doctrine having continually decayed and the impurity of it increased, the further they are removed from the time of the Apostles, and the nearer they approach towards the afore-mentioned *falling away* spoken of, as they say, by Paul.

Although the Protestants allow the Scriptures alone for the true foundation of their faith, yet they account the writings of the Fathers to be necessary, first of all for proving this *decay* which they say has happened in Christianity; and secondly, for making it appear that the opinions which their adversaries now maintain were not in those days brought into any form, but were as yet only in embryo. As for example, transubstantiation was not as yet an article of faith; notwithstanding they long ago did innocently, and not foreseeing what the issue might prove to be, believe certain things, out of which (being afterwards glossed over by passing through several languages) transubstantiation was at length concocted. So likewise the supremacy of the Pope had at that time no place in the belief of men; although those small threads and root-strings, from whence this vast and wonderful power first sprang, long since appeared in the world.

The like may be said of the greatest part of these other points, which the Protestants will not by any means receive. And that this is their resolution, appears evidently by those many books which they have written on this subject, wherein they show historically the whole progress of this decay in Christianity, as well in its faith as in its polity and discipline. And truly this their design seems to be very sufficient and satisfactory. For, seeing that they propose nothing positively, and as an article of faith necessary to salvation, which may not easily and plainly be proved out of the Scriptures; they have no need to make use of any other principle for the demonstration of the truth of it.

Furthermore, seeing that those positive articles of faith which they believe are in a manner all of them received and confessed by the Church of Rome, as we have said before in the preface to this treatise, there is no need of troubling a man's self to prove the same; those things which both parties are agreed upon, not requiring to be proved, but being always presupposed in all disputations. Yet, if any one has a wish to be informed what the belief of the Fathers was on the said articles, it is easy for them to show that they also believed all of them, as well as themselves; as for example, that there is a God, a Christ, a salvation, a sacrament of baptism, a sacrament of the Eucharist, and the like truths; the greatest part of which we formerly set down in the beginning of this discourse.

And as for those other articles, which are proposed to the world, by the Church of Rome, it is sufficient for them that they are able to answer the arguments which are brought to prove them, and to make it by this means appear that they have not any sure ground at all, and consequently neither may nor ought to be received into the faith of Christians. And this is the use that the Protestants make of the Fathers; showing that they did not hold the said articles, as the Church of Rome does at this day. So that their alleging the Fathers to this purpose only, and indeed their whole practice in these disputes, declares evidently enough, that they conceive not the belief of the Church of Rome to be so perfectly and exactly conformable to that of antiquity, especially of the first four or five ages; which accords very well with their hypothesis, regarding the corruption of the Christian doctrine. Yet no one can conclude from hence, that they allow of the authority of the Fathers as a sufficient foundation to ground any article of faith upon; for this is repugnant both to their doctrine, and to the protestation which they on all occasions make expressly to the contrary. I cannot therefore but wonder at the proceeding of some of our modern authors, who in their disputations with the Protestants endeavour to prove the articles of their faith by testimonies brought out of the Fathers; whereas the Protestants never go about to make good their own opinions, but only to overthrow those of their adversaries, by urging the Fathers' testimonies. For since the members of the Church of Rome maintain, that the Church neither has, nor can possibly err in points of faith, and that its belief in matters of faith has always been the same that it is at this day; it is sufficient for the Protestant to show, by comparing the doctrine of the ancient Fathers with that of the Church of Rome, that there is a great difference between them. Nor does this in any wise bind them to believe throughout whatsoever the Fathers believed; it being evident, according to their hypothesis, that some errors may have crept into their belief; though certainly not such, nor so gross, as have been since entertained by the Church in the ages succeeding. We shall conclude therefore that the Protestants acknowledge not, either in the Fathers or in their writings, any such absolute authority, as renders them supreme judges in matters of religion, from whom no appeal can be made. Whence it will follow, that even though the Fathers had such an authority; yet could not their definitive sentence put an end to any of our controversies; and therefore it concerns the Church of Rome to have recourse to some other way of proof, if she intends to prevail upon her adversaries to receive the aforesaid articles.

What will you say now, if we make it appear to you that the Church of Rome itself does not allow that the Fathers have any such authority? I suppose that if we are able to do this, there is no man so perverse as not to confess, that this proceeding of theirs, in grounding their articles of faith upon the sayings of the Fathers, is not only very insufficient, but very inconvenient also. For how can it ever be endured, that a man who would persuade you to the belief of anything, should for that purpose make use of the testimony of some such persons as neither you nor himself believe to be infallibly true, and so fit to be trusted? Let us now therefore see whether the Church of Rome really has so great an esteem for the Fathers as she would be thought to have by this proceeding.

Certainly several of the learned of that party have upon divers occasions let us see plain enough, that they make no more account of them than the Protestants do. For whereas these require that the authority of the Fathers be grounded upon that of the Scripture; and therefore receive nothing that they deliver as infallibly true, unless it be grounded upon the Scripture, passing by or rejecting whatsoever they propose either besides or contrary to the sense of the Scripture: the other in like manner will have the judgment of the Fathers depend upon that of the Church then being in every age; and approve, pass by, or condemn all such opinions of theirs, as the Church either approves, passes by, or condemns. So that although they differ in this, that the one attributes the supremacy to the Scripture, and the other to the Church of their age; yet they both agree in this, that both of them equally deprive the Fathers of the same; insomuch that they both spend their time unprofitably enough, whilst they trouble themselves in pleading their cause before this inferior court, where the wrangling and cunning tricks of the law have so much place; where the judgments are hard to be obtained, and yet harder to be understood; and, when all is done, are not supreme, but are such as both parties believe they may lawfully appeal from; whereas they might, if they pleased, let alone these troublesome and useless shifts, and come at once before the supreme tribunal; whether it be that of the Scriptures or of the Church; where the suits are not so long, and where the subtlety of pleading is of much less use; where the sentences also are more clear and express, and (which is the chief thing of all) such as we cannot appeal from. But that we may not be thought to impose this opinion upon the Romish doctors unjustly, let us hear them speak themselves.

Cardinal Cajetan, in his preface on the five books of Moses, speaking of his own Annotations, says thus: "If you chance there to meet with any new exposition, which is agreeable to the text, and not contrary either to the Scriptures or to the doctrine of the Church, although perhaps it differs from that which is given by the whole current of the holy doctors; I shall desire the readers that they would not too hastily reject it, but that they would rather censure charitably. Let them remember to give every man his due: there are none but the authors of the Holy Scriptures alone, to whom we attribute such authority, as that we ought to believe whatsoever they have written. But as for others (says Augustine,) of however great sanctity and learning they may have been, I so read them, that I do not believe what they have written merely because they have written it. Let no man therefore reject a new exposition of any passage of Scripture, under pretence that it is contrary to what the ancient Doctors gave; but let him rather diligently examine the text, and the context of the Scripture; and if he finds that it accords well therewith, let him praise God, who has not tied the exposition of the Scriptures to the sense of the ancient Doctors, but to the whole Scripture itself, under the censure of the Catholic Church."* Melchior Canus, bishop of the Canary Islands, having before declared himself, according as Augustine has done, saying that the

* Si quando occurrit novus sensus textui consonus, nec a sacrâ Scripturâ, nec ab ecclesiæ doctrinâ dissonus, quamvis a torrente doctorum sacrorum alienus, rogo lectores omnes ne præcipites detestentur, sed æquos se præbeant censores. Meminerint jus suum unicuique tribuere: solis sacræ Scripturæ auctoribus reservata auctoritas hæc est, ut ideò sic credamus esse, quia ipsi ita scripserunt. Alios autem (inquit Augustinus) ita lego, ut quantalibet sanctitate doctrinaque præpolleant, non ideò credam sic esse, quia ipsi ita scripserunt. Nullus itaque detestetur novum S. Scripturæ sensum, ex hoc quod dissonat priscis doctoribus; sed scrutetur perspicaciùs textum et contextum Scripturæ, et si quadrare invenerit, laudet Deum, qui non alligavit expositionem S. Scripturarum priscorum doctorum sensibus, sed Scripturæ ipsi integræ sub Catholicæ ecclesiæ censura.—*Thom. de Vio Card. Cajet. præf. in Pentat.*

Holy Scriptures only are exempt from all error, further adds: "But there is no man, however holy or learned he be, who is not sometimes deceived, who does not sometimes dote, or sometimes slip."* Then adducing some of those examples which we have before produced, he concludes in these words: "We should therefore read the ancient Fathers with all due reverence; yet, as they were but men, with discrimination and judgment."† A little afterwards he says, "that the Fathers sometimes fail, and bring forth monsters, out of the ordinary course of nature."‡ And in the same place he says that "to follow the ancients in all things, and to tread everywhere in their steps, as little children use to do in play, is nothing else but to disparage our own parts, and to confess ourselves to have neither judgment nor skill enough for searching into the truth. No, let us follow them as guides, but not as masters."

"It is very true (says Ambrosius Catharinus in like manner) that the sayings and writings of the Fathers have not of themselves any such absolute authority, as that we are bound to assent to them in all things."§

The Jesuits also themselves inform us sufficiently in many places, that they do not reckon themselves so tied to follow the judgment of the Fathers in all things, as people may imagine.

Petavius, in his annotations upon Epiphanius, confesses freely, "that the Fathers were men; that they

* Cæteroqui nemo quantumvis eruditus, et sanctus, non interdum allucinatur, non alicubi cœcutit, non quandoque labitur.—*Melch. Can. loc. Theol. l.* 7, *c.* 3, *num.* 4.

† Legendum itaque à nobis Patres veteres cum reverentiâ quidem, sed ut homines, cum delectu atque judicio.—*Id. Ibid.*

‡ Reliqui vero scriptores sancti inferiores et humani sunt, deficiuntque interdum, ac monstrum quandoque pariunt, præter convenientem ordinem institutumque naturæ.—*Ibid. num.* 7.

§ Verissimum ergo est, quod sanctorum dicta, vel scripta, in se non sunt firmæ auctoritatis, ut in singulis teneamur illis præbere assensum.—*Ambros. Catharin. lib.* 4. *Annot. in Cajet. p.* 273.

had their failings; and that we ought not maliciously to search after their errors, that we may lay them open to the world; but that we may take the liberty to note them whenever they come in our way, to the end that none be deceived by them: and that we ought no more to maintain or defend their errors than we ought to imitate their vices, if at least they had any."* And again, "that many things have slipped from them, which if they were examined according to the exact rule of truth, could not be reconciled to any good sense:"† and that he himself has observed, "that they are out sufficiently, whenever they speak of such points of faith as were not at all called in question in their time."‡ To say the truth, he often rejects both their opinions and their expositions, and sometimes very uncivilly too, as we have noticed before, speaking of his notes upon Epiphanius.§ In one place, (the authority of some of the Fathers which contradicted his opinion on the exposition of a certain passage in Luke, being objected against him) never taking the least notice of their testimonies, he answers—"That we ought to interpret and expound the Fathers by Luke, rather than Luke by them; because they cannot herein say anything but what they have received from Luke."‖ This in my judgment was very judiciously spoken; and be-

* Nos eâ, quâ par est, moderatione in divinorum hominum, sed hominum, errores, ac lapsus non tam inquirimus, quàm oblatos ultrò, ac vel invitis occurrentes, ne cui fraudi sint, patefacimus: tueri autem, ac defendere, nihilo magis quàm eorum vitia, si quæ fuerint imitari debemus.—*Petav. in Epiph. p.* 205.

† Quanquam multa sunt à sanctissimis patribus, præsertim à Chrysostomo in Homiliis aspersa, quæ si ad exactæ veritatis regulam accommodare volueris, boni census inania videbuntur.—*Id. in Epiph. p.* 244.

‡ Id. Ibid. p. 285.

§ Supr. c. 14.

‖ Nec est quod certorum patrum opponatur auctoritas, qui non aliud affirmare possunt, quàm quod ex Luca didicerunt, neque est ulla ratio cur ex illorum verbis Lucam interpretemur potius quàm ex Luca quæ ab illis asseverari videntur.—*Petav. in Epiph. p.* 110.

sides exactly agrees with what Augustine said before, and which may very well be applied to the greatest part of our differences; in all of which the Fathers could not know anything, except what they learned out of the Scriptures: so that their testimonies in these cases ought, according to the opinion of this learned Jesuit, to be expounded and interpreted by the Scriptures, and not the Scriptures by them. And this is the language of all the rest of them.

Maldonate, as bitter an enemy of the Protestants as ever was, having delivered the judgment of some of the Fathers, who were of opinion that the sons of Zebedee answered not so rightly, when, being asked by our Saviour, whether or not they were able to drink of his cup and to be baptized with the baptism that he was baptized with, they said unto him, that they were able; adds, "that for his part, he believes that they answered well."* In another place, expounding Matthew xix. 11, having first brought in the interpretations of various, and indeed in a manner of all, the Fathers, he says at last, "that he could not be persuaded to understand the passage as they did!"† Here you are to observe by the way, that the meaning of this passage is still controverted at this day. How then can this man conceive that the Protestants should think themselves bound necessarily to follow the judgment of this major part of the Fathers, which they themselves make so light of? In another place, where he has occasion to speak of those words of our Saviour, which are at this day in dispute among us, "the gates of hell shall not prevail against it," he is yet more positive, and says, "the sense of these words is not rightly given by any au-

* Malo ego credere, nec temerè, nec inscienter, sed amanter et verè respondisse, &c.—*Maldonat. in Matth.* xx. 22.

† Quam interpretationem adduci non possum ut sequar, &c.—*Id. in Matth.* xix. 11.

thor that I can remember, except Hilary."* So likewise upon Matthew xi. 11, where it is said, "the least in the kingdom of heaven is greater than John the Baptist;" he says, "the opinions of the Fathers upon this passage are very different; and to speak freely, none of them pleases me."† In like manner, upon the sixth chapter of John; "Ammonius, (saith he,) Cyril, Theophylact, and Euthymius, answer that all are not drawn, because all are not worthy. But this comes too near Pelagianism."‡

Salmeron, a famous Jesuit, says thus: "Our adversarsaries bring arguments from the antiquity of the Fathers; which I confess has always been of more esteem than novelty. I answer, that every age has yielded to antiquity, &c. But yet we must take the liberty to say, that the later Doctors have been more quicksighted."§ And again, "Against all this great multitude, which they bring against us, we answer out of the word of God; Thou shalt not follow a multitude to do evil; neither shalt thou speak in a cause, to decline after many, to wrest judgment."||

Michael Medina, disputing at the council of Trent, on the superiority of a bishop over a priest, the

* Quorum verborum sensus non videtur mihi esse, quem omnes, præter Hilarium, quos legisse memini, auctores putant.—*Maldonat. in Matth.* xvi. 18.

† Habet ex multis opinionibus quam eligat lector; sed si meam quoque sententium avet audire, liberè fatebor, in nulla prorsus earum meum qualecunque judicium acquiescere.—*Id. in Matth.* xi. 11.

‡ Ammonius, Cyrillus, Theophylactus, et Euthymius, respondent, non omnes trahi, quia non omnes digni sunt; quod nimis affine est Pelagianorum errori.—*Id. in Joh.* vi. 44.

§ Tertiò, argumenta petunt a Doctorum antiquitate, cui semper major honor est habitus quam novitatibus. Respondetur, quamlibet ætatem antiquitati semper detulisse, &c. sed illud efferimus quò juniores, eò perspicaciores esse Doctores.—*Salmer. in Ep. ad Rom.* v. *disput.* 51, *p.* 468.

|| Denique contra hanc quam objectant multitudinem, respondemus ex verbo Dei, (Exod. xxiii.) "In judicio plurimorum non acquiesces sententiæ, ut a vero devies."—*Ib. col.* 1.

authority of Jerome and Augustine being produced against him, who both held that the difference betwixt them was not of divine but only of positive and ecclesiastical right, answers before the whole congregation, "that it is no marvel that they, and some others also of the Fathers, fell into this heresy; this point being not then clearly determined."*

That no one may doubt of the honesty of the historian who relates this, only hear Bellarmine, who testifies, "that Medina assures us that Jerome was, in this point, of Aërius's opinion; and that not only he, but also Ambrose, Augustine, Sedulius, Primasius, Chrysostom, Theodoret, Œcumenius, and Theophylact, all maintained the same heresy."†

We need not here adduce any more examples: for only read their commentaries, their disputations, and their other discourses, and you will find them almost in every page either rejecting or correcting the Fathers. But I must not pass by the testimony of Cornelius Mussus, bishop of Bitonto, who indeed is more ingenuous and clear than all the rest. "O Rome (says he) to whom shall we go for divine counsels, unless to those persons to whose trust the dispensation of the divine mysteries has been committed? We are therefore to hear him, who is to us instead of God, in things that concern God, as God himself. Certainly for my own part (that I may speak my mind freely) in things that belong to the mysteries of faith, I had rather believe one single Pope than a thousand Augustines, Jeromes, or Gregories, that I may not speak of Richards, Scotusses, and Williams; for I believe and know that the Pope cannot err in matters of faith, because the authority of determining all such things

* Pietr. Soave Pol. hist. nel. concil. Trident. l. 7. p. 575.

† Michael Medina in lib. 1. de sacr. hom. orig. et contin. c. 5, affirmat S. Hieronymum idem omnino cum Aërianis sensisse: neque solum Hieronymum in ea hæresi fuisse, sed etiam Ambrosium, Augustinum, Sedulium, Primasium, Chrysostomum, Theodoretum, Œcumenium, et Theophylactum.—*Bellarm. de Cler. l.* 1. *cap.* 15.

as are points of faith, resides in the Pope."* This passage may seem to some, to be both a very bold and a very indiscreet one: but yet whoever shall but examine the matter seriously, and as it is in itself, and not as it is in its outward appearances only, which are contrived for the most part only to amuse the simpler sort of people, I am confident he will find that this author has both most ingenuously and most truly given the world an account in what esteem the Church of Rome holds the Fathers. For since these men maintain that the Pope is infallible, and confess withal that the Fathers may have erred; who sees not that they set the Pope much above the Fathers? Nor may it here be replied, that they do not all of them hold that the Pope is infallible. For, besides that those among them who contradict this opinion are both the least and the least considerable part also of the Church of Rome, these very men attribute to the Church existing, in every age, this right of infallibility, which they will not allow the Pope: insomuch that a council now called together, is, according to their account, of much greater authority than the ancient Fathers. So that the only difference between these men and the forementioned Italian bishop, is, that whereas they will have the authority of the ancient Fathers to submit to the whole body of modern bishops assembled in a general council; he will have their authority to be less than that of a single Pope alone. All that can be found fault with in that speech of his, is, perhaps,

* A quo, Roma, quærenda sunt divina consilia, nisi ab illis, quibus mysteriorum Dei dispensatio credita est? Quem ergo pro Deo habemus, in his quæ Dei sunt quicquid ipse dixerit tanquam Deum audire debemus. Ego (ut ingenuè fatear) plus uni summo Pontifici crederem in his, quæ fidei mysteria tangunt, quam mille Augustinis, Hieronymis, Gregoriis; ne dicam Richardis, Scotis, Gulielmis. Credo enim, et scio, quòd summus Pontifex, in his quæ fidei sunt, errare non potest; quoniam auctoritas determinandi quæ ad fidem spectant, in Pontifice residet.—*Corn. Muss. episcop. Bitont. in ep. ad Rom. c.* 14, *p.* 606.

his hyperbolical expression, of a thousand Augustines, Jeromes, and Gregories, all which joined together, he, in too disdainful a manner, casts down beneath the feet of one single Pope. But this height of expression may be somewhat excused in him, considering that such excesses as these are very common with all high and free-minded persons.

But the practice of the Church of Rome itself will be able to inform us more truly and clearly what esteem they have of antiquity. For if we ought to stand to the Fathers, and not to depart from anything they have authorized, nor to ordain anything which they were ignorant of, how comes it to pass, that we at this day see so many various observances and customs which were observed by the ancients, now quite laid aside? And whence is it that we find in antiquity no mention at all of many things which are now in great request amongst us? There are as it were three principal parts in religion; namely, points of belief, of ceremony, and of discipline. We shall run over lightly all three, and so far as is necessary only for our present purpose; that so we may let the world see, that in every one of these three parts they have both abolished and established many things expressly against the authority of the ancients.

As for the first of these, we have already given the reader some specimens only in the preceding chapters. For we have seen that the opinion of the greatest part of the ancient Church on the state of the soul, till the time of the resurrection, which besides is at this day also maintained by the Greek Church, was condemned not much above two hundred years since, by the Church of Rome, at the council of Florence; and a quite contrary belief there established, as an article of the Christian faith.

We have seen besides, that the opinion of the Fathers of the primitive Church, and even down as far as to the end of the sixth century after our Saviour

Christ and afterward, was that the eucharist was as necessary to salvation as baptism; and that consequently it was to be administered to little children. But for all this, the council of Trent has condemned this opinion as an error in faith; anathematizing, by a canon made expressly for that purpose, all those whoever should maintain the same. "Let him be accursed (say they) whoever shall say that the eucharist is necessary for little children before they come to years of discretion."* That the Fathers might not take offence hereat, as having so fearful an affront put upon them; these men have endeavoured to persuade both them and others, that they never did believe that, which themselves have most clearly, and in express terms, protested that they did believe, as we have before made it appear: which is, to double the injury upon them rather than to make them any reparation for it; seeing that they deal with them now, not as heretics only, but as fools also, whom a man may at pleasure persuade that they do not believe that which they really do believe.

We have abundantly heard, out of Jerome's mouth, how the opinion of the Millennarians was of old maintained by several of the ancient Fathers; which yet is now condemned as an error in faith. And indeed the number of these kind of differences in opinion is almost infinite.

It was accounted no error in those days to believe that the soul was derived from the father down to the son, according to the ordinary course of generation: but this opinion would now be accounted a heresy.

The ancients held, "that it would be opposing the authority of the Scriptures, if we should hang up the

* Si quis dixerit, parvulis, antequam ad annos discretionis pervenient necessariam esse eucharistiæ communionem, anathema sit. —*Concil. Trident. Sess.* 21. *Can.*

picture of any man in the Church,"* and "that we ought not to have any pictures in our churches, that that which we worship and adore be not painted upon a wall."† Now the Council of Trent has ordained quite the contrary, and says: "That we ought to have and to keep, especially in our churches, the images of Christ, of the Virgin the mother of God, and of the other saints; and that we are to yield unto them all due honour and veneration."‡

All the ancient Fathers,§ as far as we can learn out of their writings, believed that the blessed Virgin Mary was conceived in original sin. If now the Fathers of the council of Trent accounted them to be the judges of faith, why did they fear to be thought to hold their opinion on this point? For, having delivered their definite judgment in a decree there passed to this purpose, and declared that this sin, which has spread itself over the whole mass of mankind by propagation and not by imitation, has seized on every person in particular; they at length conclude, "that their intention is not to comprehend within this number the blessed and unspotted Virgin Mary, the mother of God:"‖ which words of theirs it is impossible so to expound, that they shall not in plain terms give the lie to all the Fathers. For if they

* Cùm ergo hæc vidissem in ecclesia Christi contra auctoritatem Scripturarum, hominis pendentem imaginem, &c.—*Epiphan. ep. ad Joh. Hierosol. t.* 2 *p.* 317. *c.* 2.

† Placuit picturas in ecclesia esse non debere, ne quod colitur aut adoratur, in parietibus depingatur.—*Conc. Eliber. Can.* 36.

‡ Imagines porro Christi, Deiparæ Virginis, et aliorum Sanctorum, in templis præsertim habendas et retinendas, eisque debitum honorem et venerationem impertiendam.—*Concil. Trid. Sess.* 25. *Decreto de Invocat. &c. Sanctorum.*

§ Ambros. August. Chrysost. &c. de quibus vide Melch. Canum de loc. Theolog. l. 7, num. 3.

‖ Declarat tamen hæc ipsa Sancta Synodus, non esse suæ intentionis comprehendere in hoc decreto, ubi de peccato originali agitur, B. et immaculatam, Virginem Mariam, Dei genitricem.—*Conc. Trid. Sess.* 5 *Decreto de Pecc. Origin.*

mean, by these words, the Virgin Mary was conceived without sin, they decidedly establish an opinion contradictory to that of the Fathers: which is the grossest manner that can be of giving them the lie. If they mean here no more than this, (which sense yet their words will scarcely be ever made to bear,) that it is not known, as a certain truth, that the Virgin Mary was conceived in sin; they, however honestly say, in plain terms, that these good men affirmed as true that which is yet doubtful, and maintained as certain that which was but problematical only and questionable.

The council of Laodicea, which is inserted in the code of the Church Universal, puts not into the canon* of the Old Testament any more than twenty-two books; excluding by this means out of this number the book of Tobit, Judith, the book of Wisdom, Ecclesiasticus, and the two books of the Maccabees. Melito† bishop of Sardis, Origen,‡ Cyril of Jerusalem,§ Gregory Nazianzen,|| Hilary,¶ and Epiphanius,** all do the same. Athanasius,†† Ruffinus,‡‡ and Jerome,§§ expressly reject these very books from the canon. And yet the aforesaid council of Trent "anathematizes all those who will not receive, as holy and canonical, all these books, with every part of the same as they are wont to be read in the Church, and as they are found in the old Latin edition, commonly called the vulgar translation."||||

*Conc. Laod. Can. 59, 60. Cod. Græc. Can. Eccl. Univers. Can. 163.
† Melit. Sard. apud Euseb. Hist. Eccles. lib 4 c. 27.
‡ Origen. apud Euseb. Hist. Eccl. l. 6. c. 26. et in Philocal. c. 3.
§ Cyril. Hieros. Catech. 4.
|| Greg. Nazianz. Carm. 33. t. 2. p. 98.
¶ Hilar Præfat. in Psal. fol. 2.
** Epiphan. l. de ponder. et mens. t. 2. p. 162.
†† Athan. ep. festal. t. 2. p. 38, 39, et Synops. Script. p. 58.
‡‡ Ruffin. Expos. Symb. inter opera Cypr. p. 552.
§§ Hæc Prol. Galeato, et Prol. in lib. Salom. ad Paul. et Eustach. et Prol. in libr. Sal. ad Chron. et Heliod. et præfat. in Esdr.
|||| Siquis autem libros ipsos integros, cum omnibus suis partibus,

Besides the affront which they have offered to so many of the ancient and most eminent among the Fathers, and indeed to the whole primitive Church itself, which received this canon of Laodicea amongst its universal rules, they have also established a position here which was not till then so much as ever heard of in Christendom; namely, that the old vulgar translation of the Bible is to be admitted as canonical and authentic in the Church of God.

The hundred-and-fifty Fathers of the second general council, and the six hundred and thirty of the fourth, were all of them of opinion that the ancients had advanced the see of Rome above that of other bishops, by reason of the pre-eminence and temporal greatness of the city of Rome over other cities; and for the same reason they also thought good to advance in like manner the throne of the patriarch of Constantinople to the same height with the former, by reason of the city where he resided being now arrived to the self-same height of dignity with Rome itself. *Τον μεντοι Κωνσταντινοπολεως ἐπισκοπον, ἐχειν τα πρεσβεια της τιμης μετα τον της Ῥωμης ἐπισκοπον, δια το εἶναι αὐτην νεαν Ῥωμην.* . . Concil. Constant. I. Can. 3. *Και γαρ τω θρονω της πρεσβυτερας Ῥωμης, δια το βασιλευειν την πολιν ἐκεινην, οἱ πατερες εἰκοτως ἀποδεδωκασι τα πρεσβεια,* &c. *Την βασιλεια και συγκλητω τιμηθεισαν πολιν, και των ἰσων ἀπολαυουσαν πρεσβειων τη πρεσβυτερα βασιλιδι Ῥωμη, και ἐν τοις ἐκκλησιαστικοις ὡς ἐκεινην μεγαλυνεσθαι πραγμασι.*—Conc. Chalced. Can. 28.

I assure you, that for all this he would now be Anathema Maranatha, whoever should go about to derive the supremacy of the Pope from any other original, than from—"*Tu es Petrus:*" and "*Pasce oves meas.*"

prout in ecclesia Catholica legi consueverunt, et in veteri vulgata Latina editione habentur, pro sacris et canonicis non susceperit, &c. anathema esto.—*Conc. Trident. Sess.* 4. *Decr. de Can. script.*

The council of Trent anathematizes all those who deny that bishops are a higher order than priests:* and yet Jerome,† and divers others of the Fathers openly hold the doctrine.

We have already told you, that the Church of Rome long since excommunicated the Greeks, because they held, that the Holy Ghost proceeds not from the Son, but from the Father only. And yet Theodoret, who expressly denied that the Holy Ghost proceeds from the Son, as we have shown in the preceding chapter, was received by the ancient Church, and in particular by Pope Leo, as a true Catholic bishop, without requiring him to declare himself any otherwise, or to give them any satisfaction on this point.

Indeed we might enumerate many similar differences between the Roman and the ancient Church: but these examples will suffice to show how the Church of Rome maintains that the authority of the opinions of the ancients ought to be accounted supreme.

We shall proceed, in the next place, to say something of the ceremonies in the Christian religion.

The first of all is Baptism, which takes us out of nature's stock, and engrafts us into Jesus Christ. Now it was a custom heretofore in the ancient Church, to immerse those they baptized in the water; as Tertullian,‡ Cyprian,§ Epiphanius,|| and others testify. And indeed they plunged them thus three times; as the same Tertullian¶ and Jerome** inform us. This is still the practice both of the Greek and

* Si quis dixerit Episcopos non esse Presbyteris superiores, &c. anathema sit.—*Conc. Trid. Sess.* 23, *cap.* 4, *et Can.* 7.

† Hieron. passim; vide supra lib. 1. c. ult.

‡ Tertul. lib. de Cor. Mil. c. 3.

§ Cypr. ep. 76, p. 211, ubi vide Pamel.

|| Epiphan. Pan. Hær. 30. p. 128.

¶ Tertul. lib. de Cor. Mil. c. 3, et lib. adv. Prax. c. 26.

** Hieron. Dial. advers, Lucifer. t. 2, p. 187. In lavacro ter caput mergitare.

the Russian Church. Yet, this custom, which is both so ancient and universal, is now abolished by the Church of Rome. And this is the reason that the Muscovites* say, that the Latins are not rightly and duly baptized, because they use not this ceremony in their baptism, which they say is expressly enjoined them in the canons of Joannes the Metropolitan, whom they hold to have been a prophet. Indeed, Gregory the Greek monk, who was, notwithstanding, a great stickler for the union, in the council of Florence, yet confesses in his answer to the epistle of Mark, bishop of Ephesus, that it is necessary in baptism, that the persons to be baptized should be thrice dipped in the water.† At their coming out of the water, in the ancient Church, they gave them milk and honey to eat,‡ as the same authors witness; and immediately after this they made them partakers also of the blessed communion, both great and small: whence the custom still remains in Ethiopia, of administering the eucharist to little children, and making them take down a small quantity of it, as soon as they are baptized.§

What have these great adorers of antiquity now done with these ceremonies? Where is the *milk*, or the *honey*, or the *eucharist*, which the ancient Fathers were wont to administer to all, immediately after baptism? Certainly these things, notwithstanding the practice of the ancients, have been now long since buried and forgotten at Rome.

In ancient times they often deferred the baptizing both of infants and of others, as appears by the history of the emperors Constantine the Great,|| of

* Cassand. l. de Bapt. Inf. p. 693.

† Greg. Mon. Protosync. in Apol. contr. ep. Marc. ep. 721. t. 4, Conc. gen. ‛Οτι μεν ἀναγκαιον ἐστι και το δια τριων καταδυσεων, &c.

‡ Deinde egressos lactis et mellis prægustare concordiam.—*Tertul. et Hieron. ubi supr.*

§ Alvarez, in his voyage to Ethiopia.

|| Euseb. de vita Constant. l. 4.

Constantius,* of Theodosius,† of Valentinian, and of Gratian in Ambrose;‡ and also by the Homilies of Gregory Nazianzen,§ and of Basil,|| upon this subject. Some of the Fathers too were of opinion, that it is proper it should be deferred; for instance, Tertullian, as we have formerly noticed.

How comes it to pass that there is not now so much as the least trace or footing of this custom to be found at this day in the Church of Rome? Nay, whence is it that they would regard a man with horror, that should but attempt to put it in practice?

I shall here forbear to speak of the times of administering baptism, which was performed ordinarily in the ancient Church, only on the eves of Easter day, and of Whitsunday; neither shall I say anything of the ceremony of the Paschal taper, and the *albes*, or white vestments that the newly baptized persons were used to wear all Easter week;"¶ because it may be thought perhaps that these are too trivial; although, to say the truth, if we are to regard the authority of men, and not the reason of the things themselves, I do not see why all the rites should not still be retained, as well as those exorcisms, and renouncings of the devil and the world, with all its pomps and vanities, which, in imitation of antiquity, are at this day, though very improperly, acted by them over little infants, though only a day old.

As for the eucharist, Cassander shows clearly that it was celebrated in the ancient Church with bread and wine, offered by the people:** and that the bread was first broken into several pieces, and then consecrated and distributed among the faithful. Notwith-

* Socrat. hist. Eccl. l. 3, c. 37. † Id. l. 4. c. 6.
‡ Ambros. Orat. de obit. Valentin. t. 3, p. 9.
§ Greg. Nazianz. Orat. 40.
|| Basil. homil. εἰς Βαπτισμον προτρεπτικη.
¶ Cassand. in hymno, p. 227, 228.
** Cassand. in Liturg. c. 26.

standing, the contrary use has now prevailed; nor do they consecrate any bread which is offered by the people, which was the ancient custom, but only little wafer cakes, made round in the form of a coin; which yet is very sharply reproved, in the old exposition or the "*Ordo Romanus*,"* &c. The same Cassander also gives us an account at large,† how in ancient times the canonical prayer, and the consecration of the eucharist, were read out with a loud voice, and in such a manner that the people might all of them be able to hear it, so that they might say *Amen* to it; whereas the priest now pronounces it with a very low voice,‡ so that none of the congregation can tell what he says; and hence it is, that this part of the liturgy is called *secret*.

We have heretofore shown,§ that the ancient Fathers concealed, as carefully as they could, the matter and the rites used in the celebration of this holy sacrament; which they never performed in presence either of the catechumens or of unbelievers. But now there is not any such care taken in this respect; for they celebrate the eucharist openly and publicly, even before Jews, Pagans, or Mohammedans, without any more regard to these ancient rules, than if there had never been any such custom. And as if the design of these men were to run counter to antiquity in all things, when the sacrament was concealed as much as possible, they show it now openly, and carry it publicly abroad every day through the streets, and sometimes also go in solemn procession with it: which custom of theirs is of very late standing among Christians, and which heretofore would have looked not only very strange, but would have been accounted rather profane and unlawful. And thus have the

* Apud Cassand. in Liturg. c. 26, p. 60.

† Cassand. in Liturg. p. 63, 64, c. 28.

‡ Conc. Trid. Sess. 22, c. 5, et can. 9.

§ Lib. i. c. 5.

customs and observations of the ancient Fathers been quite laid aside, and other new ones, which they never heard of, instituted in their place.

The same Cassander also proves,* that in ancient times they celebrated the eucharist only in the presence of those that were to communicate; and that all the rest withdrew. It is clear, that Chrysostom very bitterly reproves those who would be present at the celebration of the eucharist without communicating.

Indeed we at this day see, in the Ethiopic liturgy, that the Gospel being read, the deacon cries aloud: "All you, that will not receive the sacrament, depart: withdraw, you catechumens." And again, after the creed is sung, he says to the people, "Let them that will not communicate, depart." But now-a-days, for the most part, none of those who are present at the celebration, communicate of it: they content themselves with adoring the sacrament only, without partaking of it at all; whence you have this manner of expression:—"*to hear mass;*" and "*to see mass.*" Chrysostom says: "Whosoever shall stay here, and not participate of the mysteries, behaves himself like an impudent, shameless person. I beseech you, (says he) if any one that were invited to a feast, should come and sit down after he has washed his hands, and fitted himself to come to the table, and at length should forbear to touch any of those dishes which are served in upon it, would not this be a very great affront to him who invited him? Had he not better have forborne coming at all? It is the very same case here. Thou hast come, and hast sung the hymn, and, seeing thou hast not retired with those that were not worthy, hast thereby also professed thyself to be of the number of those who are worthy. How comes it to pass that, seeing thou hast staid behind, thou

* Cassand. in Liturg. 55, c. 26.

dost not communicate of this *table?*" &c. *Πας γαρ ὁ μη μετεχων των μυστηριων ἀναισχυντως, και ἱταμως ἑστηκως*, &c. *Ειπε μοι, εἰ τις εἰς ἑστιασιν κληθεις, τας χειρας νιψαιτο, και κατακλιθῃ, και ἑτοιμος γενοιτο προς την τραπεζαν, εἰτα μη μετεχοι· οὐχι ὑβριζει τον καλεσαντα; οὐ βελτιον τον τοιουτον μηδε παραγενεσθαι; οὑτω δε και συ παραγεγονας, τον ὑμνον ᾐσας μετα παντων, ὡμολογησας εἶναι των ἀξιων, τω μη μετα των ἀναξιων ἀναχεχωρηκεναι· πως ἐμεινας, και οὐ μετεχεις της τραπεζης.**

If any man should now preach this doctrine to the Romanists, would they not laugh at him? inasmuch as their custom in this particular is far different (as every one sees,) from what it was heretofore in the ancient Church.

It is as clear as the day, that all along in the ancient Church it was lawful for any of the faithful to take home with them the holy eucharist, which they might keep in any private place, to take it afterwards by themselves alone, whenever they pleased. Whence it is that Tertullian advises those that durst not communicate upon the days appointed for that purpose, for fear of breaking their fast, to keep the body of Christ by them. "Receiving the body of Christ (says he) and keeping it by thee, both are preserved entire; both the participation of the sacrifice, and the discharge of thy duty."†

This appears also by a story related by Cyprian, of a certain woman "who going about to open, with unworthy hands, a coffer of hers, where the eucharist was laid up, she presently saw fire breaking out thence; which so amazed her, that she durst not touch it."‡

* Chrysost. Homil. 3, in ep. ad Ephes. t. 3, p. 778, edit Savilii.

† Accepto corpore Domini, et reservato, utrumque salvum est, et participatio sacrificii, et executio officii.—*Tertul. lib. de orat. c.* 14.

‡ Cum quædam arcam suam, in qua Domini sanctum fuit, manibus indignis tentasset aperire, igne inde surgente deterrita est, ne auderet attingere.—*Cyprian. l. de laps. p.* 244.

Ambrose also, a long while after Cyprian, testifies sufficiently that this custom in his time continued in the Church; where he tells the story of his brother Satyrus, who being upon the sea, and in danger of shipwreck, "and fearing lest he should go out of the world without the holy mysteries (for he was yet but of the number of the catechumens,) made his addresses to those whom he knew to have been initiated, and desired of them to give him the divine sacrament of the faithful; not that he might therewith satisfy the curiosity of his eyes, but that it might strengthen his faith. And thus having put it into a handkerchief, and then tying the handkerchief about his neck, he threw himself into the sea, and was saved."*

If Rome indeed bears such great respect to the Fathers, as they would make us believe, why has she not then retained this custom? Why then should that which was then so ordinarily practised, be now in our days so much disliked, that they will not by any means permit the friars to keep the eucharist in their convent, nor yet in their choir, nor in any other place, save only the public church?†

Ambrose informs us moreover, that in those times they made no scruple at all of carrying the eucharist upon the sea; which custom of the ancients is so much disliked by the Church of Rome in our days, that they hold it an unlawful thing, either to consecrate or to carry the sacrament ready consecrated, upon any water whatever, whether it be that of the sea or of rivers.

This very custom of the ancients keeping the sacra-

* Non mortem metuens, sed ne vacuus mysterii exiret e vita, quos initiatos esse cognoverat, ab his divinum illud fidelium Sacramentum poposcit, non ut curiosos oculos insereret arcanis, sed ut fidei suæ consequeretur auxilium. Etenim ligari fecit in orario, et orarium involvit collo, atque ita se dejecit in mare.—*Ambros. de obit. Satyr. p.* 19, *t.* 3.

† Conc. Trid. Sess. 25, de regul. et Mon. cap. 10.

ment by them, proves very clearly that the faithful in those days received the sacrament with their hands: which is also plainly enough intimated by Tertullian; where, inveighing against those among the Christians, who were *sculptors* and *painters* by profession, he reproves them "for touching the body of our Saviour with those very hands which bestowed bodies on devils:"* that is to say, with those hands wherewith they made idols. Cyprian is clear in point in divers places;† Gregory Nazianzen also testifies the same in his sixty-third poem:—*Οὐδε χερες φρισσουσιν, ἐπην ἐς μυστιν ἐδωδην τεινεις.*‡ &c. And in the canons of the council of Constantinople in Trullo, held in the year of our Lord 680, there is one which appoints, "that he, who is to communicate, place his hands in the form of a cross, and so receive the communication of grace:" (*εἰ τις του ἀχραντου σωματος*, &c.)§ which had been the practice from the time of Cyril of Jerusalem. Yet there is no one but knows that this custom has no place now in the Church of Rome; where the communicants receive the eucharist, not with their hand but with their mouth, into which it is put by the priest.

I would also gladly be informed, by what canon of the ancient Church those *single masses*, which are now celebrated and said every day, where none communicates but the priest alone who consecrates the host, were instituted or permitted: and moreover how that respect which they pretend they bear to antiquity, can stand with that canon of the council of Trent, which says: "Whosoever shall say, that those masses wherein the priest alone communicateth sacramentally, are unlawful, and fit to be abolished, let him be

* Eas manus admovere corpori Domini, quæ dæmoniis corpora conferunt.—*Tertul. lib. de Idol. cap.* 7.

† Cyprian. ep. 56, et lib. de bono Patientiæ, p. 316.

‡ Greg.Naz. Carm. 63.

§ Synod. Quinis. Can. 101.

accursed:"* seeing that this kind of masses was utterly unknown to the ancient Church, as Cassander proves at large, in his "*Consultatio de Articulis Religionis*," written to the emperor Ferdinand.†

But that which most of all gives offence to those devoted to antiquity, is the custom which the Church of Rome has introduced and established, by the express decrees and canons of two of their general councils, the one held at Constance,‡ and the other at Trent,§ of not allowing the communion of the cup to any but to the priest who consecrates the same; excluding by this means, first, all the laity, and secondly, all the priests and others of the clergy, who had not the consecrating of it: whereas the whole ancient Church, for the space of fourteen hundred years, admitted them both to the communion of the holy and blessed cup, as well as to the participation of the consecrated bread; as those two councils themselves confess, in the preface to this New Constitution.‖ And this is still the practice also at this day among all Christians throughout the world, Russians, Greeks,¶ Armenians, Ethiopians,** Protestants,†† and all others in general, except the Latins only, who are of the communion of the Church of Rome. But besides the ancients permitting this communion under *both kinds* (as they use to speak,) it seems (which is yet much more) that unless it were in some extraordinary cases, they did not at all permit the commu-

* Si quis dixerit missas, in quibus solus sacerdos sacramentaliter communicat, illicitas esse, ideoque abrogandas, anathema sit.—*Conc. Trid. Sess.* 22, *c.* 6. *et Can.* 8.

† Cassan. Consult. ad Ferdin. &c. p. 995, et in Liturg. p. 83. cap. 33.

‡ Conc. Const. Sess. 13.

§ Conc. Trid. Sess. 21, c. 1, et 2, Can. 2.

‖ Licet ab initio Christianæ religionis non infrequens utriusque speciei usus fuisset. &c.—*Ibid. c.* 2.

¶ Jerem. P. CN. Resp. 1. ad Witemb.

** Alvarez, in his Voyage, ch. 11.

†† Confession of the Church of England, art. 12.

nicating under *one kind only.* For otherwise, why should Pope Leo give this very thing, as a mark to distinguish the Manichees from the Catholics? "When they sometimes are present at our mysteries (says he) that so they may hide their infidelity, they so order the matter, in their participating of these mysteries, that they receive the body of Christ into their unworthy mouth, but will not take into it one drop of the blood of our redemption:" and he further adds, that "he gives his auditory this warning, that they may know those men by this mark."* Should this pope now arise from his grave, and come into the world again, he would certainly believe that all those who adhere to his see, were turned Manichees, except the consecrating priests alone. How besides would you be able, without this hypothesis, to explain that decree of pope Gelasius, which says, "we are informed, that there are some, who having taken a small portion of the sacred body only, forbear to partake of the consecrated blood; doing this, as we hear, out of I know not what superstitious conceit wherewith they are possessed; we therefore will, that they either partake of the whole sacrament, or else that they be wholly put back from communicating; forasmuch as there cannot, without very great sacrilege, be any division made in one and the same mystery."†

Indeed what can you otherwise say to that story which is related by the accusers of Ibas, bishop of Edessa; that having one time made but a very scanty

* Cumque ad tegendam infidelitatem suam nostris audeant interesse mysteriis, ita in sacramentorum communione se temperant, ut interdum tutiùs lateant, ore indigno Christi corpus accipiunt, sanguinem autem redemptionis nostræ omnino haurire declinant. Quod ideo vestram volumus scire sanctitatem, ut vobis hujusmodi homines et his manifestentur indiciis, &c.—*Leo* I., *P. R. Serm.* 4, *de Quadrag. p.* 108.

† Comperimus autem, quòd quidam sumpta tantummodò corporis sacri portione, a calice sacri cruoris abstineant, &c. quia divisio unuis ejusdemque mysterii sine grandi sacrilegio non potest provenire.—*Gelas. Joh. et Maj. Episc. Decret. de Consecrat. dist.* 2, *c.* 12.

provision of wine for the service of the altar, which, after it had been begun to be distributed to the communicants, began quickly to fail: "he perceiving this, beckoned to those who delivered about the holy body, that they should come back again; because he had no more of the blood of our Saviour:"—*῾Ωστε τοις το ἁγιον σωμα διανεμουσιν ἐνευσεν εἰσελθειν αὐτους, ὡς του αἱματος μη εὑρισκομενου.**

What need was there of ordering them to suspend the business, because there was no more wine, if it was at that time lawful to distribute the bread alone, without the wine? If the councils of Trent and of Constance had accounted the authority of the Fathers as supreme, how came it to pass that they abolished that which had for so long a time, and so constantly, been observed by them? And how again does this other canon of the council of Trent agree with that deference which they pretend to bear towards antiquity; where it is said that "whosoever shall say that the holy Catholic Church has not been induced by just causes and reasons to communicate, under the species of bread only, to the laity, and even to the priests also, who do not consecrate; or that it has erred in this point, let him be accursed."†

It seems to be no very easy matter to acquit the modern Church, without condemning the ancient, their practices being manifestly contradictory to each other; the modern Church forbidding that which the ancient permitted; and the ancient Church seeming to have expressly forbid that which the modern commands.

How can you say that the one had just reasons for what it did, unless you grant that the other, in doing

* Act. Concil. Chalced. act. 16, p. 356, tom. 2, Concil. gen.

† Si quis dixerit sanctam Ecclesiam Catholicam non justis causis et rationibus adductam fuisse, ut laicos, atque etiam clericos non conficientes sub panis tantummodo specie communicaret, aut in eo errasse, anathema sit.—*Conc. Trid. Sess.* 21, *Can.* 2.

the contrary, had either no reason at all, or else but very unjust ones; seeing that it is most clear that neither the world nor the times are any whit changed, within these two hundred years, from what they were before? For it is impossible for any man to allege any reason for the practice of the moderns, which should not in like manner have obliged the ancients: nor again to produce any reason for the contrary practice of the ancients, which does not in like manner oblige the moderns. So that of necessity, either the one or the other of them must needs have been guilty either of error, or, at least, of negligence and ignorance. We may very well therefore conclude, that the Church of Rome, seeing it believes itself to be infallible, manifestly in this particular condemns the ancient Church, as guilty of ignorance, or of negligence at the least; which in my judgment seems not so well becoming those persons who do nothing else but continually preach to us the honour of antiquity. But here will all the true reverers of antiquity have an ample field for reflexion. For as for those reasons, by which the Fathers of the council of Trent were induced to make the afore-mentioned decree, how (will they say) can we know whether they were just or not; seeing that they themselves produce none at all? Whereas the reasons which induced the ancients to do as they did, which may be found in a certain discourse printed at Paris, at the end of Cassander's works, are very sound and clear, and in my judgment very full, both of wisdom and of charity.*

We need not enter further into this disputation: it is sufficient for my purpose, that the Church of Rome, in doing thus, has manifestly abolished a very ancient custom in the Church.

Besides these ceremonies, which were practised by the Fathers in baptism and in the eucharist, they

* Inter Opera Cassand. pag. 1019.

have laid aside many other also, which were formerly in use in the Church. I shall not here speak of fasting on Saturdays, which is observed by the Church of Rome, contrary to the ancient practice of the whole Christian Church, who all accounted it unlawful: because this difference in practice is as ancient as Augustine's time,* and therefore ought not to be imputed to the modern Church of Rome. I shall for the same reason also pass by what Firmilianus says,† namely, that in his time, about two hundred and fifty years after the nativity of our Saviour Christ, "those of Rome did not in all things observe whatsoever had been delivered from the beginning; and that they in vain alleged the authority of the Apostles."

I must here remark, that anciently it was a general custom throughout all Christendom, *not to kneel*, either upon the Lord's days, or upon any day betwixt Easter-day and Whit-Sunday, which custom has been generally abolished by the entire Church of Rome; and yet whether you consider the antiquity, or whether you look upon the authority of those who both practised this themselves, and also recommended it to our observance, you will hardly find any more venerable custom than this. For the author of the "Questions and Answers," attributed to Justin Martyr, makes mention of this custom, and moreover gives the reason and ground of it; and besides proves by a certain passage, which he produces out of Irenæus, that it had its beginning in the Apostolical times. *Ἐκ των ἀποστολικων δε χρονων ἡ τοιαυτη συνηθεια ἐλαβε την ἀρχην, καθως φησιν ὁ μακαριος Εἰρηναιος ὁ μαρτυς, και ἐπισκοπος Λουγδουνου, ἐν τω περι του Πασχα λογω*, &c.‡

* August. t. 2, Ep. 86, ad Casulan. p. 74 et 75.

† Eos qui Romæ sunt non ea in omnibus observare, quæ sint ab origine tradita, et frustra Apostolorum auctoritatem prætendere.—*Firmil. in Ep. ad Cypr. quæ est inter Epist. Cypr.* 75.

‡ Pseud. Just. Q. et R. Quæst. 115.

Tertullian also speaks of this custom:* and both Epiphanius,† and Jerome,‡ class it among the institutions of the Church: and what is yet more than all this, the sacred general council of Nice authorizes the same, by an express canon made to that purpose. "Forasmuch as there are some (say these three hundred and eighteen venerable Fathers,) who kneel upon the Lord's day, and upon the days of Pentecost; to the end that in all parishes, (or as we now speak, dioceses,) there may be the same order observed in all things, this holy synod ordains that (on these days) they pray standing:" *Ἐπειδη τινες εἰσιν ἐν τη κυριακη γονυ κλινοντες, και ἐν ταις της Πεντηκοστης ἡμεραις, ὑπερ του παντα ἐν παση παροικια ὁμοιως φυλαττεσθαι, ἑστωτας, ἐδοξε τη ἁγια Συνοδω, τας εὐχας ἀποδιδοναι τω Θεω.*§ This ancient constitution was revived and explained in the council of Constantinople in Trullo,|| towards the end of the seventh century; where it was expressly *forbidden to kneel* during the space of those twenty-four hours that pass between Saturday evening and Sunday evening. Every one is also aware how they have abrogated the fast, that was wont to be observed upon the fourth day of the week, that is Wednesday; which yet was the practice of the ancients, as appears by what we find in the pseudo-Ignatius,¶ in Peter,** bishop of Alexandria, and a martyr, in Epiphanius, *Τινι δε οὐ συμπεφωνηται ἐν πασι κλιμασι της οἰκουμενης ὁτι τετρας, και προσαββατον νηστεια ἐστιν ἐν τη Εκκλησια ὡρισμενη;*†† Clemens Alexandrinus,‡‡ and others.

* Tertul. l. de Coron. milit. cap. 3.
† Epiph. in Panar. in conclus. operis.
‡ Hieron. Dial. contr. Lucifer. p. 187, t. 2.
§ Con. Nic. Can. 20.
|| Synod. Quinisex. Can. 90.
¶ Ignat. Epist. 5.
** Petr. Alexand. in MS.
†† Epiph. Panar. hær. 75. Aerii, p. 910.
‡‡ Clem. Alex. Strom. l. 7. p. 317.

By the same liberty have those vigils been abolished, which were ordinarily kept by the ancient Church, and both approved and defended also by Jerome, against Vigilantius, who found fault with them;* though his opinion has now at length found more favour in the world than Jerome's. The same Father, in another place, delivers to us, for apostolical tradition, that custom which they had in his time, of not suffering the people to depart out of the Church, upon Easter-eve, till midnight was past.† What is now become of this custom, which was not only an ancient one, but was derived also from the Apostles themselves, if you believe Jerome?

We are informed, from several hands, that that command of *abstaining from blood*, and from things strangled, was for a long time observed in the Church. And it appears evidently enough, that it was most rigidly kept in the primitive times, both from the testimony of Tertullian‡ and of Eusebius.§ The council of Constantinople in Trullo excommunicates all those of the laity, and deposes all those of the clergy, who shall offend herein.|| And Pamelius, in his notes upon Tertullian's *Apologetics*,¶ informs us, that it is not long since that the observance of this custom was first laid aside among Christians, it being not much above four hundred years since there were certain penances appointed for those that should violate the same. Yet notwithstanding all its antiquity and universality, it is at length quite disused; the Church of Rome having very gently, and by little and little, laid it aside; no one, that I know of, having taken the least

* De Vigiliis et pernoctationibus Martyrum sæpe celebrandris, &c.—*Hieron. l. cont. Vigil. p.* 163.

† Unde reor et traditionem apostolicam permansisse, ut in die Vigiliarum Paschæ ante noctis dimidium populos dimittere non liceat, expectantes adventum Christi.—*Id. Com.* 4, *in Matth. p.* 121.

‡ Tertul. Apolog. p. 38.

§ Euseb. Hist. Eccles. l. 5, c. 2.

|| Synod. Quinis. Can. 7.

¶ Pamel. in Apolog. Tertull. num. 38.

notice either of the time when, or the manner how, it was done: only this we all see plain enough, that it is now entirely out of use.

The same may be said of that custom of *praying for the saints departed*, which was clearly the practice of the ancients. "We pray (says Epiphanius,) for the just, the Fathers, the Patriarchs, the Prophets, Apostles, Evangelists, Martyrs, &c., that we may distinguish the Lord Jesus Christ from the order of men, by that honour which we pay unto him." *Και γαρ δικαιων ποιουμεθα την μνημην, και ὑπερ των ἁπαρτωλων*, &c., *ὑπερ δε δικαιων, και πατερων, και πατριαρχων, και προφητων, και ἀποστολων, και εὐαγγελιστων, και μαρτυρων, και ὁμολογητων, ἐπισκοπων τε, και ἀναχωρητων, και παντος του ταγματος, ἱνα τον Κυριον Ἰησουν Χριστον ἀφορισωμεν ἀπο της των ἀνθρωπων ταξεως, δια της προς αὐτον τιμης, και σεβας αὐτω ἀποδωμεν*, &c.*

We have also some of their prayers to this purpose yet remaining; as in the liturgy of James. *Μνησθητι Κυριε θεος των πνευματων, και πασης σαρκος, ὡν ἐμνησθημεν, και ὡν οὐκ ἐμνησθημεν, ὀρθοδοξων, ἀπο Ἀβελ του δικαιου, μεχρι της σημερον ἡμερας· αὐτος ἐκει αὐτους ἀναπαυσον, ἐν χωρα ζωντων, ἐν τη βασιλεια σου*, &c.† In the Syriac liturgy of Basil,‡ after they had mentioned the Patriarchs, the Prophets, John Baptist, Stephen, the Virgin Mary, and all the rest of the saints, they at last added: "We daily send up our prayers and supplications unto thee for them." And a little after, "Lord, remember also (says the priest) all those who are departed this life, and the orthodox bishops, who have made a clear and open profession of the true faith, from the Apostles Peter and James, to this day; of Ignatius, Dionysius," &c. And then he says with a loud voice, "remember also, Lord,

* Epiph. Pan. Hær. 75. Aërii, p. 911.
† Liturg. Jacob. p. 29, edit. Par. an. 1560. apud Guliel. Morell.
‡ Liturg. Syriac. Basil.

those who have persevered even to blood, for the word of a good fear." So likewise in the liturgy of Chrysostom; "we offer unto thee this reasonable service, for all those who have departed in thy faith," &c. *Ὅτι προσφερομεν σοι την λογικην ταυτην λατρειαν ὑπερ των ἐν πιστει ἀναπαυομενων προπατερων, πατερων, πατριαρχων, προφητων,* &c. See also Liturg. St. Marc. t. 2, Gr. Lat. Bibl. PP. p. 34. *Των ἐν πιστει Χριστου προκεκοιμημενων πατερων τε και ἀδελφων τας ψυχας ἀναπαυσον, Κυριε* &c.;—*και τουτων παντων τὰς ψυχας ἀναπαυσον, δεσποτα,* &c.

Yet the Church of Rome has utterly abolished this custom, and without all question believes that you could not do the saints a greater injury, than now making any such supplications for them; and those who are curious may observe many other similar differences between the ancients and the Church of Rome, in their customs and ceremonies.

As to their *discipline* also there is not less discrepancy. One of the chief of these differences, and which indeed is the origin of a great portion of the rest, is *in the elections and ordinations of ecclesiastical ministers*, which is the true basis and groundwork of the discipline and ministry of the Church.

It is clear that in the primitive times they depended partly on the people, and not wholly on the clergy; but every company of the faithful either chose their own pastors, or else had leave to consider and to approve of those that were proposed to them for that purpose. Pontius, a deacon of the Church of Carthage, says that "Cyprian, being yet a neophyte, was elected to the charge of pastor, and the degree of bishop by the judgment of God, and the favour of the people."* Cyprian also tells us the same in several places. In his fifty-second epistle, speaking of Cor-

* Judicio Dei, et plebis favore, ad officium Sacerdotii, et episcopatus gradum adhuc neophytus, et ut putabatur, novellus electus est.—*Pont. Diac. in vita Cypr.*

nelius, he says, "that he was made bishop of Rome by the judgment of God, and of his Christ, by the testimony of the greatest part of the clergy, by the suffrage of the people who were there present, and by the college of pastors, or ancient bishops, all good and pious men."* In another place he says, that "it is the people in whom the power chiefly is, of choosing worthy prelates, or refusing the unworthy. Which very thing (says he) we see is derived from divine authority, that a bishop is to be chosen in the presence of all the people; and is declared either worthy or unworthy by the public judgment and testimony;† therefore (says he a little afterwards) ought men diligently to retain and observe, according to divine tradition and apostolical custom, that which is also observed by us, and in a manner by all other provinces; namely, that for the due and orderly proceeding in all ordinations, the neighbouring bishops of the same province are to meet together at that place, where a bishop is to be chosen; and the election of the said bishop is to be performed in the presence of the people of that place, who fully know every man's life, and by their long conversation together understand what their behaviour has been."‡

Hence it was that Eusebius, bishop of Nicomedia,

* Factus est autem Cornelius episcopus, de Dei et Christi ejus judicio, de clericorum pœnè omnium testimonio, de plebis, quæ tunc affluit suffragio, et de Sacerdotum antiquorum, et bonorum virorum collegio.—*Cyprian, ep.* 52, *p.* 97.

† Quando ipsa (plebs) maximè habeat potestatem vel eligendi dignos sacerdotes, vel indignos recusandi. Quod et ipsum videmus de divina auctoritate descendere, ut sacerdos plebe præsente sub omnium oculis deligatur, et dignus atque idoneus publico judicio ac testimonio comprobetur.—*Id. ep.* 68, *p.* 166.

‡ Propter quod diligenter de traditione divina, et Apostolica observatione observandum est, et tenendum, quod apud nos quoque, et ferè per provincias universas tenetur, ut ad ordinationes ritè celebrandas, ad eam plebem, cui præpositus ordinatur, episcopi ejusdem provinciæ proximi quique conveniant, et episcopus deligatur plebe præsente, quæ singulorum vitam plenissimè novit, et uniuscujusque actum de ejus conversatione perspexerit.—*Ibid. p.* 166.

finding fault with many things in the ordination of Athanasius, accounted this also among the rest, that it had been performed without the consent of the people.* To which, answer was made by the council of Alexandria,† that the whole people of Alexandria had with one voice desired him for their bishop, giving him the highest testimonies, both for his piety and his fitness for that charge. In like manner, Julius, bishop of Rome, among other faults which he found in the ordination of Gregory, who had been made bishop of Alexandria, adds, "that he had not been desired by the people:"—*Μη αἰτηθεντα παρα πρεσβυτερων, μη παρ' ἐπισκοπων, μη παρα λαων*, &c.‡

It appears clear enough, both out of Jerome,§ and by the acts of the council of Constantinople,‖ and of Chalcedon,¶ and also by the *Pontificale Romanum*,** and several other productions, that this custom continued a long time in the Church. But it is now above seven hundred and fifty years since the Church of Rome ordained, in the 8th Council, (which notwithstanding has been always unanimously and constantly rejected by the Eastern Church to this very day,) that the promotions and consecrations of bishops should be performed by the election and order of the college of bishops only, forbidding, upon pain of excommunication, "all lay persons whatsoever, even princes themselves, to meddle in the election or promotion of any patriarch, metropolitan, or any other bishop whatsoever;" declaring withal, "that it is not fit that lay

* Athan. Apol. 2, p. 726 et 727.

† Ibid. 726, 728.

‡ Julius ap. Athan. Apol. 2, p. 748, 749.

§ Hieron. l. 1, adv. Jovin. p. 57, t. 2, et Com. 10, in Ezech. p. 968, t. 4, et Com. in Agg. p. 512, t. 5, et Com. 1, in Ep. ad Gal. p. 271, t. 6.

‖ Conc. Const. 1, in Ep. ad Damas. p. 94 et 95, t. 1, Conc. Gener

¶ Conc. Chalced. act. 11, p. 375, t. 2. Conc. Gen. et act. 16, p. 430, &c.

** Pontific. Rom. in Ordinat. Presbyter. fol. 38, vide supr. l 1, c. 4.

persons should have anything at all to do in these matters: it becoming them rather to be quiet, and patiently to attend, till such time as the election of the bishop who is to be chosen be regularly finished by the college of clergymen."*

Thus have they, by this one *canon*-shot, beaten down the authority of the Fathers, and of the primitive Church, who always allowed to the faithful people some share in the elections of their pastors. Neither has this custom been able ever since to lift up its head; the people being (as every man knows) now more than ever defrauded of this their right, and having not the least share in the elections, not merely of popes, primates, or archbishops, but not so much as of the meanest bishop that exists.

As the people anciently had their voice in the election of their pastors, so probably also they had the like in all other affairs of importance that took place in the Church. In Cyprian's time, many, who during a very great persecution, had been forced to yield by the cruelty of the Pagans, being afterwards touched with a sense of their fault, desired to return to the Church again; but yet to avoid the shame, and the length and rigour of those penances which were usually imposed upon such offenders, the greatest part of them begged of their confessors to be favourably dealt with, and corrupted their priests, that so they might be received again into the communion of the Church, without undergoing canonical penance. Cyprian, who was a strict observer of discipline. wrote many things against this abuse; by which it evidently appears, that the people had their right also

* Neminem laicorum principum, vel potentum semet inserere electioni vel promotioni Patriarchæ, vel Metropolitæ, aut cujuslibet episcopi, &c., præsertim cùm nullam in talibus potestatem quenquam potestativorum, vel cæterorum laicorum, habere conveniat, sed potiùs silere, ac attendere sibi, usque quò regulariter à collegio ecclesiæ suscipiat finem electio futuri pontificis.—*Conc.* 8. *Can.* 22, *t.* 3, *Conc. p.* 282.

in the hearing and judging of these causes. For, in his tenth epistle he says, that those priests that had received any such offenders rashly, and contrary to the discipline of the Church, "should give an account of what they had done to himself, to the confessors, and to the whole people."* In another place, writing to the people of Carthage—"When the Lord (says he) shall have restored peace to us all, and we shall have returned to the Church again, we shall then examine all these things, *you also being present, and judging of them.*"† It is in the same epistle, and on this very point, where he adds that passage, which we have before produced, in the chapter on the corruption of the writings of the ancients: "I desire them (says he) that they would patiently hear our council, &c., to the end that, when many of us bishops shall have met together, we may examine the letters and desires of the blessed martyrs, according to the discipline of the Lord, and in the presence of the confessors, and also *according as you shall think fit.*" Hence it is, that in one of his former epistles, he protested to his clergy, "that from his first coming to his bishopric, he had ever resolved to do nothing of his own head, without their advice, and *the approbation of his people.*"‡ He who would yet be more fully satisfied in this particular, may read the fourteenth epistle of the same Father, and the twenty-eighth on the business of Philumenus and Fortunatus, two subdeacons; as also the fortieth on the business of Felicissimus; and the sixty-eighth, which he wrote to the clergy and the people of Spain jointly, commending

* Acturi et apud nos, et apud confessores ipsos, et apud plebem universam causam suam.—*Cyprian. ep.* 10, *p.* 30.

† Cum pace nobis omnibus a Domino prius data, ad ecclesiam regredi cœperimus, tunc examinabuntur singula, præsentibus et judicantibus vobis.—*Id. ep.* 12, *p.* 33.

‡ Quando a primordio Episcopatus mei statuerim, nihil sine consilio vestro, et sine consensu plebis meæ, privata sententia gerere.—*Cypr. ep.* 6, *p.* 19.

them for having deposed their bishops, who were guilty of heinous crimes.*

But that no man may think that this was the practice of the Church of Carthage only, I should state that the clergy of Rome also approved of this resolution of his, of bringing to trial, so soon as they should be at rest, this whole business, on those who had fallen during the persecution, in a full assembly of the bishops, priests, deacons, and confessors, together with those of the laity who had continued firm, and had not yielded to idolatry.† And that which, in my judgment, is very well worth our observation, is that Cyprian himself, writing to Cornelius, bishop of Rome, says, "that he does not doubt but that, according to that mutual love which they owed and paid to each other, he always read those letters which he received from him to the most eminent clergy of Rome who were his assistants, and to the most holy and most numerous people."‡ Whence it appears, that at Rome also the people had their vote in the managing of ecclesiastical affairs.

I shall not need here to add any more, to show how much the authority and example of the ancients, in this particular, are now slighted and despised; it being evident enough to every man, that the people are not only excluded from the councils and consistories of the bishops, but that, besides, the man would

* Quæ scripta est nomine 66 episcoporum: et ep. 68, et in præfat. Concil. Carthag.—*Id. ep.* 14, *et* 28, *et* 40, *et* 59.

† Quanquam nobis in tam ingenti negotio placeat, quod et tu ipse tractasti priùs, ecclesiæ pacem sustinendam, deinde sic collatione consiliorum cum episcopis, presbyteris, diaconis, confessoribus, pariter ac stantibus laicis facta, lapsorum tractare rationem.—*Epist. quæ est inter Cypr. ep.* 31.

‡ Quanquam sciam, frater charissime, pro mutuâ dilectione quam debemus et exhibemus invicem nobis, florentissimo illic Clero tecum præsidenti, et sanctissimæ atque amplissimæ plebi legere te semper litteras nostras; tamen nunc et admoneo et peto, ut quod alias sponte atque honorificè facis, etiam petente me facias, ut hac epistola mea lecta, &c.—*Cypr. ep.* 55, *ad Cornel. p.* 121.

now be taken for a heretic who should now only propose, or attempt to restore, any such thing. But I beseech you now, only fancy to yourselves an archbishop, who, writing to the Pope, should address him thus: "Most dear brother, I exhort you, and desire of you, that what you are wont honourably to do of your own accord, you would now do at my request—namely, that this my epistle may be read to the distinguished clergy who are your assistants there; and also to the most holy and most numerous people." Would not the writer, think you, of such a letter as this, be laughed at as a senseless, foolish fellow, if at least he escaped so easily, and met with no worse usage? Yet, this is the very request that Cyprian made to Pope Cornelius.

But as the bishops and the rest of the clergy have deprived the people of all those privileges which had conferred upon them by antiquity, as well in the election of prelates, as in other ecclesiastical affairs; in like manner is it evident, that the Pope has engrossed into his own hands, not only this booty of which they had robbed the people, but also in a manner all the rest of their authority and power; as well that which they heretofore enjoyed, according to the ancient canons and constitutions of the Church, as that which they have since, by various admirable means, by little and little acquired, in the space of some centuries. All this has now entirely disappeared, I know not how, and been swallowed up by Rome in a very little time.

The three hundred and eighteen Fathers of the council of Nice ordained, "that every bishop should be created by all the bishops of his province, if it were possible; or at least by three of them, if the whole number could not so conveniently be brought together; yet with this proviso, that the absent bishops were consenting also to the said ordination: and that the power and authority in all such actions should belong to the metropolitan of each several province:" *'Επισκοπον προσηκει μαλιστα μεν ὑπο παντων των ἐν ἐπαρχια καθιστασθαι*, &c.*

This ordinance of theirs is both very agreeable to the practice of the preceding ages, as appears by that sixty-eighth epistle of Cyprian, which we cited a little before, and was also observed for a long time afterward by the ages following; as you may perceive by the epistle of the Fathers of the first council of Constantinople to Pope Damasus;† and also by the discourse of those that sat as presidents at the council of Chalcedon, on the rights of the patriarch of Constantinople in his own diocese.

Notwithstanding all these things, the whole world knows and sees what is the practice of the Church of Rome at this day, and that there is not any true power or authority left to the metropolitans and their councils, in the ordinations of the bishops within their own dioceses; but the whole power, in this case, depends on the Pope of Rome, and on those whom he has entrusted herein, either of his own accord, or otherwise. Indeed all bishops are to make their acknowledgments of tenure to the Pope; nor may they exercise their functions without his commission; which they shall not obtain, without first paying down their money, and compounding for their first fruits, styling themselves also in their titles thus:—"We N. Bishop of N., by the grace of God, and of the holy Apostolical See," of which strange custom and title you will not meet with the least trace throughout all the records of antiquity; not so much as one of all that vast number of bishops, whose subscriptions we have yet remaining, partly in the councils, and partly in their own books and histories, having ever thus styled himself.

* Conc. Nic. Can. 4.

† Conc. Const. I. in Ep. ad Damas. p. 94. t. 1, Conc. Gener.

As for Provincial and Diocesan Synods, where anciently all sorts of ecclesiastical causes were heard and determined; as appears both by the canons of the councils, and also by the examples we have left us; as in the history of Arius, and of Eutyches, who were both anathematized, the one in the synod of Alexandria, and the other in that of Constantinople; they dare not now meddle with anything, except some trivial matters, being of no use in the greater causes, save only to inquire into them, and give in their information at Rome.* Nor can the meanest bishop be judged in any case of importance, which may be sufficient to depose him, by any but the Pope of Rome: his metropolitan and his primate, the synod of his province, and that of his diocese, (in the sense in which the ancients took this word,) having not the least power in these matters, unless it be by an extraordinary delegation; and having then only authority to draw up the business, and make it ready for hearing, and then to send it to Rome: none but the Pope alone having power to give sentence in such cases, as it is expressly ordained by the council of Trent.†

I shall here pass by the Pope's taking away from the bishops, contrary to the canons and practice of antiquity, all jurisdiction and power over a good part of the monasteries, and other companies of religious persons, both seculars and regulars, within their dioceses; his assuming wholly to himself the power of absolving, and of dispensing in several cases, which they call reserved cases, (though in ancient times this authority belonged equally to all bishops;) and also his giving *indulgences*, and proclaiming *jubilees;*

* Minores criminales causæ episcoporum in concilio tantum provinciali cognoscantur et terminentur, &c.—*Conc. Trid. Sess.* 24. *Decret. de ref. c.* 5.

† Causæ criminales graviores contra episcopos, &c. quæ depositione aut privatione dignæ sunt, ab ipso tantùm summo Romano pontifice cognoscantur, et terminentur, &c.—*Ibid.*

things which were never heard of, in any of the first ages of Christianity.

As for the discipline which was anciently observed in the Church towards penitents, whether in punishing them for their offences, or else in the receiving them again into the communion of the Church, it is now wholly lost and vanished. We have now nothing left us, save only a bare idea and shadow of it, which we meet with in the writings of the ancients; in the canonical epistles of Gregorius of Neocæsarea, of Basil, and others, and in the councils, both general and provincial.

Where are now all those several *degrees of penance*, which were observed in the ancient Church: where some offenders were to bewail their sins without the Church; some might stand and hear the word among the catechumens; others were to cast themselves down at the feet of the faithful? Some of them might partake of the prayers only of the Church; and others were at length received again into the communion of their sacraments also. Where are those eight, those ten, those twenty years of penance, which they sometimes imposed upon offenders? This whole course of penance, which we meet with everywhere in the writings of the ancients, is now wholly merged in auricular confession, wherein no part of the penance appears to the world.

As these kinds of punishments, which were most wholesome for the penitents, have been quite abolished by them; so have they on the other side introduced other kinds of penalties, which are indeed very beneficial and advantageous to the temporal estate of the Church of Rome, but are most pernicious for the souls of offenders; such as their *Interdicts*, when, for the offence (and that oftentimes too, rather a pretended than a true one) of one or two single persons, or perhaps of a corporation, they will deprive a whole state, wherein there are perhaps many millions of people, of the participation of the holy sacraments, which are the means by which the grace and the life of Jesus Christ is communicated unto poor mortals; an example of which kind of proceeding was practised by Pope Paul V. in my childhood, against the state of Venice. In what code of the ancient Church can you discover that any such strange kind of punishment was ever instituted, as that, for the offence of a few, many millions of souls should be damned? How can you call that power apostolical, which punishes in this manner; seeing that the apostolical power was given for edification, and not for destruction?

I would also wish to learn of any man, that could tell me, upon what canons of the ancient Church that sanguinary discipline of the Inquisition is grounded; where, after they have extracted from a poor soul, by crafty dealing, and many times also by such barbarous usage as would make one tremble to read, a confession of his being guilty of heresy, instead of instruction, they pass upon him sentence of death, and he is forthwith delivered over to the secular magistrates: to whom notwithstanding, in plain mockery both of God and man, they give an express charge, that they do not put him to death.* Yet in case they fail of so doing, and if within six or seven days after, at the most, they do not burn him alive,† (and all this without ever hearing his cause or what his offence is,)‡ they themselves shall be prosecuted by ecclesiastical censures, and shall be excommunicated, deposed, and deprived of all dignities, both ecclesiastical and temporal.

That which yet surpasses all belief is, that although the person questioned should confess his fault, and

* Nicol. Eymeric. Director. Inquis. P. 2. c. 27. p. 127. et ibi Pegna. item. P. 3. p. 512.

† Pegna in Direct. Inquis. P. 3. p. 36.

‡ Direct. Inquis. P. 3. Q. 36. et ibid. Pegna, p. 563. Comm. 85. p. 564.

should express his hearty sorrow for it, and should by way of satisfaction submit himself to the severest penance that could be; yet would not the poor wretch escape death, if he be of the number of those whom they call *the relapsed.**

O most inhuman cruelty, worthy of the Scythians and the Læstrigonians only! but very ill becoming the disciples of Him who commanded his apostle to pardon his brother, not seven times only, but seventy times seven: and as ill beseeming those who so highly boast of being the successors and inheritors of those mild and tender-hearted ancients, who taught, "that it is the part of piety not to constrain but to persuade, according to our Saviour's example, who constrained no man, but left every man to his own liberty, to follow him or not....And that the devil, as he has no truth in him, comes with axes and with hammers to break open the doors of those that must receive him. But our Saviour is so meek, that his manner of teaching is, 'If any one will follow me;' and 'he that will be my disciple;' neither does he constrain any one to whom he comes, but rather stands at the door of every one, and knocks, saying, 'Open to me, my sister, my spouse;' and so enters, when any open to him: but if they delay, and will not open to him, he then departs; because the truth is not to be pressed with swords and arrows, nor with soldiers and armed men, but by persuasion and counsel." *Θεοσεβειας μεν γαρ ἰδιον μη αναγκαζειν, ἀλλα πειθειν, και γαρ ὁ Κυριος αὐτος οὐ βιαζομενος, ἀλλα τη προαιρεσει διδους ἐλεγε πασι μεν, εἰ τις θελει ὀπισω μου ἐλθειν*, &c. . . . . *Ο μεν διαβολος ἐπει μηδεν ἀληθες ἐχει, ἐν πελεκει και λαξευτηριω ἐπιβαινων κατεαξει τας θυρας των δεχομενων αὐτον· ὁ δε Σωτηρ οὑτως εστι πραος, ὡς διδασκειν μεν, εἰ τις θελει ὀπισω μου ἐλθειν, και ὁ θελων εἰναι μου*

* Direct. Inquis. P. 3. modo 9. termin. process. p. 510. et ibi Pegna.

μαθητης· ἐρχομενον δε προς ἑκαστον, μη βιαζεσθαι, αλλα μαλλον κρουειν τε, και λεγειν, ἀνοιξον μοι, ἀδελφὴ μου, νυμφη· και ἀνοιγοντων μεν εἰσερχεται, ὀκνουντων δε, και μη θελοντων ἐκεινων, ἀναχωρει. Ου γαρ ξιφεσιν, ἢ βελεσιν, ἢ δια στρατιωτων, &c.*

The ancients also sharply reprehended the Arians, for going about to establish and maintain their religion by force; saying, "Of whom have they learnt to persecute their brethren? Certainly they cannot say that they have learnt of the saints; no, they have rather had the devil for their tutor herein." And again: "Jesus Christ has commanded us to fly, and the saints have indeed fled sometimes: but persecution is the invention of the devil." *Ποθεν ἐμαθον αὐτοι το διωκειν; ἀπο μεν γαρ των ἁγιων οὐκ ἀν εἰποιεν· ἀπο δε του διαβολου τουτο αὐτοις περιειληπται*, &c. . . . *Και το μεν φευγειν ὁ Κυριος προσεταξε, και οἱ ἁγιοι ἐφυγον· το δε διωκειν διαβολικον ἐστι ἐπιχειρημα, και κατα παντων αὐτος αἰτειται τουτο.*†

In another place they protest, that "by that very course which the Arians took in banishing (which yet is much less than burning,) all those who would not subscribe to their decrees, they clearly showed themselves to be contrary to all Christians, and to be the friends of the devil and his fiends." *Οἱ οὑτω γραφοντες, ὡστε το τελος των γραμματων αὐτων ἐξορισμον, και ἀλλας τιμωριας ἐχειν, τι ἀν εἰεν οἱ τοιουτοι; οἱ Χριστιανων μεν ἀλλοτριοι, διαβολου δε, και των ἐκεινου δαιμονων φιλοι.*‡

In like manner has another of the ancient Fathers exclaimed against the proceeding of these Arians, who made use not only of the terror of persecution, but of the enticements also of worldly riches, that thus they might the more easily draw men over to

* Athan. in Ep. ad solit. vit. ag. tom. i, p. 55.
† Athan. Apol. 1. de fuga sua, p. 716. tom. i.
‡ Athan. contr. Arian. Or. 1. t. 1. p. 288.

their belief. "But now, alas! (says this Father,) worldly suffrages recommend the faith of God: Christ is now become weak and void of power, and ambition gains credit to his name. The Church terrifies by banishment and imprisonments, &c. She, that was consecrated by the terror of her persecutors, depends now upon the dignity of those who are of her communion. She who has been propagated by banished priests, now herself banishes priests. She boasts now that she is beloved of the world—who could not be Christ's, unless the world hated her."* Agreeable to what another of them says, "That the Church of Christ was founded by shedding her blood, and by suffering reproaches, rather than by reproaching others; and that it has grown up by persecutions, and has been crowned by martyrdoms."†

Another also of the chief among the ancient Fathers reproached an Arian for having made use of the sword and axe in ecclesiastical matters. "Those whom he could not deceive by his discourse, (says he,) he thought proper to use his sword against; uttering with his mouth, and writing with his hands, sanguinary laws, and thinking that a law can command men's faith."‡ And that you may not imagine that he himself thought that lawful which he found fault with

* At nunc, proh dolor! divinam fidem suffragia terrena recommendant inopsque virtutis suæ Christus, dum ambitio nomini suo conciliatur, arguitur. Terret exiliis et carceribus Ecclesiæ, credique sibi cogit, quæ exiliis et carceribus est credita. Pendet ad dignationem communicantium, quæ persequentium est consecrata terrore. Fugat sacerdotes, quæ fugatis est sacerdotibus propagata. Diligi se gloriatur a mundo, quæ Christi esse non potuit, nisi eam mundus odisset.—*Hilar. l. contr. Aux. p.* 86.

† Fundendo sanguinem, et patiendo magis quàm faciendo contumelias, Christi fundata est ecclesia; persecutionibus crevit, martyriis coronata est.—*Hieron. ep.* 62, *ad Theoph. t.* 2, *p.* 274.

‡ Qui (Auxentius) quos non potuerit sermone decipere, eos gladio putat esse feriendos; cruentas leges ore dictans, manu scribens; et putans quòd lex fidem possit hominibus imperare.—*Ambros. ep.* 32, *t.* 3, *p.* 126.

in the Arians, he says, in another place, that in a certain journey which he made into Gaul, he refused to communicate with those bishops who would have some certain heretics to be put to death.*

The emperor Marcian, in like manner, who called together the council of Chalcedon, and was a prince that was highly commended for his piety, solemnly protests that "he had forced no man to subscribe, or to assent to the council of Chalcedon, against his will. "For, (says he) we will not draw any man into the way of life by violence or by threats." *Και ἡ μεν ἡμετερα γαληνοτης οὐδενι το συνολον ἀναγκην ἐπαχθηναι προσεταξεν, ὡστε ἠ ὑπογραφειν, ἠ συναινειν, εἰ οὐ βουλοιτο· οὐδε γαρ ἀπειλαις, ἠ βιᾳ τινα προς την της ἀληθειας ὁδον ἑλκειν βουλομεθα.*† Indeed, Hosius, bishop of Cordova, long before testified that the most Catholic emperor Constans never compelled any man to be orthodox.‡ And this is the course which is approved of by all the ancients. "God (says Hilary) has rather taught us the knowledge of himself, than exacted it of us; and giving authority to his commandments by the wonderfulness of his heavenly works, he has refused to force us to confess his name, &c. He is the God of the whole world: he has no need of a compelled obedience; he requires not any forced confession."§ These are the reasons this author brought to dissuade the emperor Constantius from using violence, and forcing the consciences of men.

* Postea cùm videret me abstinere ab episcopis qui communicabant ei, vel qui aliquos devios, licèt a fide, ad necem petebant, &c.—*Ambros. l.* 2, *ep.* 27. *t.* 3, *p.* 106.

† Marcian. ep. ad Archimandr. et Mon. Æg. in Act. Conc. Chalced. t. 2, Conc. Gen. p. 453.

‡ Hujus ep. ad Constantium, apud Athan. in ep. ad solit. vit. ag. t. 1, p. 839.

§ Deus cognitionem sui docuit potiùs, quàm exegit; et operationum cœlestium admiratione præceptis suis concilians auctoritatem, coactam confitendi se aspernatus est voluntatem, &c. Deus universitatis est; obsequio non eget necessario: non requirit coactam confessionem.—*Hilar. l.* 1, *ad Const. fol.* 84.

Ambrose says, "Christ sent his Apostles to plant the faith; not to compel, but to instruct men; not to exercise the force of power, but to promote the doctrine of humility."* Hence the observation of Cyprian, when comparing the manner of proceeding in the Old Testament with that of the New: "Then the proud and the disobedient were cut off by the (fleshly) sword; now they suffer by the spiritual, being thrown out of the Church."† Certainly then they still live, at this very day, under the Old Testament, in Spain, and Italy, and all those other places where the Inquisition is in force; and, I believe, he would find a very difficult task of it, whoever should take it in hand to reconcile this passage of Cyprian to that opinion of Pope Pius V.,‡ who said that bishops might have their officers and executioners of justice, for the causes that appertained to their jurisdiction; and might put their sentences in execution against offenders; and that the reason of their having recourse upon all occasions to the secular powers, was, not because the Church could not make use of its own proper officers of justice in such cases, but rather because it had none; or if it had any, they were so weak, and so few in number, that for the suppressing and punishing of delinquents, it stood in need of the assistance of the temporal power.

I shall conclude this subject with Tertullian, the most ancient author of the Latin Church, whom Pamelius (as we have noticed before) will have us to believe to have been a persecutor of heretics; yet he was a man that would not allow a Christian so much

* Eos misit ad seminandam fidem, qui non cogerent, sed docerent, nec vim potestatis exercerent, sed doctrinam humilitatis attollerent.—*Ambros. Com. in Luc. l.* 7, *p.* 99.

† Tunc quidem gladio occidebantur, quando adhuc et circumcisio carnalis manebat. Nunc autem, &c., spirituali gladio superbi et contumaces necantur, dum de ecclesia ejiciuntur.—*Cyprian. ep.* 62, *p.* 143.

‡ Girolamo, Catena nella vita di Pio V. p. 126.

as to draw a sword, either in a war against a public enemy, or in discharging the office of a magistrate upon offenders whom all civil laws punish with death. Hear what he says of religion. "Consider (says he to the Pagans) whether this be not to add to the crime of irreligion, to take away the liberty of religion, and to interdict a man the choice of his God, by not suffering him to worship whom he would, but to compel him to worship whom he would not. There is none, no not among men, that takes pleasure in being served by any against their will."* Some few chapters afterwards he says, "It seems very unjust that freemen should be constrained to do sacrifice against their will. For, in the performing of service to God, a willing heart is required."† In another book, when speaking of the same thing, he says: "It is a point of human right, and a natural power that every man has to worship that which he thinks fit. The religion of another man neither hurts nor profits any one. Neither is it indeed the part of religion to compel religion; which ought to be entertained willingly, and not by force; inasmuch as sacrifices themselves are required only from willing minds."‡

On this passage Pamelius gives us a marvellously rare gloss, saying, "that we ought not indeed directly to compel men to our religion, but yet we may punish them, if they will not change their opinion." Cer-

* Videte enim ne et hoc ad irreligiositatis elogium concurrat, adimere libertatem religionis, et interdicere optionem divinitatis, ut non liceat mihi colere quem velim, sed cogar colere quem nolim. Nemo se ab invito coli vellet, ne homo quidem.—*Tertull. Apolog. c.* 24, *p.* 58.

† Quoniam autem facile iniquum videtur, liberos homines invitos urgeri ad sacrificandum. Nam et aliàs divinæ rei faciendæ libens animus inducitur.—*Id. Apolog. c.* 28, *p.* 61.

‡ Tamen humani juris, et naturalis potestatis est, unicuique quod putaverit colere: nec alii obest, aut prodest alterius religio. Sed nec religionis est cogere religionem, quæ sponte suscipi debeat, non vi; cum et hostiæ ab animo libenti expostulentur.—*Id. l. ad Scapul. c.* 2.

tainly he thinks it is not compelling a man, to cause him to do a thing under pain of death. Let any man that can, reconcile the practice of the Inquisition, and the Pope's thunderbolt against king Henry VIII. and his daughter queen Elizabeth, and against some of the kings of France also, with this constant opinion of all antiquity.

Now after the Romanists have thus boldly slighted the doctrines, the ceremonies, and the discipline of the ancients, by changing and abolishing whatever they have thought good; with what confidence can they still laud the Fathers, and adduce their testimonies, and place them upon the seat of judicature, and make them the judges of our differences? Or although they still do thus, who would not be ready here to bring against them those words of Tertullian, which he made use of in another similar case? "I would be very glad (says he) that these great and religious defenders and maintainers of the laws and customs of their fathers, would answer me a little as to their own faith, respect, and obedience, toward the constitutions of their ancestors; whether they have not departed from and forsaken some of them? whether they have not rased out those things which were most necessary and most useful in their discipline? What has become of those ancient laws? &c., where is the religion, where is the reverence which is due from you to your ancestors? You have renounced your forefathers, in your habit, apparel, manner of life, opinion, and also in your very speech. You are always lauding antiquity, yet every day you assume a new manner of life."*

* Nunc religiosissimi legum, et paternorum institutorum protectores et ultores respondeant velim de sua fide, et honore, et obsequio erga majorum consulta, si a nullo desciverunt? si in nullo exorbitaverunt? si non necessaria et aptissima quæque disciplinæ oblitteraverunt? Quonam illæ leges abierunt, &c. . . . . Ubi religio! ubi veneratio majoribus debita à vobis? Habitu, victu, in-

Whether therefore they of the Church of Rome have upon just grounds dealt thus with the ancients or not, it answers my purpose notwithstanding to conclude, that by this their proceeding they have given us a sufficient testimony that they do not account their authority supreme in matters of religion. And if so, what reason have they to urge it for such, against the Protestants? Seeing they have weakened the authority of so many of those judgments, on points of religion, which have been given by the Fathers, how can they expect that their authority should pass for authentic in any one? Let us suppose, for instance, that they held that there was such a place as Purgatory. But (will the Protestant say,) if you have found their belief to be so erroneous, on the state of the souls of departed saints till the day of the resurrection, why would you impose upon me a necessity of subscribing to what they held on Purgatory? The laws of controversy ought to be equal; and therefore if you, by examining this opinion of the Fathers by reason and by the Scriptures, have found it to be erroneous, why will you not give us leave to try that other on Purgatory, by the same touchstone? Certainly, should we but speak the truth, it is the plainest mockery that can be, to cry out, as these men do continually, "the Fathers, the Fathers," and to write so many volumes upon this subject, after they have so dealt with them as you have seen.

If it be here objected that the Protestants themselves do also reject many of those Articles, which we have before noticed, we answer, that this is nothing at all to the purpose; forasmuch as they take the Scriptures, and not the Fathers, for the rule of their faith; neither do they press any man to receive

structu, sensu, ipso denique sermone proavis renunciastis; laudatis semper antiquitatem, et novè de die vivitis.—*Id. Apol. c.* 6, *p.* 31, 33.

anything from the hands of the ancients, unless it be grounded upon the word of God. If, lastly, you say that the authority of the Fathers has no place, nor is at all considerable, in the points before set down, because the Church has otherwise determined on the same; this is clearly to grant us that which we would have, namely, that the authority of the Fathers is not supreme. As for the Church, how far its authority extends in these things, that is a new question which I shall not meddle with at this time. Only thus much I shall say, that whatever authority you allow it, whether little or much, you will still find that it will very hardly be able to do anything, on the decision of our present controversies; forasmuch as you can never be able to make any use of this position, till you are assured of what and where the Church is; seeing that the Protestants strenuously deny that it is that which appears at this day at Rome; and the greatest difficulty of all consists in demonstrating this to them. For if they did but once believe that the Church of Rome was the true Church, they would immediately join themselves with it; so that there would not henceforth be need of any further dispute.

We shall therefore here conclude, that to adduce the testimonies of the Fathers on the differences that are at this day in religion, is no proper mode for the deciding them, seeing that it is no easy matter to discover what was their judgment respecting the same, by reason of the many difficulties we meet with, in the writings of the ancients; nor is it of such sufficient authority in itself, as that we may safely establish our belief upon it, since the Fathers themselves were also subject to error. Neither, lastly, is it of any force, with either party; seeing that they both regulate and examine the opinions, ceremonies, and discipline of the ancients, the one by the rule of the Scriptures, and the other by that of the Church.

Here, I find, that upon this conclusion two questions may arise. For since an appeal to the Fathers is not sufficient for the deciding of those points that are now in dispute amongst us, it may be asked, in the first place, what other course we ought to take for attaining the truth of these controversies; and then, secondly, how and in what cases the writings of the Fathers may be useful to us. Now, although both these questions are without the compass of our present design, yet as they so closely border upon it, we shall, in the last place, say a word or two in answer to them.

As for the first, it would be a difficult matter, in my judgment, to discover a better way for satisfaction on this point, than that which one Scholarius, a Greek, who is very highly esteemed by those who printed the general councils at Rome, has proposed. This learned man, in a certain oration of his, which he made at the council of Florence, for the facilitating the union which was then in treaty between the Latins and the Greeks, and was afterwards concluded, lays it down as a basis, "that we ought not to reject all those things, which are not clearly, and in express terms, delivered in the Scriptures; which is a pretext and evasion which many of the heretics make use of: but that we ought to receive with equal honour whatever directly follows from that which is said in the Scriptures; and to reject utterly whatever shall be found to be contrary to those things which are undoubtedly true." He says further, that "in those things wherein the Scripture has not clearly expressed itself, we must have recourse to the Scripture itself, as our guide, to give us light therein, by some other passage, where it has spoken more plainly." And after all this he requires, "that we should use our utmost endeavour fully to reconcile those seeming contradictions, which we sometimes here meet with in several passages; to that purpose taking notice of the diversity of times, customs, senses and the like." *Και πρωτα μεν μη παντα βουλεσθαι διαρρηδην λαμβανειν ἐκ της γραφης· τουτω γαρ και πολλους ἰσμεν των αἱρετικων χρησαμενους τω προκαλυμματι· ἀλλ' ἀν τι τοις οὑτω λεγομενοις ἀκολουθον ᾐ, και τουτο της ἰσης τιμης ἀξιουν· ὡσαυτως εἰ τι τοις ἀληθεσι, και ἀναντιρρητοις ἐναντιουμενον φαινοιτο, τουτο μηδενα παραδεχεσθαι τροπον. 'Επειτα των μη σαφως εἰρημενων, αὐτην την γραφην λαμβανειν διδασκαλον, ἐξ ὡν ἀλλοθι που σαφεστερον πραγματευεται· προς δε τουτοις την δοκουσαν διαφωνιαν ἐξηγουμενους λυειν πειρασθαι, καιρους τε, και χρειας, και διαφορους ἐννοιας, και τα τοιαυτα παραλαμβανοντας.**

Proceeding further, Scholarius says, "That the Fathers of the council of Nice after this manner concluded by the Scriptures upon the true belief touching the Son of God."† Then applying all this to his present purpose, he adds, "that the Scripture says clearly and expressly that the Holy Ghost proceeds from the Father; and that this is agreed upon by both sides, both by the Greeks and Latins." *Το μεν οὐν, ἐκ του πατρος ἐκπορευεσθαι το πνευμα το ἁγιον, κειται μεν διαρρηδην ἐν τη γραφη, ὁμολογειται δε παρα παντων ἡμων*, &c. But as Scripture has not so expressly declared itself whether the Holy Ghost proceed also from the Son or not, and as this is the thing now in question, the Latins affirming it, and the Greeks on the other side denying it, he says: "We ought therefore to prove this from some other parts, which are there more clearly delivered." *Οὐκουν ἐκ τινων ἀλλων τουτο συναγεσθαι δει, φανερως ἐκει λεγομενων.* This he afterwards performs, and indeed, in my judgment, very learnedly and happily; proving this doubtful point out of other passages that are more clear. And this was

* Scholar. Orat. 3, t. 4. Conc. Gen. p. 650.
† Ibid. p. 652 et 653.

the judgment of this great person; which will not give any offence to those of the Church of Rome, because it came from one that was on their side. Neither do I see what could have been spoken more rationally. And indeed this is the course that is observed in all sciences whatever.

If an adversary doubt of the truth of what we propose, we are to prove it by such maxims as are acknowledged and allowed of by him, making good that which is doubtful by that which is certain, and clearing that which is obscure by that which is evident. This is the rule that I conceive we ought to abide by, in the disputes that are among us at this day. The word of God is our common book; let us therefore search into it, for that upon which we may ground our own belief; and by which we may overthrow the opinion of our adversary. As for example, it is there said clearly and expressly, that what our Saviour Christ took at his last supper, was bread: and herein we all agree. But it is not at all there expressed, whether this bread was afterwards changed or annihilated. And this is now the question in dispute among us. We ought therefore (according to the counsel of Scholarius) to prove this by some other things which are there delivered clearly. And if you do this, you have got the victory: if not, I do not at all see why or how you can oblige any one to believe it.

In like manner the Scripture tells us, in terms as express as can be, that our Saviour Christ commanded his Apostles to take and eat, and to drink that which he gave them in celebrating the eucharist. But it does not at all say, that he commanded them to offer the same in sacrifice, either then or afterwards. And this is now the question: which it concerns those of the Church of Rome, if they will have us believe it, to prove by some other things, which are clearly and expressly delivered in the word of God.

The Scripture, in like manner, says expressly that Jesus Christ is the Mediator betwixt God and man: and that he is the Head of the Church; and that he purges us by his blood from our sins. Now in all this, both sides are fully agreed. But it is not at all there expressed that the departed saints are mediators; that the Pope is the head of the Church; and that our souls are in part cleansed from their sins by the fire of purgatory. Herein lies the controversy between us. The learned Scholarius's opinion herein would now be, that certainly those who propose these points as articles of faith, must deduce and collect them from some things which are clearly delivered in the Scriptures; for otherwise they are not to be pressed as truths. And although in matters of religion, or indeed in any other things of importance, a man may very well be excused for not believing a thing, when there appears no reason, to oblige him to believe it; yet, if those who reject the articles now disputed among us, have a mind to go further, and to prove positively the falseness of them, you see this author has laid down the way by which they are to proceed. He accounts those very absurd who require at your hands that you should show them all things expressly delivered in the Scripture: and this ought principally to be understood of negative propositions, of which no science gives you any certain account: forasmuch as to go about to number them all up, would be both an endless and also unprofitable piece of work. It is sufficient to deliver the positive truth. For, as whatever rightly follows thereupon is *true;* in like manner, whatever clashes with or contradicts the same is *false.* Would you therefore demonstrate those propositions that are pressed upon you to be false? Only compare them with those things that are clearly and expressly delivered in the Scripture; and if you find them contrary to any thing there set down, receive them not by any means. As for example, if a Protestant, not contenting himself with having answered all those reasons which are brought to prove that there is such a place as Purgatory, shall yet desire to go further, and to make it appear that the opinion is false; he is in this case to have recourse to the Scripture, and to examine it by those things which are there clearly and expressly delivered on the state of the soul, after it is departed this life, and touching the cause and means of the expiation of our sins, and the like. If the opinion of purgatory be found to contradict anything there delivered, then, according to Scholarius, "it ought not to be received by any means." But the brevity which we proposed to ourselves in this discourse, permits us not to prosecute this point any further.

As for the other question, it is no very difficult matter to resolve it. For, although we do not indeed allow any supreme and infallible authority to the writings of the Fathers, yet we do not therefore at once account them useless. If there were nothing of use in religion, saving what was also infallible, we should have but little good of any human writings. Those who have written in our own age, or a little before, are of no authority at all, against either party. Yet we read them, and also derive much benefit from them. How much more advantage then may we make, by studying the writings of the Fathers, whose piety and learning were for the most part much greater than that of the moderns! Augustine believed them not in anything otherwise than as he found what they delivered to be grounded upon reason; and yet, he held them in very great esteem. The like may be said of Jerome, who had read almost all of them over; and yet he takes the liberty sometimes to reprove them somewhat sharply, where he finds them not speaking to his mind. Though you should deprive them not only of this supremacy, which yet they never sought after, but should rob them also of their fame, yet would they still be of very great use to us. For books do not therefore profit us, because they were of such a man's writing; but rather because they instruct us in those things that are good and honest, and keep us out of error, and make us abhor those things that are vicious. Blot, if you please, the name of Augustine out of the title of those excellent books of his *De Civitate Dei*, or those other which he wrote, *De Doctrina Christiana*. His writings will instruct you not a whit the less; neither will you find the less benefit from them. The like may be said of all the rest.

First of all, therefore, you will find in the Fathers many earnest and zealous exhortations to holiness of life, and to the observance of the discipline of Jesus Christ. Secondly, you will there meet with very strong and solid proofs of those fundamental principles of our religion on which we are all agreed: and also many excellent things developed, tending to the right understanding of these mysteries, and also of the Scriptures wherein they are contained. In this very particular, their authority may be of good use to you, and may serve as a probable argument of the truth. For is it not a wonderful thing to see, that so many great wits, born in so many several ages, during the space of fifteen hundred years, and in so many several countries, being also of such different tempers, and who in other things were of such contrary opinions, should notwithstanding be found all of them to agree so constantly and unanimously in the fundamentals of Christianity; that amidst such great diversity in worship, they all adore one and the same Christ; preach one and the same sanctification; hope all of them for one and the same immortality; acknowledge all of them the same gospels; find therein all of them great and high mysteries?

The exquisite wisdom, and the inestimable beauty itself, of the discipline of Jesus Christ, I confess, is the most forcible and certain argument of the truth of it: yet certainly this consideration also is, in my opinion, no small proof of the same. For, pray, what probability is there, that so many holy men, who were endued (as it appears by their writings) with such admirable parts, with so much strength and clearness of understanding, should all of them be so grossly deceived, as to set so high a value upon this discipline, as to suffer even to death for it; unless it had in it some certain divine virtue, calculated to make an impression on the souls of men? What likelihood is there that a few besotted atheists, who rail against this sacred and venerable religion, should have been more successful in lighting upon the truth, than so many excellent men, who have all so unanimously borne testimony to the truth?

As for atheists, their vicious life ought to render their testimony suspected by every one; notwithstanding they may be otherwise (as indeed they conceive themselves to be) able men. For what wonder is it, if a whoremonger, or an ambitious person, cry down that discipline that condemns their vices to everlasting fire? that he that drowns himself every day, and at length vomits up his soul in wine, should hate that religion which forbids drunkennesss upon pain of damnation? The great reason that these men have to wish that it were false, must needs make any man cease to wonder at their pronouncing it to be false. To take any notice therefore of what such wretches as these may say, is the same as if you should judge, by taking the opinion of common strumpets, of the equity or injustice of the laws that enjoin people to live honestly. But the case is clearly otherwise with these holy men, who have so constantly and so unanimously taught the truth of the Christian religion. For as they were men born and brought up in the very same infirmities with other men, we cannot doubt but that they also naturally had strong inclinations to those vices, which our Saviour Christ forbids; and very little affection to those virtues which he commands. Forasmuch, therefore, as notwithstanding all this, they have yet all of them constantly maintained that this doctrine is true, their testimony certainly in this case neither can nor ought in any wise to be suspected. So that even if they had been destitute of those great and incomparable advantages of parts and learning, which they had above the enemies of Christianity, their bare word however is much rather to be taken than that of the others; seeing that these men are manifestly carried away by the force of their own vile affections, of which the others cannot possibly be suspected guilty. And as for those differences in opinion, which are sometimes found amongst them, on certain points of religion, some whereof we have formerly set down; these things are so far from disparaging the weight of their testimonies, that on the contrary they rather very much add to it. For this must acquit their *consenting* of all suspicion, that some perhaps might have, that it proceeded from some combination, or some correspondence and mutual intelligence. When you find them so disagreeing among themselves, on so many several points, it is an evident argument that they have not learnt their knowledge from one another; nor yet have all agreed upon the same thing by common deliberation; but have all of them collected it out of a serious examination and consideration of the things themselves. And if we received no other benefit from the writings of the Fathers, yet would this be considerable.

But now, that the benefit and satisfaction, which we shall receive from this consideration, may not be interrupted and disturbed by our meeting with so many different private opinions of theirs; we are to take notice, that Christianity consists not in subtleties, nor so much in the great number of its articles, as in the power and efficacy of them. A great part of these points of faith, and the end of all the rest, is *sanctification;* that is to say, a pure worship of God, and a hearty charity towards men. You may therefore boldly conclude that man to be a true observer of this discipline, whom you shall find to have a right sense and apprehension of these two points. Though perhaps he may be ignorant of those others, that exist rather in speculation than in practice, you ought not to reject him. And if, carried away by his own curiosity, or some other reason, he chance to err in some of those articles, bear with him notwithstanding. As God forgives us our sins, so does he also forgive us our errors. The hay and the stubble and the chaff shall be consumed: but yet he that buildeth therewith shall be saved, if he only hold fast to the foundation. Nor ought you to be troubled, if now and then you meet with some ignorant or perhaps some erroneous passages in the Fathers respecting these unessential points. They are not a whit the less Christian on this account, and may for all this have been most faithful servants of Jesus Christ. There is scarcely any face in the world so beautiful, but that it has some speckle or blemish in it. Yet is it not either the less esteemed, or the less beloved. The natural condition of mortal men and things, is to have some mixture of imperfection.

But now, besides what has been hitherto said, we may, in my opinion, make another very considerable use of the Fathers. For there sometimes arise such turbulent spirits as will needs broach doctrines arising from their own imagination, which are not grounded upon any principle of the Christian religion. I say, therefore, that the authority of the ancients may very properly and seasonably be made use of against the assurance of these men; by showing that the Fathers were utterly ignorant of any such fancies as these individuals propose to the world. And if this can be proved, we ought then certainly to conclude that no such doctrine was ever preached to mankind, either by our Saviour Christ, or by his Apostles. For what probability is there, that those holy Doctors of former ages, from whose hands Christianity has been derived down unto us, should be ignorant of any of those things which had been revealed and recommended by our Saviour, as important and necessary to salvation? It is true indeed that the Fathers, being deceived either by some false manner of argumentation, or else by some seeming authority, do sometimes deliver such things as have not been revealed by our Saviour Christ, but are evidently either false or ill founded; as we have formerly shown in those examples before produced by us. It is true, moreover, that among those things which have been revealed by our Saviour Christ in the Scripture, which yet are not absolutely necessary to salvation, the Fathers may have been ignorant of some of them; either because time had not as yet discovered what the sense of them was; or because, for lack of giving good heed to them, or by their being carried away with strong feelings, they did not then perceive what has since been ascertained. But that they should all of them have been ignorant of any article that is necessary to salvation, is altogether impossible. For, according to this, they should all have been deprived of salvation; which, I suppose every honest soul would tremble at the thought of.

I say then, and, as I conceive, have sufficiently proved in this treatise, that an argument which concludes the truth of any proposition from the Fathers having maintained the same, is very weak and ill founded; as supposing that which is clearly false, that the Fathers maintained nothing which had not been revealed by our Saviour Christ. For thus you might prove by the general agreement of the Fathers, that all the departed souls are shut up together in a certain place or receptacle, till the day of judgment; or that the eucharist is necessary for little infants, and the like; where every one sees how insufficient and invalid this kind of argumentation is. To say the truth, such is the proceeding of the Church of Rome, when they go about to prove, by the authority of the Fathers, those articles which they propose to the world, and which are rejected by the Protestants.

I say moreover, that to conclude the nullity or falseness of any article, not necessary to salvation, from the general silence of the Fathers respecting the same, is a very absurd way of arguing; as supposing a thing which is also manifestly false; namely, that the Fathers must necessarily have seen and clearly known all those things which Jesus Christ has revealed in his word. Such a kind of argument would it be thought among the Franciscans, if any one should conclude against them, from the silence of the Fathers, that our Saviour Christ has not at all revealed that the blessed Virgin Mary was conceived without sin. But yet I confess, on the other side, that in those points that are accounted as absolutely necessary to salvation, an argument that should be drawn from the general silence of the Fathers, to prove the nullity or falseness of it, would be very pertinent, and indeed unanswerable. As, for example, his manner of argumentation would be very rational and sound, who should conclude that those means of salvation which are proposed by a Mahomet, suppose, or a David George, or the like sectaries, are null, and contrary to the will of our Saviour Christ, (however much these men may seem to honour him) seeing that none of the ancient Christians speak so much as one syllable of it, and are utterly ignorant of all those secrets which these wretches have preached to their disciples, and delivered as infallible and necessary means of salvation. After this manner did Irenæus dispute against the Valentinians, and others of the Gnostics; who promulgated their own senseless dreams and the absurd issues of their own brain, saying that the Creator of the world was but an angel; and that there were above him certain divine powers which they called *Æons*, that is to say, *ages;* some of them making more of these and others fewer, and some reckoning to the number of three hundred and sixty-five, and an infinite number of other similar prodigies; never showing any ground for the same, either in reason or out of the Scripture. Irenæus* therefore, that he might make it appear to the world that this strange doctrine was produced from their own imagination only, undertakes to visit the archives of all the Churches that had been either planted or watered by the holy Apostles, and turns over all their records, evidences, and ancient monuments; and these *Æons*, *Achamot* and *Barbelo*,† of the Gnostics nowhere appearing, nor so much as the least part or trace of them, he concludes that the Apostles had never delivered any such thing to their disciples, either by writing or by word of mouth, as these impostors pretended they had. For certainly if they had done so, the memory of it could not have been so utterly lost. This is also the method that Tertullian followed, in his disputations against these very heretics and others of the like description, in the twenty-second chapter of his book *De Præscriptionibus adversus Hæreticos*, and in other places. The practice of these great persons, who made use of it themselves, will here serve to prove to us that this course is correct and advantageous.

Thus you see that the authority of the Fathers is of

* Irenæus, l. 3. contr. Hæ. c. 1, 2, 3, and 4.
† Id. 3. c. 2.

very great use in the Church, and serves as an outwork to the Scriptures, for repelling the presumption of those who would forge a new faith. But inasmuch as those who broach new doctrines of their own imagination, do ordinarily slight the Holy Scriptures as those very heretics did, whom Irenæus confuted; who impudently accused them "of not being right, and that they are of no authority, and speak in very ambiguous terms; and that they are not able to inform a man of the truth, unless they are acquainted with tradition, the truth having been delivered (as these men pretended) not in writing, but by word of mouth;"*—for this reason, I say, as well as others, are the writings of the Fathers of very great use in these disputes; and I conceive this to be one of the principal ends for which Divine Providence has, in despite of so many confusions and changes, preserved so many of them safe to our times.

If therefore the Protestants should propose from their own imagination, and press as absolutely necessary to salvation, any positive article which does not appear in antiquity, without question this course might, with very good reason, be made use of against them. But it is most evident that there is no such thing in their belief; for they maintain only such things as are either expressly delivered in the Scriptures, or else are evidently deduced from thence; and such as have also been expounded, the greatest part of them, and interpreted by the ancients, not in their own private writings only, but even in their creeds and synodical determinations also. They pretend not either to any particular revelation or secret tradition, or any other new principle of doctrine. Their faith is founded

* Cùm enim ex Scripturis arguuntur, in accusationem convertuntur ipsarum Scripturarum, quasi non rectè habeant, neque sint ex auctoritate, et quia variè sint dictæ, et quia non possit ex his inveniri veritas, ab his qui nesciant traditionem. Non enim per litteras traditam illam, sed per vivam vocem.—*Iren. l.* 3. *c.* 2.

only upon the most ancient, and most authentic instrument of Christianity, the Bible. Only in their expositions either of the doctrines therein contained, or other passages, they produce some few things that are not at all found in the Fathers. But these things being not necessary to salvation, the argument which is brought from the silence of the Fathers herein, is not sufficient to prove the falsity of them; time, experience, the assistance of others, and the very errors also of the Fathers, having (as they say) now laid that open to them, which was heretofore more difficult and hard to be discovered, and noticed of Divine Revelation. Who knows not that a dwarf, mounted upon a giant's shoulders, looks higher and sees further than the giant himself? It would be ridiculous in any man to conclude, that what the dwarf discovers is not in nature, because in that case the giant must also have seen it. Neither would he be much wiser, that should accuse the dwarf of presumption, because, forsooth he has told us that of which the giant said not a word: seeing that it is the giant to whom the dwarf is beholden for the greatest part of his knowledge. This is our case, say the Protestants: we are mounted upon the shoulders of that great and high giant, Antiquity. That advantage which we have above it by its means, enables us to see many things in Divine Revelation which it did not see. Yet this cannot be any ground for presumption in us, because we see more than it did; forasmuch as it is this very antiquity to which we owe a great part of this our knowledge.

It is therefore certainly clear, that as for the Protestants, and what concerns the positive points of their faith, they are wholly without the compass of the dispute. And as for those of the Church of Rome, they cannot, for the reasons before given, make any advantage of the testimony of the ancients, for the proving of any of those points of doctrine which they maintain, save only of those wherein their adversaries agree with them: and therefore, if they would have us come over to their belief, they must necessarily have recourse to some other kinds of proofs. But yet I do not see but that we may very well make inquiry into antiquity, respecting many articles which are now maintained by those of the Church of Rome: and if we find that the ancients have not said anything of the same, we may then positively conclude, that they are not to be accounted as any part of the Christian religion.

I confess, that there are some articles against which this argument is of no force; as those which they do not account necessary to salvation, and which the ancients heretofore might have been, and we also at this day may be, ignorant of. But certainly this argument, in my judgment, would be utterly unanswerable against such points as they press as necessary, and whereon indeed they would have our salvation wholly to depend; as, for example, the supreme authority of the Pope and of the Church, which owns him as its head; the adoration of the holy sacrament of the eucharist, the sacrifice of the mass, the necessity of aricular confession, and the like. For if they are of such great importance, as they would make us believe, it would be a point of high impiety to say that the Fathers knew nothing of them: in the same manner as it would be a most absurd thing to maintain, that though they did know them, they would not yet speak one word of them, in all those books which we have of theirs at this day. And if they had said anything at all of them in their writings, we have no reason in the world to suspect, that possibly those passages where mention was made of them, may have been erased, or corrupted and altered, by false hands: seeing that this piece of knavery would have been done to the disadvantage of those who had these books in their custody.

We have rather very good reason to suspect, that whatever alterations there are, they have been made in favour of the Church of Rome; as we have proved before in the first book. If therefore, after so long a time, and after so many indexes as they of the Church of Rome have put forth, and so great a desire as they have had to find these doctrines of theirs in the writings of the Fathers, and the little conscience that they have sometimes made of foisting into the writings of the Fathers what they could not find there; we can still make it appear, that they are not to be found there at all—after all this, I say who can possibly doubt but that the Fathers were ignorant of them? Who will ever be persuaded to believe, that they held them necessary to salvation? And if they were not known to be such then, how can any body imagine that they should come to be such now?

In conclusion, my opinion is, that although the authority of the Fathers be not sufficient to prove the truth of those articles which are now maintained by the Church of Rome against the Protestants, even though the ancients believed the same, it may, notwithstanding, serve to prove the falsity of them, in case we should find by the Fathers that the ancients were wholly ignorant of them, or at least acknowledged them not for such, as they would now have us believe them to be: which is a business that so nearly concerns the Protestants, that, to be able to bring about their design, I conceive they ought to employ a good part of their time in reading over the books of the ancients. Only it is requisite that each party, when they undertake so tedious and so important a business as this, should come well provided with all necessary qualifications, as a knowledge of the languages, and of history, and should also be well read in the Scriptures; and that they use herein their utmost diligence and attention, and withal read over exactly whatsoever we have left us of the Fathers, not omitting anything that they can obtain; because a little short passage many times gives a man very much light in elucidating their meaning: and not think (as some, who much deceive themselves do) that they perfectly know what the sense and belief of the ancients was, because perhaps they have spent four or five months in reading them over. But above all, it is necessary that they come to this business free from all partiality and prejudice, which is indeed the greatest and the most general cause of that obscurity which is found in the writings of the Fathers, whilst every one endeavours to make them speak to his sense; whereas in the greatest part of these points of religion, which are now controverted amongst us, these ancient authors really believed much less than the one party does, and some little more than the other does: and there are but a very few points of all this number, wherein they are fully and absolutely of the same opinion with either of the two parties. Neither is it sufficient in this business to take notice of such testimonies as either positively affirm or deny those things which we are searching after, because, however clear they may perhaps be, it can scarcely be conceived but that a quick wit will find something to darken the sense of them: as you may observe in all books of controversy; where you shall have them so baffle and make nothing of such testimonies as are brought against them out of the ancients, that you would hardly know what opinion to form.

You must also observe what are the necessary consequences of each particular article: it being impossible to conclude upon any one point of any importance, but that there will presently follow upon it divers consequences, as well within as without the Church. As for example, you are to consider what the consequences are of the *transubstantiation* of the eucharist, as now held by the Church of Rome; of *purgatory;* and of the *monarchical authority* of the Pope:

and when you have observed them well, you are then to mark, in reading the books of the ancients, whether they appear there in whole or in part. For if you find them not there at all, it is a most certain argument, that the doctrine from whence they proceed did not then exist.

I shall not, however, proceed any further in this discourse, since various others have already treated hereof at large; it being, in my judgment, no difficult matter to conclude, from what we have here delivered, how we ought to read the Fathers.

THE END.

www.ingramcontent.com/pod-product-compliance
Lightning Source LLC
LaVergne TN
LVHW011159110826
845150LV00006B/1259